P9-AOI-166

Erik Jan Hanussen

Erik Jan Hanussen

HITLER'S JEWISH CLAIRVOYANT

MEL GORDON

FERAL HOUSE

ISBN: 0-922915-68-7

Feral House
P.O. Box 13067
Los Angeles, CA 90013

www.feralhouse.com
info@feralhouse.com

Design by Linda Hayashi

10 9 8 7 6 5 4 3 2 1

Dedicated to

the late

Robert Ulrich

and his grandson,

Emerson Ulrich

AUTHOR'S NOTES

Erik Jan Hanussen went by many names. In each chapter, I have attempted to indicate the name (and persona) he was known as during that period in his career. In addition, I refer to Hanussen as the "Ottakring kid," "the Jenischmann," "the Dane," "the Master Clairvoyant," "the Mental Wizard of the Ages," "the Phenomenon of Our Time," "the Prophet of the Third Reich," and other appellations that were sometimes given to him by sympathetic or scornful acquaintances and writers.

Erik Jan Hanussen: Hitler's Jewish Clairvoyant is formatted in an unusual manner. Between each chapter, I have inserted a document that relates to Hanussen's psychological or professional development. These inserts, which explain Hanussen's tricks and thinking, were published, for the most part, at the end of his life. I have altered their printed sequence in order to provide the reader with a documentary chronicle of Hanussen's writings and those of his teachers and adversaries.

German and Czech historians who have written about Hanussen have tended to either disguise their source materials, citing no bibliographical references, or to blanket their biographies with hundreds upon hundreds of obscure footnotes. I have taken a middle path. All published sources for *Erik Jan Hanussen* are listed in the Endnote section. Important or singular references are cited within the body of the text.

ACKNOWLEDGMENTS

The author wishes to acknowledge the following individuals, who gave their time, energy, and unflagging support for this intriguing historical puzzle: Erika Steinschneider-Fuchs, Phil Steinschneider, Ernest Juhn, Mike Thaler, Ulrich Sacker (the Director of the SF Goethe-Institut), Ingrid Eggers, Tony Kaes, Ute Kirchhelle, Sharon Gillerman, Gary Bart, Genia Chef, Völker Spengler, Nina Hagen, Martin Ebon, and my father, Joseph A. Gordon, who collected and translated the Yiddish-language materials on Zisha Breitbart.

Adam Parfrey, the founder of Feral House, also deserves special mention. He understood the importance (and difficulty) of this project in all its twists and deadline-bending turns. Whenever I telephoned him, requesting an extension because yet another rare Hanussen document had fallen into my hands, he merely laughed and let me rant about its significance and place in the book. Every writer-scholar dreams of a devoted publisher like him.

I also received invaluable German and Czech translation assistance from Eberhard Scheiffele, Anne Bergstrom, Birgit Nielsen, Iveta Bartos, Heidi Blais, and André Gisiger.

Finally, the University of California, Berkeley Faculty Research Committee provided generous funding for the extraordinary costs related to the procurement and copying of Hanussen's Viennese and Berlin 35mm films thought to be "lost" or destroyed during the Second World War.

HANUSSEN
MAGAZIN
1
RM
Was bringt 1932?
2
HEFT

CONTENTS

Adolf Hitler is said to have taken a keen interest in Erik Jan Hanussen's occult practices. It was by thus interesting those in power that Rasputin gained his grip on the Czar's family. Like Rasputin, Hanussen had the power to hypnotize alluring women, who found his magnetic appeal irresistible.

True Mystic Science No. 1 (November 1938)

INTRODUCTION

Historians digging into the archives to reconstruct the chronicle of the Twentieth Century will have to deal with this strange phenomenon of Hanussen, born Herschmann Steinschneider in the humble home of a poor Jewish actor in Vienna. It will be their task to unravel a complex maze of reality and legend, myth and romance, to reach the core of the true personality of Steinschneider, alias Hanussen, and his influence on one of the most significant chapters of European history, the ascent and reign of Adolf Hitler.

Pierre van Paassen, May 1942

When Pierre van Paassen, the prominent Dutch author and foreign correspondent, wrote the above for McCall's *Redbook Magazine* in "The Date of Hitler's Fall," the "amazing exploits of Erik Jan Hanussen" were still hot international filler. What could have been more titillating than the story of a Jewish mystic who helped usher in the Third Reich and then became one of its first victims?

At least fourteen stories on Hitler's Jewish astrologer and clairvoyant had appeared in the American press beginning in 1937. Most of the articles typified the low pulp style of the period, gracing the pages of *Keyhole Detective Cases, True Detective, Startling Detective Stories, True Mystic Science, Smash Detective*, and *International Detective Cases*. Yet several exposés were penned by Germany's greatest journalists—acclaimed writers like Bella Fromm and Egon Erwin Kisch, then in North American exile.

As the German Reich expanded its borders across Central Europe in the mid-'30s, Jewish and left-wing writers attempted to outrun the Nazi dragnet through a westward migration. Those who ended up in New York, Montreal, Los Angeles, and Mexico City found that their esteemed positions and linguistic skills had vanished. The German-language newspapers and publishing houses that employed them had been closed down or "Aryanized." Most of the writers arrived in America as common refugees and were in desperate material straits. Psychologically and financially, they needed outlets for their work.

William Wagner, the president of McCall's periodical syndicate, and Bernard MacFadden, the physical culture king and magazine magnate, were among the leading—and unsung—anti-fascists in the American print media. They published shocking firsthand accounts of Nazi persecution of Jews and Communists as early as 1934. The editors of their mass-market monthlies—directed toward readers of romance, mystery fiction, fashion, true crime, body-building, and the occult—welcomed the Central European authors and tried to integrate their high artistic aspirations into their otherwise lowbrow and apolitical American journals.

The saga of Hanussen and the superstitious Führer made good tabloid reading for a Depression-era public hooked on the salacious double-dealings of master criminals, their nefarious plots, unsavory henchmen, and spectacular, Shakespearean downfalls. Who could narrate this intriguing, international morality tale better than the accredited Viennese and Berlin reporters who witnessed the events where they unfolded?

In the natural food-chain of American popular culture, the story of the unstable German leader and his Jewish patron was about to leap into a higher format, the motion picture. According to one *Redbook* author page, van Paassen's sensational five-part series on Hanussen had been optioned by a "major Hollywood studio."

But no van Paassen-Hanussen movie bio ever materialized.

In fact, the name Erik Jan Hanussen disappeared from sight after September 1942.

Exactly why is a subject of historical conjecture.

Probably the connection of any Jews or non-Germans with Hitler's coup and Nazi policies that followed was an exercise in poor political taste and had dangerous social implications. By the time the American homefront had geared up for total war in 1942, the very notion of European Jews as anything less than the targets of fascist genocide could be viewed in Washington as a form of Fifth Columnism.

The strange tale of "Hitler's Pal" (as Hanussen was tagged in two true crime periodicals) disappeared from the American cultural scene and the "Why We Fight" rationales, which pontificated on the fall of the democratic Weimar Republic, Nazism's victory, and the origins of the Second World War. Hanussen's name was stricken from the public record, only appearing in secret wartime OSS memos related to the character analysis and psychopathology of the Führer.

The Hanussen exposés written by Fromm, Kisch, and their follow refugees, which were originally issued in runs of hundreds of thousands, had been expunged from the authors' official bibliographies and archives in Boston, New York, and London during the immediate postwar period.

Even in the world of academia, it became difficult to find traces of Hanussen in the extensive English-language scholarship on Hitler and the Third Reich.

Just one example: Fritz Tobias' *Der Reichstagsbrand: Legende und Wirklichkeit* (Rastatt/Baden: Grote, 1962) is the standard historical acount of the mysterious 1933 arson that led to the dissolution of the Weimar Constitution and the imposition of the Hitler dictatorship. In Tobias' German original, there were twenty-two citations on Erik Jan Hanussen's alleged participation in the political crime. *The Reichstag Fire: Legend and Truth*, the British translation of Tobias' analysis published in 1963, however, had none. In an introduction to the Secker & Warburg text, the Oxford historian A.J.P. Taylor explained his reasons for the removal of Hanussen's name and the odd abridgment, "Some of these [Tobias' 'false trails'] have been left out, in order to spare the English reader. They do not, in my judgment, affect the general picture."

During the '50s and '60s, Erik Jan Hanussen was relegated to German folklore and racy Weimar memoirs. In both East and West Germany, an occasional Hanussen-themed novel or fantasy surfaced as a Weimar *Krimi* (or paperback crime mystery). In these noir renderings, the subterranean message was unstated yet tauntingly clear: Jews too could be held responsible for the nation's debacle and their own people's genocide. The coupling of Hanussen with Hitler helped assuage German guilt. It was a subtle whitewash, to be sure, but satisfying and deliciously ironic for the German people.

Several stage, television, and costume films publicly resurrected the figure of the Nazi Rasputin, starting in the late 1950s, but these melodramatic depictions sidestepped the issues of direct blame or ethnicity. Ivan Szabo's 1988 Hungarian-German film, *Hanussen*, for instance, avoided any references to Erik's "Israelite" origins or his known stage chicanery. In that confusing feature, Hanussen was merely seen as a sympathetic battle-scarred prophet, in the wrong place and time.

Erik Jan Hanussen: Hitler's Jewish Clairvoyant is the first attempt, outside of Germany, to take up van Paassen's challenge to "unravel" the fantastic story of Hermann Steinschneider, the Jewish psychic who, according to contemporary accounts, had altered the course of the twentieth century.

This book includes little-known or unpublished materials from private American sources and firsthand accounts from Hanussen's relatives and acquaintances. It relies heavily on the extensive print, photographic, and filmic trail that Hermann Steinschneider-Erik Jan Hanussen left in his well-documented path.

It is unabridged.

The bizarre association of Erik Jan Hanussen with Adolf Hitler and the National Socialists was brief, lasting slightly over one year.

The period discussed here, from March 1932 to April 1933, however, was certainly the most crucial and unpredictable in the Führer's extraordinary rise to power. Few believed then that the diminutive Austrian Lance Corporal could achieve his long-stated political goal—to rule Germany under a totalitarian, military regime.

Even among the Nazi elite, there were those who fretted over the national polls and concluded that their party head could never govern the country without the heavy impediment of a coalition cabinet. Hitler's inflexible persona and rabidly anti-democratic policies were an anathema to the majority of German voters. The Führer was unelectable in 1932. Moreover, the hysteric Chaplinesque figure had become a liability to the National Socialist cause, in the reckoning of the leaders of two of its three splintering factions.

Hanussen entered Hitler's life at an inauspicious and magical moment. In the summer and fall of 1932, support from all but the most steadfast followers of the Führer began to ebb sharply and nearly crash. No one, outside of Hitler's inner circle, thought the Nazi chieftain could continue much longer. Then the Danish seer appeared, offering enchanted unguents and spells, empowering agents to the exhausted and dispirited Führer. The wily Hanussen must have seemed like a Wagnerian wizard or distant Nordic twin in the unsettled year before the Nazi takeover.

Born two months and 162 miles apart in the Austro-Hungarian Empire, Hanussen and Hitler shared many life experiences and goals; they both agonized over their uncertain origins, suffered from parental neglect and petty childhood humiliations, thought of themselves as aspiring artists in a banal and uncaring world, drank in the same low Viennese bars on the Praterstrasse, wandered the lonely byways of Vienna's mammoth Lunapark in its afterhours glow, served as Lance Corporals in the Imperial armies of the Central Powers, floundered as misfits in the chaos of an eviscerated, post-World War One Germany, built cult-like followings in their image, were ridiculed by the same newspapers as foreign and kitschy impostors, and had an abiding belief in themselves as *Wundermänner* (or miracle-men).

It was said, by their detractors, that Herr Schicklgruber nudged the rule of law into the realm of god-man deification and mysticism while Steinschneider stitched prophecy and astrology to the national political consciousness.

Adolf Hitler and Erik Jan Hanussen momentarily joined forces in the tumultuous years when the Weimar Republic faded and expired. Their friendship and aid for one another would soon bring about world conflagration and destruction for European civilization and their peoples.

The two "H's" embraced each other as comrades-in-arms because of what life had placed before them: they participated in a parallel struggle, possessed a singular worldview, and trusted in the efficacy of magical thinking.

Heinrich Huter and Kurd Kisshauer, editors of two Nationalist occult journals, *Neues Deutschland* and *Die Zukunft*, however, discounted the characterological similarities between the master showmen. The German astrologers, writing in the early '30s, maintained that Hitler and Hanussen were not only descended from different racial stocks and cultures, they were also men born under divergent and adversarial star-signs.

YOU CAN READ PALMS!

As soon as you finish reading these instructions, you will be able to interpret your fate or that of your friends from the signs of the human hand. Try it and you become a Palm-Reader in just five minutes!

THE CHIRØMETER -- A Template for Palmistry!

IN FIVE-MINUTES YOUR FORTUNE!

BY ERIK JAN HANUSSEN

The Chirometer is the product of long and difficult research. It is a device that enables the layman, without any previous knowledge, to discover the future through palmistry. Follow these instructions:

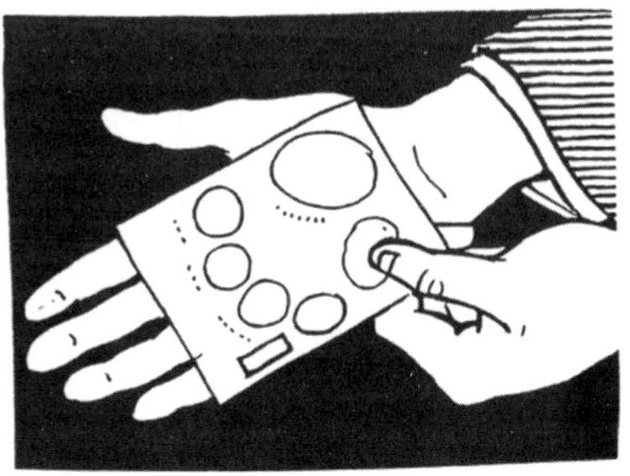

I. Cut out the Chirometer and place it carefully over your hand:

II. Set the exposed areas of the Chirometer over the eight mounds of your hand. On the surface of these mounds are tiny marks (in the rough shape of stars, crosses, etc.) that foretell your exact turns-of-fate and character-attributes.

Both palms are important. The Chirometer is first placed on the right hand, and then flipped over to the left.

III. The ten templates allow you to interpret the overall meaning of the rune-signs (i.e., crosses or stars). But each of templates deals with a single aspect of your fortune or character:

Signs of your Emotional Life (love, marriage, ideals, health) appear on the left palm. Indications of the Mind (business, occupation, money-marriage, career plans) are found on the right.

(Rune-signs are rarely formed like exact geometrical shapes -- crosses, stars, bulbs, straight lines -- but approximations of them.)

Hanussen-Magazin #2 (January–February 1932)

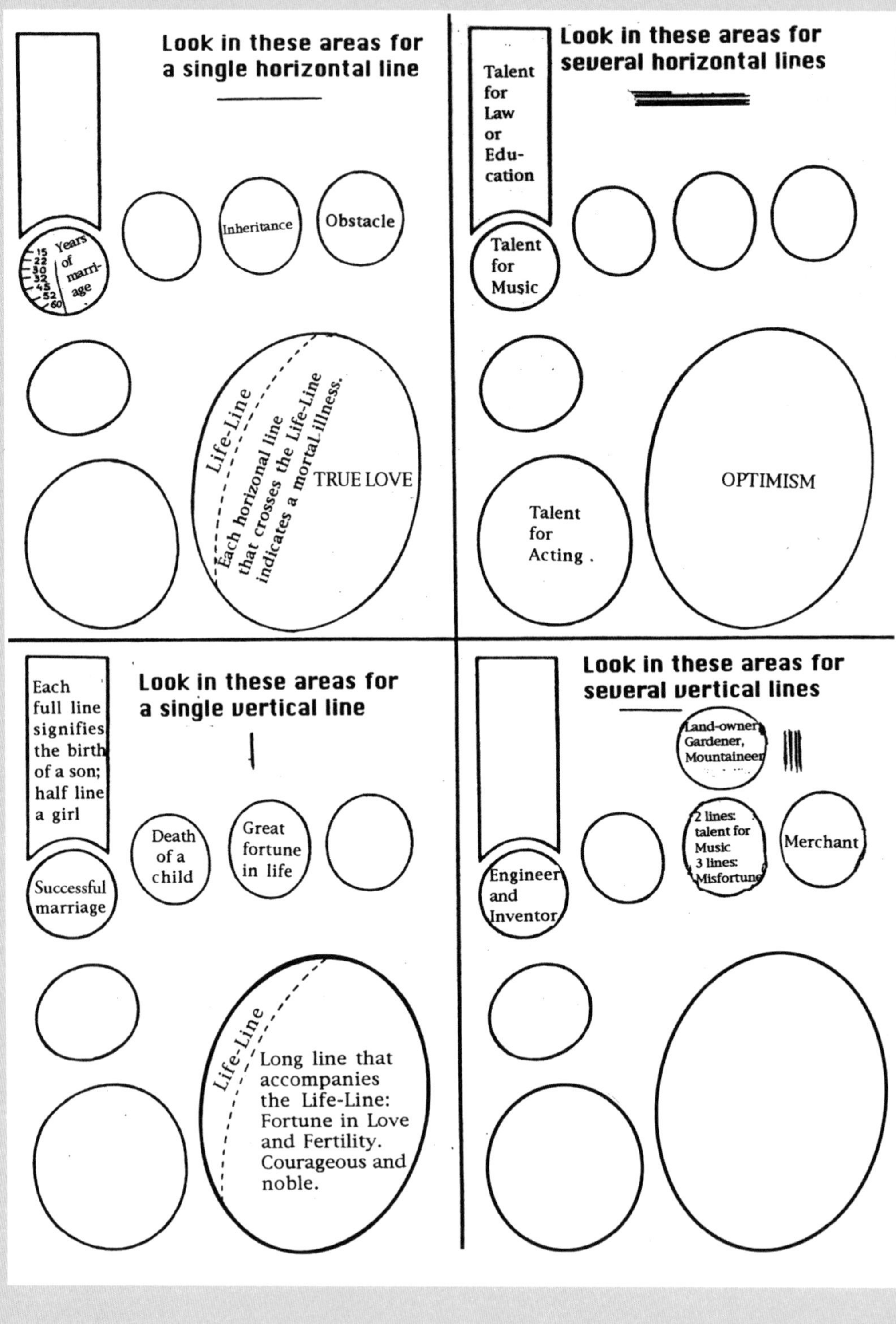
Look in these areas for a single horizontal line
Years of marriage
15
22
30
32
45
52
60
Inheritance
Obstacle
Life-Line
Each horizonal line that crosses the Life-Line indicates a mortal illness.
TRUE LOVE
Look in these areas for several horizontal lines
Talent for Law or Education
Talent for Music
Talent for Acting .
OPTIMISM
Look in these areas for a single vertical line
Each full line signifies the birth of a son; half line a girl
Successful marriage
Death of a child
Great fortune in life
Life-Line
Long line that accompanies the Life-Line: Fortune in Love and Fertility. Courageous and noble.
Look in these areas for several vertical lines
Land-owner, Gardener, Mountaineer
2 lines: talent for Music
3 lines: Misfortune
Merchant
Engineer and Inventor

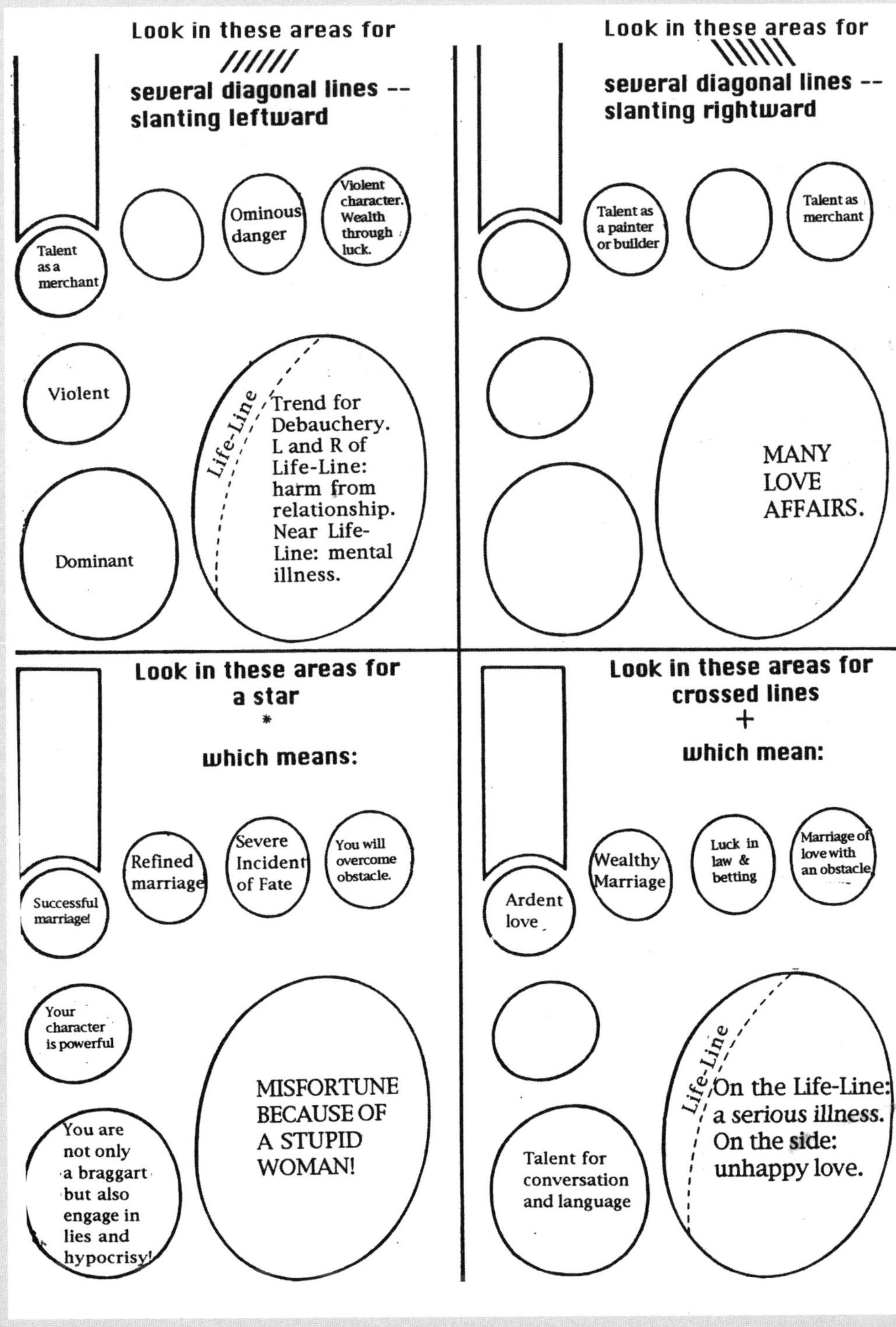

Look in these areas for
//////
several diagonal lines -- slanting leftward
Talent as a merchant
Ominous danger
Violent character. Wealth through luck.
Violent
Dominant
Life-Line
Trend for Debauchery. L and R of Life-Line: harm from relationship. Near Life-Line: mental illness.
Look in these areas for
\\\\\\
several diagonal lines -- slanting rightward
Talent as a painter or builder
Talent as merchant
MANY LOVE AFFAIRS.
Look in these areas for a star
*
which means:
Successful marriage!
Refined marriage
Severe Incident of Fate
You will overcome obstacle.
Your character is powerful
You are not only a braggart but also engage in lies and hypocrisy!
MISFORTUNE BECAUSE OF A STUPID WOMAN!
Look in these areas for crossed lines
+
which mean:
Ardent love
Wealthy Marriage
Luck in law & betting
Marriage of love with an obstacle
Talent for conversation and language
Life-Line
On the Life-Line: a serious illness. On the side: unhappy love.

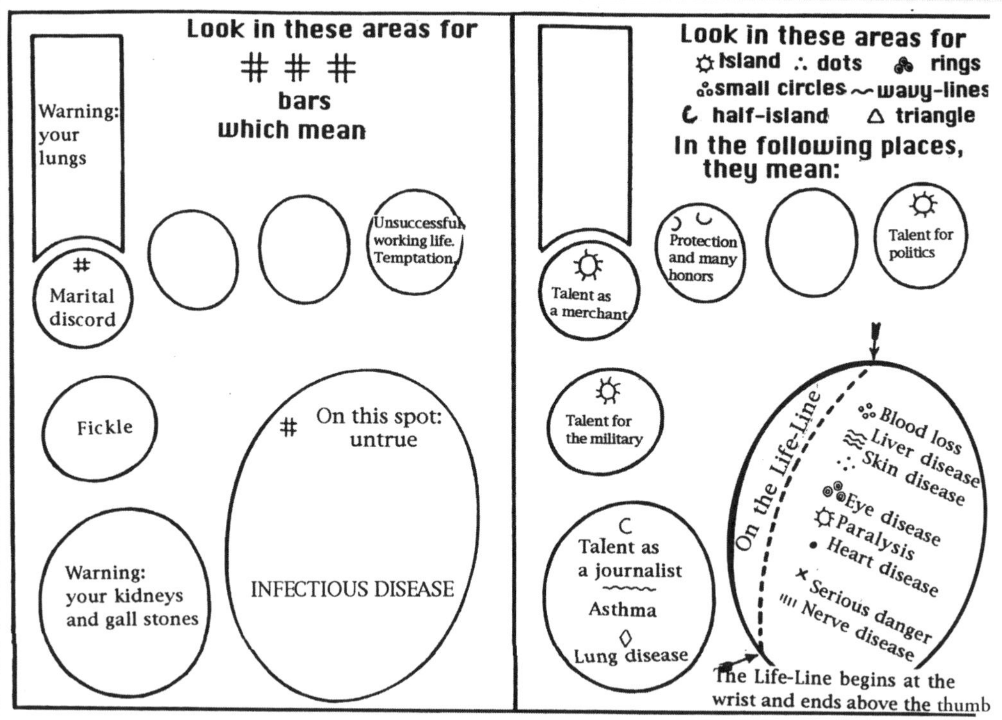

Erik Jan Hanussen's

Chirometer

For best results,
paste this template
on cardboard paper.

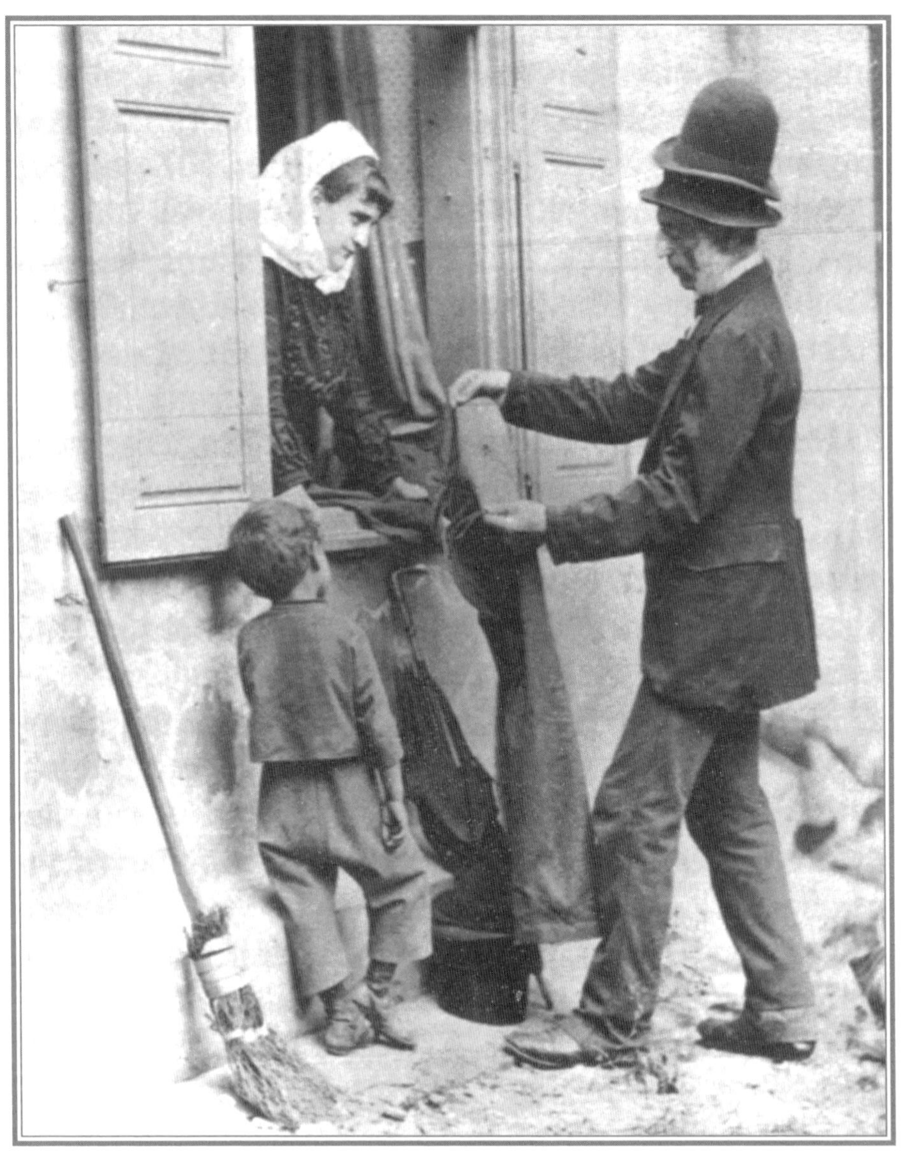

Jewish Door-to-Door Salesman in Vienna, c. 1900

CHAPTER ONE

THE CAULDRON

1889-1912

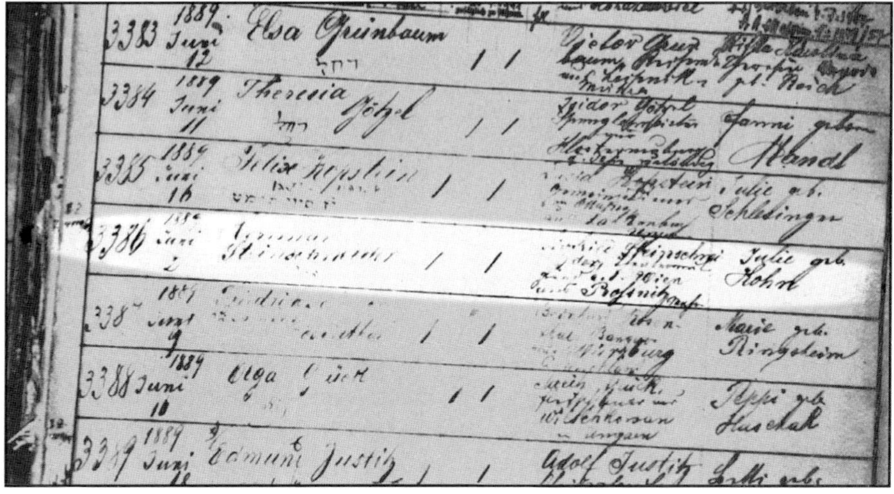

Viennese Birth Record, #386 (1889)

On the Fringes

Erik Jan Hanussen was conceived out of wedlock and delivered by a midwife in the holding cell of a precinct jail in Vienna's Ottakring district on June 2, 1889. His birth certificate (filed in the city of Prossnitz) read "Herschmann-Chaim Steinschneider. Hebrew male." It was a document that would haunt him for much of his adult life and lead to his disappearance, torture, and death in Berlin forty-four years later.

The scandalous circumstances of his birth were hidden from the impressionable Herschmann until he reached twelve. His mother, Julie Cohen, came from a thoroughly bourgeois, orthodox Jewish family. Julie's father, Sami Cohen, imported fur pelts from Russia and was proud of his comfortable living. A widower, he doted excessively on his daughter.

When the dashing, if down-on-his-luck, Siegfried Steinschneider caught Julie's eye at a Rosh Hashanah service, Sami did everything imaginable to discourage the courtship. Steinschneider was a *Schmierekomödiant*, a lowly "grease paint" actor, a mere pickup player at the Theater am Wien and parts unknown; the kind of performer who spent the better part of his life in cafés, waiting for roles that never emerged. At best, he was an itinerant *Luftmensch* and a vain flim-flam artist in the minds of Vienna's patrician Jewish upper crust but, to the sheltered Julie, the actor radiated youthful bravado and seductive worldliness. He was a feckless Romeo on the run.

Siegfried impregnated Julie during one of her father's business trips to Lodz.

The lovers stole away to Moravia, where Siegfried pounded the boards and convinced his paramour that she too possessed stageworthy talents as a *chanson* singer. When they returned to Vienna, Sami had them arrested on a phony charge of property theft. Julie was nine months pregnant and weakly defended her honor with a freshly printed marriage license.

A *droshky* (horse-drawn wagon) from the Cohen estate brought the sickly madonna home. A few nights later, Siegfried broke into the Julie's room and carried off his bride and son. Sami never spoke or communicated with his daughter, son-in-law, or celebrated grandson again. He disowned them.

Although the newlyweds were quickly booked into the cabaret circuit of German tourist traps along the Adriatic and Mediterranean coastline, life on the road became increasingly difficult. Julie had contracted tuberculosis and Siegfried wasn't able to provide a secure livelihood.

Herschmann—his parents first called him Heinrich, an obvious Germanic choice, then settled on the more racially neutral Hermann—was a precocious and adaptable child. The vagabond rhythms of quick employment and abrupt dismissal not only seemed normal, but greatly appealed to him. The rundown hotels and dilapidated boarding houses stimulated the toddler's imagination. They were no less real castles and inviting mansions than the painted images on the moldering flats which his parents used as scenery.

Hanussen's earliest recorded memory at age three is instructive.

Siegfried and Julie were engaged at a little German-speaking theatre in Nagyzeben (then called, interestingly, Hermannstadt) in the Romanian part of the Hapsburg Empire. The Steinschneider family lived in the back parlor of a *pension* on Leichengasse (or the "Alley of Corpses"). Hermann's window faced the municipal cemetery. From early morning to dusk, dirges and funeral processions were organized and straggled down the Leichengasse to the gravesites. The curious three-year-old watched the cavalcades in rapt fascination.

One moonless night, Hermann awoke in a start. "As if guided by an unseen hand," he ran from his room to the house of his landlord, a pharmacist. There, he aroused his playmate Erna, the landlord's daughter. Without a word said, he pulled her to the cemetery grounds and they hid behind a huge tombstone. After a minute or two, they heard a devastating explosion. The druggist's house burst into flames.

In his 1930 autobiography, *Meine Lebenslinie*, Hanussen declared that this was his first experience in clairvoyance. Another incident he remembered from the summer of 1891 had a more benign conclusion. The neighborhood coachman, Herr Martin, picked up the three-year-old in the afternoon and sat him on top on his manure wagon before his daily trek into the fields.

One afternoon, a thunderstorm broke out and the coachman hitched the cart to a huge tree. While Martin spread the fertilizer around the rows of fruit trees, Hermann impulsively grabbed the reins of the wagon and frightened the horse forward. A moment later, lightning struck the side of the tree, exploding its upper branches and felling the trunk forward. In a flash, the shattered arbor lay supine on the ground, ablaze on the very spot where Martin's wagon (and Hermann) was tied.

True or not—and Hanussen's memoirs are filled with such picturesque episodes—each checks out in regard to geography and time. For instance, the *Baedaker's Guide to Austro-Hungary* (Berlin, 1900) shows a detailed map of Hermannstadt with a Leichengasse leading to the city cemetery, surrounded by acres of corn fields.

As always, the theatrical commitment of the Steinschneiders ended badly. Julie's tubercular condition worsened; she could no longer perform comfortably on the stage. Siegfried moved the family back to Vienna, where he accepted a position as a door-to-door salesman, hawking Venetian blinds and other household knickknacks.

While Julie convalesced at home, Hermann was sent to the *Volksschule* on Augartenstrasse. His teacher was the rabid anti-Semite Anton Karl Seitz, fresh from the seminary and later to be the notorious mayor of Vienna, equal enemy to Sigmund Freud and the charlatan Erik Jan Hanussen.

At the *Volksschule*, Hermann experienced Jew-hatred firsthand. Not only in Seitz' schoolroom but also on the street. Neighborhood toughs chased and brutally beat the *Komödiant's* son, who soon learned the value of a quick wit and a fast getaway. There was one thing Hermann could not change: his face. The undersized pupil looked unmistakably Jewish.

Julie Kohn-Steinschneider died and was buried in a pauper's cemetery on the outskirts of Vienna. After the funeral, the hapless Siegfried brought the boy to the Moravian village of Boskowitz. The former actor now worked as an agent for Florisdorfer Textile AG, the main industry in town, and the nine-year-old Hermann was enrolled in the local grade school. His big-city swagger served him well, but it could not rescue him from taunts and anti-Semitic bullying. Yet in Boskowitz, venal persecution of the "Christ-killers" took on a more tangled, intriguing complexion. Many of the town's greatest anti-Semites were former Jews or offspring of ethnic Israelites themselves.

The Formerly Circumcised

Among the one million German-speaking Jews scattered throughout the vast Austro-Hungarian Empire at the end of the nineteenth century, nearly one in four attempted to disguise or alter their Jewish identity. Each family had a different strategy, typically starting with a invented genealogy and surname. Forged baptism papers (purchased from the local authorities or a friendly priest), intermarriage, public religious conversion, and concocted family trees frequently accompanied the travels of wealthy Jews as they migrated from small villages to Prague, Vienna, or Budapest. (In some areas of the Empire, particularly in central Moravia, the birthplace of Madeleine Albright's parents, the rate of assimilation surpassed fifty percent.)

Moneyed Jews had several clear choices at their disposal in the time of Franz Joseph's enlightened monarchy, and many managed to successfully conceal their genetic origins until the *Anschluss* or the German occupation in the independent regions of the former Empire. Other Jews, like the Steinschneider family, took a more circuitous route as bearers of the ancient Mosaic faith.

The earliest known Steinschneiders immigrated from Pressburg to the Bohemian village of Prossnitz. Daniel Prossnitz the Younger (c. 1750–c. 1800) and his son Aaron Daniel Prossnitz (1769–1809) were reputed to be *vunder-rebbes*, or Hasidic rabbis who were celebrated for their magical and curative practices. Aaron probably adapted the surname Steinschneider ("Stone-cutter") because he sold Kabbalist paper amulets, printed from engraved stone blocks. Wolf Steinschneider (c. 1790–c. 1830), who married the daughter of a local judge, and his son Aron (Adolf) Steinschneider (1823–c. 1875) remained in Prossnitz as common merchants and tradesmen.

Siegfried Steinschneider, Hanussen's father, was the scion of the family, although he more or less retained some religious vestiges of his forebears. His uncle, Moritz Steinschneider, achieved considerable renown as an Orientalist in Germany. While the Berlin professor was famous in international Jewish circles for his procurement and classification of Medieval Jewish ritual texts, Moritz always claimed to be a nonbeliever. His venerable field work was merely an attempt to preserve the remnants of an archaic, dying culture.

The Punished Hero

Fires, arson, "spontaneous combustion" were constant themes in Hanussen's life. At nine, Hermann decided to ignite the sleepy Boskowitz. He became obsessed with stories about Nero's burning of Imperial Rome and organized a gang of accomplices to recreate the event. They painted graffiti in the center of town that renamed Boskowitz as ancient Rome and set about to re-enact the Emperor's fabled deed. A previous night's rain prevented a quick incineration of the marketplace, so the "Nero Club" retired to the outskirts of town.

There Hermann poured petroleum on a bundle of rags, lighted the pile, and pitched them into the ruins of a miller's barn, which instantaneously ignited the dry straw and hay inside. Cradling a purloined shovel like Nero's lyre, Hermann led his cohorts into a cacophony of contemporary Bohemian folk ditties. Evidently none of the "Neros" were sufficiently proficient in classical Latin refrains.

Of course, neither Hermann nor his gang were aware that the miller's barn served as a temporary rendezvous for one of Austro-Hungary's most sought-after highwaymen, Heinrich Grasel. A ne'er-do-well Robin Hood, Grasel terrorized the Bohemian and Moravian countryside in the 1890s, plundering State treasury caravans as he sweet-talked local pretties into sexual servitude. Viennese authorities placed a one hundred ducat reward for his capture and deputized a special militia to patrol the Bohemian woods.

Hermann's prepubescent prank startled Grasel and his consort, the daughter of one of Boskowitz's leading citizens (the owner of the textile factory), into a confused surrender and quickly led to the outlaw's arrest and incarceration.

Municipal honors were heaped on Hermann during the subsequent heady days, although he managed to secure only five of the one hundred gold ducats due him. For his initial delinquent impulse to destroy Boskowitz, the boy-hero received twenty-five lashes on the buttocks, administered by his sadistic teacher Herr Meyer, a man who was less fond of the little Jew than the Emperor's bureaucrats in faraway Vienna. The elder Steinschneider was coincidentally fired from his position in the factory before its ownership changed hands.

In October 1900, father and the rowdy eleven-year-old returned to the Ottakring in Vienna. Siegfried married for a second time and moved in with Bertha Rieder and her two boys in an apartment on Brunnengasse. The area was by now known as Vienna's dingiest and most foreboding criminal quarter. In the newly designated Sixteenth Precinct, Ottakring teenage gangs and assorted street toughs pimped, traded loot and engaged in evening target practice in the Schmelz, an isolated parade ground for the Royal Imperial Guard. It was said that the boys could easily outshoot the best of Franz Joseph's elegantly dressed brigadiers. And the city constables consciously avoided the vast field after sunset.

Downstairs from the Rieder-Steinschneider apartment was a huge cheese factory. Hermann could never dissociate the malodorous fumes below from his adolescent loathing for his new lumpenprol circumstances and morally obedient step-family. The troubled youth spent much of his time on the street and among the scum in the Schmelz.

Slum housing in the Ottakring district in Vienna, 1900

On the other side of the Brunnengasse was the Red Bretzen, a lively tavern with a huge beer-garden. And from his father's window, Hermann could look down on the cabaret stage, where Volks-singers and dancers performed through the night. It was a world that Hermann realized he deeply missed. Days were spent in a trade school, evenings in the Schmelz, and nights staring down at the Bretzen stage.

At fourteen, Hermann fell in love. The voice of a forty-five-year-old soubrette captivated his heart. Siegfried refused the boy's pleas to attend her performances at the Bretzen, so Hermann avenged his father by tying some family heirlooms to a rope. These he managed to toss to his beloved chanteuse, waiting in the beer-garden across the street. Siegfried discovered the ruse and had to hire a team of movers to retrieve the cache of household trinkets and furniture.

Hermann's tribute and ardor must have been considerable; the middle-aged soubrette was somehow induced to elope with the teen. Hermann traded in his overcoat for a showman's morning-jacket and then pawned his bar mitzvah watch for a comic beard and fright wig. He brazenly persuaded the director of the Bretzen that he was an underage, but experienced, Volks-singer and would perform a set of original musical sketches. The comedian Kröck, a leading practitioner of the popular Viennese art form, was amused by the boy's audacity and accepted his offer. It was to no avail; the Ottakring delinquent bombed in his premiere midnight showing and was actually removed from the stage by the Master of Ceremonies using a traditional hooked cane.

Hermann's nameless soubrette and love interest vanished, yet the humiliated boy continued to nurse his ultimate fantasy to appear on the professional stage, like his once proud *Schmiere* father.

The Seven-Guilder Prodigy

In the *Neuen Wiener Tagblatt*, Hermann read a notice that the "Fink Star-Players," a Moravian theatre company in Sternberg, was auditioning for male performers.

Viennese Volks-Singers on stage, c.1900

Volks-Song by Carl Lorens (c.1900)

The advertisement energized the forlorn dreamer; still, Hermann had no financial means to travel there. He pawned his school vest along with his father's silver tie-clip. Even then, Hermann was a guilder short of train fare.

The faux performer went straight to Josef Blaha, the main publisher of Viennese sketch music. Hermann claimed that he discovered a lost manuscript collection from the estate of the late Volks-singer Carl Lorens. It was filled with cabaret songs, witty couplets, and comic dialect sketches. All original, all fantastically funny. The old Blaha was skeptical, if equally curious. They settled on a price of seven guilders, which the youth would receive upon delivery of the notebook the following morning.

The resourceful schoolboy purchased a distressed primer (with 126 blank, yellowing pages) from the backroom of a stationery emporium, set up shop in an all-night café, and frantically began to write. Whenever the pages looked too clean or his inspiration started to flag, the artist manqué merely dripped coffee on his unadorned creation. Sixteen hours later, Hermann returned to Blaha's office and presented the fabricated document as promised. Blaha studied the writings carefully. The one hundred bombastic folk ballads, sing-song lyrics, cabaret monologues, and street-savvy romantic poems were not bad. Certainly not genuine Lorens but marketable. The cautious Jewish businessman paid Hermann the seven guilders and later admitted in the decades that followed that the teenager's forged anthology made his publishing house a tiny fortune. ["Prelude to a Tyrant," *Redbook Magazine*, April 1940]

Hermann used half of the earnings to buy a suitable wardrobe—he was especially proud of the bargain he got on yellow patent-leather shoes in a used clothing store—and boarded the train for Sternberg. The theatre he found was in severe financial disarray. Frau Fanny Fink paid her ten-man company by the day according to the box-office take, which was not much. Hermann was hired as stage manager and doubled as a walk-on in such nineteenth-century operatic warhorses as August Weber's *Der Freischutz*, where Hermann zinged through the role of the mother sow. The stage-struck kid could not have been happier.

Pounding the Boards

The director of the Fink Star-Players was one Adolf Arthur, a professional leading man from Graz. The aristocratic and warm-hearted actor took Hermann under his wing and spent one year schooling the boy in the tricks of the noble theatre trade. Arthur, Hermann quickly learned, was addicted to hard drink and had nearly lost the capacity to memorize the simplest of dialogues. This explained why the handsome, urbane talent ignored the monthly entreaties from better provincial companies to leave Frau Fink's bottom-feeding "Stars." Yet when Arthur was forced to take the stage, he projected a truly poetic vitality and dark romanticism that only handsome drunks, fighting some authentic demons of the past, readily possessed.

After two full seasons, Frau Fink dismissed Hermann without warning. In nearby Neustadt, the boy thespian immediately found work with another village theatre. Yet, as much as the local impresario appreciated Hermann's enthusiastic approach, Ferdinand, the director's son, had a different feeling. During a performance of *The Death of the Serbian King*, the two youths engaged in a prolonged, roughhouse duel with rusty swords. The sabers drew real blood and Hermann was fired on the spot.

In Neustadt, Hermann experienced something new and crushing: abject poverty. He knew hunger and rejection but never both at the same time. The penniless fifteen-year-old was turned away at every door. Even the railroad station clerk banished him and alerted nearby shopkeepers and farmers of his whereabouts. Finally Hermann entered the waiting room of a medical clinic. In the midst of a room filled with moaning patients, he fell soundly asleep in a wooden chair. Unfortunately, after a few minutes of deep slumber, the doctor's receptionist called Hermann's number and wanted to know why he was there. A sympathetic town whore recognized the boy's homeless condition and graciously lent him money for breakfast and a place to stay.

In Reich-Ramming, Hermann hitched up with Zeinecke's Traveling Theater. Its classical repertoire, regrettably, was somewhat more ambitious than the theatre's stable of actors could support. The director, Bill Zeinecke, always had three versions of every play, a practical reflection of the troupe's fluctuating number of paid performers. Even the star-struck Hermann discovered that he could not convincingly embody more than three or four major parts in a single evening. He sought a more professional venue.

Under The Big Top

When Hermann heard that the Grand Circus Oriental had come to town, the gaunt kid-actor abandoned the Traveling Theater and scoped out the pristine circus encampment. To everyone's surprise, the owner, Franz Joseph Pichler, invited the boy to share his artistes' modest afternoon repast. The fresh coffee, meat dumplings, and rolls excited the teen like nothing else. Hermann picked up a fresh bundle of Grand flyers from the table and began to paste them up like a man possessed. Pichler hired the boy on the spot.

Itinerant German Circus, 1906

That evening, Harry (né Hermann Steinschneider) joined the glorious circus parade through Ramming. The entire Grand Circus Oriental consisted of six players: Pichler, who doubled as an acrobat; his towering brother Heinrich, a strongman; Pichler's wife Franziska, a sometime equestrienne, whom both brothers once courted; Pichler's grandmother, the cook and ticket-taker; and a truly evil clown, the one-eyed Mischko. The Grand menagerie was even less impressive. The animal entertainment amounted to one harebrained poodle, Sappho; two horses, Regent and Sandor; and a dyspeptic monkey, Jocko.

The Grand productions combined traditional circus numbers with Salzburg-like Passion plays. The exact nature of the drama was wisely determined by the region's dominant faith—Catholic villages required a bit more agony in the Tenth Station and a lot more Mary. Yet no matter where Pichler's family pitched their tent, the evening's program concluded with a rousing organ concert and a gala "Bengali" fireworks display.

Harry had few problems portraying Judas Iscariot in the pageants, but had to be hastily instructed in the ancient and perilous craft of circus acrobatics. During his first weeks, death-defying lessons would be given, matter-of-factly, in the wings. Over the next months, Harry proved his worth as the melodious and deft barker for the miniature operation and soon doubled as Harold, the world-renowned British horseman; then as Marini, the sole surviving member of an Italian tumbling troupe; then as the tragic, bearded trapeze-artiste, Herr Gari; and finally as the hilarious Auguste clown, Mr. Clapp-Clapp. In the dramatic curtain call before the fireworks finale, Harry stepped forward as the nonpareil Austrian stage marvel, Hermann von Brandenburg.

Ritually, every one of Harry's circus days began with a curse. The multi-charactered roustabout slept in a wooden shed, lying between the horses and Heinrich the Giant. Herr Direktor Joseph awoke at sunrise and tossed a pail of icy water across the heads of the four huddled quadrupeds and bipeds. Like a military reveille, Pichler shouted his morning prayer, *"Janenisch verplah'n!!!"* ("All life is shit!")

In an underworld Balkan patois, composed of raw Romany, Viennese street slang, and a rich assortment of obscenities from Yiddish and Romanian, or Jenisch, Pichler intoned the following: "All life is shit! God gave you no money, no place to rest, no friends outside this room, no skills, and only whores for companions. It is time to face this shitty day!" Pichler then returned to his trailer still mumbling in the private lingua franca of Europe's peripatetic showmen, pickpockets, circus folk, thieves, white slavers, and prostitutes.

Harry spent much of the morning securing or disassembling the circus side-tents and the big top. Later in the day, he went house to house, hawking crudely printed sheets of medieval saints. Only when he discovered the creed of his potential client did he reveal the identity of the generic paper icon. For his devout patrons, he also offered—for an extra fee—to invoke magical hexes or counter-spells on their disbelieving neighbors. Like Grandma Pichler, Harry accepted payments in foodstuffs.

Harry also designed the Grand posters and had to assist the alcoholic Mischko, who paraded around village squares wearing Harry's painted sandwich board over his chest. When the shaky Mischko fell on his back in a drunken stupor, Harry could relax. The locals had no trouble reading the evening's attractions. But when the one-eyed clown tipped face downward, Harry was obligated to flip him over so the townies could view the board, yet another bit of circus derring-do for the Viennese youngster. The wretched Mischko clawed and bit like a ferocious snapping turtle and often bloodied his companion.

Henrich the Giant was the acknowledged star of the circus and Harry's cherished mentor. It was from him that the Jewish runaway acquired the basic craft of stage illusion as well as all the legerdemain tricks, carnival gaffes, and confidence schemes that formed the stock-in-trade of each and every traveling Central European circus and freak show. At first trained as a stable-boy and lowly geek, Harry learned the timeless arts of eating glass shards, biting off the heads of chickens, knife-throwing, and sword-swallowing. He practiced fire-eating and juggling, worked the trapeze bars fearlessly, and cared for the tiny circus zoo.

Harry adored Regent the Wonder Horse. He slept cheek-to-neck with the white-maned mare, groomed her faithfully throughout the day, shared his beloved dumplings with her, and in the open fields, pretended the horse was his stage partner in the Grand biblical extravaganzas. (Decades later in interviews, Hanussen claimed that among God's creatures, only Regent truly understood him and could actually read his thoughts and make sense of his adolescent anxieties.)

Heinrich Pichler was a cocksman par excellence. Open-faced peasant girls and educated shopkeepers' daughters visibly trembled at the sight of the hulking strongman, who smiled knowingly and communicated with few words. His love escapades on the road were legendary.

In the Upper-Austria town of Lobenstein, Heinrich initiated Harry into carny seduction and female psychology: women were weak and wanted to be controlled sexually. From the haughtiest archduchess to the most naive milkmaid, all females of the species fawned before signs of cold masculine strength and secretly desired a scenario of erotic humiliation and violent rape. Most female spectators who came to the circus had the mindset of complaisant whores; money, silly gifts, smooth flattery produced at the right moment could be exchanged for their passionate and immediate carnal surrender. Heartfelt declarations of love, romantic tête-à-têtes, extended wooing through notes and letters were thoroughly unnecessary. Effective sexual domination required mastery of the moment and surprise.

According to Heinrich, these manly erotic qualities were manifested in flawless physical movement and self-assuredness. The time-honored skills of the circus ring and the street-con were identical to those of the boudoir. Some women, of course, had to be humored or manipulated into acquiescence and corporal degradation with more ingenuous strategies. These too Heinrich promised to teach the boy. Harry laughed appreciatively.

Heinrich's world view both enthralled and frightened the rambunctious fifteen-year-old. *Jenischmänner*, priests, Moravian townspeople, peasants, Jews, whores, anti-Semites, teachers, door-to-door salesmen, the Emperor's officials—all were involved in an endless scheme to dominate and deceive. Even Harry's pure image of the animal kingdom was not immune to Heinrich's cynical exegesis.

Why are lion-tamers careful only to work with the male cat, Heinrich queried Harry one evening. Because, Heinrich answered with rhetorical glee, the male lion can be controlled through masturbation as well as through fear of the whip. To make the jungle beast sexually dependent on his human master, the male is manually stimulated before each show. Even feral animals will quietly submit to a sharp mind and quick hand. Harry attempted a laugh. The Strongest Man in the World was a font of witty observations. The robust pair continued to hammer away in the dark. The paltry Grand was on the move.

Yet something shattered inside the boy's brain that night: the good, the sacred, the nonsexual did not exist. Erik Jan Hanussen was being born.

The Ropes

In Bad Hall, Harry exacted revenge on his worldly tutor. Heinrich, all out of character, fell head-over-heels in love with the comely daughter of the local brewmaster. Harry offered to act as Heinrich's Cyrano and wrote phony letters to her that comically negated the strongman's sincere profusions of love and affection. Heinrich suffered like a schoolboy, turning restlessly for nights like a young bull elephant. Harry had his philosophical comeuppance.

A few weeks later, Grete Pichler, the widowed sister-in-law of Direktor Joseph and Heinrich, came to visit the Grand in Upper-Austria on family matters. She cast a long eye at Harry and invited him to manage her traveling amusement park, the Electric Carousel. As Grete promised, if Harry left the Grand, there would be no more stables to clean—the horses were wooden—and he might be granted ownership of the entire unit should he prove able and savvy enough. Grete also assured the ambitious lad full meals and an improved wardrobe, befitting an employee of means.

Sneaking away from his one caring family, Harry hiked for five hours to reach Grete's establishment. At the Electric Carousel, labeled the "Most Modern Merry-Go-Round of Europe," Harry received some unexpected bad news. The so-called Electric Carousel was powered by five or six children, hidden beneath the contraption and concealed by a tarp covering. The only "electrical force" of the Electric Carousel was generated by a team of child laborers.

Harry had human problems too. Grete's right-hand man, Leopold, was a hateful punk with few talents, other than an endless capacity to complain and swear. The now-husky Harry bowled the roadie over with a punch to the stomach and a swift kick to the face.

Frau Pichler was not impressed. Her sweet-talk and seduction of Harry was a cruel ruse. She wanted Heinrich's amorous attentions and figured her dim-witted brother-in-law couldn't live peaceably without his constant aide, Harry. And she was right.

The gargantuan Heinrich came looking for his Viennese disciple after a few days and slavishly confessed his affection for him. Grete dragged the teary-eyed giant into her trailer, where a night of brutal love-play ensued. Over the next few days, Harry surreptitiously pocketed the Carousel subscription receipts and high-tailed it with Heinrich back to the Grand.

They crept into the old circus stable and re-established their bedding between Regent the Wonder Horse and Sandor, the Amazing Human-Brained Stallion. When Joseph saw the four of them there the next morning, he nonchalantly shook the water pail over their faces and pronounced his regulation Gypsy curse.

After the final performance of Pichler's *Blondin's March Through Thin Air*, Harry received a second wakeup call in Bad Hall. An attractive schoolteacher's daughter sent him a note. Instead of an invitation for an evening stroll or a lusty tryst, she admonished him, "You are much better born than to be a clown. Promise me that you will go home soon. Soon!"

Harry looked at himself in a stage mirror. His green-striped pants, Schiller shirt, and rubber collar, topped off with a stiff straw-boater made him a ridiculous figure. Who could take him seriously as a suitor or lover? Harry decided to leave the Grand Circus Oriental. When the circus wagons departed Bad Hall at dawn, Harry hid in the bushes and, from his concealed encampment, waved an invisible good-bye for the last time to Regent and Heinrich. The tramp-performer was determined to return to civilization.

Into the Lion's Den

Carrying his earthly possessions in a cigar box, Harry applied for a job with the mammoth Circus H., a three-ring outfit with nearly one hundred employees, forty

Lion's Cage in German Circus (1920)

horses, and a full menagerie of Arctic bears, lions, tigers, and trained dogs. The British owner, Mr. Johnson, a faded circusman covered in hideous scars, needed a lion-tamer as a replacement for himself. In the interview, Harry claimed that he had years of experience caring for wild beasts and, remembering Heinrich's story, asserted his proficiency in the lion's den.

Four days later, Harry, armed with a short whip and service revolver, entered the Johnson Big Top during a matinee performance. A team of beefy lions trotted to their striped platforms in the main ring. The disciplined felines mostly followed their routines and only one, Sultan, sensed Harry's fear and unexpectedly sprung at the sweaty, top-hatted teenager. The novice ringmaster cracked the snarling creature on the snout to the cheers of the sympathetic staff. Harry's audacious bluff resulted in no serious injury.

With Johnson's Czech wife, Harry fared a bit worse. The old, cross-eyed shrew had designs on him. The Jenisch-boy departed Circus H. and joined the Carl Hagenbeck Circus in Hamburg. Again he entered the ring as a lion-tamer; unfortunately, he was no match for Hagenbeck's professionals.

Back in Vienna in 1908, Harry had a happy rapprochement with his father. Siegfried's condition by then was not good. The former actor-salesman-representative was confined to his bed in the Ottakring dump. Franz Joseph's Imperial Army, unfortunately, caught up with the twenty-year-old prodigal there. Harry Hermann Steinschneider was drafted into the infantry, where he served for one year in Sarajevo, the capital of the newly incorporated province of Bosnia. However, a severe bout of hydrocele, which flooded his sperm ducts, landed Harry into sickbay. The jaunty Schweik negotiated a honorable dismissal. His commanding officers probably did not even notice the private's absence.

Journalist and Bum

In Sarajevo, citizen Harry Steinschneider embarked upon a brand new career. An uncle, Dr. Max Arminski, used his bureaucratic connections to secure the ex-soldier a minor editorial job at a government newspaper, *Der Drau*, in the Croatian backwater town of Essegg. Harry covered local events, such as they existed, and wrote *faits divers*, as he could find them. For the first time, Harry searched out paranormal topics and volunteered to be hypnotized by a Professor E.K. Hermann.

After a second year in the Yugoslav wild, Harry made his way back to ever-beckoning Vienna. His job prospects were not particularly sunny, but he managed a day-to-day bohemian existence, scribbling out *chansons* on napkins and comic monologues for Vienna's newest entertainment discovery, the literary cabaret. In 1910, Vienna boasted seven or eight such intimate establishments. Every Viennese performer—especially those at the bottom rung—needed fresh material by the week. And like the absinthe-addled street-poets of Montmartre, Vienna's itinerant wordsmiths took to the cabaret trade like madcap miners in a goldrush.

Harry hung out at the Café Louvre. The restaurant-cum-poolhall could not be found in any *Baedeker* or *Grieben* guidebook of the city. It was one of dozens of twenty-four-hour cheap bars, or *Nachtlokals*, on the Praterstrasse. Stretched out on the Louvre's distressed sofas and the graffiti-etched tables were pick-pockets, bar-girls, their pimps, cat-burglars, free-lance prostitutes, down-and-out writers, revue dancers, and restless salesmen and merchants on the slum. When the better dining and drinking emporiums closed for the night, teams of restless cooks and waiters dropped in for the latest illicit action.

Steinschneider's gang was the youngest of the deadbeat raconteurs. They gambled, kibitzed around the pool table, and spent much time hoodwinking innocent novices who hoped to break into Vienna's lustrous variety and cabaret world. A favorite amusement involved convincing a desperate would-be performer to sing her routine into an unconnected telephone receiver and then command her to show her legs as if the invisible theatre manager at the other end of the line could actually see them.

Harry peddled his obscene ditties to various singers and producers. Each received "exclusive performing rights." Once Harry sold a single "exclusive" *chanson* to five unknowing performers within one week. Interestingly, although Hanussen thought little of his lyrical achievements when he wrote about them in 1930, his Viennese contacts, like the old man Blaha, remembered Steinschneider's improvised artistry with considerably more enthusiasm.

Kurt Robitschek, the eminent director of Berlin's famed KaDeKo cabaret, left Nazi Germany in 1933 and landed in New York five years later. Interviewed about Hanussen, Robitschek claimed the twenty-two-year-old Steinschneider was "clever as they made them, he was. And his gift for writing risqué couplets was

Leo Singer and twin midget performers on Praterstrasse, 1913

something extraordinary. For a hundred kronen he would supply me with half a dozen songs—all hits, mind you." [*Redbook Magazine*, April 1940]

Harry loved the Louvre life. He had his share of erotic adventures and easy laughs. On off-nights, he patrolled the nearby Prater, where sausage wagons, girlie sideshows, Ferris Wheel rides, and other fairground amusements vied for loose working-class kronen. On Praterstrasse, dimestore phrenologists, astrologers, graphologists, palm and tea-leaf readers, and necromancers cast fortunes for giddy lovers and servicemen. One could also view a thousand-and-one human oddities: Leo Singer's family of midgets, the Three-Leg Virgin of Circassia, the Living Mermaid, the Double-Necked Bushman from the Kalahari, the Bearded Venus; see Gypsy women perform hooch shows, and drink good local *Dunkelbier* or *Kirschwasser*. The fact that most of the freaks were fake or artificially created only heightened his interest.

Like his future partner, Adolf Hitler, with whom the cabaret-writer probably stood shoulder-to-shoulder in the Prater crowds, Harry was fascinated with the booth-show barkers. The *Spielers'* constant patter, their ability to draw crowds, instinctive understanding of how humor and humiliation worked inexplicably to wring money from resolute strangers, peculiar eloquence, and juggling of emotional homilies reminded the playful artist of his former struggles on the road. Naturally the big-city skills and super-competitive allures of the Prater ballyhooers were considerably better honed. They used indelible, garish images on canvas and scientific terminology to transfix and hook their ambulant marks. (Of course, Hitler despised the Prater's multinational strollers; in his eyes, the naive herd were uncouth Czechs, Serbs, Croatians, Poles, Slovaks, Romanians, Slovenes, Galician Jews, Hungarians—*Untermenschen*. For Harry, the street johns were *Jenischmänner* bait, suckers that Vienna attracted toward the end of every payday.)

At the Louvre one night, Harry's best friend Max Moritz, a music publisher, and a veteran member of the gang, told the restless twenty-two-year-old that his father was looking for a seasoned journalist.

This paper was more to Harry's taste. It was a con.

Hymns, Vienna's Wedding Newspaper existed as a private newspaper without subscribers or newsstand sales. In the first issue of the unusual journal were three tony-sounding articles: "The Mercantile-Ranking and Its Meaning," "Austria and Its Importance for European Trade," and "The Emperor and Commerce." These economic ripostes reappeared unerringly in every issue. What changed was the date on the masthead and the manufactured reportage on page five. On the blank Society Page, old Moritz set flattering photographs and approbations about a future bride and groom. Wealthy relatives, worried about the social standing of the about-to-be-married couple, paid Moritz for the phony edition, which was then distributed at the wedding feast.

Hymns looked no different than any of Vienna's two dozen traditional daily or weekly rags. Its irregular publication and stodgy analysis only enhanced its worth to Vienna's vain nouveau riche and arrivistes.

Almost Bourgeois

Harry assisted Moritz as the gumshoe reporter and secretive ad man. Once again, Steinschneider was back in the publishing racket, writing inconsequential tidbits and laying out type and pasting up photographs fresh from the developing studio. Yet just when Harry reentered the legitimate workforce, his father's physical and financial condition suddenly worsened.

Back in the Steinschneiders' malodorous Ottakring apartment, fifty-year-old Siegfried arranged his own death. Embracing a desk (one that young Hermann lowered to his soubrette years ago), the invalid father leaped from the second-story window and smashed into the pavement below. Bertha Rieder, widowed for a second time, committed suicide shortly after Siegfried's funeral. Both were interred in pauper's graves near the Schmelz.

On May 19, 1912 Harry Steinschneider married Herta Samter, a prompter from one of Vienna's small cabarets. How they met is unknown—Herta was expunged from Hanussen's autobiography and later writings—but they officially took their sacred vows before a rabbi at the Viennese Jewish Community Council. It was the first of three marriages that Hanussen consummated in a Jewish ceremony.

Herta was three years older than Harry and probably pregnant at the time of the wedding. Their male-child was delivered stillborn in the late summer and Harry parted from Herta not long after.

As a final rejection of his dreadfully somber middle-class existence, the newly-orphaned and newly-separated Steinschneider quit his job at *Hymns* as well. He was ready for the world.

ARE YOU A MEDIUM OR A HYPNOTIST?

AN OCCULT TEST CREATED BY ERIK JAN HANUSSEN

First, what is a Medium? In layman terms, he or she is a person who has a particularly fragile ego and consequently is easily guided by a stronger individual. The Medium's psychological tendency can result in a complete dissolution of the self; the Medium thinks, feels, and does only what the stranger commands. The Medium literally enters into the psyche of the master and can never be free from this dependency. A release is only possible when a greater power than the first Hypnotist enters the scene. Only then can the Medium be free from the chains of the clinging relationship.

If the servile state is foisted upon the Medium while fully conscious or awake, it is not a case of a true hypnotic mediumship.

The Hypnotic Medium is no longer consciously dependent like the Suggestive Medium; instead, he is in a perfectly abnormal trance-state which, once invoked, takes control of the Medium when he (apparently fully awake) executes his daily chores, takes care of his business, eats and drinks, laughs with other people, gossips and speaks—in short, when externally evoking the image of a normal and fully independent human being.

This second condition is a trance-state. In order to generate the trance, a hypnotic session is required. (How this is performed and executed shall be explained—expertly and precisely—in later columns.)

For this article, it is sufficient to say that inducing someone into trance is only possible after long, careful, and precise preparation. Remember that amateur hypnosis can be a great danger for the hypnotized. One cannot warn urgently enough about the dangers of hypnosis. The usual jovial attempts to hypnosis, at parties and such, should be avoided in every case. Anyone who, even as a joke, allows himself to be hypnotized, will have surrendered himself to the Hypnotist's will, as well as those around the Hypnotist who are stronger in will than the Medium.

In general, most people, especially females, underestimate the depth of their own suggestibility or mediumship. They often say, laughing, "It would never work with me. Go ahead and try to hypnotize me, I'd like to see if you succeed!" and offer themselves to such seemingly playful games. The result is that once hypnotized, the Mediums may, at a later time, become easy marks of a stranger who dazzles them with a hypnotic gaze. The victims may be bewitched anywhere or anytime in their life: in the theater, in the tramway, on a walk, in the middle of the day, by a second Hypnotist whom they have never seen before and who can inflict a spell of hypnotic dependency.

At my consultation sessions, I often meet such people who simply do not know what has come over them. At a certain point in their lives, they feel insecure, i.e. they experience a longing for some person whom they cannot physically imagine. They dread some impending disaster that they cannot comprehend. They fall into melancholy, they brood, lose interest in work and often experience—wholly inexplicable to themselves—a weariness of life that has in many cases leads to suicide; the causes for their self-inflicted wounds appear mysterious. It is therefore advisable to dissuade medium-inclined individuals from participating in such pastimes.

The examination below is not dangerous. It is a just test of suggestibility and cannot induce the subconscious dependent-relations that I have described above. The purpose of this small amusement is merely to determine the degree of one's medium qualities. Not every person is a Medium, and fortunately there are in general far fewer Mediums than one supposes. For every thousand people, there is only one true Medium. Correspondingly, there are also far fewer Hypnotists than one generally assumes. Possessing a piercing gaze alone will not suffice. The power of hypnosis is something inborn, innate. A true Hypnotist must emerge into the world as such. He can increase his skills, deepen them, refine them; under no circumstances, however, can he train himself from books to be a Hypnotist if he is not predestined for it.

Dear student, before answering the questionnaire, sit in a comfortable chair and read only one question at a time. Then, without too much thought, record the answer in the designated space.

Afterward count the points and you will discover your aptitude to be a true Medium or Hypnotist.

1st Experiment

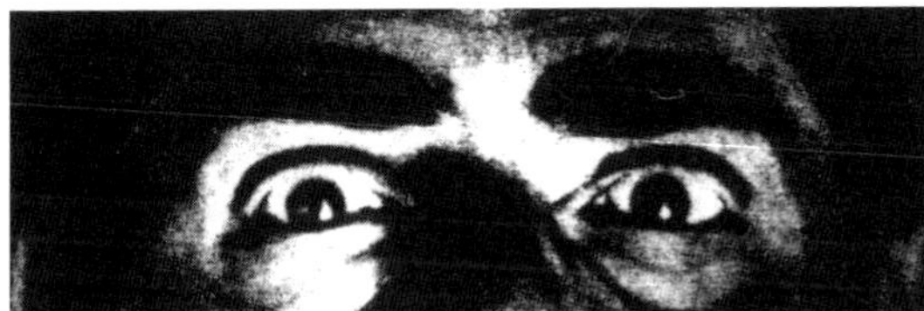

LOOK DEEPLY INTO THESE EYES!

QUESTION:	ANSWER:
I. Do these eyes frighten you?	
II. Turn your head to the left and then to the right. Did you sense that the eyes were following you?	
III. Focus sharply on the bridge of the nose without looking away. Count. How many seconds before you blink or look away?	

I. Analysis: Yes = 20 Medium Points. No = 1 Hypnotist Point

A high score of twenty is awarded for Medium Points, since only a very suggestible person can experience fear from the mere image of a clairvoyant's eyes. The low score of a single Hypnotist Point is conversely justified. An individual need not be of exceptionally strong will to feel no fear from staring at a drawing of a pair of eyes.

II. Analysis: Yes = 1 Medium Point. No = 20 Hypnotist Points.

Why? It is natural to imagine that these penetrating eyes are following your glance as you turn from side to side. To fully eliminate this imaginative power, a very strong will is required, thus the high score for the Hypnotist.

III. Every normal person should easily be able to focus on the base of the nose in the picture for about forty seconds.

Every second below 30 = 1 Medium Point.
Every second over 30 = 1 Hypnotist Point.

2nd Experiment

Pick one of these cards quickly!

QUESTION:	ANSWER:
Which card did you select?	

Analysis: Ace of Clubs = 2 Medium Points.
Eight of Spades = 1 Medium Point.
Eight of Clubs = 1 Hypnotist Point.
Jack of Spades = 2 Hypnotist Points.

3rd Experiment

PICK ONE OF THE HIDDEN CARDS QUICKLY!

QUESTION:	ANSWER:
Which of these ten cards (counting from the left) did you select?	

Analysis: Fifth card from left (outer most) = 10 Medium Points. [A very strong, uncritical disposition is necessary to not have smelled the bait. The card was clearly outstanding in a provocative manner.]
Fourth card from left = 2 Medium Points.
Third card from left = 1 Medium Point.
Second card from left = 5 Hypnotist Points.
First card from left = 3 Hypnotist Points.
Second card from right = 20 Hypnotist Points.
[Seldom chosen since it lays hidden; this indicates a strong resistance.]

4th Experiment

Quickly pick a number between

Three and Ten

QUESTION: ANSWER:

Which number did you pick?

Analysis: Seven = 3 Medium Points. [Most common choice.]
Eight = 3 Hypnotist Points.
Six = 5 Hypnotist Points.
Five = 5 Hypnotist Points.
Four = 5 Hypnotist Points.
Nine = 8 Hypnotist Points.

5th Experiment

Quickly think of a geometric figure

QUESTION: ANSWER:

Which shape did you think of?

Analysis: Triangle = 3 Medium Points.
Circle = 1 Medium Point.
Rectangle or Square = 3 Hypnotist Points.
Any Other Shape = 5 Hypnotist Points.

6th Experiment

Quickly think of a color

QUESTION: ANSWER:

Which color did you think of?

Analysis: Red = 5 Medium Points. [A sign of unusually strong suggestibility.]
Green = 1 Medium Point.
Black = 1 Hypnotist Point.
White = 5 Hypnotist Points.
Blue = 1 Hypnotist Point.
All Non-Primary Colors = 10 Hypnotist Points.

7th Experiment

If you wanted to hypnotize this woman . . .

QUESTION:
Would you consider this seating arrangement correct?

ANSWER:

Analysis: The positioning is perfectly correct (although most people would not think so). A true Hypnotist seats himself casually across from the Medium, since he wants to avoid frightening her. On the contrary, he wants to inspire trust and converses first in an amiable and social manner with his Medium.

If you answered the question with "false," this shows that you are an exceptionally good Medium, since you expect from the position of the clairvoyant something unusual and that would affect you badly.

False = 5 Medium Points.

If you answered the question with "correct," then you have much talent towards becoming a Hypnotist.

Correct = 20 Hypnotist Points.

8th Experiment

Please stand now!!!

QUESTION: ANSWER:

Did you stand up?

Analysis: If you really stood up, you are a Medium non plus ultra.
Followed my command = 20 Medium Points.
Did not stand up as a first impulse = 20 "pro" Hypnotist Points.

9th Experiment

Write down one of the five women's names!

BARBARA
EMMALIESE
ELEONORE
MARIE
CLOTILDE

QUESTION: ANSWER:

Which name did you write?

Analysis: Marie = 5 Medium Points. [I congratulate you on your mediumship.]
Clotide = 8 Hypnotist Points.
Emmaliese = 10 Hypnotist Points.
Eleonore = 2 Hypnotist Points.
Barbara = 1 Hypnotist Point.

10th Experiment

Think of a Great German Statesman!!!

QUESTION: ANSWER:

Which statesman did you think of?

Analysis: Bismarck = 10 Medium Points.
Any other statesman (except Stresemann) = 1 Hypnotist Point.
Gustav Stresemann = 5 Hypnotist Points.

1
2
3
4
5
6
7
8
9
10
11
12
13
14
15
16

Final=Experiment

The Magnetic Scale

Concentrate! Then place your index finger on level "16" of the scale and glide your

finger swiftly and without thinking

up the rungs of the scale until you command yourself to

"STOP"

QUESTION:

On which number did you stop?

ANSWER:

Analysis: 7 = 10 Medium Points.
8 = 10 Medium Points.
6 = 5 Medium Points.
5 = 5 Medium Points.
4 = 5 Medium Points.
3 = 5 Medium Points.
10 = 1 Medium Point.
9 = 7 Medium Points.

15 = 20 Hypnotist Points.
1 = 5 Hypnotist Points.
14 = 15 Hypnotist Points.
13 = 10 Hypnotist Points.
12 = 8 Hypnotist Points.
11 = 5 Hypnotist Points.

For the Other Part of the Experiment

Perform the experiment with an acquaintance in the following manner:

While you move your finger up the scale, this person should quickly think

"STOP"

and you should point to a square (without any forethought).

If you succeeded in stopping where the Medium thought "STOP," then you have telepathic talent and great potential to become a Hypnotist.

Analysis: Number of Consecutive Successful Attempts (out of four):
4 = 30 Hypnotist Points.
3 = 20 Hypnotist Points.
2 = 10 Hypnotist Points.
1 = 5 Hypnotist Points.
0 = 10 Medium Points.

ABSOLUTE MEDIUM = 110–135 MEDIUM POINTS.
ABSOLUTE HYPNOTIST = 180–200 HYPNOTIST POINTS.

Hermann Steinschneider, c. 1914

CHAPTER TWO

THE OTHER WORLD

1912-1914

Journey to the Orient

In September 1912, Harry Steinschneider changed his name once again and bluffed his way into still one more occupation for which he had no natural qualifications. He became a basso-singer in a traveling opera company. To do so, Harry metamorphosed into the living persona of the Viennese Bass singer Aloys Beyerl.

At the Louvre, Harry learned of a choral audition for the Vienna Opera Polensky. The traveling company needed a few more minor singers for its proposed tour of Greece and Turkey. The wifeless, homeless, and kronen-shy man walked over to a café on Josephstädterstrasse at 8:30 in the morning.

In the rear of the coffee shop, Polensky's audition call was nearly concluded. Twenty soloists and twenty chorus members were already rehearsing around a conductor's piano. Harry glided into the circle and began to mouth the words of the company's obscure opera libretto. Polensky and his secretary arrived.

The director announced the schedule: a final meeting at the Central Bahnhof at six the next morning; a train ride to Trieste; a three-day sea journey to Athens, where they would perform for one week; and a second week in Constantinople. The secretary bellowed out names and roles from his audition notebook and handed each singer a contract to sign with a monetary retainer.

When Herr Aloys Beyerl failed to respond after his name was called twice, Harry stepped forward and initialed the secretary's papers. Ignoring the excitement and general tumult around him, the novice first-bass Steinschneider graciously accepted his sixty kronen advance payment.

Early the next day, Aloys (né Harry) was on his way into the lands of antiquity. (Coincidentally, Adolf Hitler was also thinking of abandoning Vienna at this time. After eight months of unremitting struggle, he finally put away his water-colors and stack of postcards, and embarked from the same train station for happier points north, to the neoclassical Mecca of Munich.)

In Athens, Aloys-Harry got a break. Polonsky rented the outdoor arena of the Marmor Theatre, but unseasonable heavy, cold rain forced the cancellation of opening night. The skies soaked the unprotected garden-theatre each and every evening during production week. The Vienna Opera Polonsky could never draw a paying audience and never even attempted a première performance. The smug Aloys and his ensemble mates sailed on to Constantinople.

In the Turkish metropolis, war fever was growing. Serbia, Bulgaria, Romania, and Greece—all former entities or provinces of the Sultan's empire—were preparing for the next Balkan War. Turkish troops menacingly paraded through Constantinople's central thoroughfares and Ottoman naval units blocked all traffic south of the port. The mood in the city visibly soured from the time of the troupe's arrival.

At the Theatre Petit Champ, Polensky's company innocently presented Franz Léhar's *The Merry Widow*, the lighthearted, sure-fire operetta mainstay. Its tunes were heard everywhere in Vienna at the time. (*Widow* remained Hitler's favorite non-Wagnerian opera.) Unfortunately the Montenegro colony viewed the Ruritanian puff-piece as an insult to their nation's honor; it caricatured the private lives of Montenegro's noble house and the loyal subjects of the Sultan. When the colony's leaders were unable to legally close down Polensky's buffoonery, other Montenegrians took a more activist approach. They bombarded the Petit Champ stage with ink-pots, a good number of which struck Polensky's lead performers.

Harry and the lesser lights gladly replaced the Viennese stars, who departed overnight. The Vienna Opera Polensky was still not saved. The Second Balkan War broke out three days later on October 17, 1912. Polensky went bankrupt. Fifteen of the seventy-some members, including Harry, were left stranded in the warring city. The Austro-Hungarian consulate in Constantinople showed little sympathy for their plight. It then had more pressing matters to deal with at the moment.

Under Harry's guidance, the down-and-out Austrian artists rallied and managed to rent a theatre on the tourist island of Kadikai on the Bosporus, just a stone's throw from Constantinople proper. Without musical accompaniment or the artistic means to carry it out, Harry announced the premiere of a new Léhar opera, *Lumpazius Vagabundus*. In addition, Léhar himself—astonishingly—would be in attendance. The Greek manager of the theatre was unmoved. Harry studied the man's face and informed him that an elaborate fire-display would conclude the evening. The Polensky rockets would patriotically spell out the initials of the Sultan Abdul Hamid from four directions. The skeptical Greek took in Harry's civic-minded proposal. After all, Greek-speaking merchants in Turkey, despite the war, were loyal subjects of the Empire too. *Lumpazius* could go on if the cash-box filled with the ticket receipts remained on the stage at all times.

In mad desperation, Harry assembled the production—without Léhar, without a musical libretto, without scenery or costumes, without operatic talent, without proper advertising, even without the chauvinist fireworks. Greek, Armenian, and Turkish music-lovers and curiosity-seekers bought tickets to the faux Austrian extravaganza. Of course, someone stole the money from the cash-box before the performance and Harry's actors vanished before the grand fusillade finale; the remaining ensemble climbed the backstage wall and sailed out to sea, leaving their inventive impresario behind.

Harry had to face his enraged and bewildered audience alone. The Kadikai merry-makers were impatiently rustling in their seats, waiting for the long-

Turkish Island of Kadikai, c.1915

promised open-sky spectacle. They suffered through the bare-bones musical farce; now they expected some real explosive action.

There were no fireworks, Harry informed them, because his company had no funds to purchase them. In a soaring voice, the desperate singer-cum-director bared his soul and told them of his true predicament, the pathetic story of the Polensky comedians. There was an excruciating silence in the Concert Garden Theatre. Then, out of nowhere, spectators began to throw coins at Harry. The opera-lovers stamped appreciably and applauded for over two minutes. The formerly dour Greek theatre owner jumped up and announced that Harry could keep the entire (empty) cash-box. Suddenly an excited Armenian vendor dumped two hatfuls of Turkish pounds on the stage. Harry Steinschneider (aka Aloys Beyerl) was at that moment a solvent man. It was also virtually the last time he would be honest with any stage audience.

Back in Constantinople, Harry purchased a third-class ticket for the coveted journey back to Vienna. The first five days of the trip were on the luxury liner, the *Baron Beck*, which docked in Trieste after four ports of call. In Constantinople, Harry met another starving Viennese performer, Betty Schostak. She would become the love of his life.

A cabaret chanteuse from the Viennese Chat Noir, Betty also could not find a steady livelihood in Constantinople. The exiled White Russian community formed their own nightclubs and *Lokals* since the Revolution. Many of the former Russian aristocrats and Czarist officials became overnight music-hall magnates and impresarios and, naturally, had nothing but contempt for saucy entertainers from Central Europe, poaching on their sparse Turkish terrain.

During her short and fruitless stay in Constantinople, Betty contracted tuberculosis. Harry also discovered that Betty was the sister of an old Schmelz acquaintance, Franz Schostak. Her brother was currently working the tables at the Café Louvre as a head-waiter and a known buyer of purloined goods. Harry bought Betty a ticket for passage on the *Baron Beck*.

The Psychic Detective

Before boarding, Harry saw the entourage of high society in the upper decks and was determined to move to a first-class cabin. He informed the Captain that he was none other than the celebrated baritone, Titta Ruffo, from the Milan Scala. The *Beck's* naive Captain was amazed at his luck and accepted Harry's offer to perform an evening of arias in exchange for an upgraded fare. Calculating quickly, Titta-Harry told the Captain that his performance would take place on the fifth—and last—night of the trip. Harry then went into his traditional over-the-top risk mode. He would brainstorm some elegant solution to cover his preposterous claim before showtime approached. Maybe a throat infection.

In a lower deck was an uncommonly exotic passenger, an East Indian fakir. It was rumored that the entertainer on his way for a revue engagement at the Vienna Apollo Theater. The Indian obsessively carried a straw basket shaped like a beehive. Inside were three poisonous viper snakes, to which he fed live mice in full view of the other passengers. The Indian made no secret of the glass-snakes' lethal ability; a single bite from one of them meant an instantaneous, as well as horrific, death. When the wild-eyed fakir approached the sun deck with his basket, the second-class riders yielded him a very wide berth.

The Captain got wind of the dangerous cargo and ordered the Indian to disembark as quickly as possible, the next evening in Corfu.

Harry noticed other curious passengers aboard the *Beck*. In the first-class compartment was the Count Montegazza, a charming bon vivant who apparently spoke every language, knew every city, and dressed with immaculate care. By his side was an ever-attendant and worldly valet. At the communal meals, Count Montegazza and his valet were the intense focus of both the Captain and his elite charges. Nearly every first-class patron jostled his set sitting arrangement to be near the striking Italian raconteur. And whenever the subject of opera or music came up, the consummate aesthete Montegazza winked knowingly at Titta-Harry and inquired about the baritone's obviously declining vocal health. (At every public function, Harry appeared with a noticeably thicker scarf around his neck.)

The night before the *Beck* docked in Corfu, the scandalous story of the fakir and his basket animated the dinner conversation at the Captain's table. Taking in the society ladies' fearful thoughts, Count Montegazza made an outrageous suggestion: the sequestered East Indian should give a last performance on the promenade, where everyone could watch the vipers' fantastic dance to the hypnotic

Tourist Steamer in the Constantinople Harbor

rhythms of the fakir's flute. It would be an amusing contrast to Ruffo's lofty *a cappella* concert to follow, the Count maintained.

The Captain had his misgivings, but the first-class passengers, especially the women, were easily swayed by the fun-loving dandy and insisted on the daredevil entertainment, despite their earlier apprehension. The Captain sent his purser to inform the Indian of the last-minute project and ordered chaise-longue chairs and colored lights to be placed on the promenade deck for the next night.

The Count was in a particularly jaunty mood the following day. When the Mediterranean sun was about to set and the time for the snake-charming enactment arrived, he enthralled the *Beck's* socially distinguished patrons with humorous anecdotes about his many travels in South Asia and the Far East. Suddenly the outcast Indian appeared. He was a unusually handsome man with luminescent dark eyes set off against perfect bronze-colored skin. The fakir greeted the awed spectators Hindu style and returned to the galleyway to retrieve his caged reptiles. Everyone sat still in anticipation.

Then it began.

First a horrible shriek sounded from below the deck. Then the thud of panicked people in flight. More high-pitched commands. Eventually two frightened sailors emerged from the stairwell. The Indian pushed through them and shouted to the perplexed crowd that his malignant vipers had escaped.

The promenaders sat paralyzed in their lounge-chairs for a fraction of a second. Then hell broke loose. A pair of matrons screeched hysterically as they attempted to find higher ground. The men scouted for escape routes while the Captain stared silently at the Indian, totally aghast.

Only Count Montegazza remained calm. He assured the terrified passengers that poisonous glass adder-snakes preferred moist, darkened environments and probably had not traveled far from the Indian's room. As long as the passengers stayed under the bright lights of the deck and made no inviting noises, they had nothing to fear. Stepping on a viper or irritating it, of course, would solicit a deadly response. So no one was to speak or move. No one.

Next the Count demanded a bowl of warm milk, which a trembling steward quickly procured. The Indian was to bring his flute and entice the creatures from their hiding places on the second deck. The fakir, almost rigid from shock, nodded in agreement. Count Montegazza promised the Captain to return in a mere quarter of an hour with the reptiles in tow. Carrying the pan of milk—with the somnambulant fakir close behind—the Count stealthily opened the hatch-door and treaded carefully down the stairs. He flashed a toothy grin to his frozen admirers before disappearing below.

At first, almost every spectator commented glowingly on the Count's ingenuity and daring. A few of the men wondered, however, if the Italian's self-confidence was misplaced or recklessly exaggerated. The Captain sheepishly apologized for his mishandling of the potentially disastrous event. Only Harry said nothing.

Ten, fifteen minutes elapsed. A ghostly silence overcame the merry-makers. Only the monotonous churning of the sea against the streamer and the gyration of the ship's engines could be heard. The men and women in their fancy evening attire were transformed into enchanted statues.

Count Montegazza pushed open the hatch-door with a flourish. Behind him was the beehive cage. Wiping the perspiration from his forehead, Montegazza lifted the hutch and dropped it on a table under the colored lights. The glass-snakes were recaptured and secured in their basket. The crowd applauded their resourceful savior. The beaming Count offered to show them the runaway vipers; the Captain, however, barked at the Indian to swiftly remove the hideous beasts from his deck.

The lights of Corfu glistened behind the celebrants. The luxury liner was approaching land. In ten minutes, the *Baron Beck* would be anchored and rid of the clumsy fakir and his venomous pets. Only Harry protested. He insisted the Count and the snake-charmer remain in place and the performance continue.

Montegazza's face fell. When Harry moved toward the table, the fakir flashed a dagger that he had hidden in his loincloth. Harry struck him in the face before the warrior could manipulate it effectively. The Count hoarsely shouted that Harry was a fraud, this man was not Titta Ruffo. Harry acknowledged the unwelcome disclosure, explaining that he was no more a Scala baritone than Montegazza was an Italian viscount.

In a startling denouement, Harry unlatched the wicker basket and pulled out three long wiggling snakes. The astonished crowd gasped. They were, according to Harry, a trio of harmless sand-vipers. What made them different from their garden-variety siblings was their extremely rich diet. With his other hand, Harry retrieved from the bottom of the basket: a tangled string of gold watches, a diamond brooch, a gold cross, and two fistfuls of assorted jewels and precious stones.

Members of the promenade audience recognized the secreted valuables at once as their own. Montegazza and the Indian had looted their valises and suitcases from the ship's first-class storage in the hold during the fifteen-minute snake escapade. The Captain ordered the immediate arrest of thieves and their accomplice, the valet.

Harry, for the second time in his life, was a legitimate hero.

While the *Baron Beck* docked, Harry described the method of his fantastic detection. The Indian fakir exuded a strange but familiar smell. It was the unmistakable odor of a special stage makeup, the kind of greasy cream that actors and carnies use to tint their skin a darker shade to play Asians or aborigines. A few days earlier, Harry had surprised the Indian in a shower-room while he was applying the tint to his upper body. On the Indian's pale left shoulder was a tattoo with an inscription in Jenisch. The man was a Gypsy and most likely a con-artist.

Later during the trip, a girl from Dresden asked Titta-Harry to sign her autograph book. Harry noticed that the Indian's signature and Count Montegazza's were both unusually similar and came from lefthanded writers. That aroused the old carnie boy's interest. He never suspected Montegazza was anything other than the real McCoy. Nonetheless, he then decided to investigate a bit further. Sure enough, on the Count's left shoulder was a faded Jenisch tattoo, although possible surgical attempts were made to remove or disfigure it. Finally, Harry realized the pair's identity.

They were the Pirelli Brothers, a criminal team who once worked the Balkan circuit as acrobats. Circus postcards of them were passed from carnival to carnival, warning owners of their depraved activities. Harry clearly remembered their exuberant grins and sparkling eyes. Additionally, Harry knew from his days at Circus H. that snake-charming was an absolute hoax. Reptiles cannot hear or feel musical vibrations; they only follow the flute as a defensive instinct. Any scheme that involved a flute and locating poisonous adders in the dark had some serious flaws. Harry also knew the fakir's dreaded snakes were about as innocuous as reptiles came.

The passengers were mesmerized by Harry's explanation. It was more exciting than any Arthur Conan Doyle story or sleight-of-hand music-hall number. The richest of them gathered in a circle and anted up a considerable fund in Austrian kronen as a token of their gratitude. The Captain wanted to know Harry's real name and that of his female companion. H. B. Marinelli, a Broadway entrepreneur, handed the amateur detective his business card and encouraged him to enter the variety stage as a comic psychic or a fast-draw graphologist. Harry chuckled at the suggestion but kept the card. (Twelve years later, Harry would show up at Marinelli's New York office, reminding him of the invitation.)

Around the Ring

Back in Vienna, Harry relied on Betty's show-business contacts. He worked as a runner for a local talent-scout and joined the newly-established Viennese revue,

Simplicissimus. At the Simpl, Harry recycled his Louvre-inspired *chansons* and probably performed in the cabaret sketches with Betty as the wacky love-interest.

In the spring of 1913, Harry returned to tabloid journalism and to life on Vienna's rougher edges. He became a reporter for *Der Blitz*, a notorious "revolver-journal." The five-year-old scandal sheet exposed—in delicious detail—the secret nocturnal life and sexual escapades of the Duo-Monarchy's most prominent citizens. Its front pages unveiled the petty machinations of corrupt city officials, disclosed the bourgeois patronage of venereal disease clinics, reported the full arrest records of prostitution and narcotics cases, and reveled in outing Vienna's closeted homosexuals and cross-dressers.

Much of *Der Blitz's* hard income came from proposed or advance-copy articles that never ran. The subjects in question paid hush-money to ensure that accounts of their embarrassing peccadilloes were killed in the press room. Advanced proof sheets were handed to prospective victims, who were then offered the opportunity to compensate the journal for its prepublication expenses. *Der Blitz's* editor-in-chief, Gustav Georg Leitner, made a substantial living from this out-and-out extortion.

Unfortunately some of *Der Blitz's* assertions were blatantly false and, on several occasions, Leitner found himself defending the honor of his regal profession against charges of slander and defamation in municipal court. As a result, Vienna's vice police were ordered to confiscate offending editions of *Der Blitz* before they reached the newsstands.

At the beginning of May 1913, *Der Blitz* changed its format from a haphazard tabloid to a "pictorial weekly." In its newest incarnation, it featured a photographic list of staid clients who frequented a high-class brothel with indications of dates and financial transactions.

Writing under the pen name "Faun," Harry's first column appeared on May 28. It announced the publication of two serialized novels to appear in future editions: *The Memoirs of a Snake-Dancer* (based on the actual diaries of a Viennese-Berlin courtesan and official police documents) and a twenty-one-part roman à clef, *The Adventures of Major Quitsch*. In the June 4 issue of *Der Blitz*, Faun was elevated to the position of co-editor.

Harry's *Major Quitsch* series was a semi-fictional exposé of Vienna's pleasure clubs and illicit Prater establishments. Quitsch and his sidekick Erasmus Pankratius Rosskopf chased around shadowy Vienna, visiting recognized hotels, restaurants, *Lokals*, and classy fashion shops. After being notified that their emporiums were on Quitsch's infamous list, *Nachtlokal* and restaurant owners were encouraged to pay blackmail à la *Blitz*. Harry also added a *Hymns*-like element: payment could be made for flattering portraits as well.

On August 14, 1913, *Der Blitz* bizarrely exposed itself. Harry Steinschneider and Leitner (aka Quitsch and Rosskopf) were arrested by the vice officers at the Phoenix-Palast, a Prater pimp-bar and brothel. The procuress-owner Amalia Swoboda ungraciously refused their blackmail request and turned the two characters over to the authorities, who had observed *Der Blitz's* techniques first-hand. Naturally, Leitner threatened to retaliate by revealing the nocturnal "secrets" of the Prater police-commissioner.

Berlin's Night-Asylum

By October, Major Quitsch and his trusted companion Rosskopf completed their last adventure. The journalist Harry had somehow crossed the line of acceptable criminal behavior with the Viennese vice squad, and even Leitner was growing impatient with his reckless co-editor. Harry was advised to seek a new venue immediately. Harry agreed. His newfound prosperity had been frittered away during his nightly forays at a Prater casino and entertaining the girls of Café Louvre. It was definitely time for something new.

In addition, Betty's physical condition deteriorated precipitously. The former chanteuse was now unable to perform. Viennese physicians declared her TB incurable. Harry heard about a radical treatment in Berlin. Once again, Harry departed from the Central Bahnhof and dropped the critically ill Betty at Berlin's main charity ward. Meanwhile he pursued new career possibilities. Within three days' time, he was broke and thoroughly despondent.

After reading a newspaper ad for a "singing waiter," Harry showed up at the Night-Asylum, a North Berlin dive on the Neue Friedrichstrasse near the Alex. Harry bluffed his way past forty other job-seekers and appeared in Jacob Schlesinger's dingy office. The proprietor promptly showed the Viennese upstart the door. Then Harry threatened blackmail. He knew the Night-Asylum did not have a certificate to sell liquor. Schlesinger recoiled; how did Harry know that? Harry claimed to be a clairvoyant. He knew all.

The ever-flexible Schlesinger hired Harry on the spot and handed him a Russian blouse and a sash. Harry Steinschneider was now Ivan, a muzhik-clad singing waiter. The old opera hand's repertoire was limited but hardly noticeable in the tumultuous atmosphere of Schlesinger's clip-joint. Its three different specialty beers were all drawn from the same tap and no one complained.

At midnight, the Night-Asylum transformed into a curio cabinet-cum-haunted museum of nineteenth-century Germania. Guests were led into a darkened antechamber, where Schlesinger pointed to desiccated objects and identified them as sacred cultural relics: a sand-filled glove was worn by Schiller when he penned *The Maid from Orleans*; a discolored cotton ball lying on a pillow was the inspiration for Goethe's *Faust*, and so forth. When Harry-Ivan took over for the proprietor one night, a new and unexpected lecture unfolded.

Cradling the fragile artifacts in his palm, Harry envisioned the real owners and their tragic histories. The weighted glove was not a literary souvenir from the *Sturm-und-Dranger's* salon, it was the property of a suicidal actress who wore it the day before her demise. The pillow that supported the cotton fist, the greased cucumber, the broken doll, each had a strange and tragic history that Harry inexplicably surmised.

Neither the drunken revelers nor Schlesinger took to Harry's uncanny technique or spooky revelations. He was fired that evening. (Hanussen later claimed in his autobiography that this was his first experience in the psychic analysis of objects and the histories of their owners, or Psychometry.)

The next day, Harry visited Betty in the TB sanitarium. Her once creamy-skinned face had become waxy and sunken; her fulsome lips now contracted into a mute tight line; and her formerly luminescent blue eyes bulged uncomprehendingly from their darkened sockets.

Harry applied for a job as a stage magician in another North Berlin *Lokal.* He purchased a handbook on credit from the wizened conjurer, Janos Bartel, in his shop at the edge of Friedrichstrasse and attempted to master the trade in a day. Harry's first performance ended disastrously. But the *Lokal* owner didn't dismiss the fake legerdemain-meister as Harry dreaded.

The North Berlin audience loved the Viennese's unintentionally comic act. Watching Harry Steinschneider's incompetent arrangement of objects and earnest fumbling of paper flowers, coins, handkerchiefs, and eggs brought tears of laughter to the delighted spectators. The tavern's manager never heard so many rounds of applause in his miserable, dank cellar. Harry received a two-week contract.

Harry returned to Bartel to learn a phony telepathy and fortune-telling routine with tarot cards and a hidden mirror. He studied the master's various formulas (six for each of "mankind's fifty personality types") and practiced on the edge of Betty's bed in her charity ward room. It was useless. When showtime approached each evening, Harry forgot the basic mind-reading formulas. And his beer-addled audiences now were not so forgiving. Harry's prognostications were not only clumsily drawn but also without waggish humor or charm.

Café Spectators, c.1915

The Magician's Grief

Harry was dismissed and began his mind- and fortune-reading routine again in a still more northern, out-of-the-way variety-bar. A sympathetic agent tried to assist him by suggesting a more upbeat, punched-up patter. Harry resisted. On stage, his mind went blank, and his demeanor before the ready-to-laugh audience radiated a visceral contempt. Harry's winning comic persona had utterly vanished.

One night, Harry began with the usual Bartel card-guessing trick. He offered the deck of oversized playing cards to a man in a front-row seat. After Harry turned his back, the gentleman was instructed to hold the card high and display his selection for the general audience's viewing. Harry would then magically intuit the man's choice. Naturally, the trick involved a tiny mirror secreted on the stage table. That night, however, the magician's mirror tilted downward and detached from its mooring. Harry was lost.

In his panicked imagination, Harry saw Betty, not the gentleman or the card. He visualized her in the TB ward, attempting to stand and mouthing his name. Crimson drops trickled from the sides of her ashen lips and she collapsed back into her blood-soaked mattress. Betty Schostak had finally given up the struggle.

Harry turned and looked hard at his audience. The comic telepathy number that he so painfully memorized no longer seemed to matter. Instead Harry lashed out at his tormentors. Pointing to one hellishly-grinning spectator, Harry harangued him to stub out his cigarette; he was a consumptive and slowly infecting his girlfriend by letting her share his beer glass; the man's father was a drunkard and his mother a prostitute. In addition, the galahad's employer was about to have him arrested for embezzlement.

Shifting to another table, Harry warned a frightened drinker that it was time for her to return to her hovel and forget about her cherished lottery dreams and pray. The woman's pregnant daughter, unbeknownst to her, was walking the streets of the Friedrichstadt at that minute.

An elderly man sitting with his wife was Harry's next target. The henpecked husband had consulted a gypsy that afternoon, Harry screamed, to see how much longer he had to wait before his wife's death. Finally in his true state of clairvoyant rapture, Harry grabbed the tarot deck from the lap of the front-row man and ripped up the magic cards like confetti.

The enraged owner of the *Lokal* rose from his table and struck Harry in the stomach. And before Harry could gather his coat to exit, the entrepreneur pulled down the magician's hand-drawn poster and shredded it in disgust.

Harry pushed his way out and fled to the nearest streetcar stop. He got off at the main Friedrichstrasse station and ran down Karlstrasse. The crazed magician frantically rang the night bell of the Charity Hospital and was led downstairs to the basement morgue. There Harry was shown Betty's emaciated corpse.

It was only on his return trip to Vienna that Harry's hysteria and grief subsided. If fortune-telling was a low stage con, he wondered, how did he foresee Betty's fated hour? Were his manic visions of the Night-Asylum museum artifacts and the cabaret customers' personal histories authentic insights, or Bartel's chicanery run amok?

Harry later confessed that he was more than confused; the *Jenischmann* was frightened. If clairvoyant ability truly existed, did he possess it? That idea worried him. Knowing too much about the future could lead to danger. Still, another flipped childish fear gnawed inside Harry Steinschneider's overheated brain: suppose clairvoyant powers were available to some chosen individuals but he was not among the elect? That was the worst thought of all.

The Next Path

On New Year's Day 1914, Leitner's *Der Blitz* temporarily ceased publication due to a printers' strike. Three months earlier, the pictorial weekly had published Harry Steinschneider's salacious account of Berlin's gay bars. Leitner accepted his prodigal correspondent back into *Der Blitz'* fold. Now Harry had to brainstorm safer and more legally ambiguous schemes to survive. He discovered one at the Café Louvre.

Eugen de Rubini (né Leo Rubiner) was a clairvoyant from Brünn who performed at the Ronacher variety theatre and frequented the artists' clubhouse. His specialty was a form of telepathy known as "Hellstormism." The phenomenal Rubini could locate concealed objects, hidden by audience members in his absence, through pure "thought transference." The spectator who secreted the tiny item was designated by Rubini as his "medium." The telepathist then asked the volunteer to mentally concentrate on the location of the article. Holding the medium's wrist, the clairvoyant Rubini quickly led the spectator through the variety hall to the spot in question. Rubini's magical efforts were unfailing. Every item, no matter how small or well concealed, was ferreted out by the Great Rubini. Vienna's audiences were stunned by the seamless display of paranormal detection.

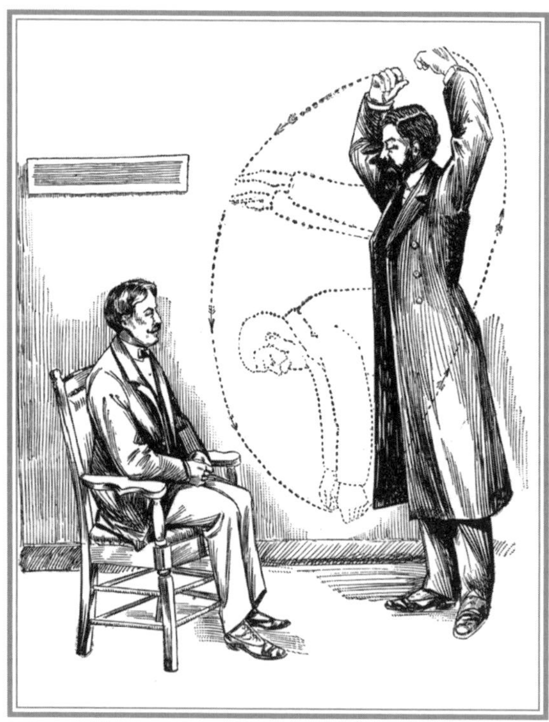

A Hypnotic Pass from the **Flowers Kollektion** (1910)

Joe Labéro, the People's Enlightener

Joe Labéro

In February 1914, Joe Labéro appeared at the Café Louvre. The "Experimental-Psychologist" from Munich badmouthed Rubini's telepathic sleuthing as fraudulent mentalism and lackluster showmanship. Suddenly Harry realized a scoop in the making and introduced himself as the editor-in-chief of the newly re-established *Der Blitz*. (While Leitner battled the unions, Harry forged ahead with his own pasted-up version of the weekly.)

Harry offered Labéro 200 kronen for an open letter exposing Rubini's deception and the secrets of his mind-reading tricks. Labéro complied and (writing under the thinly-disguised pseudonym of Joe Sabeo) accused Rubini of pseudo-telepathy and flat-out charlatanism. Rubini's psychic acts were nothing more than misappropriations of American "muscle-reading," a scientific turn-of-the-century discovery that correlated muscular contraction to conscious brain activity.

Harry ran Labéro's inflammatory letter, "The Telepath Rubini Exposed!" on the front page of *Der Blitz* in his final February edition. Naturally, Leitner publicly denounced Steinschneider and his ersatz "revolver sheet." Meanwhile Harry himself became intrigued with Labéro's provocative thesis and asked him, days after the accusation appeared, to instruct him in the techniques of muscle-reading. Harry assured the German parapsychologist that he would neither display them in any commercial arena nor reveal the method to anyone else.

"Muscle-Reading"

The term "muscle-reading" was coined by Dr. George Beard in 1874 to explain the astounding telepathic demonstrations of Jacob Randall Brown. Like hypnosis and graphology, Brown's mind-reading performance was a nineteenth-century phenomenon that confounded American scientists, who discounted its spiritualist origins, yet could give no easy rational explanations for it.

Brown's subjects merely had to think about the whereabouts of their hidden articles and the Missouri showman could read their minds and retrieve the objects. Beard watched how Brown made physical contact with his subjects as he inquired about the hiding places. The mystifier was not really reading their mute thoughts, Beard reported, but was detecting their slight and nearly imperceptible ideomotor responses to his questions. Beard, despite his hocus-pocus introduction and otherworldly ratiocination, was a skilled interpreter of unconscious nervous impulses generated by the human brain. His psycho-physiological theatrics would have a profound impact on the skeptics in the medical world and among the new breed of criminologists. It would be the basis of William James' Objective Psychology and the lie-detector machine in all its crank antique renditions.

Other American vaudeville magicians and stage occultists borrowed from Brown's methodology and fanned out across the country. Mind-reading, telepathy, clairvoyance, and out-and-out spiritual quackery became standard and implacable elements of American popular entertainment until the 1950s when television variety shows diminished their enduring live appeal.

By 1905, mind-reading (via muscle-reading) had reached the European continent, where it mixed with fakirism, "Second Sight," psychometry, animal mesmerism, "thought-wave" communication, stage hypnosis, auto-suggestion, psycho-graphology, and flashy sleight-of-hand table magic. Hellström (Axel Vogt) and Ernesto Bellini were the acknowledged kings of Mental Telepathy in the German-speaking world. Both Rubini and Labéro studied the same American and British texts and spent time with their *Mitteleuropa* masters. Hence Rubini and Labéro were natural adversaries.

Muscle-Reader and Medium, 1914

Labéro's Lessons

Labéro refined the basic muscle-reading procedure. The selection of the medium was crucial. Young, enthusiastic, good-looking women in general, he felt, were more suitable than, say, stout men, who were the least appropriate and most likely to fear ridicule. The medium had to be cooperative, a thoroughly willing subject, comfortable on stage, even physically submissive. He or she had to possess some overt spiritual or naive quality and then demonstrate sensitivity to the telepath's commands—usually determined in a group hypnotic test before the number began.

Instead of thinking of the location of the hidden object directly, Labéro instructed his mediums to break their thoughts into short unspoken commands, like "Two steps right," "Now the center aisle," "Out that door," "Under the seat," and so forth. The telepath also needed to be intensely focused on the minute involuntary twitches of the mediums' hands and arms, always stepping ahead of them. Finally, the mind-reader had to exhibit great confidence in his psychic abilities—not only to convince the medium of his intuitive powers but also to more sharply focus his own perceptions. [See "Ten Rules for Muscle-Reading," pp. 52.]

Labéro also taught Harry "Telepathy without Bodily Contact." The task was more difficult, yet the principles were similar. Watch for facial tics and unconscious directional clues from the medium's body. Walk slightly behind the subject, always asking questions, observing the tiniest movements of the medium's shoulders and neck, arm gestures, and shifts in posture.

Harry was a model student. On his first outing, he found a coffee-spoon that his friends secreted in the Louvre's billiard parlor. The *Jenischmann* instinctively knew aspects of human behavior that were foreign to the middle-class, show-business mind-readers. How a potential medium shook his hand already indicated to Harry the willingness of the subject. Barking insulting, ego-threatening demands; deep inflection in the voice; rapid-fire questions; and teasing comments softened the resistance of even the stoutest, most skeptical nay-sayers.

Labéro's greatest contribution to Harry's future education as a clairvoyant was his lessons in "Pseudo-Telepathy," or "Echolalia." [See pp. 52.] Muscle-reading alone could not account for many of Rubini's most spectacular "thought-transference" stunts. Stage assistants—both known and invisible to the audience—secretly communicated with the Great Rubini through a system of sound or visual cues.

As a proof of Rubini's magical power of "Second Sight," he would have himself securely blindfolded by a volunteer and then positioned with his back to the audience. Meanwhile Rubini's partner would walk through the aisles, gesturing silently for random objects from the spectators. Rubini's stooge would then majestically hold up the article and ask the blinded clairvoyant to identify it through his telepathic reading of the assistant's projected thought. Although Rubini feigned confusion and an inability to visualize the selected item at dramatic moments, he always guessed right in the end. Audiences adored the number and even skeptics were baffled.

The Rubini's Second Sight trick was quite simple, according to Labéro. Rubini's confederate conveyed the object through a verbal system of codes. Each object was indicated through the aide's first word. So, "Guess what I am holding now, Master?" meant the partner selected a watch. Rubini's assistant reportedly avoided children because they were known to carry weird objects, like dead mice or frogs, on their person: items that could not be easily imparted through common codewords.

Similar visual codes, which were used for the "Non-Contact Muscle-Reading" Act, involved hand signals and minute facial gestures. To indicate that a needle, for instance, was hidden in the hat of a woman in the fifth seat of the eighteenth row, Rubini's helper, standing at the back of the house, would lick his lips (female), flash a one and eight with his fingers (18), then flutter five fingers (5), and finally pass his hand over his head (a hat). With a little effort and encouragement from Labéro, Harry created his own intricate and more advanced Pseudo-Telepathic glossaries.

Labéro believed there was still a more profound aspect of telepathy: the telepath's superhuman ability to memorize finite details of people, places, and dates. For this, he created a series of mnemonic devices that fixed objects to numbers or to nonsensical sentences. [See Labéro's Mnemonic Chart, pp. 53.]

Clairvoyant-In-Training

In May, as soon as Labéro returned to Munich, Harry challenged Rubini to a contest in Mental Telepathy at the Café Louvre. The amateur Ottakring kid won hands down. Chagrined that he placed second to an amateur, Rubini took Harry on as an assistant for his summer provincial tour.

Back on the road in Moravia, Harry perfected his mind-reading experiments and began an intense study of hypnotic suggestion and other psychological-occult stunts. The young telepath built and displayed a "Palmograph" from the designs of Dr. Wilhelm Preyer, a German physiologist from the University of Jena. The Palmograph, a Rube Goldberg-like apparatus, measured tiny muscular contractions in the arm and could be utilized like a primitive lie-detector machine. The scientific-supernatural instrument never failed to astonish and dumbfound the local constabulary.

Hanussen demonstrates his Palmograph, 1914

In Prossnitz, Siegfried Steinschneider's hometown, Harry successfully exorcised a deranged milk-maiden of a recurring religious visitation. The girl was possessed by nightmarish visions of the Virgin Mary and babbled in unintelligible dialects. Harry was amazed by the ease with which the peasant woman fell into his hypnotic trance and finally returned to her normal state. The villagers celebrated the wondrous healing experiment with their best slivovitz and local delicacies.

Hanussen and Hypnotized Subject

According to Géza von Cziffra, who claimed to have seen Harry's diary entries from the Rubini tour, the budding telepath met Sigmund Freud in Prague after his success in Prossnitz. There, in a deserted lobby at the Hotel Flora on June 2, the two Viennese strangers, abandoned by their hosts and starved for late-night conversation, kibitzed about the efficacy of hypnotic treatment. Harry maintained that the founder of Psychoanalysis seemed pleased with his fieldwork and wished him good luck after a pleasant game of pool. [Like many of von Cziffra's anecdotes about Hanussen published in *Hanussen. Hellseher des Teufels* (Munich/Berlin: Herbig, 1978), the story was probably apocryphal, charming nonetheless and certainly an exquisite specimen of Hanussenia in its post-World War Two phase.]

Keeping to his predictable pattern of assiduous fealty followed by impetuous insubordination, Harry broke with Rubini and returned to Vienna. He may not have known it just then but the drill fields and firing ranges of the Schmelz outside his father's old apartment resounded with incessant activity. Europe in the summer of 1914 was preparing its armies for war on a scale yet unimagined in human history.

10 RULES FOR MUSCLE-READING by Joe Labéro

1. Be very cautious from the very beginning. If you are performing in an unelevated room, start in the corner. On stage, always position yourself in the center. That way, you can maintain your focus, by relying on your reflexes for a smashing conclusion.
2. Relax. Make yourself light. Sharpen your senses. Become loose. DO NOT FIGHT AGAINST YOUR REFLEXES. Also do not try to dismiss them.
3. Never let the Medium know that you are the leader. Make him think that only he is the one determining the event.
4. Never let the Medium lead you. Stride ahead of him or, at the very least, stop in order to be in line with him!
5. In uncertain moments, keep in constant hand contact. This will allow for precise probing and location of the details.
6. Make the search seemed so fated that your Medium stops believing in his own abilities.
7. Never lose your nerve if you make a mistake. Restart the entire experiment if necessary.
8. Before the experiment, always give your Medium (and spectators) an elementary explanation of Mind-Reading.
9. If you have to search under more pressing conditions, divide the mission into discrete parts.
10. Work out all initial probes through hand-contact. When you are certain of the location, lead with your free right hand. The effect will produce a more sensational conclusion.

JOE LABERO'S PSEUDO-TELEPATHIC KEY

OBJECT	SIGNAL WORD	NUMBER	SIGNAL WORD
Woman	"Here"	1	"Then"
Man	"And here"	2	"And"
Child	"Still here"	3	"Tell"
Ring	"Look"	4	"Now"
Watch	"Guess"	5	"Likewise"
Hat	"Concentrate"	6	"Also"
Key	"Divine"	7	"Again"
Gold	"From what"	8	"Quickly"
Silver	"Where from"	9	"Please"
[And so forth ...]		0	"Fast"

Wundermänner, Ich Enthülle Eure Geheimnisse! (1933)

Joe Labéro's Memory Key

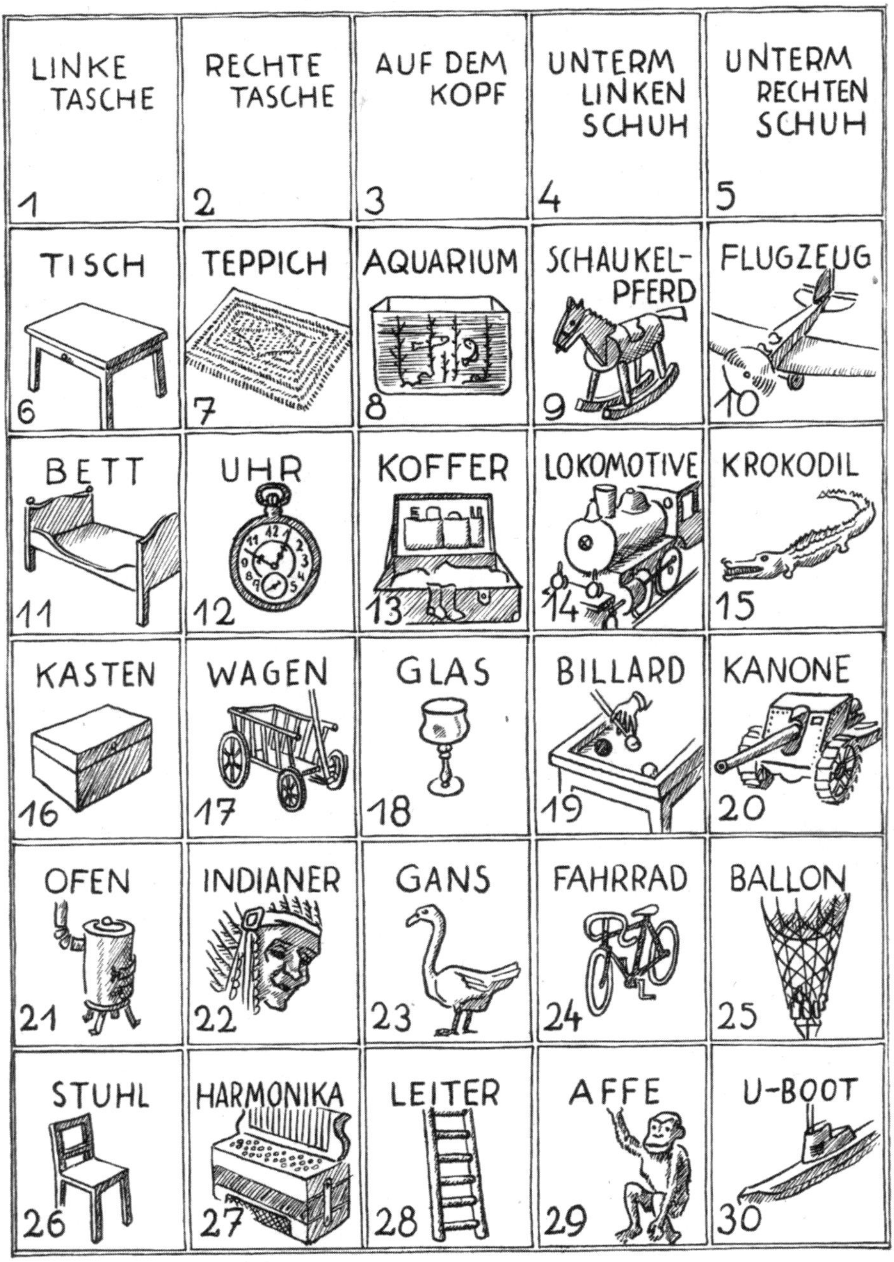

LINKE TASCHE 1	RECHTE TASCHE 2	AUF DEM KOPF 3	UNTERM LINKEN SCHUH 4	UNTERM RECHTEN SCHUH 5
TISCH 6	TEPPICH 7	AQUARIUM 8	SCHAUKEL-PFERD 9	FLUGZEUG 10
BETT 11	UHR 12	KOFFER 13	LOKOMOTIVE 14	KROKODIL 15
KASTEN 16	WAGEN 17	GLAS 18	BILLARD 19	KANONE 20
OFEN 21	INDIANER 22	GANS 23	FAHRRAD 24	BALLON 25
STUHL 26	HARMONIKA 27	LEITER 28	AFFE 29	U-BOOT 30

Words in Chart: 1. LEFT POCKET, 2. RIGHT POCKET, 3. ON THE HEAD, 4. UNDER LEFT SHOE, 5. UNDER RIGHT SHOE, 6. TABLE, 7. RUG, 8. AQUARIUM, 9. HOBBY-HORSE, 10. AIRPLANE, 11. BED, 12. WATCH, 13. SUITCASE, 14. TRAIN, 15. CROCODILE, 16. CASE, 17. WAGON, 18. GLASS, 19. POOL TABLE, 20. CANNON, 21. STOVE, 22. INDIAN, 23. GOOSE, 24. BICYCLE, 25. BALLOON, 26. CHAIR, 27. ACCORDION, 28. LADDER, 29. MONKEY, 30. SUBMARINE.

Harry Steinschneider, Lance Corporal, 1917

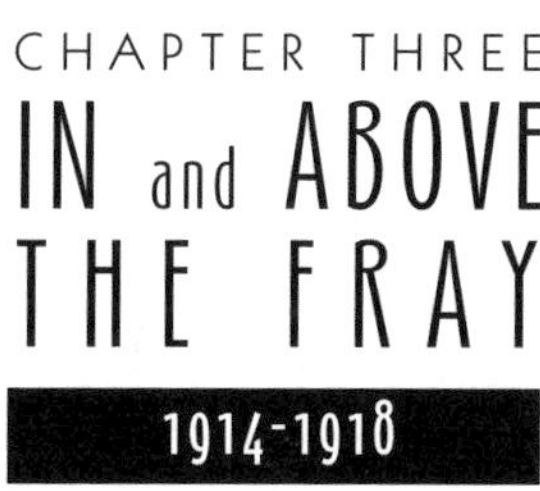

CHAPTER THREE

IN and ABOVE THE FRAY

1914-1918

Private Steinschneider, First-Class

Two months after the Serbian Black Hands assassinated the Archduke Ferdinand and his wife in a side-street in Sarajevo, the Great War finally arrived to the delight of Europe's general staffs and frustrated revolutionaries. Germany now had an excuse to push its overextended Russian and French adversaries headlong into a continental battle royale. Austria and Turkey were assured by Kaiser Wilhelm II that an Entente victory would rescramble the fractious boundaries of their empires into expanded and more governable national zones.

Harry Steinschneider was immediately conscripted into the Austro-Hungarian 54th Infantry Regiment, known as the "Old Starhemberg," and was stationed in the garrison town of Olmütz on the Eastern Front.

Harry's official rank was that of Private First Class, due to his previous stint. His superiors, however, treated him little better than the peasant cannon fodder that comprised the bulk of Franz Joseph's Imperial troops. Their contempt was a predictable response to Harry's insolent Ottakring manner. He perfected a maddening incompetent soldierly image by seeming to agree to all military commands with an open-faced enthusiasm but actually carrying none of them out to their proper and logical conclusion. Harry was just one of the many Sergeant Schweiks that doomed the Austro-Hungarian Army and stymied the Central Powers' Great Six-Month Offensive.

Private Steinschneider's Moravian sergeant despised the Praterstrasse denizen. He assigned him to latrine duty, which Harry, of course, accepted with smirky ebullience. Unfortunately, after his commanding officer fell victim to nervous exhaustion, Harry's passive-aggressive antics were no longer tolerated and he was resigned to the disintegrating Galician front. The Southern Russian Army had penetrated fifty miles eastward, nearly engulfing the entire Carpathian plain. The first-class private with unwashed gloves and a sunny disposition welcomed the change of venue gladly.

Harry was stationed in Lemberg, the home of the 11th Army. From there, the Old Starhemberg was ordered to reinforce the medieval city of Przemysl against the Czarist onslaught. Over 160,000 soldiers, mostly Hungarian Cavalry units, stood fast, in hastily constructed fortresses and underground mazes, against the Russians' punishing artillery and battle-fresh troops. Besieged Przemysl was the key to Galicia and a gateway to Hungary.

Harry, careless and carefree, was wounded several times in the trenches. At the Przemysl military hospital, his madcap behavior was contagious and welcomed. Harry organized evenings of cabaret sketches, magic tricks, lice-races, and a British version of bingo. The maw of war was not about to grind down his frenetic Viennese sense of humor and joie de vivre. Harry's injuries and childish pastimes could not trump the Eleventh Army's orders; Private Steinschneider was always remanded back to his original outpost.

Harry's closest buddies also fought the boredom by clowning around in the earthen bunkers. To accompany their accordion recitals, they manipulated helmets with sticks and had them dance along the foxhole perimeters. Russian troops, across the field, provided a ringing musical counterpoint with their rifles.

The greatest enemy of the Galician conscripts was thirst. Some one hundred Austro-Hungarian and Russian soldiers, crawling to a beckoning waterhole in no-man's-land, were picked off by sharp-shooters from opposite sides. Ultimately, a Russian contingent organized a private truce.

At six in the evening, Austro-Hungarian and Russian troops met at the well for potable water, some pidgin-language prattle (except for the Jews who tumelled maniacally in Yiddish), and barter. Harry remembered the loaves of fine Russian bread he received for cigarettes. The commanding officers on both sides, of course, were soon informed of the treasonous idyll and quickly put an end to the seditious affair. The senseless killings had to continue.

One of Harry's funniest associates, and delousing comrade, was Dovidel Zwillinger. An enormous bear of a man—Harry claimed that he needed three sets of pants, stitched together, for his regulation uniform—Zwillinger demonstrated exceptional courage in the service of his multinational motherland. When Harry teased him about his risky maneuvers in the trench, Zwillinger replied that as a Jew he could not afford that supreme luxury of cowardice. In Przemysl, he represented his accursed race.

The Ottakring bon vivant returned to his fetal-like position in the muck only to witness Zwillinger's demise; a bullet pierced the Hebrew Goliath's cranium. Zwillinger was rolled into a mass grave with the rest of Old Starhemberg's heroic defenders. Harry later commemorated the stalwart giant in a cabaret ditty, "Kohn, the Old-Year Volunteer." [*Was so über's Brettl ging* . . . (Olmütz: Josef Groák, 1915)]

The Commander of Corpses

By February 1915, Harry lost his enthusiasm for frontline combat and faked an incapacitating bout of shell-shock. The military doctors back in Olmütz could detect no organic damage to his brawny exterior, but the first-class private Steinschneider trembled nonetheless with or without their medical permission.

Only by chance did the imaginary invalid miss the fall of Przemysl on March 22. The Hapsburgian officers were unable to sufficiently rally the city's defenders

Gorlice Burial Unit

and ward off the Southern Russian Army's final savage assault. 110,000 of the Emperor's battle-tested soldiers surrendered en masse; the rest died in the chaotic nighttime retreat or in the bloody internecine mutiny that followed.

In May 1915, Harry was shipped to Gorlice, an Etappe city one hundred miles to the east that had been devastated even more horribly than Przemysl during the Russian spring offensive. Over 60,000 Imperial Austro-Hungarian, German, and Czarist troops were slaughtered in the streets and fields of Gorlice. Mangled corpses and detached body parts lay scattered in grotesque compositions everywhere. Fieldmarshal Paul von Hindenberg's wonder weaponry—mobile cannon nicknamed Big Bertha—proved its lethal worth and then some.

Harry led a special burial squad of Austrian noncombatants and Russian prisoners of war. The heaps of fallen soldiers, all in a state of putrefaction, had to be identified, placed in wooden crates, and then interred in Gorlice's pliant marshy soil. Many of the cadavers had no personal markings left; high-velocity shrapnel charges and Moravia's rapacious bacteria obliterated those. Naturally, the gallant officer corps of the three armies had to be segregated from the common soldiery in order to receive the recompense of a Red Cross. These august markings were penciled over selected pine coffins by Harry's battalion. It was ghastly and mind-numbing work. Names and ranks of the anonymous and headless torsos had to be constantly fabricated.

Austria's best architects and stage designers received orders to devise geodesic mausoleums honoring the departed warrior-gods of Gorlice. The gruesome project, which meant vaster graveyards and further reburials, took nearly a year to complete. The Empire's sentimental endeavor was said to be the zenith of the Vienna Session movement and much acclaimed in the capitals of the Duo-Monarchy. It was yet another concrete example of Franz Joseph's unparalleled humane temperament in the midst of world war. Even Kaiser Wilhelm was supposed to visit the sacred, artistic grounds in 1915 but never appeared.

Séance in the Ruins

In the late autumn of 1915, Harry befriended one Russian POW, a talented poet and a painter. However, the overall situation in Gorlice was growing pathetic. The thousands of Russian captives, a fading concern of their own government, were laboring under slave-like conditions. Harry decided to raise money for the prisoners' welfare as a Christmas gift. He offered to conduct a telepathic séance and use the spectators' receipts as the basis of a food fund for his Russian platoon-workers.

The commanding officer of Gorlice, Precinct Captain Mitschka, a lawyer in peacetime, had an unmilitary-like fondness for Harry. (The Viennese conscript taught the Captain tennis, photography, and rabbit breeding.) Mitschka was also an amateur occultist. The idea for a seasonal charity event with supernatural overtones greatly appealed to him. He designated the officer's casino as the private's theatre-hall and commandeered additional funds from local oil magnates.

Harry's evening telepathic evening was a phenomenal success. With the help of two aides, whom he instructed in Labéro's codes, Harry discovered the whereabouts of hidden needles and other such objects. He also made a spectacular prediction: Mitschka's wife had just bore him a son.

Five days later, the clairvoyant prognosis came true. The CO was so overjoyed with the telepath's abilities that he gave Harry one hundred gold kronen and promoted the plucky seer to the rank of Lance Corporal. Harry had to split the monetary reward with Willie Graubundner, a confederate in the field postal department. Harry's silent partner was a military censor; he read the celebratory postcard from Mitschka's family and passed the information to Harry five days before it was released to the Captain in the general mail call. Hence, the amazing five-day foreknowledge.

No matter. Harry Steinschneider now attained the exact same military standing as Adolf Hitler, the German lance corporal defending his adopted homeland on the stalemated Western Front in January 1916.

The clairvoyant delayed-letter ploy established Harry's magic credentials with the Gorlice regulars. Besides entertainment, it acted as a desperate psychological boost. Frustration with the war's unheralded lack of progress and ever-expanding lists of casualties inspired otherworldly pursuits among Vienna's elite military classes. Rudolf Steiner, the founder of the New Age "scientific religion," Anthroposophy, and Madame Sylvia, a doll-faced society clairvoyant, engrossed Franz Joseph's generals and their tactical advisers with the battlefield premonitions, based on astrology and other occult means of divination. The amateur con on the Eastern Front was only following in his betters' footsteps.

Front-Line City Cracow

Lance Corporal Steinschneider was reassigned to a machine-gun unit in the 13th Regiment. Once again he was wounded in a leg and, after a long period of convalescence, sent to serve in the safe haven of Cracow as a railroad guard and military policeman.

Harry's activities in 1916 are curiously undocumented. Labéro thought he saw the AWOL corporal in Vienna during his engagement at the Circus Busch in the winter of 1915-16. According to the master teacher, Harry had gone back on his word never to imitate the telepathic lessons; Labéro's brash pupil had reentered Vienna's show-business arena and "was already capable of performing some acceptable experiments in muscle-reading." [*Wundermänner, Ich Enthülle Eure Geheimnisse!* (Leipzig: Verlag Wahrheit Ferdinand Spohr, 1933)]

Whether Labéro only imagined the petty betrayal or Harry stayed fixed in place on the steps of the Cracow train station remains unclear. No matter. Lance Corporal Steinschneider's star as a psychic was about to rise.

At the beginning of May 1917, Harry conducted several telepathic experiments at the Cracow Nerve Clinic at the request of the squadron head of the Austrian Army. The results were stunning and the captain of the military news service, a Viennese newspaper editor and book dealer in prewar times, invited Harry to demonstrate his clairvoyant skills at the main officers' club. Harry accepted the challenge and hypnotized a high-ranking lieutenant. He also duplicated the movements of a major, who executed a number of simple actions in an adjoining room while mentally communicating with the telepath. (Harry mastered this clairvoyant transaction by observing the gestures of a shill, trained in one of Labéro's codes, who signaled the major's activities to the lance corporal.)

Telepathic Experiment in Cracow, May 1917

A few weeks later, on May 17, 1917, through his usual fast-talking manner, the penniless Corporal Steinschneider managed to rent the city's mammoth, 800-seat Sokol Hall for three evenings. Two of the three nights sold out with surprising ease; the third was nearly filled. After expenses and money for glad-handing and under-the-counter promotion, Harry collected over 3,000 kronen in pure profit.

Harry's humorous demonstration both revealed the tricks of run-of-the-mill telepaths and clairvoyants and then displayed his own "true feats" of thought-transference. One professor from a local academy, who examined Harry on stage, was convinced that the lance corporal, despite his cavalier mix of moods and playful demeanor, actually possessed a "sixth sense."

Not everyone enjoyed the comedy or the shattering of their cherished beliefs; some of the hoodwinked turned their furor at the crafty enlightener. More troubling, the Austrian officer corps was uncertain in its reaction to this difficult-to-define Jew.

Entertaining the Troops

An advisor for the Austro-Hungarian Army Widow-and-Orphan Fund heard of Harry's Sokol evenings in Cracow and invited him to make a six-week tour of the front with his "morale-building" telepathic production. The *esprit de corps* in the Imperial and Royal Army had sharply fallen by June 1917. The venerable 86-year-old Emperor Franz Joseph had died six months earlier, and his little-known nephew Karl I succeeded him to the throne. In the third year of warfare, 500,000 Imperial troops were captured and one million were missing or dead. Czech and Ruthenian nationalism was growing in the East. Italy had joined the Allied crusade in the South.

Harry signed a contract to remit fifty percent of his ticket proceeds to the Widow-and-Orphan Fund—or a minimum of 4,000 gold kronen. Olga, a pretty, vixen-faced Polish servicewoman, with whom he flirted at the main train station, accompanied Harry as his impresario, medium, abettor, and ticket vendor. They set off for Lublin in a first-class couchette and were performing at the front in a few days. For the pale lance corporal in borrowed evening dress and his heavily made-up assistant, the six-week expedition was a pleasant diversion, a kind of traveling honeymoon. Even a Russian pilot's attempt to demolish Harry's makeshift theatre, in the middle of one of the shows, was treated with whimsy. With or without a roof, the magical exercises in thought-transference continued.

To the standard muscle-reading acts, Harry added a telepathy number that involved Olga's complicity as a trained medium. After Harry was led out of the theatre hall with a trio of audience volunteers, the remaining spectators were asked to write down simple amusing activities for the telepath to enact. These were scribbled on a sheet of paper, which then was placed in an envelope. The envelopes were presented to Olga, who read them silently as she sat in a chair. Harry re-entered the stage with his "Supervisory Committee" and then stared at his mysterious "thought-bearer." In a wordless trance, Olga communicated the contents of the selected letters to Harry, who proceeded to accomplish each of the series of written tasks as she sat in the chair and he turned to study her face.

One evening, for example, Harry followed Olga's psychic instructions (made possible through a prearranged code of tiny, virtually imperceptible movements): to demand a coin from a soldier in the tenth row, go to the theatre buffet and order a glass of liquor, return to the auditorium, hand the glass to another spectator, and request that he toast the patron soldier, whose coinage had paid for the drink. The result was what one would expect, even under peacetime circumstances: rapturous.

Unfortunately, the seductive Olga was much better at Labéro's psychic glossaries and flashy mediumship than collecting money. The tour came up several hundred kronen short of its contracted goal. In disgust, Major General Borislav von Wolfzahn, Harry's humorless CO, dispatched the corporal back to his original machine-gun unit.

Before Harry was re-outfitted in combat fatigues, he wrote and distributed a booklet, *Worauf beruht das—?! Telepathie, ihre Erklärung und Ausübung* (Cracow: Self-Published, 1917) [*On What Is It Based—? Telepathy, Its Explanation and Practice*], which catalogued Labéro's clandestine techniques and explained Harry's menu of pseudo-magical tricks. If there was such a thing as a mystical "sixth sense," author "Hary Steinschneider" wrote, it was based on the telepath's magical belief in his own extraordinary powers. The pamphlet was just the first of several incidences of Erik Jan Hanussen's odd enterprise in revealing his own tricks under the cover of exposing frauds.

Back in the field, Harry once again assumed the role of battalion jester; moreover, his hocus-pocus amusements went beyond fortune-telling and stage telepathy. He added a demonstration of dowsing, the occult art of detecting pockets of water or mineral ores deep in the ground with the aid of a bifurcated branch or a twisted metal rod. In his first comic enactment, Harry circled a machine-gun nest three times and then followed the thrust of his divining stick to an empty barren patch a hundred meters away. Two feet below the hard ground surface was indeed a fresh-water spring. Harry admitted that he was as startled as his cheering comrades.

The Divining Rod

Scholars of esoteric science claimed several different countries as the cradle of dowsing technique: ancient Rome, China, France, Abyssinia, Italy, Great Britain, the United States, and Germany. Each nation had its adherents and origin histories for the magical use of wooden switches or curved metal bars. Cicero wrote about forked sticks that trembled uncontrollably in diviners' hands, pointing downward to symbolic images drawn on the earth. The supernaturally charged wooden apparatus foretold personal futures and impending calamities. In the Bata-Toga villages of east Abyssinia, self-entranced "Lebascha-Boys" employed V-shaped branches to ferret out criminals and locate lost treasure. The violently palpitating fixtures, not the foaming boy shamans who merely held them, "smelled" wrong-doing or the place of riches. German miners in the Saar region were said to use dowsing rods as standard exploratory tools for countless generations.

By the late seventeenth century, court scientists in Western Europe investigated the folk phenomena and began to publish their findings, which in the main were extremely favorable. A second period of dowsing mania erupted in Europe around the early 1900s. It was one of many paranormal subsets that evolved from the science of magnetism and wave theory. During the Great War, the Italian Army—and Australian troops, stranded in the Turkish port of Gallipoli—used it to great success. God, luck, or science was on their side.

In Vienna, the acknowledged expert was Dr. Moritz Benedikt, a fuddy-duddy professor who wrote two classics in the field, *Leitfaden der Rutenlehre* (Vienna: Leipzig Verlag, 1916) and *Ruten- und Pendellehre* (Vienna: Leipzig Verlag, 1917). Benedikt would be the stimulus for a vast scientific literature on this subject in the German-speaking world, the formation of international dowsing societies, and a respected monthly journal that lasted into the middle '30s.

Exactly how or when Harry discovered Benedikt's pioneering works can only be surmised. Harry probably read the basic primer sometime in 1916. Just two years later, the celebrated scientist and the telepathic corporal had certainly collaborated. In Vienna and in Bosnia, Harry bragged to reporters about their intimate relationship. He maintained that Benedikt called him his "successor" and willed the lance corporal all his worldly possessions. No doubt there was something to Harry's claim; Benedikt wrote publicly of the Corporal's special psychic talents, although the pedantic professor also thought "H.," or "Hanussen-Steinschneider," had a tendency to overdramatize his paranormal experiments. (The mad pacing of the muscle-reading numbers, especially, reminded the old man of a police dog off his leash.)

Cover of Booklet on Dowsing (1928)

Behind the Lines

In the Winter-Spring of 1918, Harry incorporated dowsing into his growing arsenal of occult practices and taught the technique to Austro-Hungarian military policemen of the First Army, who were excited by the arcane craft. Harry called his dowser-apparatus the Bagetta-Magica.

Like Benedikt's wooden fork with attached metal balls and Professor Schermuly's spiral rod, it was a device of surprisingly simple construction. The Bagetta consisted of thick, welded steel wire twisted into the shape of a horseshoe. Harry distinguished his execution of dowsing from that of his competitors in another way as well: the shape and material of the diviner's rod, he declared, was less important than the heightened state of the dowser. Smell, sensitivity to the climate, self-confidence, primal instinct, shamanistic belief—these were the best tools of the dowser. And find water Harry did.

In a chauffeured automobile and assisted by a canine unit, Harry claimed to uncover "extraordinary reserves" of anthracite coal and petroleum deposits in northern Galicia and Bohemia. His rate of success was uneven, yet no worse than the Austrian Army's professional geologists.

Major General Wolfzahn was not amused or impressed by Steinschneider's extrasensory expeditions and, in early April 1918, sent the feckless lance corporal on a wartime mission to Albania. An entire platoon of Czech conscripts had abandoned their frontline posts and, after court-martial proceedings, were to be interned in a brig on the Dalmatian Sea off occupied Albania.

Harry confided to the leader of the Czech deserters that their journey could be made pleasant and leisurely if they promised not to flee and followed his lackadaisical orders implicitly. It was even possible that an armistice would be declared before they reached the Durazzo fortress. And for every prisoner who escaped, Harry explained, he was to receive three months in the same military brig as punishment. Each party had reason to support the other. The Czech nationalists cheerfully agreed to Harry's good neighbor policy.

Hanussen as Dowser in Cracow, March 1918

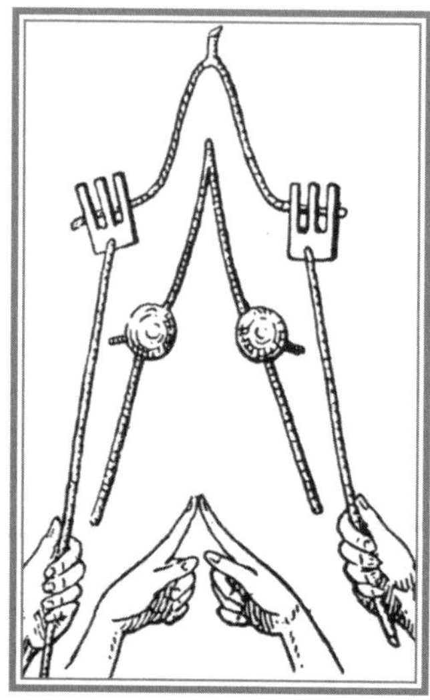
German Divining Rods, Seventeenth Century

The four-week journey could actually be completed in half of the allotted time, Harry calculated correctly. In cattle-car transport, Harry and his convoy left Cracow for points south: Vienna, Budapest, Fiume. At each train station, the prisoners were free to scrounge for food and beer, which they successfully accomplished through cargo theft and barter.

Satisfied that they could survive for a day or two without him at the Viennese Bahnhof, Harry stole away to the northern village of Lundenburg, where, in civilian attire, he gave a lucrative lecture on telepathy. When the lance corporal returned to his charges, he discovered the jailbirds huddled in a drunken stupor inside a boxcar; they traded his rifle, bayonet, and military boots for beer and were still sleeping off the effects of their good fortune.

Ten days later in Fiume, Harry dutifully handed over his forty thieves to the platoon commander of the Marsch Company. The Czech prisoners, true to their pledge, remained with Harry. Within minutes of their official military transfer, however, they utterly disappeared into the Adriatic night. The stumble-bum infantrymen were finally liberated from the horror of the Imperial and Royal Army and so was Harry: at least for two unaccounted weeks. He hightailed it home to Vienna.

Peppi's Offer

On the train car to the Imperial capital, Harry met Josef "Peppi" Koller, a former Viennese character actor and an ever-hopeful impresario with a pronounced Yiddish accent and *Luftmensch* mentality. Peppi had rented the mammoth 3,000-seat Konzerthaus on April 30 for a dance concert starring the Danish erotic sensation Ronny Johannsson. But with only four days until showtime, sales were unnaturally slow.

Peppi listened to Harry's self-promoting ramble and quickly hatched an elegant solution to his imminent financial calamity. Here was an esoteric angle to shore up the overreaching artistic presentation: Harry the legendary wizard of the Imperial and Royal Army would perform his telepathy act as an awe-inspiring conclusion to the overly upscale evening. Telepathic stunts and other paranormal delights fit the temperament of the times better than Expressive Dance and might even attract Vienna's elite, who weren't likely to frequent the Rubini and Labéro music-hall venues.

Harry was certainly beguiled. He had finally befriended someone more ambitiously reckless than himself. Yet receiving permission to perform in Vienna would not be so simple or legal; even an army entertainer couldn't wantonly abandon the field without severe punishment.

Peppi suggested an intriguing deception: Harry would be introduced as "Erich Jan Hanussen," the master clairvoyant of Copenhagen. No one would know a lance corporal from the Imperial Austro-Hungarian Army had gone AWOL. And the entire evening could then be a patriotic salute to neutral Danish culture.

Harry felt compelled to take the dare. He invented hundreds of outlandish names for the faceless corpses of Gorlice; why not an aristocratic Scandinavian moniker for himself?

It was the last time Herschmann Steinschneider, aka Heinrich Steinschneider, aka Harry Steinschneider, aka Mr. Clapp-Clapp, aka Nelly Fink, aka Aloys Beyerl, aka Titta Ruffo, aka Faun, would change his name. ("Erich" would soon be altered to the more hardy, Northern European "Erik.")

Enter the Dane

Posters announcing the additional presence of Telepath Hanussen to the Ronny Johannsson event were plastered on kiosks throughout Vienna. And Peppi's hastily-printed notices had their desired effect.

The Danish evening on April 30 at the Konzerthaus turned into a gala affair. Chauffeured sedans and horse-drawn carriages blocked the main entranceway to the baroque palace. 3,000 ticket-holding spectators filed into the massive hall.

Journalists, the reigning stars of the classical Hofburg Theater, and members of Vienna's top 400 were ushered into the front-row seats. Each clique gathered in

Viennese Konzerthaus Stage

its private circles to discuss the pressing matter at hand. Even the Imperial Family was heavily represented in the Royal Lodges. On the left balcony was the Archduke Leopold Salvator, Archduchess Bianka Immaculata, Archduke Eugen, and the supreme Army-Commander Archduke Friedrich himself.

Ronny performed and an intermission was announced. Then a bell rang to signal the second part of Peppi's program: Erich Jan Hanussen.

In a rented morning coat and with slicked-back hair, Hanussen faced his first venerable audience, which he knew would determine his fate for some long time to come, and instinctively regarded it as an adversary to be tamed and conquered.

The Danish clairvoyant began with a public solicitation. He requested that the restive, if curious-to-skeptical, audience choose a trusted representative to ensure the integrity of the telepathic experiments and direct the activities of the spectator-volunteers during his offstage absences. The flamboyant Hofburg actor in the front row, Georg Reimers, was the public's unanimous nomination. Reimers hoofed to the Konzerthaus rostrum and bowed as if he were taking a festive curtain call.

After some stage pleasantries with Reimers, Hanussen explained how the remainder of the evening would unfold. There would be five experiments in thought-transference and the paranormal: Finding Four Concealed Needles; Guessing Four Simple Actions Suggested by the Audience; a Dowsing demonstration; a display of "Second Sight"; and the enactment of an interactive occult sketch, *The Spy*. Besides the volunteer host, Hanussen also needed two mediums and a team of esteemed scientists to act as a supervisory panel. They would accompany him to a sound-proof chamber.

Two prominent Viennese personalities accepted the role as Hanussen's mediums. A scientific commission of physicians, including the chief doctor of the Municipal Hospital, assembled to oversee the offstage proceedings.

Hanussen handed Reimers four needles. First, spectators were to hide these in the auditorium. Secondly, Reimers was to query the audience for interesting, unrelated, actions that could be performed on the Konzerthaus stage and amateur players to enact them.

With his committee of physicians in tow, the pasty-faced clairvoyant retired to an isolated greenroom.

Reimers and the giddy audience followed Hanussen's instructions sequentially. After announcing his selections, the Hofburg ham nodded to a stage hand to ring the intermission buzzer and the telepathic seer was led back to the proscenium.

Using his standard muscle-reading method, Hanussen held the wrist of his first medium to check for ideomotor responses and asked him specific questions about the needles' locations. Meanwhile the Danish maestro dragged his medium around the theatre, dashing left and right, shouting constantly for silence, and admonishing the frightened medium to think more sharply. All four needles were discovered in a matter of minutes. The mind-reader then turned to the improvised series of tasks concocted by the audience and their designated participants.

Briskly walking through the Konzerthaus aisles with the other medium, Hanussen peered carefully across the seated spectators and pointed. "That woman!" He led a giggling matron to the stage and directed her to the grand piano, "Play!" While she performed a standard waltz piece, Erich pointed to a man and a woman in the front section, "You! And you! On the stage. Quickly!" The two good-naturedly acquiesced, joining the matron. Hanussen gave his final command, "Kindly, dance, my subjects." The Viennese audience roared. Three of their random suggestions were now manifested magically through pure thought-transference.

Hanussen dismissed the musical trio and his pair of mediums. Reimers stepped to the side and the supervisory committee sat attentively on chairs upstage from the master. Hanussen changed the mood. He started to lecture solemnly on dowsing and its crucial wartime function. (Never mind that Denmark was a non-combatant nation.)

In his hand, Hanussen waved Dr. Moritz Benedikt's steel divining fork. He demonstrated its supernatural use and invited its inventor to the stage. Benedikt, unaccustomed to public acclaim, arose and mounted the platform unsteadily. Hanussen embraced the old professor and vigorously shook his hand. A few of Benedikt's colleagues from the University, who were seated near him, were ordered to stand and receive homage for their work. The Danish clairvoyant's reverence for the scholars further improved his standing among the awestruck theatregoers. It was their fourth secret suggestion.

Next Reimers blindfolded Hanussen with a thick black cloth. Suddenly, the bottom of Erik's face reddened and began to turn away from the audience. The clairvoyant's hands trembled and he spoke incoherently. The Dane pawed sharply at the air for an instant as if he were attempting to retrieve his mystic powers that were expiring from his unseeing face. The obviously frightened seer paced fitfully and appeared distraught. Maybe the psychic jig was up. All 3,000 spectators held their collective breath.

Then Erich stood still for an instant as if his composure and self-confidence were miraculously returning. In the booming voice of a Prater *Spieler*, Hanussen barked that Hugo Thiming, the head of the Hofburg Theater, should step to the stage. Thiming sprinted up the ramp and stood before the panting mentalist. Hanussen ordered Thiming to remove his necktie. The audience, including the Royal Family, went wild. That was their fifth task.

Hanussen's other psychic feats, including a "scientific" demonstration of dowsing and an audience-participation detective play, were even more spectacular.

The last experiment of the program, essentially, was a parlor game with a telepathic component. Hanussen claimed the idea for his *The Spy* scenario came from a real-life drama. The sketch was only a playful enactment of an astounding undercover military exploit.

In Cracow, a defense lawyer for a man accused of being a murderous secret agent hired Hanussen to prove the innocence of his client. Besides saving the life of a helpless patsy, the desperate lawyer wanted to serve the cause of Hapsburgian justice by exposing the true foreign operative and recover the State's purloined confidential files.

Naturally, Detective Erich went into heroic Lebascha mode, unveiling the actual culprit, together with his cache of stolen papers before they could be dispatched to the nefarious enemies of the Imperial Empire. (Again, no one questioned what a Danish stage clairvoyant was doing in wartime Cracow, home of the mutinous 1st Army.)

The Spy involved a round of "psychic detection" and required spectators to take a variety of roles: defense lawyer, victim, and deadly spy. Moreover, the scene of the crime, the weapon used, the stolen State documents, and a code-word were to be determined by a coordinator while the telepath and his committee absented themselves yet again.

The psychic detective motioned to his paneled gang of physicians and, in a single marching unit, majestically exited the Great Hall.

Volunteers from the audience assembled on stage. One was selected to be the rube, another the insidious thief, and so forth. They decided the murder weapon was a needle, which was hidden behind a column; the crime site a bank; the State document a spectator's book, which was concealed under an industrialist's chair in the audience; and the secret code-word, known only to Reimers and the coordinator-medium, was a word they pointed to in the "confidential" book.

Hanussen re-entered, holding Benedikt's divining rod, and made short work of their elaborate stratagem. The female medium telepathically (and without any muscle contact) led him to the imaginary cast of characters, who were invited back to the stage, the needle weapon, and the book.

On stage, Hanussen held the medium's wrist and flipped through the book. In a few minutes, the clairvoyant ascertained the identity of the spy and Reimers' secret word.

The Vienna public stamped their feet in approval. Roaring shrieks, shouts of bravo, and—if we are to believe Hanussen's teasing memoirs—even fainting accompanied the applause.

Herschmann Steinschneider had found, at long last, the undeniable success that so often eluded him in his many shifting personas and unlovely vocations. For twenty-eight years he struggled as a menial Steinschneider, the son of a Jewish-Moravian *Schmiere* actor; now chance and relentless ambition presented to him a new self, that of Erik Jan Hanussen, the dapper scion of Danish nobility, later to be the Clairvoyant of Berlin and Prophet of the Third Reich. The enchanted metamorphosis was to persevere for exactly fifteen years.

Imperial Fascination

Backstage, Peppi hugged his treasure, his creation. Both impresario and star were bathed in sweat. "His Majesty wants to meet you," Peppi crowed.

Waiting calmly in their private lodge was the Royal Family. In the seats and stalls below, hundreds of spectators lingered as well. They wanted to see what would happen next. Possibly a real natural miracle.

Hanussen and Peppi were warmly greeted by the Archdukes and Archduchess. Hanussen realized that the Imperial court was addressing him by his Christian first name, a bizarre familiarity, as if he was an old friend who had come to unwind after a late-night performance.

The two showmen remained in the Royal Lodge for nearly an hour, about as long as the entire occult Konzerthaus program. Hanussen amused the Archduchess Bianka Immaculata, the Emperor's niece, with simple muscle-reading tricks.

The first succeeded: the Seer of Copenhagen located a needle that Bianka hid in her vanity case. The Princess, enthralled by now with Hanussen's unwavering ability to perform the marvelous, attempted her own telepathic experiment—she mentally commanded him to touch the third button of Archduke Salvator's military jacket. Hanussen misinterpreted the message. Bianka then concentrated on another task: she willed the mind-reader to take a paperback book from the Archduke's satchel and deposit it into the coat pocket of his Wing Adjutant. This silent missive Hanussen guessed correctly and carried out. Peppi burst into hysterical fits of laughter.

The Austrian General Staff was forced to listen to the trashy music-hall duo brag about their nonpareil achievements. To their horror, Peppi committed one major faux pas after another. He touched the arms and legs of the Royal Family. And in his unmistakable Jewish lilt, the impresario deigned to compliment the Royal Highness on her skills as a medium and telepathic potential.

At the conclusion of the congenial tête-à-tête, the Archduke Leopold Salvator offered to drive Erich to his hotel. The Danish telepath wisely demurred. Instead he went off with Peppi to a Praterstrasse *Lokal.* When the two exited the Konzerthaus, they were astonished to see several queues of Viennese police officers impeding street traffic around the playhouse.

The Commissioner of Police was alarmed to learn that the members of the Royal House had tarried for more than an hour in the music-hall emporium. When the police chief was told of the reason for the purposeful delay, however, he discreetly ordered a thorough investigation of Erich Jan Hanussen, which would take days of circumspect sleuthing. This telepath could be fake, the cautious official opined, maybe a Slovene or Ruthenian anarchist posing as a Danish nobleman.

When the AWOL Lance Corporal and the former character-actor reached their streetcar destination a few blocks away, Peppi daydreamed some fanciful consequences, "I don't know if they shall give me the Franz-Joseph Medal for tonight or a café concession in Leopoldstadt (the old Jewish quarter)!"

Meanwhile, the two had more than enough money for a plate of sausage and beer. They were rich by the relative standards of the time but without any further prospects.

Steinschneider-Hanussen

Vienna's respectable newspapers and weeklies played up the "occult phenomenon" of Hanussen for four or five days running. Like the performance itself, their articles provided a fascinating exotic diversion for a war-weary capital. Neither the crude maps illustrating the Austro-Hungarian Army's wondrous breakthroughs on the mountainous Italian frontier nor the vapid official communiqués (which frequently contradicted the newspaper diagrams) stimulated the dubious populace to steadfast belief in their leaders. With the overall scale of casualties in the Imperial Army slowly approaching the shocking rate of fifty percent and no fast cessation to the conflict in sight, the paranormal delivered a rejuvenating bounce to a public weighed down by hard, impending loss.

Hanussen, the Grand Telepath himself, enjoyed a few days of celebrityhood in Vienna. Eating breakfast in an outdoor café, he was surrounded by youthful worshippers. At first, he didn't know why the crowd was staring at him. Maybe it was his poor Ottakring table manners or something dropped in his lap. Then he realized that the wide-eyed schoolchildren were merely admirers. Hanussen signed their autograph books, unsure about the proper spelling of his own name. The lance corporal made a mental note to memorize it.

After May Day, the adventure terminated. Steinschneider boarded a train for Cracow. He was officially "missing in action" for a total of eleven days and now subject to immediate arrest. The wizard-cum-platoon commander retrieved what was left of his corporal's uniform at the railroad station Garderobe and bid goodbye to a still-undaunted Peppi. The diminutive impresario promised to petition their mutual patron, the Archduke Salvator, and start the machinations for Hanussen's release.

At the Cracow fortress, General von Wolfzahn studied Lance Corporal Steinschneider's report. The charges against the recalcitrant NCO were dropped; Harry was redetailed to his old machine-gun unit. The platoon commander quickly fell into the old regimen—barracks maintenance and drills in the morning, gun instruction in the afternoon, and mayhem in the evening. Besides organizing cutthroat poker tournaments at the officer's club, Steinschneider read tarot cards for his superiors and their restive consorts.

Bartol's old fortune-telling system more or less ignored the vagaries of the magical shuffle and metaphoric arrangement of the playing cards; instead, it emphasized the character of the suppliant. Altogether, there were six formulas for each of the fifty basic personality types, a total of 300 prognostications to be learned. Steinschneider could not retain Bartol's precise characterology scheme for more than a few hours—he had a life-long block against tarot cards—and sometimes made a mess of the readings.

The wife of a high-ranking colonel, for instance, complained that Steinschneider's Gypsy cards foretold two utterly incompatible destinies for her in the same week. It was only one of dozens of charges and accusations against the lance corporal that reached von Wolfzahn's desk. Other reports hinted at

Steinschneider's public flirtations with married women and possible adulterous affairs. The man was a nuisance.

Meanwhile Peppi was not idle.

The music-hall agent ran himself ragged in Vienna's military compound, attempting to pull the proper strings to have his telepath re-engaged at the Konzerthaus' Great Hall.

First, Peppi arranged a private conference with his old pal, the Archduke Salvator, but the Imperial Highness' mood had suddenly changed. Having learned that Hanussen was no Danish grandee, only a common platoon commander on leave, the Archduke told the impresario, instead, to convince Steinschneider's sergeant to discharge the stage magician from active service. Yet before their brief tryst concluded, the wily Peppi got his bemused protector to allow him one thing: he could proclaim the Royal House's enthusiasm for a second Hanussen evening.

Without a moment's delay, Peppi sent off a telegram to Major-General Wolfzahn, stating Archduke's princely wishes for Hanussen's immediate reassignment. The decree was signed by the mono-appellation "Koller," an emphatic and mysterious State official. Possibly an little-known major general or fieldmarshal or someone even higher in the Austrian War Ministry.

Von Wolfzahn and his associates ignored the royal command. However, other telegrams followed. These were signed by recognized authorities, namely Major Wiedring, a Wing Adjutant to the Emperor, and Secretary of War Czap. Steinschneider-Hanussen was to be sent to Saravejo for work in Emperor Karl's Entertainment unit, with one week off for family leave in Vienna.

The High Commander of the Cracow garrison, General Schroiter, sat on the Viennese orders for two weeks. Like von Wolfzahn, he was confounded and enraged by the fantastic wartime request. Steinschneider was left to molder at the front like the rest of his inglorious minority shirkers and lackeys. Eventually, the lance corporal's well-placed advocates prevailed and Steinschneider-Hanussen was shipped off on a second-class train for the sedate Bosnian front. On May 24, 1918 the man with two names disembarked in Vienna.

Command Performance

Once again, Peppi did his magic. He rented the Konzerthaus, contacted Archduchess Bianka's secretary, and notified the press of the great event to take place on May 26.

Hanussen wisely added a new feature for the top of the evening, the Telepathic Post. Blank sheets of paper and envelopes were handed out to members of the audience and they were to address messages to other spectators in the hall, seal them in the envelopes, and Hanussen would conjure his telepathic power to deliver the letters to the intended subjects. It was another variation on muscle-reading, with an in-house comic lunacy. Even the shyest of spectators could be dragged into the proceedings. And it took up lots of stage time.

The public mood of the second Konzerthaus performance was darker, more cynical, even oddly hostile. Peppi's ceaseless promotion and boasting had a boomerang effect. Both the press corps and the general audience viewed the Danish telepath with hard, disbelieving eyes.

Hanussen took the first two writers in hand, pulled them through the theatre, and delivered their letters to the correct destinations. Yet no applause, virtually no audience acknowledgment, followed Erich's telepathic achievement.

Then a servant from the Royal Box handed Hanussen a sealed envelope. It was from the Archduchess.

Now Hanussen faced a strange quandary. The postal stunt involved muscle-reading, physical contact, and a bit of hectoring toward the participant—"Think more sharply," "A real medium must have more intelligence than a milk-cow. Please, concentrate!" and so forth. It would be unseemly and self-defeating, worse than a Peppi social blunder, to subject the Emperor's niece to that. Hanussen decided to wing it. He studied the sealed envelope and glanced at Bianca's face.

Hanussen jumped off the stage and stopped at the sixth row. He turned again to Royal Lodge, making eye contact with the Archduchess, and then sauntered back one row. The seer paced back and forth in the fifth row for a while and finally remitted the envelope to a startled white-bearded gentleman in a center seat. It was Professor Kerzl, the personal physician to Emperor Karl II and a Viennese councilman.

Archduchess Bianca's thin voice pierced the heavy atmosphere, "Amazing! You are correct, Herr Hanussen! Correct!" Strained silence gave way to a kind of audience euphoria.

The remainder of the evening unfolded like the program from the previous month, only with several wrong guesses, telepathic missteps, and fewer scientific explanations. Naturally, it didn't matter. The Konzerthaus audience, after the Telepathic Post routine, was determined to believe.

Bosnia

Lance Corporal Hary Steinschneider-Hanussen drove to Sarajevo in the last week of May. The garrison there was a decided improvement over Cracow. Emperor Karl's Charity Fund, the replacement for the Widow-and-Orphan organization, featured more upscale entertainers and was the center of civil and military cultural activity. Besides, the war against the British and their Greek allies in the South had subsided into small-arms hit-and-run operations. The guerrilla warfare was more or less contained by special units of the Bulgarian Army, a ferocious element in the Central Powers' Balkan defense.

Hanussen announced his presence in the *Bosnischen Post* with a "telepathic séance" to be given at the Vereins-Theater on June 4. Three days earlier, Hanussen demonstrated his hypnotic and dowsing skills at the central military clinic. Dr. Max Ostermann, a famous researcher in hypnosis and "waking suggestion" from Vienna, was impressed with Hanussen's legerdemain. Of course, like his University colleague Benedikt, Ostermann frowned at Hanussen's razzmatazz approach. Still, the boy had great promise. Ostermann treated Hanussen like a prize student.

In June, Hanussen-Steinschneider gave two telepathic performances—facsimiles, more or less, of his second Konzerthaus sensation. He also began to write his first full-length book, *Das Gedankenlesen/Telepathie* (Vienna: Waldheim-Eberle A.G., 1920) [*Mind-Reading/Telepathy*], which would be published two years later in Vienna.

One cavalry officer, Captain Bruno Rechinic, remembered Hermann's entry into Sarajevo's refined social world. The telepath requested a joy ride in Rechinic's two-seater aeroplane. The Captain explained the Army prohibition against such frivolous uses of his valued war machine. Hanussen insisted and Rechinic, for the one time in his professional career, took the dowser on a tail-spinning flight over the city.

Later that evening, Hanussen and Rechinic were dinner guests at a Viennese concert-player's house. Professor Käsisoglich, who resisted all previous entreaties to entertain friends at parties, got up in the middle of the meal and ran into the next room and started to pound the keys of his piano furiously. A variety-actress at the table then began to scratch her body uncontrollably as if she were infested with lice. The diners' eyes widened.

When the Captain assured Hermann that such occurrences did not normally occur in polite Austro-Bosnian society, the newcomer responded with a satanic grin and whispered back, "How could they? The events here and this afternoon were all of products of my hypnotic suggestion." (The officer remembered the disquieting evening for years and reported it at Hanussen's trial in Leitmeritz in 1929. All three prosecuting attorneys accepted the validity of the Captain's incredible story without comment. Just listening to the decorated pilot's unvarnished words, they knew it was true.) [*Heinrich Wissiak, Der Leitmeritzer Hellseher=Prozess Hanussen* (Teplitz-Schönau: Self-Published, 1931)]

The Emperor's Dowser

The Austro-Hungarian Commander of the 4th Army, Colonel General Sarkotitsch von Lowcen, befriended Hanussen and had Police Chief Homer officially designate him Royal Dowser of Bosnia-Hercegovina. With a military guard and translator, Hanussen was to travel around the barren province and coastal Dalmatia, searching for potable water and raising money for the Emperor Karl Charity Fund. Hanussen negotiated one more additional accessory, a female auxiliary.

On July 1, Hanussen put his paranormal theories and invented past to use. With the aid of his Bagetta-Magica, he unraveled the mysterious case of Muhamed Aga Dzinic, a wealthy Turkish landowner who was murdered in his own harem,

Hanussen Teaching the Secrets of Dowsing in Mostar

The notorious crime, on which the Royal Dowser spent only a few hours, had frustrated the Austro-Hungarian experts for nearly one year. On the very next day, Hanussen was called to Travnik, seat of the old Turkish capital and the Imperial Army's sub-headquarters in Bosnia-Hercegovina. Police Chief Homer had another unsolved homicide for the psychic detective.

Sarkotitsch's commission allowed Hanussen to double dip into the Charity receipts and avoid the many unpleasantries of army life. He outfitted his crew with phony braids and meaningless medals. He commandeered auto and donkey transport, going to balmy sites far from the zones of combat or twentieth-century civilization; he gave lectures that were practically unintelligible to Croatian and Italian-speaking peasants and then blamed his translator when the Bagetta-Magica came up short. Better still, Royal Dowser Hanussen ignored the orders of the incredulous military authorities.

Hanussen with Assistants in Dalmatia, August 1918

By October, Hanussen had antagonized too many local administrators. He was denounced in Mostar and Spolato on a military technicality—employing a soldier with whom he was having sexual relations—and unceremoniously stripped of his command. At the Savajevo HQ, Hanussen again faked a lethal illness and was sent to recuperate in a brig-hospital.

Yet before the lance corporal was to be remanded to the front as a common foot-soldier, a political miracle transpired: the mighty Bulgarian Army surrendered to British and French forces in Salonika. The monarchy in Sofia toppled. In a matter of days, Czechoslovakia declared its independence. And the entire Austro-Hungary Empire began to fracture into national ethnic conclaves. Both Kaiser Wilhelm and Karl's General Staff realized the political and military gravity of the situation. Their Great War to defeat Britain and France had become hopeless.

On November 3, the warring armies in Europe agreed to a general armistice.

Hanussen and the inmates from the prison-hospital were among the first to be liberated in Bosnia. Like runaway slaves, they hoisted themselves into waiting military railroad cars and headed toward Vienna, the capital of the new rump Republic of Austria. Hanussen was especially delighted that while he and his fellow invalid-prisoners luxuriated in first-class couchettes, General Sarkotitsch von Lowcen and his staff were relegated to the back of the train, to third-class accommodations.

Hanussen, right in the Harem of Muhamed Aga Dzinic, 1918

Elements of Mind-Reading

by Erik Jan Hanussen-Steinschneider

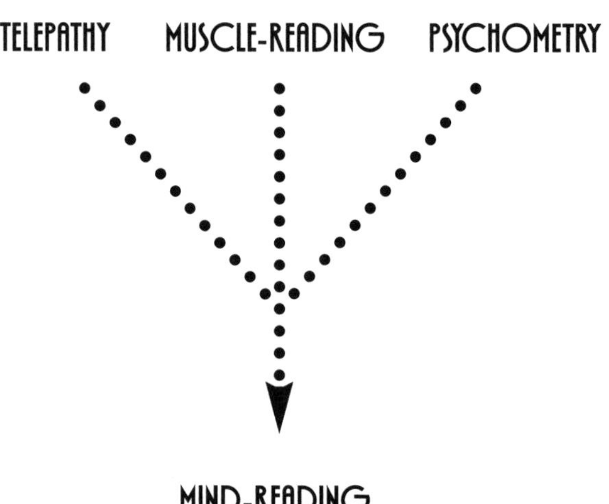

Das Gedankenlesen/Telepathie (Vienna: Waldheim-Eberle, 1920)

Grand Konzert Saal

November 11, 1918

ERIK JAN HANUSSEN

PROGRAM

Introduction

Formation of the Supervisory Committee

The Palmograph (Mechanical Telepathy)

Guessing a Series of Random Dates

Arithmetic through Telepathy

Name Guessing

Experiments with Contact

Experiments without Contact

Long Distance Experiments—tasks will be selected at random and remain secret

"Lebascha"—the Indian fakirs' method, first used by Hanussen with great success in aid of criminal investigations

The Divining Rod—Hanussen-Steinschneider's own. Used for police service and in his state expeditions to discover ground water in Bosnia, Hercegovina, and Dalmatia.

Experiments in Conscious Suggestion

Hanussen Portrait, (1919)

CHAPTER FOUR

SHOWMAN, PSYCHIC DETECTIVE and STUDENT OF THE OCCULT

1918-1922

Bigger and Better

Vienna lacked electrical power and coal in the month following the Armistice. Starving German-speaking villagers and hollow-eyed conscripts flooded the city. Proletarian committees overpowered factory officials and defied police and private militias to stop them. Tuberculosis, smallpox, syphilis, and a half-dozen contagious diseases that had no name forced entire neighborhoods into medieval-like seclusion. Hanussen's aristocratic benefactors were nowhere to be found. The thousand-year-old Duo-Monarchy had been deposed and the specter of Bolshevik insurrection haunted the Ringstrasse.

Somehow the Eden-on-the-Danube was determined to remain jocular. Candlelit nightclubs and cafés still drew their familiar clientele. The food and drink may have been ersatz, yet the entertainment continued to sparkle. Even the major theatres stayed open as best they could, mounting breezy matinee specials before the five o'clock shutdown.

Peppi arranged two Hanussen programs at the Konzerthaus on November 11 and 17, 1918. This time Hanussen added a stronger intellectual format to the production, probably an adolescent response to Benedikt and Ostermann's Old World academic critiques.

The Danish clairvoyant started with a demonstration of the Palmograph as an example of science in the service of telepathy and concluded the full-length program with a mass experiment in "conscious induction."

Audience members were put into a light hypnotic trance, then told they couldn't raise their arms over their heads or unlock their interlaced fingers. When the lights came up, Hanussen tested the spectators' suggestibility by commanding his devoted public to hold their arms up or hands out. A surprising number of theatregoers were unable to break Hanussen's "wide-awake" spell. They had to be hypnotized a second time in order to regain full muscular control.

Later, instead of a comic premise to endow the evening with an interactive finale, Hanussen utilized the Conscious Suggestive Induction as a prelude to the Telepathic Post. In that way, he could decipher which spectators were highly

Cover of **Close Your Eyes!** (1920)

susceptible to his commands and therefore prime subjects to assist him on stage as volunteer mediums.

The director of the Pan Nightclub, Alexander Rotter, realized Hanussen's potent draw in a more intimate dining setting and hired him to fill out his standard cabaret program of humorous sketches and vaudeville dance. For the month of December, Erik delivered sealed envelopes via his Telepathic Post, found needles concealed in women's hair or pinned inside men's high collars, and other lightning-like displays of muscle-reading.

At the Café Westminster on Mariahilferstrasse, where the restless showman set up shop after the cabaret performances, Hanussen bragged to his friends that he was beginning to think that possibly he possessed real clairvoyant powers, not just the ability to astonish and delight the Pan's free-drinking habitués through carny tricks and misdirection.

Rotter was naturally intrigued and decided to test Hanussen's bold assertion. He showed the telepath the first three lines of a letter written by his fiancée from Karlsbad. No one knew of Rotter's engagement and the note was unsigned. Hanussen declared the writer was a woman who was tiny and somewhat unstable; she was not related to Rotter by blood but, nevertheless, extremely close to him. The scribe had long dark hair and wore a gold chain around her neck. While writing this letter, she also wore a light-colored dress with dark stripes.

Rotter immediately wrote to his financée about her last letter. She confirmed Hanussen's graphological analysis. Each of his physical descriptions of her was accurate. The normally jaded nightclub owner, long after he departed Vienna for the Bohemian hinterlands, retained an enduring belief in Hanussen's supernatural capacity for telepathic vision and psychometry. [*Der Leitmeritzer Hellseher=Prozess Hanussen*]

At the Apollo

Ben Tiber, the artistic director of the Apollo Theater, Vienna's largest variety palace, also saw a financial windfall in Hanussen's innovative magic numbers and manic presentational style. Unlike Rubini and Labéro, Apollo celebrities from the Emperor Joseph era, or the latest sensations, Paulsen, Dr. Leopold Thoma, and Hermann the Great, Hanussen toyed with audience expectations, mixing edgy scientific babble with equal doses of Prater irony, sexual innuendo, and New Age-like mysticism.

Tiber engaged the clairvoyant-about-town for a four-month run, beginning New Year's Day 1919. Hanussen's sixteen weekly performances at the Apollo sold out, playing to 48,000 spectators. They netted the fabled institution over one half-million kronen in ticket sales. Only Enrico Caruso had surpassed Erik Jan Hanussen's dizzying record at the Apollo. The arbiters of waltzy Wiener Kultur were perplexed.

The Danish clairvoyant had become such a household name by April 1919 that Peppi had to publish a notice in the theatrical trades, threatening stage imitators (who were using similar phony Scandinavian names) of legal prosecution. There was only one true Erik Jan Hanussen!

Freud's Vienna

On his free days, Hanussen studied and practiced at a Viennese medical clinic, the Institute for Breath Therapy and Physical-Healing Techniques. Under Max Ostermann's expert tutelage, the showman headed the institute's hypnotic unit and would soon branch out to found his own school of hypnosis and the occult arts. Hanussen's students came from all walks of life. One group consisted of a manufacturer, an actor, an attorney, a physician, and a factory laborer. Altogether, thirteen of them were introduced on the Apollo stage, where were duplicated the "para-psychological experiments" of their master.

Hanussen also demonstrated his system of "absolute telepathy" at the League of Viennese Physicians. In the auditorium of Vienna University, Dr. Alexander Pilcz, a respected professor of neurology and indefatigable researcher in "borderline science," designed a rigorously controlled experiment to test the telepath's claims. In an adjoining room, Hanussen was to guess four digits drawn on the lecture-hall blackboard.

Erik got two numbers of four numbers right. The odds of such an occurrence happening at random were exactly twenty-to-one. (In a statistically unlikely aside, Pilcz reported that his test-case, a non-clairvoyant doctor, also guessed two of the numbers correctly.)

The Hanussen Academy, 1919

The Viennese psychiatrist Paul Schilder, Freud's heir apparent, examined Hanussen separately in his university laboratory. Schilder thought of the image of a round table. The Ottakring clairvoyant, sitting across from him, jotted down a circle with five arrows, each darting out from a center point. Schilder marveled at the exploit and wrote up the experiment for future study. ["Psychopathology of Everyday Telepathic Phenomena," [1934] in George Devereux (ed), *Psychoanalysis and the Occult* (New York: International Universities Press, 1953)]

Ten years later, Ostermann testified at Hanussen's trial at Leitmeritz that his former pupil was an exceptionally sharp observer of human behavior. At the Spitalgasse nerve clinic, Hanussen proved highly persuasive and scrupulously honest in his dealings with the patients. As for Hanussen's famed telepathic abilities, Ostermann refused to pass judgment. The patriarchal scientist didn't believe that paranormal clairvoyance actually existed.

The Austro-Hungarian State Bank Printing Theft

Shortly after the Armistice, hundreds of thousand-kronen bills had mysteriously disappeared from the Austro-Hungarian State Bank's printing plant. The subterranean factory employed over 300 workers and none had previous criminal records. The repeated thefts were significant enough to eventually endanger the solvency of the new Austrian currency.

The municipal police were slow to respond and appeared to be strangely disinterested in the Bank's growing predicament. After three months of documented shortfalls, the board of directors began to panic.

An official at the bank, Franz Hlavinka, suggested that they contact Erik Jan Hanussen, the miracle-man and self-proclaimed psychic detective whom he had

Hanussen in the Printing Works Vault, February 1919

Canteen of the Austro-Hungarian Bank Printing Works

seen at the Apollo Theater. Already at his wit's end, the bank chairman Hellerbarth agreed with little hesitation. The robbers had to be found and the missing funds retrieved. The investigative means no longer mattered.

On February 10, 1919, Hlavinka brought Hanussen to bank headquarters. Hellerbarth greeted the mystic profusely and explained how he discovered the bill theft. There were not many relevant details, only hundreds of uncut lithographed sheets of thousand-kronen notes were absent from the state coffers and nowhere to be found.

Hanussen requested a map of the printing works. He would return the next day with an aide and some equipment. The Dane estimated that his psychic investigation would take about ninety minutes, certainly no more than two hours. Hellerbarth asked if he needed any police assistance or protection. Hanussen waved him off with a smile. The two shook hands and Hlavinka drove the clairvoyant back to his apartment in the Sixth Precinct.

At ten o'clock sharp the following morning, Hanussen showed up at the entrance to the State Bill Printing plant. By the telepath's side was his trusted African servant, Ali, who carried a dowsing rod and a photo-stand with an attached camera. The bank officials and a nervous team of Viennese police inspectors were also there. A small contingent of journalists stood between them. The hostility between the two warring federal camps could not have been more palpable.

A criminal lawyer from the central police station immediately objected to the black man's presence; Hanussen insisted that he stay. In that instant, the bad blood between the Viennese Police Commissioner Schrober and Hellerbarth was now deflected onto the vaudeville seer and his Eritrean companion.

Unbeknownst to Hanussen, it was a momentous occasion. The seemingly inconsequential spat would later set in motion Herschmann Steinschneider's greatest career-changing trauma, his expulsion from Vienna, the city of his birth, and a permanent life of exile.

Once entombed in the underground bill factory, Hanussen, the *Lebaschmann*, was in his element. Like a lion with the scent of zebra in his nostrils, Hanussen trotted the vaulted hallways headlong, peering in every sideroom and staring menacingly into the faces of the busy plant workers. Many of them did freeze in their tracks like exposed prey but not because of the bushy-browed psychic. It was Director Hellerbarth, standing behind the clairvoyant, that they feared.

Hanussen reasoned that the theft had to be an inside job. The internal bank audits showed too many instances of large-scale losses of the thousand-kronen notes, followed by intermittent petty pilferage of smaller currency sheets. This wasn't consistent with the pattern of a daring gangland-type burglary. The real giveaway was the missing hundred-kronen bills. And since bank security frisked the employees at the end of the day, Erik calculated that the sackloads of money were probably still in the building. Only someone with access to empty adjacent areas during the day would have the ability to stash them in a hidden corner unnoticed.

Hanussen asked Hellerbarth for a list of workers who failed to show that morning. With Ali holding the dowsing rod and a patrolman watching, the psychic detective made a second examination of the press works, starting at the vault, where the manufactured paper proofs were finally deposited.

Coincidentally, one of the men who hauled the flat car to the safe called in sick; the other, Josef Prokesch, was alone in his partitioned booth. Hanussen had his man. In an ecstatic state that looked to all to be trance-like, he quickly notified Hellerbarth to thoroughly search the secluded rooms around the walk-in vault.

Meanwhile Prokesch and two other suspicious employees had already been body-searched by a Detective Ondrowics during the previous half-hour. Prokesch's coat hung in the factory's Garderobe and Ondrowics went upstairs to rifle through it.

Hanussen requested the police-observer to empty Prokesch's pockets. Thin shreds of lithographed paper were pulled out. Before Erik could begin his conclusive questioning, Ondrowics reappeared with Prokesch's money-stuffed jacket in hand and had the irritating psychic removed from the room. Hanussen left in amazed protest.

Both sides claimed victory. Prokesch confessed, after a violent interrogation, to being the State Printing Works thief and Hellerbarth, following Hanussen's *Lebasch*-hunch, unearthed the bulk of the forfeited cash.

The Viennese journalists and the bank's board of directors went with the telepath's miraculous version. Hellerbarth mailed Hanussen a 2,000-kronen reward for unveiling the culprit and an extra 2,000 kronen for locating the cache of bills. In addition, Hellerbarth wrote two public letters testifying to Erik's proven paranormal abilities. Police Commissioner Schrober was outraged; his detective alone had solved the crime. Schrober spoke privately with Mayor Richard Weiskirchner and both took measures to exact their revenge against this Ottakring Jewish poseur. [Friedrich Mellinger, *Zeichen und Wunder* (Berlin: Neufeld & Henius Verlag, 1933)]

Vienna Bans Stage Hypnotism

The unlikely solution to the Austro-Hungarian State Bank theft and the resulting defamation of the city's Police Department created delicious sensation and scandal for the establishment newspapers and tabloids. Both events reinvigorated the "phenomenon of Erik Jan Hanussen." Tiber wasted no time profiting from the once-in-a-generation publicity. He made transparencies of Hellebrath's letters and projected them on the Apollo Theater's motion-picture screen during every intermission.

Hanussen added a new feature to his act. He invited a man and woman to the stage and hypnotized them into believing that they were a feuding dog and cat. As soon as the miracle-man clapped his hands, the man and woman dropped to their knees and furiously chased one another around in a circle. Over their shrill snarls and meowing, Hanussen compared the human quadrupeds to Schrober and his Police Department. It was a good laugh line.

On February 20, two days later, the Viennese Police Commissioner announced a city-wide prohibition against public hypnotism. The order was to take effect that day. Vienna, the birthplace of Franz Mesmer, became the first municipality in the world to issue such an odd blanket decree. Schrober, at the risk of international ridicule, had launched his initial barrage against the impudent Prater showman.

Hanussen responded by writing to all ten major papers about his certified scientific work in telepathy, dowsing, spiritualism, mass suggestion, and hypnosis. He held a "private" hypnotic lecture-demonstration at the Apollo, which he thought proved the harmlessness of the stage novelty.

Every time he was about to induct a subject into deep trance, the Dane teasingly interrupted his magical countdown to assure the audience that this was only a scholastic exercise, not an actual hypnotic display.

Hanussen With Hypnotized Man, 1919

On stage, Hanussen went through his usual series of spells and post-hypnotic suggestions: he sat a little boy into a chair and hypnotized him into remaining there despite all entreaties to raise; he induced two women into holding each other's hands, which they could not break despite all efforts; he hypnotized another woman into making two fists, which she was unable to open; and finally Hanussen found, through muscle-reading, a cigarette can concealed in a police commissioner's hip pistol-holster.

More significantly, Hanussen, deeply stung and agitated by Schrober's personal jabs, penned a confessional essay about his secretive techniques and why they succeeded. It was entitled "How I Work" and appeared in the *Neue Wiener Journal* on February 22, 1919. The article was a classic example of Hanussen's fascinating tendency to disclose, or "leak," his otherwise shrouded background and methodology.

For a Jew born in Vienna and a known con-artist from the Café Louvre, Hanussen's self-exposure of his mysterious foreign masquerade was a strange and dangerous game. Obviously, the non-Danish speaking Erik had little psychological resistance to the double thrill of duping his public on stage and then revealing his stunts in print. And like a mania for Russian roulette, it was a self-destructive impulse that could not sustain repeated attempts.

In the German Sky

In the fall of 1919, Hanussen drove to Prague, capital of the Czechoslovakian Republic, which was about to celebrate its first year of autonomy.

Through a Hungarian impresario, Ernst Aranyi, Hanussen broke the prohibition against German-language entertainment. He gave five lectures—with a Czech translation—on telepathy and the occult. Bruno Frei, a left-wing journalist and later one of Hanussen's most rabid critics in Berlin, reported that Erik, in order to ingratiate himself with an audience at a Prague Zionist Club, described his lineage as thoroughly "Czech-Jewish" and himself as a proud descendent of "a wonder-rabbi from Prossnitz." [*Hanussen: Ein Bericht* (Strasbourg: Sebastian Brant, 1934)]

Franz Hlavinka, who had previously received a small reward from the Austro-Hungarian State Bank for the Hanussen's psychic wizardry, arranged for the free-lance detective to meet with bank officials in Prague. They also had suffered an enigmatic loss of state funds. Unfortunately, the clairvoyant was in Germany then.

The director of the Apollo Theater in Nürnberg-Fürth, Otto Hiller, hired Hanussen to perform at his variety house for the entire month of October. The telepath negotiated the incredible salary of 12,000 marks for his lecture-demonstrations. Nonetheless, according to Hiller, the four-week engagement proved troublesome. [*Der Leitmeritzer Hellseher=Prozess Hanussen*]

While Hanussen's performances drew overflow audiences and stimulated an eerie atmosphere of otherworldly suspense, Hiller received bitter letters from several of the volunteer-mediums. They complained of intense headaches and dizziness after their evening service. Hanussen was obliged to conduct private sessions in his hotel room to relieve them of their symptoms of post-hypnotic stress.

A greater and more public scandal erupted on October 15. The Bavarian Aviation Association announced a benefit program for German POWs still interned in Allied camps. Hanussen offered to conduct a new telepathic experiment following the afternoon air show. He was to pilot a two-seater and mentally "read" the directions of his impresario on the ground. Hanussen's team wagered 10,000 marks that the miracle-man could accomplish the sensation in a single pass. The Association rejected the stunt as insufficiently controlled and potentially dangerous. Instead, Hanussen, in the field, was to respond to clairvoyant messages from a professional aviator flying above him.

When Hanussen drove his automobile to the show, he was stormed by a crazed throng, many of whom waved sealed envelopes containing tasks that the pilot was to communicate to him. Hanussen instinctively put his car in reverse, which the crowd interpreted as a cowardly attempt to escape and chaos ensued. Finally, Hanussen's secretary "selected" one envelope from the hands of twenty irate participants and passed it on to the swashbuckling airman.

Outside his automobile, Hanussen waited for the telepathic command being issued from the circling plane 1800 feet above in the German sky. The clairvoyant then cranked the engine of his car, flashed his lights, and tooted the horn. The

Hanussen, the Telepathic Pilot, August 1919

smiling pilot swooped down low over the spectators and shouted, "Good, very good!" The dramatic feat was achieved, yet few left the air show satisfied. Skeptical newspaper reports trailed back to Vienna even before the Dane could make his faux triumphant return.

In November, Peppi eked out special permission for Hanussen to perform once more at the Konzerthaus. Again hypnotic and mass-suggestion "demonstrations" were staged. Unfortunately, the Viennese public was obviously tiring of the stunt.

The Second Frau Hanussen

On the Konzerthaus stage, with the Hanussen pupils, was a fresh, attractive face. It was the Bürgertheater ingenue, Theresia Luksch (known professionally as Risa Lux). Hanussen met her in the spring of 1919 while she was on her way to the playhouse. Wearing a fashionable, narrow skirt, Risa couldn't lift her leg to the height of the streetcar rung. Hanussen hoisted the big-eyed flapper from behind and dropped her on the back-platform of the trolley. Instead of thanking the local celebrity for his spontaneous assistance, Risa pretended not to know who he was. Hanussen was intrigued with her arrogant repartee; he invited her to the Apollo. After the show, the perky soprano accompanied him to the Café Westminster.

Risa Luksch and Hanussen, August 1919

Hanussen pursued Risa through the fall and winter of 1919. Although his eyes and hands gravitated—Frankenstein-style, according to his café buddies—toward any pretty thing in reach, Hanussen was insanely jealous of Risa and accused her of unfaithful behavior in the most innocent of circumstances. Hanussen had a winningly boyish and unusually generous temperament, however, so Risa overlooked his unhealthy suspicions and crude manners. For instance, among the headliners at the Apollo and the Vienna's other variety venues, Erik alone seemed authentically warm and personally attentive to the stagehands and the rest of the lowly front-of-the-house workers. [Theresia Luksch, "Unpublished Diaries," (1919–1924)]

One of Hanussen's social proclivities truly vexed Risa. The Ottakring telepath was obsessed with gold. He wore thick gold chains around his neck and slipped flashy gold rings on his fingers before leaving the apartment. Moreover, Hanussen carried gold coins and a huge gold nugget in his jacket pocket. Invariably, the golden objects would be fished out during the evening and exhibited publicly on café tables—to the astonishment of bustling waiters and Prater onlookers. Risa wanted to die at those moments.

The devoutly Catholic Risa believed in Erik's supernatural abilities. During his clairvoyant experiments, she watched his body tremble and break into glistening coats of perspiration. In the middle of every evening, Hanussen had to change shirts and afterwards his face appeared ashen, his muscle tone visibly strained. He was silent and ate very little on the days he performed. To her, Hanussen was a kind of miraculous saint who only pretended to be a Balkan charlatan or boisterous, merry-faced con-man.

Once in the early hours at the Café Westminster, Hanussen became strangely agitated. He demanded that Risa change seats immediately; she supposed that it was another of his insipid fits of jealousy. Risa rose and allowed herself to be pulled to a corner table. She stared angrily at Hanussen's bloodless countenance, which registered absolute fear. Nothing happened for a few minutes.

Then an argument erupted in the far side of the room. A woman hurried out of the restaurant. One of the Westminster waiters, evidently her lover, stood, brandishing a pistol. He placed the shaking revolver to his head and fired three times. The first two shots somehow missed their target. The third killed him. Risa's eyes scanned the room. One of the stray bullets had shattered the windowpane just above the chair where she had been sitting.

By New Year's 1920, Risa and Erik were an established couple on the theatrical after-hours circuit. Risa attempted to introduce the mysterious paramour to her father, a minor city official (and apostate Jew); sadly, the endeavor turned calamitous. When the upstanding Luksch realized this Erik was none other than the Great Hanussen, the mocker of Mayor Weiskirchner and Commissioner Schrober, he chased his future son-in-law from his apartment with a dog-whip. Risa had nowhere to go but to remain with Hanussen; she was pregnant.

The lovers waited until the death of Risa's father before marrying.

On July 19, 1920, Erik petitioned the Viennese authorities for a formal divorce from Herta Samter. In addition, Hanussen obtained a *get*, a religious document dissolving the union, from the Jewish Community Council. After converting to Judaism, the religion of her ancestors, Risa wed Harry Steinschneider-Erik Jan Hanussen at the Viennese Branch Synagogue on August 3. Five weeks later, Risa gave birth to a daughter, Erika. At home, Risa practiced the Hebraic rituals that she had just learned. Naturally she was more pious than her thoroughly assimilated husband. The mother and daughter remained Jewish for six years.

The New Decade

Hanussen was clearly an entrenched stage luminary in Vienna by 1920, yet—as always—he still was unsettled about his public persona. Was the Master Dane a mere variety clairvoyant, two steps up from the Prater; a certified psychic detective; a high-minded enlightener of people's foolish superstitions; or a multi-talented writer-journalist, long ignored by the reigning intelligentsia? In various corners of the city, Erik enjoyed a reputation for at least one of the above callings. Of course, his renown as a legitimate artist and writer was the weakest and most ridiculed of his shifting identities. Hanussen was now determined to disprove his many detractors.

In early 1920, Erik Jan Hanussen-Steinschneider completed his grand masterwork, *Das Gedankenlesen/Telepathie.* It was an attractive softcover manual, interspersed with charts and hand-drawn diagrams of his tricks, reproductions of testimonial letters, and eleven photographs. Several months later, Erik finally dropped the old "Steinschneider" appellation and reissued his anthology booklet of pre-war and wartime cabaret lyrics under a more enticing title of *Schliessen Sie die Augen!* (Vienna: Nestroy-Verlag, 1920) ("Close Your Eyes!").

The Tricks of Erik Jan Hanussen

Erik Jan Hanussen was almost always considered to be an accomplished variety artist and telepath. Yet few reviewers or spectators ever placed him in the upper tier of magicians who dazzled and amused European audiences in the major music halls or vaudeville stages. There was absolutely something different about Erik. For one, he was difficult to define.

Typically, a stage magician or clairvoyant created a clear persona or mood when he or she appeared on stage. The music, lighting, set pieces, and especially the costume informed the audience pretty much what to expect. A performer with serious occult intentions might enter in an eerie fog or unexpectedly from a mirror-like closet; a comic type might begin with a mishap or leap up from the orchestra pit, wearing inappropriate clothing.

Hanussen fit none of these archetypes. His mood normally shifted sharply from serious to playful to taunting to shocking and mysterious. Erik could be a skeptic, a comic monologist, an exciting professor on tour, a friendly trickster. Yet invariably, he concluded his act with unabashed mystification, as if he himself had just realized his occult powers—the very subject that he scientifically outlined, then mocked and toyed with forty minutes before.

Reading full transcriptions of Hanussen performances or listening to people who witnessed them startles. The Ottakring clairvoyant understood audiences.

Erik's tricks can be catalogued accordingly:

1.Belief-Confidence-Personality-Humor

Hanussen studied his spectators attentively. Nearly all of them, especially the cynics, wanted to believe in the invisible, ineffable powers of the human mind and its ability to communicate through time and space. Without this kind of magic, there was no religion, no soul, no meaning outside desire and struggle, only Jenischism. Erik symbolized belief, in the twentieth century, to Central Europeans by his erudite commingling of popular science and stage sleight-of-hand, personal involvement with the public, and signature humor. What made it blend was his daredevil self-confidence. Erik felt that it was his conviction in his mysterious abilities, especially under duress, that sometimes created the real magic and connection.

Hanussen Program Cover (1928)

2. Observation-Psychology

From time immemorial, Gypsy fortune-tellers learned to pick up on minute facial or bodily reactions of their clients, during readings, to make seemingly amazing biographical pronoucements. Erik used this craft unerringly.

3. Muscle-Reading [See "Ten Rules for Muscle-Reading," pp. 52.]

4. Hypnosis-Suggestion

5. Surprise-Confusion-Hectoring

Unlike most stage mentalists, Hanussen rarely treated his subjects with restraint or affection. To him, they were stray children who desired discipline, punishing demands, a master to please; lost souls in search of a commanding leader whose occasional compliments and passionate threats meant he seriously cared about them.

6. The Abettor-Research

Most of Hanussen's astounding feats were accomplished through abettors, or paid assistants. Weeks before a show, they would ferret out private information about potential spectators or fascinating events from little villages or from innocuous discussions with audience members (or the coat checkwoman) during the preshow or intermission. The secrets of audience members could be signaled from the back of the house (through the menus of codes). If Hanussen was detained by a supervisory commission, the abettor could scribble the messages on the outside of rolled cigarettes, left in a backstage washroom or on a magician's table during the intermission. In the bathroom or during the performance, Erik would read the note on the cigarette and then destroy the evidence by lighting up.

In the "One-Ahead Trick," Hanussen took sealed envelopes from the audience and revealed their contents before opening them. He never missed because he was always "one ahead." His first fake divination was "confirmed" by an abettor. When

"Question-Logic" Trick (1920)

Thought-Reading by Hanussen-Steinschneider

"Is it a something you can touch?" "Yes."
"Can you find it in this room?" "No."
"In Vienna?" "No."
"In Germany?" "Yes."
"Can you find it in a building?" "No."
"Is it an object?" "No."
"Is it a person?" "Yes."
"A living person?" "No."
"A dead person?" "Yes."
"Male?" "Yes."
"A political leader?" "No."
"A famous person?" "Yes."
"A scholar?" "Yes."
"Did he write books?" "Yes."
"With spiritual content?" "Yes."
"Plays?" "Yes."
"Was he from Prussia?" "No."
"Are his works still presented?" "Yes."
"Are they classics?" "Yes."
"Did he die young?" "No."
"Old?" "Yes."
"Very old?" "Yes."
"Did he live in Weimar?" "Yes."
"Goethe?" "Yes."

Das Gedankenlesen/Telepathie, 1920

Erik tore open the first envelope in question to verify his guess, he memorized the contents of the question and then repeated its words when he held up the second sealed envelope. A real spectator (the author of the first letter) would, almost always, excitedly verify Hanussen's second "telepathic vision." And so forth.

7. Mnemonics-Memory Training

Hanussen had a prodigious mind with a superhuman ability to memorize the smallest of details and retain the most complicated series of dates and names. This helped immeasurably in the "One-Ahead" stunt and dozens of other telepathic routines. Erik practiced these mental feats relentlessly through mnemonic devices and exercises in concentration and recall.

8. Logic-Psychology

Another aspect of Erik's psychic ability was his simple use of refined logic. In the fewest number of questions, usually never more than thirty, he could determine any name or object that a spectator wrote on a concealed board. To the right is a transcription of a typical exchange.

Film Star and Director

Like many stage magicians worldwide, Hanussen was fascinated with the commercial and artistic possibilities of the motion picture. Film was not only the latest novelty in entertainment, it also seemed to be an enchanted analog to the magic show in its seamless displacement of time and space. In Central European music halls and variety houses, short subjects were being replaced by feature-

Hypnosis: Hanussen's First Adventure Film Poster, (1920)

length cinematic presentations. Occult topics were a specialized subset, like documentaries, but a growing competition to star-studded romances and detective thrillers. Erik toyed with the idea of a composite feature, which, like his performances, would use elements from every genre.

Gaston fights the Fakir and dies to save a soul.

A few weeks before Christmas 1919, Hanussen began to organize a film company that would promote his real-life experience as a psychic detective. He would undertake the positions of producer, director, and lead actor. It was called *Hypnosis: Hanussen's First Adventure*. By spring, all the pieces were in place and shooting commenced in a tony Viennese neighborhood. Although the visual and acting style was traditional Belasco realistic-melodrama, the theme of *Hypnosis* mined other popular and avant-garde hits, especially *Fantomas* and Hans Janowitz and Carl Mayer's Expressionist *The Cabinet of Caligari.*

Hanussen played a thoughtful, pipe-smoking, Sherlock-Holmesesque private detective, Gaston. His evil nemesis was a turbaned Indian fakir, who had the ability and means to hypnotize naive Viennese girls into sexual slavery and replicate their lissome bodies with zombie-doubles. By the fifth act, the Indian was dispatched into the wholesome air of the Vienna woods and his original harem-beauties freed. Gaston, in the final moments of the film, suddenly realized the woman he took for his beloved, in fact, was one of the fakir's erotic automatons. In order to return the Wienerin's soul to her body, the detective extinguished his own life-force and slipped to the floor as the girl awoke from the Indian's hypnotic spell.

Hypnosis opened at the Vienna Circus Busch Cinema in September. It received little notice and probably played the small town and village circuit before it hit Berlin and then virtually disappeared. Hanussen rarely referred to the feature; still his interest in motion pictures and advanced recording technologies continued until his death.

Hanussen, the Psychic Plaintiff

In March 1920, Erik received a new commission. Ludwig Zauner, a Viennese engineer, panicked when he spotted his luxury automobile missing from a garage warehouse. After placing a 5,000-kronen reward in a daily newspaper for its retrieval and prosecution of the thieves, Zauner contacted Hanussen. The telepath met with Zauner the same day.

Hanussen arrived in a chauffeured limousine, carrying his trusted Bagetta-Magica. Together they scrutinized Vienna's sidestreets. Embarrassingly, the hired car soon ran out of gas and stalled in the roadway. The comical turn of events did not speak well for the omniscient clairvoyant. Hanussen manipulated his dowser: it pointed in the direction of Stammerdorf. That was where the stolen sedan was located. The Dane then advised Zauner to withdraw his public notice and, instead, offer to drop all charges against the burglar if he returned the vehicle promptly.

The embittered Zauner had his doubts, but finally acquiesced to the detective's curious plan.

The next day, Hanussen disguised himself as an underworld car-dealer and made a tour of criminal dives. By the end of the day, he found his car thief and convinced the man to bring the said automobile back to Zauner and then collect the remuneration for his seemingly honest efforts. The burglar thanked the unscrupulous stranger for his cunning advice and departed. Hanussen informed Zauner that he had a premonition that his car would be restored to its owner within twenty-four hours.

In the morning, two teenagers appeared at Zauner's house. They had located his car in a barn in Stammerdorf. Instead of paying a reward, however, Zauner had them arrested. The police retrieved the sedan although they had no proof that the boys were involved in a criminal scheme.

Now it was the teens' turn for legal retribution. They sued Zauner for reneging on his promise of payment. At the August 29 proceeding, Hanussen was called to testify and demonstrate in the courtroom his divining techniques. He maintained that it was the Bagetta-Magica that led to his discovery of the clandestine whereabouts of Zauner's cherished automobile.

At that point, Zauner retaliated against Hanussen. He refused to fully reimburse the psychic for his services. Hanussen ascertained the car's hiding place through ratiocination and common detective work, Zauner maintained, not by telepathy as agreed upon. Therefore, like the boys, Erik was forced to press breach-of-contract charges against the recalcitrant engineer.

The *Hanussen v. Zauner* trial did not take place until December. It was just at the time when Erik appeared at another prominent venue, the Great Music Union Hall. At his end-of-the-year New Year's production, Hanussen again chose to play the fatherly enlightener. He proffered a cautionary message to his fans: clairvoyance, hypnosis, and dowsing, as enacted by the Danish master, were confirmed scientific realities, although spiritualism and most exhibitions of stage telepathy—that is, the routines of his competitors and adversaries—were based on fraud and crafty artifice. The noble Hanussen, naturally, revealed the mechanics of how the oily gurus ingenuously duped their faithful clientele with mentalist schemes and subterfuge.

Leopold Thoma

Meanwhile, the Viennese municipal court selected one of their own, Leopold Thoma, as an expert examiner to verify Hanussen's paranormal boasts. Thoma—then known as Dr. Leopold Thoma or by his wonderfully exotic pseudonym of "Tartargula"—occupied a unique position in Vienna's professional life. Unlike Hanussen, he slickly traversed the normally stationary spectrum of university professor, clinical therapist, police bureaucrat, playwright, legal scholar, science journalist, and stage hypnotist. Discovered in his youth by Prof. Julius Wagner von Jauregg, Europe's leading authority on hypnosis (as well as Pilcz's and Ostermann's superior at Vienna University), Thoma headed the Psychology Unit of the Vienna Police in 1920 and, one year later, founded the private Institute for Telepathic-Crime Research.

Thoma often worked with the Polish-Jewish medium Megalis and had great success in mass suggestion and the promising field of psychic criminology. During one experiment at the University, Thoma put 180 physicians into trance, while blindfolded and facing a wall. The Renaissance man's specialty was "mechanical hypnosis," which used recording and film devices for dream-induction. And unlike the Dane, Thoma had few enemies.

Leopold Thoma at Vienna University, 1923

It was little wonder that Hanussen marveled at the list of Thoma's accomplishments and his felicitous connections. At a historical moment when most champions of borderline-science and extrasensory communication were widely perceived as duplicitous cheats, sex-maniacs, or religious confidence-men, Thoma remained unscathed. One decade later in Berlin, Erik would designate him to be his personal companion, ghost-writer, political go-between, and chief editor. And, characteristically, Thoma always stood above the murderous fray that would surround his Ottakring boss. [Leopold Thoma, *Hanussen: Hinter den Kulissen eines mysteriösen Lebens* (Aufbau-Verlag: Berlin, 1933)]

To corroborate Zauner's accusation that Hanussen could not locate stolen merchandise through purely psychic means, Thoma devised a double-blind test. He drove a supposedly "hot" automobile from one garage to another and wrote down the name of the second enclosed station on a sheet of paper, which he placed in a sealed envelope and deposited with the court reporter.

The following day, December 30, Hanussen came to the courthouse, armed with a dowser. The telepath got into Thoma's car and sat next to a chauffeur. In the back seat were the district attorney, the judge, and Thoma. For two hours, the *Lebaschmann* indicated to the court-appointed driver which Viennese sidestreets to negotiate. Finally, in a collapsed and exhausted state, Hanussen abandoned the daytime search. The experiment continued on December 31, but since the "stolen" vehicle was moved during the previous night for a second time, there was confusion on both sides. Hanussen, however, correctly surmised the identity of the original "thief." It was one of the police chauffeurs who accompanied him on the quest.

After the tainted hunts, the judge of the municipal court declared Hanussen an extraordinary observer and fine detective while indeterminately psychic. He was to keep Zauner's March retainer, not the total promised reward.

Merchants of War

True to his itinerant roots, Erik did not stay long with Risa and daughter. He left Vienna in the spring of 1921 for a year-and-a-half trek around the colonial rime of the Eastern Mediterranean. He also took several off-the-path excursions to the mystic oases in the distant east and south. Hanussen toured the great metropolises of Greece, Turkey, Egypt, and Saudi Arabia, and explored many of the new colonial protectorates and mandates awarded to victorious France, Britain, and Italy. It was a fanciful and impulsive adventure, a journey totally unnecessary for Erik's material or career benefit and clearly more suitable for the feckless gratification of a teenager, not a thirty-two-year-old father and minor European entertainer.

The Oriental journey began with someone else's confidence scheme.

The hedonistic Hans Hauser was the proud inheritor of the Austro-Hungarian foreign tobacco concession. In Maffersdorf, a village outside Vienna, Hauser's family owned the town's largest estate and their cigarette fortune made them more respected than any landed gentry. Even in the financially shaky postwar era, the Hausers lacked no physical comforts.

At the Hausers' usual Midis-like evenings with princely spreads of imported delicacies and other rich dishes, however, Hans found that he could not tolerate a single morsel of food. The family scion suffered from globus hystericus, the inability to swallow.

Treatment from Vienna's most illustrious physicians and psychologists merely isolated and identified Hans' malady. The tobacco tycoon fell into a state of perpetual panic; every mouthful of solid food caused his throat to contract and gag. After a few maddening weeks, he showed up at Ostermann's clinic. Hypnotic therapy, as administered by Erik Jan Hanussen, went directly to Hauser's problem, a deeply-rooted fear of suffocation while dining. The curative sessions with the Master Dane had a miraculous result. In Erik's presence, Hauser was able to eat. The king of Maffersdorf returned to his sumptuous repasts, but he required the constant therapeutic company of the telepath.

In March 1921, the restored Hauser hatched a wild business scheme. He used his pre-war contacts in the Austrian government to purchase boxcars of surplus army goods at cut-rate prices. These would be his barter for Greek tobacco. Most of the Royal and Imperial Army supplies were then practically worthless—even the locomotives that transported the banged-up artillery, crates of saddles and backpacks, and befeathered helmets were in a sad state of disrepair. Yet, Greece, alone among the European powers, was gearing up for war. It needed substantial military equipment for its fourth (or fifth) armed conflict with its traditional archrival, Muslim Turkey.

To dine in the manner to which he was accustomed, Hauser still required Hanussen's hypnotic services. That was reason enough to cart the burly clairvoyant to Athens. In addition, the wily capitalist was convinced that Erik's amazing powers of suggestion could be useful during negotiations with the Greek Secretary of War. A man who could outperform Rubini and Freud would have no problem with distracted Balkan bureaucrats. (Hanussen was Vienna's real secret weapon, in Hauser's demented world view.)

Inside the national military compound in Athens, the simpatico tobacco trader presented the Greek War Minister with suitcases of ornamental rifles and showy relics from the deposed Emperor's antique war chest. It was a mistaken opening gambit. The Greek Army craved modern armaments, not the artistic vestiges of lost campaigns. And Hanussen's furtive hypnotic passes proved hollow and utterly unsuccessful. Suggestion necessitated either the hypnotiseur's concentrated will or the acquiescence of the subject. At the Ministry, there was neither.

Meanwhile the frustrated Hauser spied a dark-eyed Armenian beauty at the Hotel Angleterre, where the arms-traders were staying, and fell madly in love with her. He sent her bouquets and a diamond cross pendant, but the exotic creature returned them all without a word. Erik too was greatly attracted to her. She spurned both of their clumsy advances. Then the old Ottakring delinquent went into action.

He asked the tobacco dealer what the Armenian woman's affections were worth. Hauser offered Hanussen one of his luxury sedans if he could change her heart.

At the Angleterre lounge, Hanussen announced an experimental evening of the occult arts. The oily telepath inveigled several high-living Greek matrons into having their fortunes publicly read through chiromancy and, a half-hour later, the Danish telepath found a needle hidden under the bar by a tourist.

Hanussen walked over to the implacable Armenian enchantress and took her hand. He needed a medium for his final act of hypnosis. She followed him willingly and, with three snaps of his fingers and a few hypnotic passes over her slim body, the dark-eyed woman, unlike the Secretary of War, fell into deep trance.

The story made the rounds the next day and local journalists swarmed over the Viennese miracle-man. Hanussen was back in his element. He rented the Dymotikon Theatre. The sales from the premiere alone brought in almost 40,000 drachmas, enough to pay for the otherwise ill-fated trip. Hanussen played at the Dymoitkon for four more evenings and another two in the larger Royal Theatre. The Athenian dailies hailed the foreign hit show. And the Greek Music Hall even produced a lavish number about the European clairvoyant, a parody that Erik remembered as hilarious.

Now with money in his pocket, Hanussen began to court Hauser's Armenian dream-girl. The tobacco merchant withdrew the automotive reward and decided to drive back to Maffersdorf, where he was the uncontested lord of the manor. Evidently, Hans Hauser's eating disorder, as well as his unbridled martial enthusiasm, were checked.

Back to Asia

In 1921, over half of Salonika, including most of its extensive Jewish Quarter, had been destroyed by fire. Hanussen heard that interest in the supernatural, therefore, was rife among the multi-ethnic city's inhabitants. An engagement at Moses Avramiko's Theatre was set. For fourteen days, beginning on April 15, Erik played in German to sold-out houses. It was here also that the miracle-man discovered hashish, and an addictive form of retsina called Dusiko.

On May 1, Hanussen crossed the Dardanelles into the Asian side of Constantinople. Again he rented a theatre, the Lehman, for a two-week run. This time, his luck turned sour. No one came to the magic show. Hanussen had completely gone through the fortune he collected in Greece.

With one Turkish pound remaining and a trunkful of magic props, Erik boarded a freighter to Smyrna, the Greek port city in Asia Minor. Like Salonika, it was also devastated by a biblical-like conflagration and its townspeople were slowly recuperating physically and spiritually.

In a harbor pawnshop, Erik sold his last valuable, a gold pen, a gratuity that Uncle Hans bequeathed to him. At least now he had a grub-stake. Acting as the Berlin impresario Franz Müller, Hanussen then rented a hall for himself and printed up street posters. He played under the Arabic name El Sah'r (The Wizard) and managed to recoup some of his losses.

At Xantos, another Greek possession wrenched from the Ottoman Empire, Hanussen teamed up with the director of the Operetta Athens. El Sah'r was to accompany the troupe to Alexandria and perform during its six-week run. In the midst of packing, Hanussen had a visit from some new friends, a Greek band of hashish smugglers. The head gangster found Erik's steamer trunk an ideal receptacle for his wares. It was just one of 300 theatrical costume and flat-crates. The likelihood of it being controlled by British customs was statistically remote.

In Athens, Hanussen embarked on the *Isminia* with his tainted property chest. The steamer ship, however, unexpectedly ran into a ferocious storm system and was unable to disengage itself. For four days off the Cretan coast, the *Isminia* struggled to keep itself afloat. Rising tides and torrential rains flooded the decks.

Alone among the Greek singers and superstitious Levantine travelers, the Danish telepath refused to pray and petition the angry gods for forgiveness and sanctuary. Instead Erik demanded food from the chief steward. At that moment, bolts of lightning streaked across the Mediterranean sky. This was a clear sign to the terrified passengers that an emissary from the Devil was in their midst.

The *Isminia* crew efficiently organized a judicial council to eliminate the unholy contagion before their badly listing ship utterly capsized. A human sacrifice had to be made. El Sah'r was to be bound and tossed into the churning, wine-darkened waters. Hanussen's comic rejoinders and comradely appeals fell flat before the agitated lynch party. Finally, the magician elicited from his pursuers a full thirty minutes to calm the storm and steady the endangered craft. With a fixed smile, Erik retreated to his cabin where he kept a Browning automatic pistol. And while the sailors waited for El Sah'r to reappear on the poop deck, the storm actually subsided. Both the *Isminia* and Hanussen were saved.

At the customs warehouse in Alexandria, Erik retrieved his trunk. Neither the blocks of Syrian hashish nor his 3,000 English pound consignment were inside. The omnipotent Wizard had been played for a common sucker.

Another Luftmensch

Freed from the Athenian Operetta commission, Hanussen wandered the cosmopolitan backways of Alexandria. It wasn't long before he found himself a new German-speaking sidekick and impresario, Philip Neufeld. A fellow *Luftmensch* and colorful jack-of-all-trades from Galicia, Neufeld (known as Maki) managed to communicate in fourteen languages and make himself indispensable to the British colonial authorities and the indigenous ruling classes of Egypt and the Sudan.

When they met, Maki ran the canteen at one of the British Army officer's club, which was fast becoming insolvent under the Galicianer's typical laissez-faire style of management. He also owned British railroad stock, being the one shareholder who was conversant in Arabic, English, Hebrew, and Yiddish—the languages of Mandate Palestine, the gemstone of the reconfigured British Empire. Unfortunately, the civic authorities in Egypt were a bit puzzled over Maki's Levantine accounting methods. The impresario with mismatched sandals needed a quick change of locale.

Maki claimed to know all about Hanussen from newspaper clippings and proposed a partnership. He would arrange a series of evenings throughout the Near East, where the Dane could work his wonders in commercial halls and inside the courtyards of amusement-starved potentates. Erik agreed. Maki was the least polished of con-men; in fact, Hanussen had never met one so transparent or ridiculous in appearance. That was Maki's unique charm and the unlikely means of his success.

For their first project, the Jewish roustabouts entertained the French viceroy at his palace in Damascus. After a vexing three-day negotiation, Maki rented a theatre for a month-long rendezvous in the city proper. The local populace, however, did not take to the foreigners' occult shenanigans. Arab audiences were more resistant to hypnotism than the Greek ministers and rarely laughed at El Sah'r's lighter routines.

In Aleppo, the situation worsened. A nightclub owner, who received a fifty percent share of the ticket sales, personally rebuffed the Wizard's entries of hypnotic induction on stage, insuring a disagreeable opening night and mutual financial farrago. He explained his adversarial—and self-destructive—behavior afterwards. It was better for an Arab to lose his profits and investment than sully his sense of honor by giving up control of his mind.

In the Land of Zion

Hanussen decided to find greener, more European environs. He would conduct his business in Jewish Palestine. It was one of several places that Maki, because of the British railroad stock imbroglio, had to avoid. El Sah'r went it alone. The twosome decided to reunite in Cairo.

Hanussen performed in Herzlia, Jerusalem, Jaffa, Haifa, and a half-dozen Jewish cooperative colonies and kibbutzim. High Zionist officials accompanied him on his forays in the Sharon Valley and Erik even made an attempt to lecture in fractured Hebrew. His memory of the ancient tongue from pre-Schmelz days was sorely challenged and he was encouraged to communicate instead in his Viennese-inflected German or *Mitteleuropa* Yiddish.

Hanussen especially marveled at the Chalutzim, the idealistic European Jews who shed their mercantile and urban origins to work the harsh and malaria-infested soils of Palestine. Overall, the tour revitalized Erik's fatigued spirits, temporarily reshaped his ethnic identity, and filled his pockets. The Wizard arrived in Cairo with 1,000 British pounds.

Spiritualist and Spy

The further adventures of Maki and Erik took them to Kos, an idyllic isle once home to Socrates and site of the Aesklepeon, the fabled hospital fortress from the time of Pericles. Split peacefully between 1500 Greek and Turkish inhabitants, Kos was then under the rule of Italy. The Italians used the ruins of the Aesklepeon for their garrison. The entire military crew consisted of a garrulous old sergeant and his two underlings.

Uncharacteristically, Hanussen and Maki relaxed on the do-nothing fleck of paradise for two weeks. Waiting for the next Italian freighter to dock and deliver the mail, the miracle-man charmed the locals with little more than a few tales and the technological magic of his wind-up gramophone. One of the enchanted Kosians was a sweet-faced Turkish prostitute. Both Erik and Maki pursued her as if she were a classical vision come alive.

Amidst the ruins of the ancient Aeskulap temple, Hanussen performed a midnight séance. For the Danish impostor, the event seemed truly mysterious. His invented incantations conjured up sharply-detailed materializations of ancient beings in all their diaphanous, spiritual wonder. The Kosians saw the images too and pronounced El Sah'r a living god. An old Greek man, the island's poet laureate, penned a 3,000-line ode to Hanussen. It was one of the happiest and most serene moments in Erik's life.

On Rhodos, the Austrians did not fare so well. The Italian police refused to allow them to disembark. The island was a transit point for Italian arms being shipped to Turkey. The station commander assumed the two were Greek spies. Hanussen narrowly convinced the skeptical Italian that they were merely entertainers; his international production would boost the defenders' morale.

Maki made arrangements for a performance at a pension, the Hotel Bellavista. Assuming that his notoriety would draw a larger audience, Hanussen contracted for 200 additional chairs from a Turkish café. The Bellavista's patio-garden was filled with onslaughts of curious spectators that night, including the station commander who sat in the front row, taking notes.

When the Turkish café owner came to pick up his chairs the next morning, though, the cocky telepath attempted to renegotiate their contract. The Turk indignantly refused and Hanussen cursed him. Erik handed the shopkeeper his piasters, warning him that lightning would strike his house and cornfields and all of his sheep would soon sicken and die.

Twenty-four hours later, a throng of hundreds of Turkish peasants, wielding pitchforks and muskets, surrounded the pension. The Italian hotelier pounded on the Austrians' door. There was a problem.

Hanussen stepped to the balcony and gazed at the howling mob below. The Turkish café owner screamed to El Sah'r that he wanted his sheep back. Two of them had died mysteriously the last night. The clairvoyant smiled wanly.

Some of the Turkish farmers gawked in fright; they recognized Hanussen's smirk as the taunting countenance of a witch. Others demanded that the Devil's quarters be torched altogether with his European accomplices.

El Sah'r tried to remain calm. Yes, he was a wizard, a supernatural being. In fact, he had the ability to bewitch and destroy all of the sheep on Rhodes, maybe all of the world's sheep. However, he also had the means to resurrect the beasts. If the café-owner wanted his sheep restored, he only had to refund half of the 200 piasters.

Hanussen's proposal quieted the pugnacious mob. For an instant, they were stunned. A circle, three deep, formed around the coffee-man and the community leaders. Half of the peasants wanted to see the resurrection; the firebrands in the circle equally pleaded for retaliatory arson or some other murderous revenge.

After fifteen minutes, the Islamic wisemen prevailed. El Sah'r was to undo his evil spell and resurrect the lifeless creatures. The Demon Effendi would receive thirty piasters if he succeeded; people's justice if the experiment failed.

A dead sheep was carried to the pension wall on the backs of the peasants and hoisted up to the balcony. Maki dragged the carcass across the room, down the hotel stairway, and dumped it in a manure pit, well hidden from the crowd. Outside in an animal pen, Maki grabbed one of the Bellavista's sheep by its muzzle and stealthily carried it back to the master's room.

Hanussen ordered a straw-fire to be lighted under his balcony for the hellish ceremony. While the villagers gathered and prepared the combustibles, Maki took black dye and a brush from Hanussen's make-up case and painted the snout of the corralled beast to exactly duplicate the distinct markings of the lifeless animal buried in the muck.

The straw-fire burned with a dense cloud of black smoke, which enveloped Hanussen's balcony. When the fumes cleared, Maki released the animal's muzzle and the resurrected sheep bleated and stammered nonstop. The Turkish peasants were beside themselves with joy. The astonished café-owner inspected his treasure. This was worth fifty piasters, not thirty, he exclaimed. His dignity and soul intact, Erik graciously accepted the reward.

Along the Coasts

Maki and Hanussen sailed south to Tripoli, then a dusty backwater administrative town and the gateway for the Italian reconquest of the old Roman Empire. Neither the Arabs nor the Italian troops cared much for El Sah'r esoteric feats.

Hanussen reverted to a traditional carny dare. He announced a 1,000 pound reward for any man who could lift him off the floor. Maki rented a cabaret space and insisted that secret hooks and steel cables secure the miracle-man to the ground. Erik protested that the trick involved only mechanical advantage and his rapid transfer of weight. In the end, he allowed for Maki's gaffed construction.

When the stunt was exhibited before a sold-out audience, however, a local strongman feigned an upper body attack and then lifted Hanussen straight from his hips. The hooked metal hinges, which Maki nailed into the cabaret stage, were yanked from the rotten floorboards with Erik's body. It was a form of levitation but not a profitable one.

The pair struck out for Oran in French Algeria, where they studied Arab dervishes and fakirs in the Casbah marketplace. The fearless mountebanks juggled fire, swallowed shards of glass, charmed snakes, pierced their arms and cheeks with rusty spikes, drank molten wax, laid face down on beds of nails, and contorted their faces and bodies into grotesque shapes and haunting expressions. The Austrians were greatly impressed with the superhuman displays and had difficulty separating the explainable tricks from body magic.

Alone

In early 1922, Hanussen returned to Cairo, via Malta and Corfu, and was employed as a detective for the British colonial police. He tracked down a gang of hashish smugglers to Damascus, where they imprisoned him. Later he managed to escape and collect a £200 reward.

In Beirut, Erik fell head-over-heels for the daughter of a Turkish importer. Maki volunteered to assist in the delicate mediation, even dressing as an Arab marriage-broker. The seemingly innocuous ploy backfired twice over. Maki was arrested for fraudulent impersonation and, once out of jail, betrayed his master by proposing himself as the intended groom.

Philip "Maki" Neufeld and Erik Jan Hanussen parted ways over the incident of the merchant's daughter. They would not see one another for two years. By then, the Beirut affair would be another comic anecdote of their common Oriental adventure.

El Sah'r continued on to Baghdad and Shiraz. By this time, Hanussen was much more a pupil of the paranormal than a purveyor of it. The experience at the Oran Casbah strangely affected him. There was much to learn about illusionism and the fakir's physical orchestration of body and belief.

In Hillah, an Arab village near the ruins of Babylon, Hanussen witnessed (and secretly photographed) the Indian Rope Trick. It was a fantastic and unerring blend of sleight-of-hand magic, unusual acrobatic skill, and spectator manipulation.

Oran Fakirs, (1923)

Hanussen in Giza.

With an Egyptian Magician, 1921

Crisis and Discovery

Erik concluded his Oriental journey back in Egypt. In Tanta, a city north of Cairo, his skills of divination were challenged by an Arab commodities trader. If the Dane possessed infallible clairvoyant powers, why didn't he play the stock market himself and acquire some plum dividends? Why wasn't he a rich man, instead of an empty-pocket, always-on-the-run, middle-aged entertainer? The worldly investor offered Hanussen a lucrative stake for his advanced insights. He wanted to know if Egyptian cotton futures would rise or fall. Should he dispose of them? More to the point, could Hanussen factually ascertain their exchange value on, say, May 15? Erik objected to the gross application of his legerdemain.

The entrepreneur's questioning was incisive and touched the miracle-man in ways that he didn't expect. Most of Hanussen's talents, naturally, involved out-and-out chicanery and optical tricks—just like the Arab fakirs. But some fell into a gray area, like his ability to influence people through hypnosis and psychic detection—again like the Berber and Arab seers. Or was it all just magical thinking on his part?

In Tanta, Erik experienced nagging self-doubt and underwent a full spiritual crisis, possibly a mental breakdown. A sympathetic Indian introduced the manual exercise of "worry-beads" to comfort the ailing clairvoyant. As irrational and silly as the strings of polished wooden beads appeared, handling them helped Hanussen recover from his psychological malaise. The Persian version of rosary beads, which Hanussen labeled the Gomboloy, was an ancient and effective form of therapy. In postwar Europe, it would replace the Bagetta-Magica as the Dane's signature metaphysical apparatus.

Ali, his Eritrean compatriot from Vienna, found Erik in the Egyptian city and brought him to his sister's summer palace in Asmara, near the Red Sea coast. There, after watching parades of Ethiopian folk dances and trance-inducing orchestras, Hanussen finally beheld the real *Lebaschmen*, the teenage Bali Sea shamans who mastered the craft of auto-hypnosis and detected soul-vibrations with the aid of flawless branches from fruit-bearing trees.

Although Hanussen alternately toyed with dowsing as an efficacious scientific art and then as an ingenuous stage novelty, here in Asmara, Erik was beguiled by the preliterate world's authentic paranormal teachers and practitioners. They were truly capable of ineffable wonders, even in the open-air grounds of the Queen's palace.

The *Lebaschmen* achieved their miraculous results from sources other than sham machinations and misdirection. These simple villagers never doubted their preternatural gifts; they accepted, from the ancestral gods of the forest and sea, the divine curse and blessing of their exalted vocation. That was the *Lebaschmen's* primal secret.

It was a fitting conclusion to Erik's seventeen months of wandering and self-discovery.

Lebasch-Dowser

Warning!!!

Attention! **Directors and Agents** **Attention!**

I have severed all contact with the telepath **Erik Jan Hanussen**. My current stage shows are now directed by **Mister Rex**. I am warning all managers and agents of fakes and imitations. I am the **Original Martha Farra**, the strong woman who recently received such tremendous acclaim in Vienna (Apollo-Theater), in Zagreb (Music-Hall Orpheum), in Budapest (Fövarosi-Zirkus and Tabarin), in Teplitz-Schönau (Variety Imperator). **This autumn I will perform in Prague (Theatre Variety Divadlo)** and am not longer associated with Hanussen! I **alone am authorized to use the name Martha Farra,** which is registered under the number 18962 by the I.A.L. (International Artists League). **Whoever uses my name without authorization** will be immediately reported to the I.A.L. and **turned over to the proper authorities!** I, the **Original Martha Farra**, the talk of Vienna and rival of Breitbart, was born in Vienna on October 31, 1903. My family name is Martha Kohn; I have blonde hair, dark eyes, and possess a long, slim figure (see photograph).

Directors and agents, do not deal with Herr Hanussen and kindly honor the above statements!

My great success in Prague has been extended to October 15th at the

Theatre-Variety Divadlo, Prague.

My forthcoming tour, with Mister Rex, is currently available for booking anywhere in the whole world!

Free after October 15, 1923!

What does Martha Farra do?

Martha Farra, a 19-year-old girl, can perform all of the phenomenal stunts that the Iron-King Breitbart executes onstage!

Martha Farra

the world renowned Iron-Queen

(This picture has been confirmed by the directors of the Apollo-Theatre Vienna, the Music-Hall Zagreb, the Fövarosi-Zirkus Budapest as the Original Martha Farra.)

Those wishing to contact me (before October 15, 1923) may write my impresario Ferdinand Oesterreicher, **Theatre Variety Divadlo, Prague.**

Das Programm, October 7, 1923

Breitbart the Mighty Man

BREITBART is a youthful Pole, derived from the best blood of Poland: handsome, intelligent, modest. He is said by the scientists of Europe, who have taken personal and professional interest in his amazing feats, to be both the strongest man of modern times and records and, also, the most unaccountable. His ways and habits are those of an unspoiled boy. Endowed with super-normal muscular and nervous power he achieves feats of strength never before attempted by the bulky "lifters," wrestlers and physical giants of the past. His quietude, his distinguished appearance, his modesty, his unselfconsciousness are all so untheatrical as to make his performance the more amazing. Every wonder he performs "looks easy" because there is always the quality of effortless ease about it. Breitbart is a graciously "peculiar" individual. Interest in him waxes with knowledge of his personal and social attainments.

New York Hippodrome Souvenir Program (1923)

CHAPTER FIVE

THE BREITBART YEARS

1922-1924

Alt Wien

In the autumn of 1922, Hanussen once again emptied his pockets at the customs desk of the Vienna Bahnhof. Social life in the gay metropolis had deteriorated considerably since Hauser had chaperoned Erik through the sequestered compounds of Greece's War Department. The Great Inflation, which transformed the German mark into worthless blocks of paper, now descended over the Austrian economy and the once sprightly escapades of nocturnal Vienna. Child beggars stationed themselves in front of the entrances of bakeries and cafés. Prostitution became rampant and black-market barter was the commercial norm. The rhetoric of both anti-Semitism and revolution burst from neighborhood *Lokals* and disturbingly punctuated the menacing orations from Austria's leading parliamentary speakers.

Continuing his separation from Risa, Hanussen rented a small apartment on Esterhazygasse. Peppi arranged for some magic programs at the Music Club and the Konzerthaus. Beneath the pipes of the Konzerthaus' monstrous organ, Erik burned incense and planted a mango tree seed in a ceramic urn. He blathered some Arabic incantations in his best spell-binding facsimile of an Egyptian sorcerer—really a turbaned flim-flam artist that Hanussen observed as a tourist by the Great Pyramid in Giza.

The fabled Indian trick on the Konzerthaus stage, however, came up short. No stem arose from the pot, no branches jetted out from the trunk, no leaves untangled and sprouted, no flowers blossomed, and no exotic fruits germinated in fast-forward motion and dangled from the tree. When the cloud of cheap incense dissipated, it was clear to the new generation of tabloid journalists that the mango tree (as well as Hanussen's nonpareil powers) had failed to materialize. A few of Erik's hardcore devotees, of course, swore they spotted misty outlines of the exotic fauna in bloom.

The aborted stunt, surprisingly, did not much dampen the miracle-man's spirits. Stage telepathy and clairvoyant shows were quickly losing their appeal in the depressed capital. Finding a concealed needle, guessing the contents of sealed envelopes, no longer shocked or amused. Even the Telepathic Wonder considered relinquishing his title as Vienna's premiere magician. There were better outlets for the Dane's new philosophical musings and cynical wit.

Legitimate Venues

Waldheim-Eberle, the Viennese publisher of *Das Gedankenlesen/Telepathie*, announced four companion books in their Hanussen-Steinschneider series: *Hellsehen und Fernfühlen* ("Clairvoyance and Distant Feeling"), *Wachsuggestion und Hypnose* ("Conscious Suggestion and Hypnosis"), *Der Wünschelrutengänger* ("The Dowser"), and *Die Weltseele* ("The World-Soul"). It is unclear today which of the booklets were actually penned, printed, or distributed. Unlike *Gedankenlesen*, the runs must have been uncommonly small and probably reflected a declining interest in occult and practical magic during the Inflation. Scheduled for a winter 1922 release, *Die Weltseele* presumably elucidated Erik's most recent theories on the conundrum and limitations of scientific methodology, primitive belief-systems, and human behavior. The very topic would be recapitulated in later writings.

In December, Hanussen composed, directed, and starred in an occult melodrama at the Bürgertheater. His play, *Dr. Svengali*, was a direct and conscious borrowing from the 1897 British potboiler *Trilby*, which Paul Potter had adapted from George du Maurier's popular novel. The Bürgertheater version transposed the action from music studio to hypnotist's clinic.

Hanussen's character, Dr. Svengali, avenges himself on a caddish rival by seducing the man's wife through hypnotic induction. Over time, Svengali realizes that he deeply loves the will-less lass and undergoes an ego-shattering crisis. Should he release her from his insidious spell and chance losing her physical charms? Or should he keep her in hypnotic bondage? In the end, the ethical Svengali empowers the woman with free choice. She walks out of his clinic and the defeated hypnotist collapses in despair.

The Viennese critics were unkind to the production but generally praised Hanussen's portrayal as dynamic and sharply drawn. Less welcome was the playwright's flat depiction of the minor characters. Each of the three scholarly scientists in *Dr. Svengali* was an obvious echo of a contemporary Viennese figure in Hanussen's life: the inflexible Professor Wallner was a stand-in for Erik's adversary, Prof. Julius Wagner von Jauregg; the saintly Prof. Moritz Benjamin could be none other than the dramatist's benefactor, the saintly Moritz Benedikt; and Dr.

Umstecker, who switched allegiances to Svengali in the last act, mimicked the pixie-like gait of Dr. Leopold Thoma, an erratic confidant of the Dane.

By the end of December, Hanussen returned to the world of variety. An old wartime colleague from the Emperor Karl Charity Fund, Moritz Rosner, needed an established personality to fill a slot for his vaudeville program at the Ronacher Theater. Erik would be the number two attraction on the New Year's bill. Heading the evening was Sigmund Breitbart, an international sensation who was widely heralded as "The Iron King" or the "Polish Goliath."

The Modern Samson

Zisha (or Sigmund) Breitbart was already a phenomenon in German variety-houses and circuses by 1922. A Yiddish-speaking strongman from Poland, Breitbart executed breathtaking sideshow feats like twisting steel bars into ornamental shapes, severing one-inch-thick chain links, pounding spikes into heavy boards with his bare fists, lying on a bed of nails as he supported a spinning carousel of children, and hoisting a *droshky* of spectators in the air. With a helmet of wavy blonde hair and an imposing, if modest, physique, the Tarzan-clad Zisha hardly resembled the mustached, muscle-bound Adonises that Central Europeans long associated with taciturn circus-giants.

Breitbart projected something gentle, almost feminine, in his sunny stage persona and was often compared with the silent film star, Rudolph Valentino. Moreover, Zisha's proud and unassimilated espousal of his Mosaic faith (through his scenic characterizations of Goliath, Samson, and Hebrew gladiators, together with his Zionistic proclamations in Yiddish) represented a fresh archetype: twentieth-century Jew as noble savage.

Born in 1883 and raised in Starovitch, the hard-scrabble proletarian quarter of Lodz, Breitbart trained as a blacksmith and learned to combat anti-Semitic injustice through brute strength and guileless confrontation. At thirteen, he joined a Jewish circus that passed through the city and soon developed a reputation as a powerful and inventive showman. On a bet, Zisha could lift cumbersome iron blocks with one hand and balance stools in the air that were weighted down by hefty, incredulous gangsters. He challenged railroad workers, equipped with sledgehammers, to smash tombstones laid on his chest and allowed himself to be buried in airless coffins for ten-minute intervals. Breitbart wrestled fairground bears and held shaking troikas in place.

Poles and many Jews doubted Zisha's Herculean prowess. He must have utilized a secret deck of Gypsy ruses. Yet when they attempted to replicate Breitbart's barroom exploits, bloodied hands fumbled, anvils crashed from the dissembling embrace of unsteady arms, and rib-cages cracked. Zisha was unassailable and quickly became a legend in the crammed Jewish ghettos and shetlakh of Russia's Pale of Settlement.

In a decade, Breitbart would be the subject of at least two dozen Yiddish and Polish hurdy-gurdy songs. (Some were still sung in alleys of Manhattan's Lower East Side in the late '20s and early '30s, years after Breitbart's death.) Like a Jewish Madonna, his image was a treasured icon in the groschen-bags of Warsaw's kaftaned porters and street peddlers. And vagabond entertainers in eastern Poland knew a surefire brand name and began to hawk themselves as Breitbart the Second, or, in even more faraway climes, Breitbart the Third. [*Zishe Breitbart: Der Moderner Shimson Hagibor* (New York: Ferlag Hagvira, 1925)]

During this early period, Zisha continually added stunts to his circus repertoire. The iron rods he bent freehand were now wrapped around his left arm in eight equidistant loops—a visual citation of the leather tefflin straps religious Jews bind around their arms each morning. Other metal bars were twisted into shapes easily recognizable to the ghetto dwellers—like Friday night candleholders or in Sabbath egg-bread patterns—but culturally opaque to gentile audiences.

Breitbart also increased the size and theatricality of his performances. Typically, in large halls, he came riding on the stage in full Roman regalia while an orchestra played a heroic fanfare. Toga-clad assistants slavishly carted on and off the podium Zisha's many props and helped select volunteers from the audience to examine the solidity of Breitbart's chains and other objects of demolition. Crowds of ten, twenty, or forty were even led to the proscenium in order to stand on the superhuman fulcrum or ride in a *droshky* that would roll over Zisha's steel-plated chest.

In 1916 German soldiers started to frequent productions of the Hebraic curiosity and Breitbart's entourage moved westward with Hindenburg's retreating armies. At the war's end, Breitbart was in Prussia. The Circus Busch hired the Polish strongman for their traveling Three-Ring Extravaganza and lavishly promoted him as the "World's Mightiest Human."

The mythic powerhouse acquired fame and wealth in the midst of Germany's collapse. Illiterate by traditional Jewish standards, Breitbart assembled a 2,000-volume library on ancient Rome and spoke glowingly of the Zionist enterprise in British-liberated Palestine. In 1918, the androgynous titan married and fathered a son. With his substantial earnings from tours in Hamburg, Dortmund, Munich, and Breslau, the King of Europe's *Ostjuden* purchased an estate in Friedrichthal, outside Berlin.

In the winter of 1922, Rosner engaged Breitbart for a three-month run in Vienna. The former Imperial capital, a prime destination for Galicia's disposed, quickly transformed into one of the newest and most disparate Jewish communities in Europe. West of the crumbled Czarist Empire, that old Prison House of Nations, there was no other region so changed by internal immigration. An organized counter-reaction among Austria's beleaguered nationalists churned ominously, by the month, to the surface. Their intimidating invective reverberated far beyond the cordoned halls of the xenophobic Reichs-Assembly. Vienna's considerable populace of assimilated, clandestine, and baptized Jews was suddenly threatened by an unfolding ethnic upheaval.

The Man of Iron

Rosner had regularly tested the waters of the city's public taste. In times of political stress, Vienna reverted unerringly to sport and musical buffonade. And, in the waning weeks of 1923, international negotiations on Austria's fate in Geneva had taken many bad turns. New Year's 1924 was an ideal moment for sportive challenge and racially-charged gaming. The Jewish Samson from the East had come to the multi-ethnic Gaza to shake the pillars of Erich Ludendorff's Pan-Germanism or slink away in shame. For his efforts, the boastful Hebrew was to receive one billion (inflationary) kronen.

At noon on December 31, 1923, in front of the Ronacher Theater, huge crowds of celebrants gathered at Johannesgasse Square. Doubtful clerks and their bosses peered from the windows of the surrounding office buildings. An orchestra belted

"Modern Samson," **Illustriertes Wiener Extrablatt** (January 3, 1923)

out a brass overture, the "Breitbart March." From around the corner, a carriage bedecked in gold and green and drawn by two snowy-white horses came into view. Breitbart descended from the carnival wagon and threw off his cape. He stood before the multitude in the dazzling garb of a Roman gladiator.

Next Zisha took the metal brace attached to the harness of the Schimmeln horses and placed it in his mouth. He settled onto the edge of a flatbed cart, which held forty standing passengers. Other than Breitbart's oral connection, this second vehicle lacked any means of locomotion. A stall master behind Breitbart tugged the reins of Zisha's steeds and the show-horses propelled the cart forward as Breitbart clutched the single bridle-chain firmly in his mouth. The Ronacher wagon magically spun down the street led by the prancing Schimmelns.

The curious mechanical effect of a human mouth-harness stupefied the crowds and got Vienna's journalists writing. The band was soon drowned out by a torrent of shrieks and applause. This strongman was more than human or beast; he had the strength and agility of a machine. Breitbart frenzy exploded on Day One and would not be easily stymied.

Rosner knew his Viennese milieu.

The Ronacher bill in the first weeks of January 1924 sold out completely. Even standing room was scarce.

The tenth and final act of the evening, the Breitbart number, was the chief draw and overshadowed everything before it. The Roman-helmeted Zisha bent short iron bars into horseshoes, pounded carpenter nails into thick boards with the flat of his hand. Then, in the costume of a slave, he stretched out supine on stage. A protective wooden plank and several enormous boulders were stacked on the iron-man's chest. Next a nail-board was slid under Breitbart's back and blocks of granite replaced the stones. A selected team of blacksmiths heaved their sledgehammers against the gray rock, which shattered into fiery airborne fragments. After a dramatic pause, Breitbart emerged unharmed. His finale included biting through the links of a steel chain.

Under Rosner's skilled direction, Zisha became the instant talk of Vienna. His name comically popped up in newspaper ads: "Breitbart and Us! Super-Reliable!!!" He was the topic of silly schoolboy riddles: "Did you hear how Breitbart stopped the express train from Prague? He pulled the emergency cord." Charities, sporting leagues, Jewish immigrant associations inundated him for endorsements and contributions. Journalists reported that women's eyes "sparkled" at the mention of his name and professional athletes "blanched."

Austria's heavyweight champion Scherz decried in the second week of the Ronacher smash production that Breitbart used special "cartridges" to bend the iron-rods; however, he was unable to prove his claim. One week later, he publicly apologized to the Polish Wonder and congratulated him on his "unique" talents.

Even Hanussen, practically forgotten as the Number Two Attraction, knew top-drawer showmanship and, at first, admired Breitbart's art.

The Jewish Mind and the Jewish Body

Hanussen and Breitbart grew up as outcasts and experienced similar lowly rites of passage. Their fathers were ne'er-do-wells, divorced from the spiritual and social palliatives of synagogue and from the secular brotherhoods of revolution and Socialism. The young men survived the Great War as non-combat entertainers and went on to scale the obstacles and vagaries of postwar European popular culture. Despite their auto-didactic backgrounds, they obsessed over books (the rarer the better) and claimed to cherish animals above people. The *Luftmenschen*-cum-costumed headliners were basically overachieving loners.

Hanussen and Breitbart, the mysterious Jewish Mind and the mysterious Jewish Body, also shared one other quality. They were both cheats.

The believability of Erik's telepathic stunts and parapsychological experiments was constantly undermined by his glib patter and sardonic humor. It was easy to discount the tuxedoed Dane and his scientific claims. Spectators either submitted to Erik's weird and aggressive mentalism in whole or struggled to unravel his webs of trickery and counter his rude theatrics.

Yet to European audiences, Hanussen was the avatar of modern psychological science—his appellation and manner of dress were those of a university professor. The Dane used blackboards, tabletop machines, and selected panels of doctors and assorted intelligentsia to "verify" his human "experiments" and "lecture-demonstrations." Moreover, he consorted with the funeral-attired commissions as if they were all part of the same arcane academic fraternity. Hanussen, the smirking puppeteer of souls, must have seemed to the Viennese like a music-hall representation of Freud and his Psychoanalytic Circle.

Breitbart was another matter. His presentation of self was equally egomaniacal, yet unguarded and childish. Audiences, especially Jewish audiences, openly identified with him and saw his *balagan* challenges and travails as a pictorialization of some personal awakening or a series of dramatic tableaux symbolizing the Hebrew Renaissance. Breitbart was the Jewish Body as envisioned by Theodor Herzl and Fredrick Winslow Taylor. Zisha's enemies (both real and imagined) were the enemies of progress and the despoilers of his adoring fans' fantasies.

The strongman numbers that Breitbart enacted were mostly boilerplate ballyhoo; essentially, displays of athleticism from the time of Peter the Great remounted as silent-movie spectacle and Old Testament erotica. Some of Zisha's extravagant routines—certainly the ones that incorporated the fakir's bed of nails and his body as a pivot for bridges and platforms—borrowed directly from the repertoire of Arab street entertainers.

What was new in the Breitbart evenings were his patently superhuman feats, like biting clear through chain-hoops or finger-thick metal bars as if they were salt-pretzels. These could not be duplicated easily by Breitbarts Two and Three or other pumped-up Slavs because they were beyond the jurisdiction of the human body. They were acts of fraud.

The Wager

In just two weeks, Erik's prominence in Vienna's demi-world faded. The Polish Behemoth replaced him.

Erik knew Breitbart seamlessly blended fakir and carny tricks with bouts of real physical might. Simple-minded skeptics like Scherz were unable to untangle Zisha's muscular craft from the hokum. The Indian board of nails, for instance, was so densely studded with metal tips that anyone could lie on it without drawing blood. Breitbart's miraculous sustenance of the anvil blows or boulder-smashing was accomplished through a bracing of the body, based on contortion of the lower torso and the support of a small pedestal under his back. Even the weight of an automobile, which was driven on a bridge-like ramp over Breitbart's glistening chest, could be deflected with a series of swift, focused kicks to the right and left planks. And any iron bar could be bent if the mechanical advantage was correct and the center-point thin enough.

What Breitbart actually possessed was a formidable stage presence and raw sex appeal. His overall persona of a man-child and Biblical reincarnation metamorphosed the number into a music-hall knockout. Theatrical lightning, dramatic drum-rolls, and perfect timing distinguished the twenty-minute exhibition from all others. Individually, Zisha's strongman stunts were commonplace bits.

On the night of January 20, Hanussen sat brooding with his friends in the Café Payer. Erik wagered that he could make the next person who entered the coffeehouse a civic sensation more glorious than the Mighty Pole. And the process would only take five days. Hanussen's drinking buddies insisted that criminality not be involved. Erik concurred, but when the proprietor's dog, a drunk, a crazy charwoman, and a gust of rain successively passed through the Payer's portal, all the gamblers agreed that the only next entrant could be Hanussen's subject.

Martha Kohn, an unemployed nineteen-year-old seamstress, walked into the café. Hanussen approached the pretty Jewish waif and explained that he had come from the Fourth Dimension to change her life. Hoping for at least a free drink and hot meal, Kohn listened attentively to Erik's rap. It was, to be sure, an original proposition.

For five excruciating days, Hanussen trained the 120-pound girl in his apartment to simulate Zisha's Ronacher tricks and body-defying displays. Erik had still not solved how Breitbart ground through five centimeters of metal with his God-given teeth, so he surreptitiously traveled to Pressburg, where the Iron Man kept his magical properties in storage. Hanussen assumed that the link chains had concealed catches, which Breitbart manipulated with his tongue. Instead Erik discovered that the trick was achieved through a manual bit of legerdemain.

Zisha snapped the loops imperceptibly with his hands as he brought the metal cord to his mouth. Breitbart used "Viktor," or cow, chains that had an indented stamp in the middle of each tie. Twisting the weak part of one link against another, he severed the iron with a lightning-like torque of his wrists. By the time the

chain was placed in the Iron-Man's teeth, the iron loop was already cracked. [See "Fakir Magic/Phony Magic," pp. 127.]

With that knowledge, Hanussen was ready to out-Breitbart the Giant from Lodz.

Iron Queen

At 9 PM on January 25, before the cue for his telepathic number was called, Erik brought Rosner into the green room of the Ronacher. He introduced the slight blonde in a skimpy toga as Martha Farra, his new medium. Hanussen announced that his medium, under his command, could wrap steel poles around her shapely arms and execute all of Breitbart's variety hits, many of which were simple carny ruses anyway. The Artistic Director responded cautiously; he would happily guarantee the new team a year-long engagement if they could perform exactly as promised.

Rosner rounded up four of Breitbart's iron rods and handed them to Farra. She managed to bend two of them into horseshoe shapes. Erik assisted her with the third; the last bar could not be bowed or deflected from its rigid state. At that strained and ill-fated moment, Zisha burst into the room and demanded an explanation for the backstage audition. A buzzer sounded and the master clairvoyant from Copenhagen rushed to the stage.

As soon as the curtain fell on the telepathy number, one of Breitbart's servants beckoned Hanussen into the strongman's dressing room. Zisha wanted to know if Erik intended to copy his act. The Dane replied sarcastically, "Your act cannot be duplicated!" The Man of Iron rose from his chair and catapulted Hanussen into a wall. He ranted, "I'll smack you dead, you pig!" and walloped him on the side of his head. Erik staggered from the room, shouting for the Ronacher security.

The next morning, Hanussen briskly marched into the executive suite of the rival Apollo Theater. In his arms was a small crate of metal rods. Martha coltishly stood at his side. Tiber, the Apollo owner and a Café Louvre acquaintance from prewar days, welcomed the telepath and his friend with a fixed grin and wary eye.

After some pleasantries in the Apollo office, Erik opened his box and had Farra demonstrate a couple of numbers from her strongwoman act. The testy Tiber sat up straight in his seat. He ordered a contract to be drawn up at once and, by nightfall, the first ad for the mystery "Iron-Queen" appeared: "In a few days, the whole city will be talking about the nineteen-year-old Viennese girl, MARTHA FARRA!"

More notices were placed in the dailies during the week, each larger and more garish than the last. Martha was hailed as the "Queen of Will," "a weak nineteen-year-old maiden who bends iron spirals and horseshoes, lies naked on iron spikes, bites through iron chains and nails, pounds spikes through wood with her hand. Not through the Power of Her Muscles, but only through the POWER OF HER WILL!"

On January 31, the night before her official premiere, a press preview was given at the Apollo. Martha pulled off her skirt and stood on stage in revealing bloomers and a backless blouse. She picked up a six-foot iron rod and twisted it into an extended coil, "like a soft Christmas candle." Then a professor from the Technical College and the chairman of Vienna's Blacksmith Society inspected Farra's nail-bed to check its construction and the sharpness of the spikes. Each man touched the nail-points and yelped an agreeable "Ouch!"

The Iron-Queen reclined on the fakir board. A cushion and anvil were placed over her breasts. Two smithies walked onstage and pounded the anvil with their trusty sledgehammers. When they completed their mission, Martha arose, smiled, and was examined by a white-bearded physician. He announced to the reporters that Farra's pulse was perfectly normal.

The blonde Queen of Will grabbed a one-inch-thick plank, placed a six-inch nail over it, and struck the metal head with her palm. The nail penetrated the board. Martha pulled a pencil-sized nail out of her pocket, placed it in her mouth, and, after a few false starts, bit cleanly through it. Finally, a gang of portly wrestlers put an iron-studded "bridge" over her body and weighed it down with cement blocks. One of the smiths hoisted a steel hammer in the air and smashed the cubes with his blows. The iron bridge was removed and Martha Farra took her curtain call.

After the slim nineteen-year-old retired to the wings, Hanussen stepped to center stage. He explained to the journalists that all of the supernatural powers they just witnessed were the product of his hypnotic commands.

Martha reappeared at her master's side in a stylish hat and seal fur pelt. Out of nowhere, a Breitbart devotee rushed to the proscenium apron and theatrically presented Farra with a steel shaft from the Ronacher production. The smartly-dressed seamstress stared at the metal piece and politely declined his challenge. The Breitbartite exchanged it for a second bar. This the nineteen-year-old accepted and held over her knee for a moment, and bent it slightly after strenuous effort.

The newspaper writers were ecstatic. The Farra-Hanussen program gave new life to the mawkish, month-old Breitbart mania. The winsome Martha radiated pert female sexuality. The surprise provocation at the end also added a novel touch.

With the Danish telepath peering darkly from stage right at his guileless pupil, the already gamy proceedings became submerged in occult atmospherics. A battle royale between the iron-biters was confectionery journalism, front-page ambrosia.

Tiber's Folly

Like Rosner, Tiber luxuriated in his good fortune. The Farra premiere on February 1 was heaven-sent. Taped across the Apollo box-office window was a banner "sold-out" posting. Before the booth, a frantic stream of customers pleaded for tickets to a dozen alternate dates.

The stage-shy Martha was naturally anxious on the day of her debut. Erik also was worried. He wondered if he were playing out his melodramatic *Dr. Svengali* scenario for real.

The Breitbartian intrusion at the press show's conclusion did not augur well for the challengers. The aging Ottakring kid began to prepare for an aggressive counter-response. If the first night went smoothly, sans Breitbart interference or some scenic shortfall, he could weather the storm. But that was wishful thinking. The open-faced Samson exuded generosity, kindness, and an exuberant love of humanity to the Viennese public. Yet inside the merry exterior, Hanussen believed, was a vicious and wounded Hebraic core. There would be vengeance.

Martha Farra, the "Wonder of Vienna," was the last attraction on the Thursday program. A note in the playbill invited spectators to be members of an "expert commission," which would examine Farra's strongwoman properties and evaluate her performance up close.

Forty-some volunteers, almost all young muscular men, gathered at the edge of the orchestra pit after the ninth number. The "experts" seemed to know one another and were arranging themselves for some sort of organized mayhem. A mood of intimidation from the impatient and unruly mob near the stage radiated throughout the auditorium.

Police were called to disburse the rowdy clique. This, however, further antagonized the Breitbart fans in the hall. When Hanussen looked to see what was causing the commotion, a block of protesters in the first ten rows whistled and jeered at the pale Dane. The Breitbartites seized the moment and started to chant their Polish hero's name.

Finally the curtain was drawn and Erik mounted the Apollo platform. He shouted above the tumult for audience volunteers. It was time for the formation of the Farra control group. Hanussen limited the pool to recognized locksmiths, blacksmiths, and physicians. When a number of Breitbart toughs refused to budge from the line, Erik again restricted the applicants to whose who could present professional certificates.

An exceptionally tall man, who looked surprisingly like the Modern Samson, leaped over the stage railing and attempted to harangue the audience. Theatre security arrested him. The house responded with catcalls and a deafening bellow.

Nervously, Hanussen led the selected "experts" around the podium to view the various piles of stage equipment. Taunts and charges continued unabated from the front rows. Martha disrobed under the spotlight and bravely tried to ignore the uproar, but the venom from the mob was taking its toll. The dolled-up seamstress visibly trembled. When her iron bars were carried to stage center, the heckling redoubled.

Uncertain how to proceed, Erik felt that the best way to restore calm and win over the crowd was through some magnanimous gesture. Against his Jenisch instincts, he allowed a few of the least abrasive Breitbart devotees admittance to the supervisory panel. They upended the first of Martha's stunts, by pilfering the stage stocks behind the strongwoman and bending the iron-rods themselves. The steel strand that Farra ground down with her teeth, one of them announced, was not the same piece that the jury inspected. The devious Dane had exchanged the metal sticks through a sleight-of-hand operation.

The Apollo olio curtain was rapidly lowered before the surprised faces of the bickering panel and then raised again. Erik implored the police to release the Breitbart lookalike whom they had arrested at the beginning of the number and bring him to the stage. Hanussen asked his new partner to watch carefully as the torturous Chair of Nails, a seat dotted with nail-points, was being assembled for another daredevil display.

The Breitbart fanatics used this new occasion to protest Hanussen's maniacal contraption. He was hooted offstage and the show, for a second time, stumbled forward.

When the Queen of Will stretched out for the sensational bridge number, a new herd of Breitbartites hurdled themselves over the orchestra pit and tossed the allegedly 100-pound stone cubes around like medicine balls. One of the toughs clumsily dropped a block on his foot and, in a perfect turn from a circus clown finale, hobbled off, red-faced, holding his toe. The rioters who remained on stage were not nearly as amusing.

The music-hall curtain fell for the last time. The Apollo staff tried to usher out the playgoers although many were perplexed and remained seated for another half-hour. Finally, the management announced that an unblemished commission of expert witnesses would determine the veracity of Martha Farra's powers at a five o'clock showing on Friday. That closed the show.

Outside the variety palace, scuffles erupted and mounted police separated the Breitbartites from their opponents, the "Farrans." Martha and her master waited in their dressing room until two o'clock to exit from the backdoor. On Mariahilferstrasse, they spied a lonely Wurst-vendor scrubbing down his stand. Hanussen purchased the last of his wares: one sausage and a torn bun. The two famished headliners laughed as they split their meager repast. Like street urchins, they jumped around in the cold to keep warm.

The Boy from Lodz, the Girl from Vienna

Vienna's newspapers mostly favored the Breitbartian position: he was the authentic phenomenon of the age and Hanussen's "suggestive willpower" was the usual unsubstantiated rubbish concocted by a jealous interloper. Regarding the character of Martha, there was considerable sympathy and personal interest. The flapperish teen was described as charming, fresh-faced, and demure. (The conservative papers thought the dressmaker revealed a little more ambition and flesh than her station allowed.) Overall, Farra fit snugly into the new Hollywood mode of the emboldened heroine; she was an innocent lass, who fought only to disentangle herself from scandal and dislodge the evil, grasping figures in her path.

Tiber gambled that the Friday afternoon examination would keep the profitable controversy alive and that Martha herself would improve. He was basically correct.

The greatly anticipated program filled every one of the 1,200 Apollo seats. Tiber's distinguished jury included two university professors, a court counselor, a psychoanalyst, an academic painter, an architect, two engineers, a sports columnist, and three chairmen from Viennese athletic associations. The panel's findings on both Farra and Breitbart, a slide projection on the Apollo screen promised, would be publicly released and published.

When Hanussen joined the team of neutral observers, the old cries of fraud and swindle greeted the telepath's entrance. The Dane appealed to the audience's sense of fair play and affection for Martha. The fragile girl was unaccustomed to the limelight; she needed absolute silence. Disruptions, Erik warned, could also cloud the judgment of the Apollo's exquisitely chosen panel. Shouts and verbal assaults from the Breitbart lobby continued nonstop.

The Two Iron-Biters and Their Fans, **Illustriertes Wiener Extrablatt** (February 11, 1923)

During Farra's biting number, a protester in the balcony was ejected from the theatre. And when another vociferous heckler lambasted the partiality of the testing, a Farran responded to the Breitbartite with an anti-Jewish epithet.

Miniature battles erupted throughout the hall, with Farra's angry supporters and their equally irate opponents reduced to face-slapping and other childish altercations. It was the first time anti-Semitism manifested itself overtly in the contest of the iron-biters. Although all the participants were nominally Jewish, Zisha naturally symbolized the Palestinian revolutionaries; Martha and Erik, the defenders of the Double Eagle and Holy Trinity.

After the melees subsided on their own, Hanussen tried a new tactic. He pleaded for silence because Farra's work, unlike that of the Galician, was no mere muscle-flexing stunt; she required mental concentration to receive Hanussen's "transference of will." The ploy was a mistake. Whatever sympathies the spectators still had, they were affixed to Martha, not to her presumptuous teacher.

After a brief discussion, the panelist head and chairman of the Vienna Boxing League, Willy Kurz, faced the audience. He pronounced Martha as a superior, although not extraordinary, athlete, who, nonetheless, could not be compared to the Great Breitbart. As for Hanussen, she would be better without him or his fraudulent management.

The commission visited the Breitbart show that night at the Ronacher. Weiner, a locksmith from the Freihaus Workshop, the same store where Farra's tools were manufactured, submitted an English steel chain to the strongman. Should he gnaw through a single link, the machinist offered to donate one million kronen to charity. One of Breitbart's lackeys pulled the cable from the locksmith while two others unceremoniously gave Weiner the bum's rush.

The interruption hardly deflected from the high-spirited mood. Kurz' commission claimed they were equally satisfied with Breitbart's performance. Both productions were first-rate exhibitions of human strength. No deception was uncovered. The contest was a wash. Only the engineer, Willfort, recognized that the breaking of iron chains could not be achieved through "biting." The loops were shattered by skillful twists and torsion.

On Saturday, the more Mosaic-sounding hyphenated "Erich Jan Hanussen-Steinschneider" published a four-part challenge to Herr Breitbart in *Der Tag*. Hanussen declared Zisha's iron-biting a "public disgrace." Ten million kronen would be deposited in the Rescue Services account in the Mariahilf Bank if Breitbart could sever an iron chain (of Erik's choosing) with his teeth. A second ten million would be added to the philanthropic award if Martha failed to withstand Breitbart's fakir bed with an anvil placed on her chest. And another million kronen wager was offered if the "weak maiden" could not safely lie under his stone board or if Hanussen was unable to find twenty non-athletes who could deform Breitbart's steel bars and flat-iron sheets.

Erik gave Breitbart 48 hours to accept the dare or risk exposure and a legal suit for libelous remarks. Hanussen's demand ended on an ominous note for Zisha:

the Yiddish Samson had already defaulted three years earlier on a similar charge at the International Artiste's Lodge in Hamburg.

Mutual Destruction

On Monday, February 5, 1924, "Jan Hanussen" was summoned to police headquarters. Senior Officer Kozdas informed Erik that as "Hermann Steinschneider," a resident of Prossnitz, Czechoslovakia, he was persona non grata and subject to immediate expulsion. The order for his deportation was not directly related to the Breitbart affair. The Steinschneider-Hanussen police files swelled with more than a decade's worth of citizen complaints and allegations of misconduct and fraud.

As far back as 1913, the *Blitz* editor was accused of extortion and coercion. Featured prominently in the rap sheets were Erik's confidence schemes, involving blackmail, feigned telepathy, disrespect of the civil authorities, and generally repellent behavior. For instance, it was noted that, as Martha Farra's impresario, he failed to sterilize her nail-board with proper antiseptic. This alone, negligently and ruthlessly, endangered the young woman's health. Vienna's undercover police kept ample and detailed records on their man.

Hanussen in Court, **Illustrierte Kronen-Zeitung** (February 24, 1923)

And there was the old 1919 Austro-Hungarian Bank provocation.

Hanussen's hand in the latest Apollo swindle, Kozdas confided, had merely tipped the judicial scales slightly to the side of decency and public safety.

Erik-Hermann listened uncomprehendingly as the charges were read. It was as if he were back in the Orient. How could someone born and bred in Vienna lose his Austrian citizenship and suddenly be declared a Czech national? There was no legal or common-sense basis for the decree. In fact, Erik barely spent a weekend in Prossnitz, his father's—not his—birthplace. Hanussen's enemies in the mayor's and the police departments had gone too far, finally overreached themselves. The native Wiener would turn the tables on them in the county courtroom.

Meanwhile Breitbart continued to enlarge his program and social image. It kept the Ronacher legend in the news. He invited reporters to observe the filming of his feature motion picture, *The Iron King*, and complained about the financial burdens his boyish and irresponsible philanthropy had caused.

Under Hanussen's direction as her "personal conferencier," Farra teasingly imitated every one of Zisha's bold inventions at the Apollo. As "The Living Carousel," she balanced a merry-go-round of children with her shapely legs; supported a loaded automobile of adults, which drove over her Bareback Bridge. The newspaper editors dubbed her the "Auto Queen." Like most of Vienna's males, they were growing fonder of their local avatar of Will.

Breitbart's lawyers filed a slander suit against Hanussen. The music-hall plaintiffs and defenders met in Vienna's Criminal Court on February 23. Erik used the widely-publicized occasion to countersue: the temperamental giant struck him viciously in a Ronacher dressing room on the night of January 24.

When Farra testified that she witnessed the brutal assault from a backstage corner, the strongman's face contorted and he lashed out furiously like a wronged suitor. He accused her of lying. The judge admonished Zisha and his attorney for inappropriate behavior, for turning his civil court into a vaudeville arena. Martha added another circus element to the story: Erik was thrown toward one of Breitbart's nail-boards, but the agile telepath vaulted around it.

And when Hanussen's physician told of the life-threatening consequences of the Breitbart blow behind Erik's left ear, the Goliath could no longer restrain himself. Policemen had to accompany him out of the courtroom. [Sharon Gillerman Collection]

The other witnesses (both pro and con), including Erik, gave sworn testimony; they all told a similar story. Breitbart attempted to shrug off the entire proceedings as a waste of time and an act of infantile extortion. At the end of day, the condescending giant was fined 250,000 kronen and Erik was expelled from Austria for a ten year period.

One month later, Farra sued Breitbart for his slanderous remarks in the Criminal Court. The case was written in the judicial roster but dropped when Martha failed to show. She was with Hanussen in Prague.

Betrayal

Erik and the Queen of Will arrived in Prague in March and played to good houses at the main revue-house, the Theatre-Variety Divadlo, for two months. Steinschneider-Hanussen, a prodigal son of Moravia, was hailed as a national hero and dramatically received his new passport. Unfortunately he could not read it. Like most Jews from Emperor Joseph's Czech-speaking provinces, Erik never needed to communicate in anything more sophisticated than a Slavic pidgin-patois. As for the written language, he could decipher Turkish, Arabic, or Ladino more fluently.

How Prossnitz became Hanussen's new place of birth in 1889 was unclear. Probably, a proud Siegfried Steinschneider sent a Yiddish copy of the certificate to his hometown bureau to be filed with other family documents. Herschmann-Chaim Steinschneider was determined to make the best of it.

In Vienna and Prague, Breitbart's film *The Iron Man* was presented as a variety novelty and made the rounds in Zionist fund-raisers. A one-reel parody of the Zisha-and-Hanussen rivalry, "Schmalbart Versus Kann'utzen" also trailed in its path. The story had staying power and Zisha toured Prague.

In June the master clairvoyant and the Queen of Will received an engagement in Budapest, where the German-speaking community still held cultural sway, despite political demands from Hungarian nationalists, church leaders, and local anti-Semites. Hanussen arranged several engagements at Tabarin, the massive entertainment palace, and Fövarosi-Zirkus. Still his bad luck streak continued unabated.

Sweet Martha Kohn tired of Erik's abuse and fell in love with a Hungarian showman, Stefan Réthey. The randy Budapester, who went by the stage name "Mister Rex," stole the maestro's coveted strongwoman props along with the strongwoman herself. The lovers escaped to Neutra in upper Hungary, where they performed the Farra Show with a new MC.

Within a week, the wronged Dane-Czech hunted the lovers down and battered them with a dog whip. The local police arrived on the scene and hustled the feuding variety artists off to court. Erik charged the grifters with the theft of his valuable, handmade stage properties. The judge ruled that Rex had to return the stolen equipment but, after hearing about the phony strongwoman act from both sides, refused to press further charges against the couple. Rex and Martha wisely left the country for Zagreb, Teplitz-Schönau (Czechoslovakia), and back to Prague. They ultimately settled in Seville.

Hanussen returned to Budapest, chagrined and partnerless. He punched up his old one-man clairvoyant demonstration with its usual mocking features and occult surprises. However, Hungary was not free-wheeling Vienna; the nationalist Archbishop of Budapest declared Erik's stage performances blasphemous. The newspapers reported that Hanussen had hypnotized one unfortunate volunteer into believing that he was Jesus Christ being nailed to the Cross. When blood began to gush inexplicably from the man's palms, spectators stomped their feet in disbelief.

Martha Farra II

Backstage at the Fövarosi-Zirkus, Erik's luck turned. He found his next Martha Farra: a neurotic equestrienne of British and Italian origin named Rose Presl. This potential Queen of Will, a beautiful and troubled twenty-three-year-old, had badly injured herself in a circus accident a few weeks earlier.

In the middle of her trick-riding act, Rose saluted the audience with one leg in the air and the other fixed in the stirrup. The metal clamp cracked from the weight and the young woman tumbled to the ground. Her dexterous horse panicked, galloping wildly around the arena. While the stunned Rose lay unmoving in the sawdust, the frightened beast circled back, and kicked the lithe artiste on the top of her head. Rose suffered a major concussion and a nervous condition that left her prey to violent headaches.

Then in the summer of 1923 Hanussen came.

He confronted a jubilant Rose one night as she dashed triumphantly from her curtain call to her private dressing stall. Waiting by the door of the tent enclosure was Hanussen in Svengali mode. The equestrienne saw only a set of piercing gray eyes framed by strange, shaggy brows. She was simultaneously shaken, disgusted, and creepily excited by the hypnotist's satanic stare. Flushed and confused, Rose demanded to know what Hanussen wanted. To possess her, Erik replied. This cheap enactment from the *Svengali* script, at least, went according to plan.

Rose gestured him away but could not stop thinking about the mysterious clairvoyant once inside her tent. The sight of the intense, charismatic man made her head throb. Rose later recalled the haunting moment as "cyclonic," like an explosion that roared in and outside her bandaged scalp. [Marta Fara, "My Life as Marta Fara, the 'Strong Woman,' Was Fake and Torture," *New York Saturday Graphic* (September 1924)]

Now Erik reverted to his circus roots. He pursued Rose through flattery and afternoons of brutal sex play. The hysterical girl surrendered totally to her relentless stalker. No other man had possessed her with such force and self-assurance. Rose's incapacitating brain spasms ceased.

Following Erik's direction, the top-billed star packed her belongings and vanished from the canvas realm of the Fövarosi. At Hanussen's secret "love nest" a few blocks away, she was given a new name: Martha Farra.

Despite her superior physique and radiant stage persona, Rose had few of the vivacious charms of the original Martha. For Hanussen, however, this Farra was a better match: her psychological dependence on him, her clear devotion, her robotic appearance as a "love slave" increased his theatrical participation and the compelling eroticism of the production. No reviewer or judge would advise Rose to sever her bounds with the master showman. No lover would hustle her away for a midnight rendezvous or romantic escapades.

For three months, Farra II was initiated into the tricks and bluffs of the strongwoman routine. In the cramped, dusky studio, Hanussen taught her to bend, twist, pulverize, and tear the Breitbartian metal tongs and iron pieces. He steeled her body to receive the shocks of hammer-blows and stacks of granite blocks. Instruments that resembled the tools of Torquemada were applied to her compliant flesh.

Martha II attempted to satisfy Erik's increasingly sadistic commands although her body resisted. Welts, dark bruises, muscular contractions, and slow-healing scratches surfaced along her joints, spine, and breasts. Hanussen sweet-talked her into ignoring the corporal signs of abuse. To fail on stage was worse punishment than any agony that he could conceive of in rehearsal.

Erik coached her to snap iron bars as naturally as a peasant's wife would crack kindling with her knee. At an early lesson, Farra II placed a thick construction rod over her bent leg and tugged at it with all her strength, but the metal shaft did not give an inch. Then Hanussen placed his knee behind the small of her back and pulled her wrists in a furious rotary movement. The added force splintered the bar into two pieces. Martha shrieked in pain. Spread across her kneecap was a smarting bloody gash. The equestrienne fainted.

In time, the black and blue welts callused over, forming a protective epidermal layer. Martha could snap ten poles of varying thickness with ease. The taskmaster's tortures slowly became commonplace exercises and the fainting stopped. The Farra II show was ready for public viewing.

In more tender moments, Erik refashioned Rose's stage appearance. He clothed the circus star in elegant furs, had her hair shorn in the latest German pageboy mode, and—if Hanussen's memories are to be believed—gave her lessons in proper table etiquette. [*Meine Lebenslinie*]

The Tour

In September 1923, Martha Farra II presented her debut at the Liebich-Theater in Breslau. Hanussen introduced the exotic girl as his hypnotic subject and assured the audience that in her somnambulant state she was impervious to all pain. A musical prelude ushered in the trim Trilby-like artiste. Martha began energetically with the usual preliminary Breitbart stunts: bending rods into horseshoe shapes, twisting iron bands around her arms.

After the applause died down, the Queen of Will stretched out on the nailboard. Erik invited two men from the audience to strike a 300-pound anvil that had been placed on Farra's chest. He encouraged them to hit as hard as possible. They did and, somewhere in the house, a woman screamed in sympathetic horror. It covered a genuine moan from Martha. The apprentice strongwoman was hurt. Hanussen slapped a medical gauge on her back to conceal the bloody marks.

Stage hands replaced the anvil with four 100-pound slabs of sandstone. The volunteer smiths delivered the requisite blows. Martha sank into unconsciousness. Hanussen revived her halfway through the number. The circus stalwart smiled and issued a pro forma stage bow. In the greenroom, Martha lost control; she picked up a horseshoe (a real one) and banged it against her forehead in a petulant act of rebellion. Erik lifted her off the floor. Her premiere was a success.

Slowly other bits were tacked on to the show. Ten men, five on each side, bent a twenty-foot railroad tie over Farra's padded head. Hanussen held a publicity stunt in the Breslau public square: a shameless facsimile of the Breitbart New Year's feat in Vienna.

Farra took the harness cable from a team of dray horses in her mouth. She was expected to secure the force of the horses with her teeth and draw a wagon of twenty Breslauers down the street. When the driver shook the reins and whistled to his steeds, the chargers jerked forward, tearing the cable from Martha's determined grip. Blood dripped from her mouth; half of her teeth were dislodged.

Over the next six weeks, the duo appeared in tony revue houses in Nuremberg, Leipzig Insterburg, Dresden, Hannover, Magdeburg, Hamburg, Cologne, Elberfeld-Barmen, and Brussels. Their routine gained in professionalism and was highly regarded on the variety circuit. Laberó saw his industrious student at the Hansa-Theater in Hamburg and tried to meet Hanussen backstage. The next day, he sent the Dane a complimentary message. Erik ignored both of Laberó's requests to discuss his evolution. [*Wundermänner, Ich Enthülle Eure Geheimnisse!*]

At its height, each Hanussen-Farra spectacle garnered thousands of marks for its sprightly creator. The German mark, however, was fast losing its value. Erik spent their most of their earnings on expensive meals, limousines, fine clothing, and girls. The angry, love-sick Martha again attempted suicide, slicing her wrists with a pair of scissors.

Circus Berlin

Erik's Farra number was picked up by the eminent Circus Busch Berlin. Stenciled in crude Expressionist typeface, a multi-colored poster depicted the imaginary backstory (or the magical retelling) of Breitbart, Farra, and the Dane in Vienna: on the toppled body of a medieval colossus stood a victorious blonde nude; to her left was the demonic gaze of a man-god.

Martha's strongwoman act was entered as the final evening attraction, the circus' top billing.

The artistic director of the Busch, Otto Friedländer, doled out salaries to his company in an oft-repeated morning ritual. The circus staff and performers immediately ran out to acquire food and material objects with their fluctuating marks; by afternoon, the inflated scrip often lost fifteen to fifty percent of its purchasing power.

Hanussen insisted on payment in Austrian credits to Friedländer's foolish delight. Erik then used the foreign bank notes to obtain stock in hard currency-shy German firms. Overnight, the clairvoyant-turned-entrepreneur amassed a real fortune in barter as he adroitly demanded factory goods for his paper certificates. The exchange brought in four fur coats, porcelain, a ten-carat diamond ring, assorted evening apparel, two carloads of motion-picture equipment and film stock, silk stockings, a sailboat, gramophone boxes, and an automobile.

With his newly acquired merchandise, Hanussen shot and developed short films of himself as a telepathic detective with superhuman abilities. Martha played the saucy medium. The occult featurettes sold well in the inflationary madness. Professional movie studios in Berlin even employed the hypnotist-about-town for dashes of local color in their full-length productions.

Meanwhile, Erik and Martha continued to draw throngs to the Circus Busch throughout the last month of the national financial crisis. During the intermission of one of those performances, an usher hurried backstage to announce an unusual mendicant. A decrepit and cantankerous beggar was demanding to see the Great Clairvoyant. Hanussen wandered to the Big Top entrance and observed the turmoil.

Arguing with the Busch ticket-taker was Maki—El Sah'r's former impresario. Erik had not seen or heard from him since Beirut. The hapless Galiziner looked much the worse for wear. And before the ecstatic headliner could embrace his old travel companion, Maki waved Hanussen off; the miserable *Luftmensch* was lousy with fleas.

Erik led Maki to a bathtub in his dressing room and ordered a barber to wash and cut the bum's matted hair. The expansive showman then revealed the pièce de resistance, his inflation wardrobe: elegant shoes, gloves, hats, jewelry, and forty suits. Maki was to take all he needed. And to complete the fairy tale-like fantasy,

Erik implored Philip Neufeld, aka Maki, to be his personal secretary and manager. The freshly scrubbed pauper accepted.

Improvements and Scandal

In December 1923, Hanussen escorted his new entourage to outlying regions that had never seen the Breitbart production and, more importantly, paid fees in non-German funds. They began in Bratislava, Czechoslovakia, and on December 3 performed for five days at the Miramar Variety in the independent municipality of Königsberg.

The enhanced Hanussen-Farra show added an equal number of telepathic experiments to the strongwoman displays. Erik demonstrated his practiced Thought-Transference routine, followed by the Telepathic Post and Needle Search. After the intermission, Farra did her act. She bent a fourteen-millimeter-thick iron pole "like a wax stick"; twisted rods into curved ornaments; supported an anvil on her chest, which was struck by sledgehammers; bit through a four-and-one-half-millimeter chain; and, while the hypnotized Queen lay rigid on the fakir bed, endured a pounding with the sandstone slab, administered by eleven hefty volunteers.

This time, the skin punctures on Martha's delicate back and her chipped teeth were grandly exhibited to the commission of selected "experts." The Miramar audience was astonished.

Two days later, members of the University of Königsberg issued a statement testifying to the supernatural qualifications of Fräulein Farra and Erik Jan Hanussen. Maki procured the effusive document and sent it to variety agents in Berlin.

The trio moved on to Memel, a German-speaking territory that the League of Nations bestowed to the fiercely sovereign Republic of Lithuania. There, the identical show fared worse. Hanussen's posters promised sensations that never took place.

Farra, the flyers claimed, would accept any metal chains from the audience and tear them apart "like paper." She would lift 2,000-pound weights and dance on a nail-board in her bare feet. The Woman of Will would drag ten local athletes across the stage in a juried tug-of-war. And, finally, cars and trucks would drive back and forth over her unprotected body.

When none of the above stunts was demonstrated on opening night, the police were called to investigate. The oversight committee leader, patrons complained, was too drunk to notice the discrepancies in the program. Martha's chain-biting number was also disputed.

It seemed, while she stood on a chair to receive the iron links, giving the spectators a better view of her magical exploit, Hanussen monkeyed with the metal cord below her. All eyes were on the regal, half-naked artiste. It was, according to one journalist, a classic case of misdirection. [Fred Karsten, *Vampyre des Aberglaubens* (Berlin: Verlag Deutsche Kultur Wacht, 1933)]

The Memel police raided Hanussen's hotel room on the third night and dragged the pair and their paraphernalia to the Criminal Commissar's office. At the police station, the master and his medium were unable to duplicate their stage feats. The ever-vigilant Commissar quickly signed a decree, banning them from further performances in his district. Lithuania was the second country to prohibit Erik from working or residing inside its borders.

Hanussen and team could not have been too upset about the legal wrangling or its shotgun outcome. Maki had secured a contract from H. B. Marinelli, the representative of the B. F. Keith Vaudeville Circuit in Berlin. With their old friend, Leo Singer, the Prater Midget King, they were to play at the Hippodrome Theatre in New York City during its Christmas and January seasons. Their proposed tour in New York and other American cities was to run for a minimum of eight months. Best of all, the salary for the Hanussen-Farra act was a phenomenal 1,000 dollars per week.

America

Erik arrived in New York City with his usual over-the-top vivaciousness and sense of purpose. Other European troupes (especially the great theatre ensembles) had broken the cultural and linguistic barriers that separated Old and New Worlds. Jacques Copeau's theatre, the Moscow Art Theatre, Max Reinhardt's Company, Berlin's *Blaue Vogel* cabaret, the Parisan Grand Guignol, even Breitbart were financial hits in Jimmy Walker's free-wheeling jazz metropolis.

But with three decades of street smarts, the *Jenischmann* soon changed his mind about the city of skyscrapers and boundless optimism. It was the one place where he was conned and thoroughly fleeced.

E. F. Albee, the president of the Keith vaudeville empire, was a universally reviled and secretive tyrant. He detested variety artists, and, in his Manhattan lair high above the Palace Theatre, the robber baron of the American entertainment industry conjured up dozens of schemes to humiliate and defraud them. Albee especially despised Europeans.

Keith's agents panned across the continent looking for minor music-hall sensations, much like Hanussen's. The fast-talking American scouts offered huge salaries and long engagements. After the naive artistes completed the transatlantic journey, they were hustled off to Hoboken, to a special Keith Theatre. The papered audiences there consisted of a special Albee claque: they were groomed to feign boredom and apathy in response to the most breathtaking foreign stage displays. Afterwards the shocked vaudevillian stars were informed that while their divertissements might have dazzled European playgoers, regrettably, in America the enactments had little appeal. New contracts and greatly reduced wages were instantly arranged.

In Hoboken, Hanussen's hopes were shattered. Both Erik and Martha (now renamed "Dr. Hanusen" and "Marta Farra, the Italian Strong Woman") were

MARTA FARRA
Italian Strong Woman

stunned by the New Jersey spectators' indifference. The Dane blamed it on American stupidity and lack of imagination. As he was later to learn, the opposite was true. Albee, the villainous recluse, and his entertainment lawyers duped Maki into renegotiating the terms of the agreement. The original weekly fee was whittled down to the hundreds. [Vaclav Pavel Borovicka, *Vrazda jasnovidce Hanussena* (Prague: Svoboda, 1968]

For the attorneys, it was business as usual.

At the New York Hippodrome, the "largest playhouse in the world," Breitbart was the major solo attraction and the producers were uncertain where to place Farra on the ticket. She auditioned her bridge and fakir-bed number. A horse-drawn wagon passed over her wooden platform while the Hippodrome stagehands held the structure in such a way that little weight actually pressed down against the girl. It was decided that the act needed more work. Erik and Marta were sent to the sticks, Philadelphia and Norfolk, Pennsylvania, the railroad capital of the East.

The Philadelphia engagement proceeded uneventfully. In Norfolk, however, Farra's bridge was poorly constructed by the stage carpenter and collapsed in the middle of the performance. Two of Marta's ribs fractured under the tonnage of the rolling wagon.

She was hospitalized for two weeks and then returned to New York.

Erik, always looking for another angle to differentiate the Farra act from Breitbart's, added chorus girls and an elephant. Marta would pull a bevy of showgirls across the Hippodrome stage—this she could do—and hoist an elephant off the ground, using only a simple harness and her Herculean might; that was a ruse.

In the middle of Times Square, the tiny equestrienne lifted the hitched-up pachyderm by means of a Rube Goldberg-like pulley and spring system. Despite the mechanical chicanery, it was an arresting sight. Less successful was what followed. The elephant, under Hanusen's telepathic command, was supposed to walk over the fearless medium, who bedded down on her nail-board. The mammal stepped, however, directly onto Farra's swollen rib-cage. The recipient of so much pain could not win for losing. Rose planned her escape and covertly wrote to Marinelli. He offered to represent her properly in his private vaudeville roster once her legal obligations were settled.

In February, the Hippodrome's Director General featured "Hanusen and Fara" as a single occult, hypnotism number, totally separate from the European Man of Iron. Sparks between the two European antagonists flew everywhere outside the stage. They glowered at each other in the wings and dressing rooms. At Gartner's Pub on Broadway, Zisha challenged Erik. Before a brawl could ensue, Martinelli separated the rivals. They should save their enmity, he barked, for the Hippodrome performance and everyone's mutual riches.

Breitbart, Erik, and Marta began to organize a single competitive number. An odd thing happened during the New York rehearsals, however: the iron-biters and telepath discovered much common ground and a growing admiration for one another. Variety performers in Europe were highly treasured and worked only in the evening. In American vaudeville, artists were expected to perform three, sometimes, five times a day and the spectators often slept through whole shows, knowing their favorite acts would be repeated in the next set. The visceral antipathy between Zisha and Erik practically disappeared.

"Hanusen and Farra" were sent to the DeKalb Theatre in Brooklyn in March while Breitbart took his act to St. Louis and then to scattered venues around the country. Marta's unhappiness increased with the loss of Zisha's moderating presence. She checked into a hospital for five days and implored Marinelli to rescue her.

Meanwhile, smarting from the deterioration of his relationship with Rose, Erik wandered around Manhattan and spent time observing Rahman-Bey, the Egyptian

Farra at the New York Hippodrome

holy man, who, after Houdini, had taken America by storm with his new brand of mental magic and fakir demonstrations. Bey could do all the regular fakir magic: poke long steel hairpins into his cheek and out through his lips, lie rigid on the points of two swords. In addition, the fakir could stop or desynchronize his pulse at will, go into a complete physiological state of catalepsy, tolerate incisions to any part of his body and impede the flow of blood.

Erik watched the miracle-man being sealed into an airtight coffin and lowered into the Hudson for thirty minutes. Like the committee of journalists and physicians who conducted the experiment, the Viennese trickster was fascinated.

In Brooklyn, Hanussen received a telegram from Vienna. Risa urgently demanded his return. Erik understood it to be a call for divorce. It was another blow to his fragile ego. He blamed it on the United States venture.

The last "Hanusen-Farra" appearance in America was mounted in Boston in April. Marta finally announced her resignation and Maki made plans for Erik's departure.

Coda

Marinelli redesigned Marta's solo performance. He portrayed her as the latest feminist icon. In the New York Hippodrome and at the 61st Street Theatre, Farra showed society women how to develop and beautify their flabby bodies. Through an interpreter, Marta lectured on the physical culture movement and methods to ward off rheumatoid disease. The undernourished, squeamish creature became an advocate of health regimens and exercise machines. Marinelli also cheated her, retaining eighty percent of her income and controlling every aspect of her personal life.

It was business.

Marta caught up with Breitbart in the summer of 1924. He nobly took the depressed actress under his wing. Zisha also parlayed his front-page celebrity into a newly profitable direction. His New York office in the Gotham Bank Building became a center for body-building, marketing weekly mail-order lessons and "Breitbart's Muscle Meters" to skinny, Jack Dempsey wannabes. The cable-address was "Superman-New York." [*Breitbart's Physical Culture Course* (New York: Self-Published, 1926)]

In September, Fara (she dropped another letter in her name) exposed her sham career as a strongwoman with "Hanusen" and Marinelli and her "sexual enslavement" in the national tabloid *The Saturday Evening Graphic*.

Later the Queen of Will moved in with a paper-box manufacturer in Queens. And, according to Franz Polgar, the popular Hungarian hypnotist, who visited her in the mid-'30s in the Catskill mountains, Rose spent her final years as an entertainer in the Jewish resorts of the Borscht Belt. [*Story of a Hypnotist* (New York: Hermitage House, 1951)]

In August 1925, Zisha, then an American citizen, returned to Warsaw, possibly as a result of hounding from the AMA and U.S. Post Office. During a performance in Poland, he contracted blood poisoning from a rusty nail. The Man of Iron died in Berlin on October 12. His lucrative enterprises and legendary exploits outlived him. It was his vital portrayal as an ethnic redeemer and tragic death, not the battle or reconciliation with Hanussen, that entered into Jewish folklore. [*Zishe Breitbart: Der Moderner Shimson Hagibor*]

Onstage at the Hippodrome

FAKIR MAGIC
phony MAGIC

BY ERIK JAN HANUSSEN

Voluntary Regulation of Blood Circulation • Chain Biting • the Stone Slab • Bloody Tears • the Miner Diebel • Buried Alive • Fakir in the Trunk • the Living Gasometer

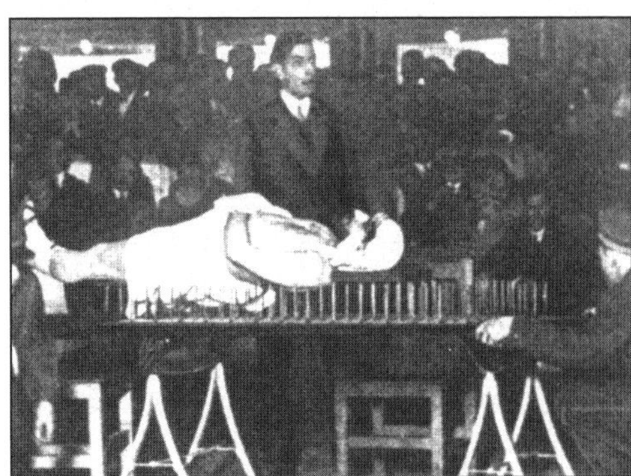

BED OF NAILS

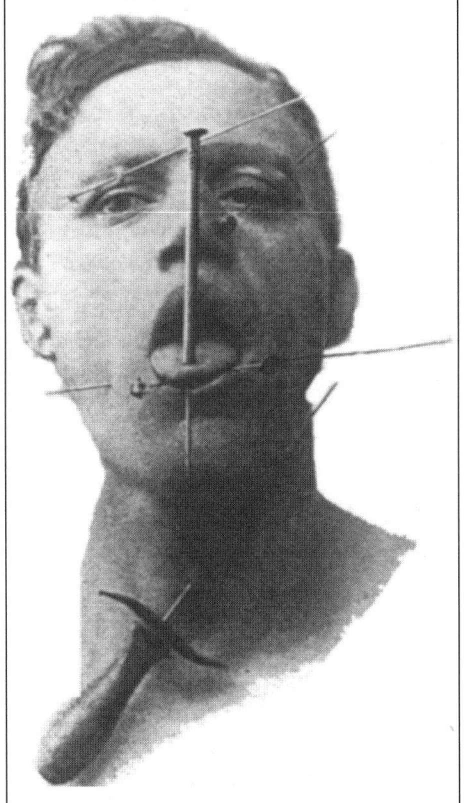

JABBING OF LONG RUSTY SPOKES THROUGH THE CHEEKS AND TONGUE.

Last year I wrote an article on the "Mango Tree Miracle," in the *Berliner Illustrirte Zeitung*. In the piece, I described my adventures with Oriental fakirs and revealed the famous fakir trick. The exposé sparked numerous replies from all parts of the world.

My BIZ explanation encourages me now to write another series on fakir magic. This attempt at demystification, however, should not be seen as an attack on the truly supernatural abilities of certain fakirs. I am convinced, because of my many trips to the Orient, that there really are such individuals whose feats that can't be explained by natural means.

Since I have always had a burning interest in the supernatural, my turbulent life has made it possible for me to meet many famous fakirs and mediums and to examine their feats.

For example, both the Miner Diebel and the Living Gasometer fooled me.

I myself tried being "buried alive," as well as the wonder of swallowing fire, eating glass, and the melting of red-hot sealing wax on my tongue; in short, overall I am speaking here from my own experience when I explain these things.

Several years ago, a big stir was caused by demonstrations by men whose supernatural willpower allowed them to achieve these apparent feats. That is how an artist in Vienna showed off: by crushing iron chains with his teeth.—I still remember with great pleasure how, in the capital city of the Austrian Empire, serious scholars of international ranking, for example Professor Stranski, or the psychologist, Professor Wittels, allowed themselves to be persuaded that a man could crush chains with his teeth.

One can't even crush a little piece of wood between one's teeth. Try squeezing a toothpick or a match between your teeth and biting through the wood without bending it: it will be impossible.

THE CHAIN BITING TRICK

unfolds as follows: for such experiments, only so-called Viktor-chains can be used; they are figure eight chains (see our picture).
These chain pieces have two loops to the left and right of their middle link. One places a third piece between two chain links to create leverage, that's how one can spring open the knot of the middle link on one side. It is caused by torsion. It has to be done incredibly fast. While the artist apparently lifts the chain to his mouth, he can easily twist the chain link and stick it into his mouth already split open. A small movement to the left with the chain link is sufficient, the rupture opens itself and the chain is "bitten through."—Incidentally, in the January 1926 edition of Uhu, I presented an illustrated article on the subject.

The phenomenon with the so-called BED OF NAILS occurs just as naturally. The many iron points that project from the board are, in reality, not nearly as dangerous as they appear. Precisely because there are so many spikes, a person can easily lay on his back over them without injuring himself. The weight of the body is distributed evenly across the many nails, so that each individual nail supports only a minimal amount of weight. Because of this, the nails are easily prevented from breaking the skin. Therefore, the more nails there are, the less dangerous it is; the fewer nails, the more dangerous the experiment is.

One can easily lie on a bed of nails from which 500 sharpened tips project, but no person is capable of lying on a bed of nails from which only five or six points protrude.

What also looks very dangerous is the EXPERIMENT WITH THE STONE STAB Here, a stone slab with a very heavy weight on top is placed over the athlete's chest. (See the picture.) Not as dangerous as it appears! Under the athlete's back is a wooden pedestal. Together with his legs, which are braced against the floor, an absolutely secure human buttress is achieved. One wouldn't believe what enormous weights one can bear with the back in this position.

Another really horrible-looking fakir trick is the JABBING OF LONG RUSTY SPOKES THROUGH THE CHEEKS AND TONGUE. Even though it does not appear enjoyable, the pain caused by sticking a spoke through the cheek is very easy to bear. Try it with a sewing needle. It stings a bit but, when all is said and done, it is bearable. If the needles are sharp enough and pierce the cheek quickly, the incision will not cause bleeding.

This fakir trick, however, has nothing to do with the special WILLPOWER THAT REGULATES BLOOD FLOW. Since blood does not flow near certain areas of the epidermis, the tearing of tiny pores in the skin may result in no bloody eruptions. If the fakir were to pierce muscle tissue, instead of the skin that is pulled away from the muscles, then this self-inflicted act would be considerably more painful and more likely to cause blood poisoning. The fact that these needles are frequently rusty doesn't play any role in this slight injury—besides one does not become infected from rust, but rather from dirt.

A very clever trick was invented by the Miner Diebel, whom I was able to observe some time ago. He allowed BOLTS TO BE SHOT AT HIS CHEST FROM AN AIR GUN from a relatively close distance. That looks very dangerous. But if one shortens the spring of the air gun beforehand, thereby reducing the its velocity, as Diebel did, then the bolts won't cause any extreme pain; they may prick a little, that's it. However, if a bolt ever struck an eye, the fakir would suffer a severe injury and the eye would be lost—but no fakir in the world would let anyone shoot at his eye!

Diebel made use of an out-of-the-ordinary trick with his DISPLAY OF BLOODY TEARS at the Berlin Wintergarten. This was part of Diebel's competition with the Seeress from Konnersreuth. Fearful that his trick would be revealed, Diebel later blamed his impresarios for the deceit and gave the following false account to journalists. Diebel claimed that he inflicted small cuts in the corners of his eyes with a razor blade, and, in this way, forced streams of blood to flow down his cheeks. If Diebel had done this just three times in a row, then he would have lost his eyes. The correct explanation is much simpler. Diebel obtained red-colored chalk from a pharmacy. He placed tiny fragments of the chalk in the corners of his eyes before his performance. Then he held a handkerchief soaked in ammonium chloride against his nose. This stimulated the mucous membrane of his eyes to tear. The tears absorbed the red dye from the colored chalk, secreted in the corners of his eyes. In order to prove that the tears were really blood, Diebel appeared to blot his face with a cotton gauze. The red gauze was then inspected by physicians (sometimes with a microscope), Diebel, however, always switched the first cotton square with a different prepared square. The second gauze piece was in fact covered with drops of his own real blood. (Diebel obtained this blood by pricking a finger.) Also, to demonstrate his ability to "sweat blood" from his thighs or ankles, Diebel merely dripped blood from his finger on the "stigmatic" area. Many times, when not enough "blood was in supply," Diebel quickly dealt with this by fetching a razor blade, which he wore hidden under his belt, to scratch the skin. He did this with such skill that, for the longest time, I was completely convinced of his gifts and actually believed in his phony magic.

BURIED ALIVE The secret technique of this fakir stunt is quick simple. A concealed rubber hose, with one end above the soil, is slipped into the coffin and buried with the fakir. One must pay close attention that the tubing doesn't become filled up with dirt, otherwise the fakir will suffocate. This is what happened to a few poor devils in Central Germany and Beacaman in Argentina. The manager or impresario holds one end of the rubber hose in the hollow of his hand; the man in the coffin places the other end in his mouth. In this way, the fakir can live quietly from the air he breathes through the hose; even better he can receive a little bit of chicken broth every once in a while. But this must take place secretly at night, since during the day a visitor would be able to notice the ruse.

Still simpler, from a physical standpoint, is the experiment of the fakir Tachran—Bey, in which he allowed himself to be SOLDERED INTO A METAL COFFIN AND LOWERED INTO THE HUDSON RIVER for thirty minutes. Naturally, this requires courage, but no excessive talent on the part of the fakir. The amount of air in a large coffin contains enough oxygen to sustain the fakir for one hour. The exhaled air is blown toward the bottom end of the coffin and, for a time, will not recirculate toward the other side.

When I tried this experiment on a young man, as a preliminary exercise, I locked the "FAKIR" IN THE TRUNK He remained without further complaints for more than half an hour in the trunk, and he would have remained squatting inside even longer if I myself had not become afraid.

A very impressive trick of many fakirs is ARRESTING THE PULSE To do this, one must put a billiard ball under the armpit and, at the right moment, apply pressure to the artery. Then the pulse is apparently interrupted. Naturally it doesn't stop altogether, but it becomes so weak and inaudible that one could believe that the pulse beat had completely come to a halt.

Finally, another really amusing stunt is the "LIVING GASOMETER" One day a young man came to me and showed me an amazing experiment. He placed a big steel siphon supposedly filled with acetylene gas in front of me, attached a tube to it, opened the valves, and apparently pumped his stomach full of flammable gas. He took an ordinary gas hose, which was attached to a Bunsen burner, and then, he ignited it. The gas—that was supposedly coming out of his stomach—flared up with bright, brilliant flames. The same stunt allowed the young man to cook two fried eggs on a gas stove from the gas, issued from a hose in his mouth; the Wonder-Man also ignited a lamp, using ribbed tubing that was several meters long.

I was enraptured and awed by the feat until I was let in on the trick. Before the experiment, the Gas-Man places a sponge that is generously soaked in gasoline in his mouth. The fumes that are produced in the mouth feed the various combustibles. The whole time I wondered why my Living Gasometer was always so silent before his production started, today I don't wonder any more.

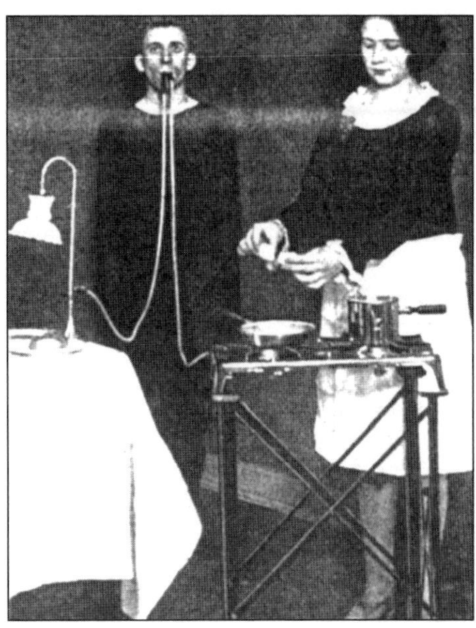

CHAPTER SIX

AT THE EDGE

1924-1928

The Empty Nest

Erik and Maki returned to Europe in the spring of 1924 with no European contracts in hand and few American press clippings to show for their four-month effort. But they were flush with hard currency dollars in an economically depressed France and settled into a swank hotel suite in Paris. For a few memorable and restorative weeks, they pursued the City of Lights' naughtier pleasures. Like spoiled progeny of Scandinavian industrial magnates or Jazz-Age American bon vivants, they drank and cavorted boisterously in the cafés, cabarets, music halls, and *maisons de tolerence* of Montmartre.

In May, the Keith dollars ran out. Maki and the maestro separated. The devoted secretary journeyed to Berlin in search of a third Martha Farra; Hanussen quietly retreated to forbidden Vienna for a dreaded face-to-face accounting with Risa.

The domestic encounter took place in his old Esterhazygasse apartment and lasted only one hour. Risa demanded a divorce. Erik's public dalliances and duplicitous persona were more than she could bear; Risa wanted a normal life for her daughter. Besides, the former showgirl was being courted by a wealthy Austrian brewer, Hans Fuchs. He offered to take her and Erika to live at his estate in Meran, in northern Italy. But, in order to secure annulment papers from Fuchs' friends in the Vatican and remarry, Risa had to baptize their daughter and make punctilious amends to the church.

Hanussen assessed the situation from a more primitive point of view. The clairvoyant was a poor provider. Risa had a right to happiness although he predicted her union with the merchant to be a brief respite from loneliness and despair. Erik acquiesced to Risa's wishes and boarded the train out of Vienna for the last time.

Farra the Third

Maki had secured the services of a new Iron-Queen, Anna Schedel, a slim bourgeois girl from the Rhineland. Unfortunately for Erik, Maki was sweet on her. The trio ceded Berlin and Hamburg to Breitbart and his reorganized German company. (Scandalously, Zisha's twelve-year-old boy assistant turned out to be a menstruating lass, who bled through her leather shorts during an opening night stunt.)

In the second part of 1924, the old Martha Farra numbers—as recreated by Anna—pulled in audiences at the variety houses in Chemnitz, Dresden, Leipzig, Nuremberg, Cologne, and Barmen. Maki made plans for a grand tour of Poland, Hungary, and the Balkans, yet they only got as far as Warsaw. After New Year's 1925, Hanussen became dangerously ill and had to return to Berlin for an operation and a stay of convalescence.

The love-smitten Maki, like Mister Rex before him, made off with Erik's Martha and the hand-crafted circus props. The Iron-Queen expedition continued without its ailing creator.

In the spring of 1925, simultaneously in Seville, New York, and Budapest, three Martha Farras bent metal bars, bit through chain links, and balanced horse-drawn carriages with their bent legs and steely thighs. The hydra-headed Farras existed in triplicate and were finally severed from the master's controlling strings.

Another Wager

Hanussen's hospitalization was lengthy. Eventually, he recovered his physical health and ability to perform, but months had passed and the Dane was now reduced to his last 100 marks and practically alone.

The thirty-six-year-old survived as a stone-faced fakir in the Rahman-Bey mode. It was Erik who chewed and swallowed glass shards, poked rusty spikes into his cheeks, and sealed his tongue to his upper palate with hot bubbling wax. It was Erik who consciously suspended or slowed his pulse and laid stoically on nail-beds. And it was none other than Erik Jan Hanussen himself who was tucked into an airtight coffin. The fakir act with all its challenges was simple and cost close to nothing to produce. It also played in the lowest Lunapark venues and paid workman's wages.

One night at the end of October, Erik sat in the Café Kempinski with a drinking companion, an industrialist of some note. Bored by Hanussen's sad sack whining about the course of his diminished career, the capitalist began to mock the soothsayer's predicament. Here was a man who claimed to have the divine gift to peer into mankind's future but could not make a sustainable living for himself. Once upon a time, two years ago, Erik enriched traders and brokers with his numerical prophecies in the international commodities exchange. The Berlin Borse was soaring. Use your magic, play the market yourself, the industrialist laughed.

It was a familiar refrain. Yet the afterhours ridicule shook Hanussen from the paralysis of his post-Farra malaise.

Erik bet his partner that he could produce more money in the next two hours than the capitalist himself pulled in over an eighteen-month period. It was a curious wager, so outrageous that the industrialist hesitated at first. Naturally, his shocked and unsober sense of honor forced him to accept the challenge.

The game for Erik's psychic preservation was afoot.

Hanussen raced down the block to Kochstrasse, the site of the Ullstein publishing conglomerate. Somehow, the mad Dane talked his way past security and into Hermann Ullstein's office. Sigmund Breitbart had died in Berlin on October 12, two weeks ago, and was the subject of countless glowing and maudlin European and American obituaries. (Even the venerable *New York Times* mentioned the strongman's death as a sidebar in an October editorial page.)

Erik's description of the storybook celebrity was entirely different. Breitbart was a magnificent entertainer, to be sure, but also an ingenious fraud. Hanussen offered an illustrated article, exposing Breitbart's signature tricks. It would be entitled "You Too Can Break Chains!" and there was no one alive to sue him for the professional breach.

Ullstein studied his list of assigned features. There was an opening in the January 1926 issue of *Uhu*, Ullstein's general interest pictorial monthly. They concluded upon the unusually high honorarium of 500 marks, half of which would be paid that night.

Downstairs in the Ullstein lobby, Erik waved 250 marks in the industralist's face. There was only one hour left.

The two taxied to the newly-opened Hotel Alhambra on the fashionable Kudamm. Hanussen sketched out a freakish number, involving combustible fumes, a tableful of gleaming machinery, iron tubing, a stove, and a human repository of acetylene gas. The manager of the hotel nightclub (later to be christened the Club Palm-Beach) nodded and signed a slip for a 3,000-mark advance. Hanussen's rival rolled his eyes twice when he saw the contract.

Finally, Erik rushed to the Friedrichstadt post office. He wired the manager of the Drei Linden Variety in Leipzig. It was the same pitch that he delivered at the Alhambra. This time Hanussen demanded 6,000 marks for a month-long engagement. After a few hours, Erik received a 2,000-mark retainer. By breakfast, the Dane had 5,500 marks in his pocket. He won the bet.

Omikron, the Living Gasometer

Hanussen reverted to an old carny trick. As usual, it involved fire and misdirection. He found an unemployed Berlin artist, Fritz Jung, and trained him in a few sessions to be "Omikron, the Living Gasometer." (In his later writings, the Wizard of All Ages naturally claimed that his self-created geeks always approached him and he was as beguiled as his audiences by their trickery. [See "Fakir Magic/Phony Magic," pp. 127.]

The Gasometer stunt itself was marvelously simple. Yet, as always, Erik added an interesting format and his own dark humor. The production dazzled even before the conferencier and Omikron appeared. On stage was a laboratory—or kitchen—of the future. Bowed flanks of metal tubing, reading lamps, a line of meters with mysterious dials and switches, and other pieces of equipment were set on and around a long zinc table. At one side were huge steel cylinders, marked "acetylene gas" and "oxygen." A stylish young woman in a black silk blouse arranged what looked like a modern gas range.

Hanussen introduced the routine in his traditional Jenisch manner, orating on the human mystery, the wonder of the mutated body, and other such hocus-pocus, and then beckoned the Omikron to the stage. Costumed in a loose black gown (a probable fashion "borrowing" from the Berlin vegetarian cult of Madzananism, popular among Bauhaus devotees), Jung resembled nothing so much as the sleep-walking Cesare from *The Cabinet of Caligari.*

Erik quickly put the Omikron into a "suggestive state." A thin rubber hose from the "acetylene" canister was placed in Jung's mouth. Hanussen twisted the valve and the "gas" poured into the somnambulist's stomach. A series of double hoses replaced the first. The Living Gasometer was now a flesh tank of natural gas. The remainder of the performance had the Omikron blowing ignitable vapors into a Bunsen burner, lamps, and a miniature stove. The high point had the stage assistant boiling water and frying two eggs.

The energy to light the burners did not come from Jung's "acetylene-filled" stomach. Just before entering the stage, the elfish Berliner merely put a sponge, drenched with petrol, in his mouth. The entire production was little more than a fire-eating act with a few droll scientific-occult touches. Altogether the stage novelty worked well.

In November, Hanussen brought the Omikron to Varieté Drei Linden in Leipzig. The local police requested a private demonstration and were evidently satisfied with the results. Shortly after the Drei Linden gig, the hapless Jung dropped out of sight.

Hilda, the Hunger Artist

The talk of Berlin in February 1926 was a singular character, Siegfried Herz, otherwise known as Jolly the Hunger Artist. At the working-class Rheinish restaurant, the Hackepeter, Jolly sat in a locked glass booth, in a voluntary fast and surrounded by bonded "observers." While the Hackepeter diners gorged themselves with minced pork and schnitzel, the immodest Jolly—he wore only a diaper-like covering—chain-smoked cigarettes and sipped from a glass of seltzer water. On the hour, a midget bellowed into a megaphone the exact number of hours and days the unshaven Hunger Artist had refrained from eating.

Although journalists condemned the proceedings as yet another example of Berlin's penchant for mindless kitsch and cruel entertainment, hordes of curiosity seekers flocked to the North Berlin eatery and paid the extra fifty pfennig to marvel at the reptilian oddity.

Jollymania grew, especially after a biblically miraculous forty days of starvation passed. Various imitators popped up across the city. Harry and Fastello performed as a “team fast.” They beat Jolly’s forty-four day record by twenty-four hours.

A “Danish” hunger pro, Eriksen, opened up shop in Berlin’s Linden-Passage arcade, a site teeming with pubescent boy hustlers. After eight short days, Eriksen’s body rebelled, and he wanted to quit. Hanussen told the faster’s manager about the Rahman-Bey coffin trick: removing a screw in the wooden frame and surreptitiously pumping bouillon through a concealed straw. The manager incorporated the wise counsel and Eriksen’s fast went uncontested.

Hanussen toyed with his own hunger artist production. Like the Breitbart extravaganzas, the Jolly/Harry/Fastello/Eriksen demonstrations were missing one vital show-biz element: erotic appeal to men. A beddable Mädchen in a cage had greater voyeuristic possibilities than any jaundiced-eyed consumptive.

An entrepreneur from the industrial city of Chemnitz, Harry Markowitsch invested start-up funds for Hanussen’s Female Hunger Artist show. Erik had little trouble finding a proper vehicle; he chose a sexy Berlinerin, Hilda, who jumped at the chance of being paid ten marks a day to starve.

In Chemnitz, Hanussen had posters printed that defied Jolly’s now-passé forty-four day binge. Townspeople could soon marvel at a corporal marathon in which Hilda would break the world’s record for self-imposed starvation. Before the supervisory commission, led by the editor of the city’s newspaper, Erik proudly announced in his stentorian basso that every thousandth visitor would be allowed a special viewing of the hunger artist.

Before the official committee, the lusty Hilda smiled sweetly and entered the isolation booth. Nothing had prepared her for the ordeal to follow. Hanussen had difficulty following through with his plan to secrete a pig’s bladder filled with chicken broth into a hidden receptacle in a corner of the cage. A committee of bonded guardsmen patrolled Hilda’s booth around the clock. The girl began to starve for real. [See “Fakir Magic/Phony Magic,” pp. 127.]

After twelve days, Erik brought Hilda out of the glass cage, using the excuse of the Hunger Artist’s twenty-third birthday. In the planned chaotic interval—as police, watchmen, photo-journalists, and fans pushed to see her unwrap gifts—Hanussen restocked the booth’s tiny larder.

One week later, on day 19, a randy member of the guardsmen committee proposed marriage to Hilda. Newsmen and crowds came to witness the lovers’ public embrace. (And again, Erik managed to covertly pump cold soup into the pig bladder.) On day 32, Hilda became nearly psychotic from hunger and smashed the glass panes of her Chemnitz prison cell.

Despite its shocking finale, the sadistic charade was quite profitable. So profitable in fact that the Chemnitz police charged Hanussen with tax fraud and a host of other improprieties.

Diebel, the Stigmatic Miner

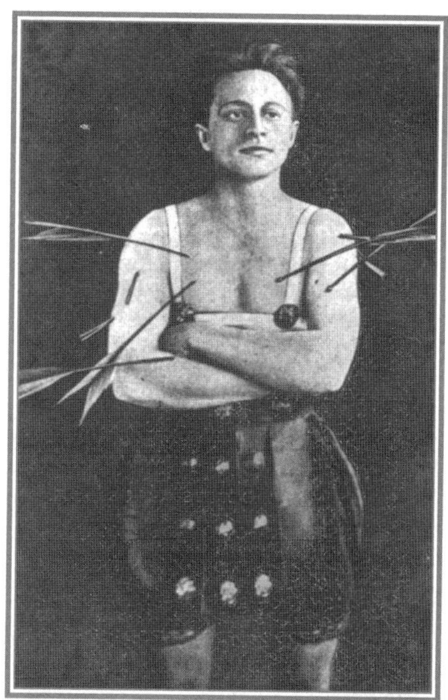

Paul Diebel at the Berlin Wintergarten, 1927

The third and last of Hanussen's panoply of freaks, Paul Diebel, was potentially the most troublesome and the only one to achieve a moment of international fame. A strikingly handsome miner from Silesia, Diebel made his appearance during the Christmas season of 1927 at the famed Berlin Wintergarten. But Diebel was more than a fakir in contemporary garb; he shockingly duplicated, parodied and ultimately threatened the phenomenon of Therese Neumann, the first stigmatist of the modern age and one of the most enduring and controversial candidates for German sainthood.

Born in 1898 in Konnersreuth (a border village that would soon be indelibly linked with her miraculous and time-traveling abilities), Therese was a simple-minded peasant who cured herself of blindness and severe leg and spinal injuries through devotional exercises and prayer. In 1925, she began to receive otherworldly visions from the Savior himself and speak in a language akin to Jesus' Aramaic.

On April 21, 1926, the Konnersreuth (as Therese came to be known) bled spontaneously from her palms, and thick rivulets of blood poured from her eye sockets. Three months later, the bedridden woman stopped drinking and eating completely. For the next thirty-five years, it was claimed, she sustained herself solely on a humble and heavenly-sanctioned ration of weekly Communion wafers.

The Konnersreuth held Friday sessions between Easter and New Year's, when she channeled Christ's Stations of the Cross and recapitulated in vivid detail the suffering of saints and preachers of the Gospel. And then Therese would fall into a stigmatic trance, spotting her sheets with massive pools of blood from invisible wounds. Afterward she imparted blessings and divine homilies to astonished supplicants. Local priests and physicians testified to the Konnersreuth's authentic supernatural state of grace. A medical commission rigorously observed Therese for fourteen days. During their watch, the miracle woman not only refused all forms of nourishment, she managed to actually gain weight.

By August 1927, Therese Neumann had become an international luminary. German universities and the Vatican itself sent special investigators to witness the Konnersreuth wonder and conduct closed-door examinations. Major newspapers, including *The New York Times, Der Tag*, and the *Vossische Zeitung*, dispatched seasoned journalists to the German Lourdes. Their findings were similar to that of the religious consuls: no evidence of fraud.

Two Lutheran physicians (with their skeptical families in tow) as well as Bernard Karpeles, a Jewish Social Democrat, converted to Catholicism after beholding the living miracle. Others followed their lead. Konnersreuth became Central Europe's lodestone for petitioners of the lost and afflicted, non-denominational occultists, fervent petit-bourgeois Catholic pilgrims, German-Americans from Milwaukee and Chicago, relic-hunters, and assorted riff-raff. In 1928, Lillian Gish, America's Sweetheart, paid her respects to the bleeding saint, requesting heavenly intervention for her dying mother. [Josef Teodorowicz, *Mystical Phenomena in the Life of Therese Neumann* (London: B. Herder Book Co., 1940)]

Like Therese Neumann, Diebel claimed an accident—although, in his case, either in a mineshaft or a Russian POW camp—caused his ineffable condition. Diebel was impervious to pain and could bleed at will. He pierced his face and limbs with hairpins and thin daggers. And when the instruments were withdrawn, no blood or traces of the incisions could be found. Diebel allowed metal bolts and feathered pellets to be shot from a crossbow into his chest. He sat bunched in a chair for six minutes and forced blood to seep from his knees and ankles in a concentrated act of superhuman will. When he stood, a cross-shaped wound mysteriously appeared on his back. He touched his eyes and crimson tears rolled down his face. Doctors from the audience affirmed the unlikely: the coagulating mess was in fact human blood. The Man from Waidenberg was just as bafflingly stigmatic as the Maid of Konnersreuth.

In Munich, Diebel stopped the show with a bizarre finale: he was crucified on stage. The Silesian played the scene for grotesque laughs, puffing on a cigarette while bantering with spectators. Diebel's manager, then Kurt Juhn, boasted that he could remain in the Lord's position for up to ten hours.

The Viennese authorities banned Diebel altogether, compelling him to confess the disingenuousness of his act to the foreign press. The Stigmatic Miner agreed, inventing even more outrageous explanations for his bloody witchcraft. Reporters loved the confession.

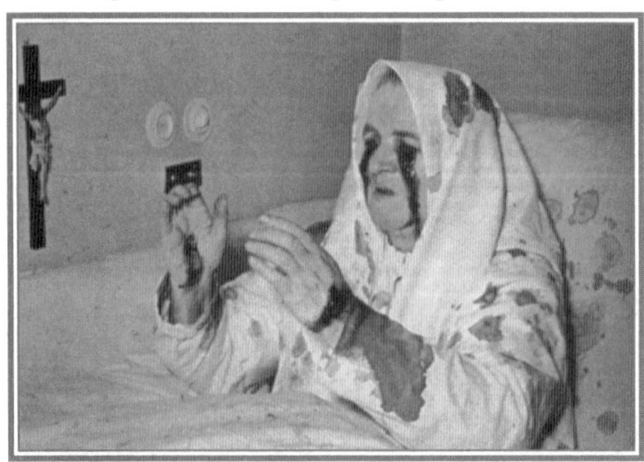
The Stigmatic Therese Neumann

Needing an established thrill for his Czech tour, Hanussen hired Diebel but trimmed the comedic repartee. In the now-standard Hanussen framework, it began with hypnotic induction, in which Diebel would be mentally transformed into the figure of Therese Neumann. After the spellbound miner trembled uncontrollably and sank to his knees, the Dane informed his mesmerized subject that he (as the Konnersreuth) was now witnessing a visitation of the Holy Virgin.

The stricken Diebel-Neumann rose from the floor like a marionette, his face and body spotted in ever-widening circles of blood. Audiences were utterly spooked. That, Erik felt, was a more satisfying beginning to an evening of miracles. To dispute the Hanussen-Diebel routine could be nothing less than a petulant affront to certified science and established religious belief. [See "Fakir Magic/Phony Magic," pp. 127.]

The Last Frau Hanussen

Berlin's considerable community of novelists, playwrights, literary agents, graphic artists, and journalists made the Romanisches Café, near the Kaiser Wilhelm Memorial Church, their five o'clock-to-midnight headquarters. The presence of so many notables also attracted a secondary crowd: star-struck teenage girls, middle-aged hangers-on, and hundreds of cultural wannabes and gawkers. The ring-like architecture of the massive glassed-in café-restaurant allowed for various groups to dine in separate spheres with the ability to spy on one another when necessary. The maître d' and fast-draw waiters at the Romanische permitted the regular guests hours of uninterrupted time to nurse mochas and read from the extensive racks of newspapers.

Erik adored the Romanische and normally held court there during his Berlin productions and holidays. He vigilantly maintained a café table where he interviewed and auditioned his revue-house accomplices. It was there he met his third and last wife, Elfriede Charlotte Rühle.

The twenty-three-year-old Fritzi (or Friedel) came from a traditional middle-class Berlin family. Her father was an army officer and she worked at the Federal Post Office as a telephone operator. When Fritzi first met Hanussen, the effervescent *Nutte* was engaged to be married. Overnight, however, she succumbed to the Dane's romantic charms. (Her fiancé, Walter Zobel, immediately filed a specious complaint against Hanussen for "erotic seduction through hypnosis.")

Fritzi assisted in Erik's shows, creating sexy female walk-ons and other backstage roles. For the naive Berlinerin, it was great fun and something of an adventure.

While Erik courted Fritzi, his fortunes improved markedly. By the summer of 1926, he possessed two fancy automobiles and bragged about a substantial bank account. But he remained uneasy about his personal life and relationships. Could it be that Fritzi only loved him for his money? In a variation on the *Svengali* theme, Hanussen decided to free her from his external control, so he tossed away his hard-earned lucre, luxury cars, and stable employment. That is, he squandered all of his assets in one evening of gambling at the Marmorhaus and Ecarté-Klub casinos.

In the morning, with five marks in his pocket, Erik asked Fritzi to leave Berlin with him. To the *Jenischmann's* utter surprise, the well-mannered woman agreed and he drove her to the Postal Department, where she gave notice after four years of service. Still, the emboldened Fritzi could not face her father. The lovers bought tickets at the Schliessen Bahnhof for Breslau, a lucky city for the telepath.

In Breslau, Erik deposited their luggage at the railroad station Garderobe and he sat with Fritzi at a nearby café. The Wizard Who Knows All did not have the heart to tell his trusting companion that he could not even cover her coffee bill. He assured Fritzi that the director of the Anglo-Bank would lend him a thousand marks or so. Then Erik hit the street.

After a dispiriting *Bummel* around Breslau, Hanussen spied a poster for the Brothers Hirschberg Kosmos Cinema and Variety. He trotted to the Hirschberg office. No one would take an appointment with him. Finally, Erik burst into the variety inner sanctum and clairvoyantly announced that their season would be ruinous without him. He expounded mystically to the brothers that they would make a profit of 15,000 marks from his guest appearance. The Hirschbergs were impressed with the Hanussen moxie. The soothsayer left with his thousand-mark advance.

The question of breakfast was now resolved. But he fell into a deep depression, worrying incessantly whether Fritzi loved him, whether he could continue as a performer. For months after the Kosmos engagement, Hanussen slept around the clock and refused to leave his pension. He could neither pay the modest rent nor the food bills. All day long, Erik read Karl May's pulp frontier novels and Maurice Maeterlinck's Symbolist tracts. He studied graphology and palmistry manuals. The fact that Fritzi stayed unquestioning at his bedside at least proved his cardinal human worth.

Finally, Erik went through his crate of press-books and testimonial letters. The Danish Galahad, whom reporters and paranormal enthusiasts once hailed as an agent of the supernatural, was not him, only a cocksure stranger. Slowly, his doubts subsided: yes, he was Hermann Steinschneider but also the performer Erik Jan Hanussen.

Steinschneider-Hanussen steeled himself and once again was ready to face the world. The manic telepath cajoled a typographer in the pension to lend him his last 100 marks.

Two days later, Erik made it to Czech Bratislava (formerly the Moravian capital of Brünn), lecturing on the occult. And a few months later, on Christmas 1926, Erik Jan Hanussen could be considered a rich man. He drove a Mercedes-Benz around town and refurbished Fritzi's wardrobe with furs and high-collared velvet dresses. Meanwhile, the precious savings of the Breslau typographer were repaid along with the benediction of a windfall gratuity.

A Restricted Profession

At the foot of Spielberg Mountain, Bratislava was still a German-speaking town in 1927 and Moravia's manufacturing hub. Hanussen received permission from the local authorities there to lecture and "demonstrate" exhibitions of fakirism and chiromancy for a six-month period. He was expressly forbidden to discuss or engage in anything related to spiritualism, hypnosis, telepathy, or human magnetism. Additionally, Erik soon realized that he was expected to "donate" funds to the local constabularies in the surrounding villages. His old stomping grounds had reverted to Slavic Orientalism. Even in sophisticated Prague, telepathy and hypnosis exhibitions were formally banned.

Erik either ignored the prohibitions or found flimsy means to circumvent them. His "Séances of the Occult" flyers advertised his supernatural abilities to look into the past or future destinies of mankind through the shape and design of the hand, graphological analysis, or "psychic transportation." And since auto-suggestion was not considered a form of hypnosis, Hanussen added his Gomboloy (48 black beads and one red bead on a string) to the act. He called it a "Hypnoscope" and had spectators handle the Egyptian rosary as he led them into "self-induced" trance-states.

In Bratislava, Hanussen befriended a decrepit fortune-teller, "Princess" Leila Hanuma, and her husband, "Doctor" Fränkel, who doubled as her secretary. The two also played the small-town Moravian circuit.

As soon as the Fränkels arrived in a city, they wined and dined the editor-in-chief of the local paper and the Princess proceeded to read his palms. Judging from the man's basic demeanor, dress, vocal and facial response, Leila could give a fairly accurate character analysis and fantasy prognosis. (Her M.O. was that there were only so many personality types and each had their own bank of irrational longings and fears.) An exuberant article on the front page almost always followed their appearance.

The Fränkels set up daily consultation sessions in the village's downtown hotel. The Doctor interviewed the clients in a foyer, learning about their livelihoods and backgrounds, and then signaled the information to his wife. During the initial days, a stream of patrons paid top fees. Later, when interest in the magical business drastically receded, the Princess offered special discounted sessions for the poor and "less spiritually developed."

A Chiromantic Reading

Erik adopted the Princess' chiromantic readings to his ductile program and added the consultation sessions to his after-hours income. On stage, Hanussen dazzled audiences with the latest scientific explanations. The fakir demonstrations were examples of affirmed yogic mind-body willpower, not merely muscular or physiological feats. The graphological analyses came from years of intense psychological study. In no way could they be considered random guesses.

The updated ballyhoo yielded abundant box-office receipts and a bit of stardom for the itinerant Dane, yet no relief from the ultimatums of impatient authorities. Erik earned thousands of Czech kronen from his "scientific" lectures and personal readings. But by June 1927, Hanussen's public and private undertakings were again officially prohibited in Moravia and Prague. Success had caught up with him.

Erich Juhn, the Impresario and Secretary

The Bohemian spa resorts in Karlsbad and Marienbad, where international trade and affluent clientele flocked, offered the big money. Nightlife, except for the elevated café-concert and kitschy vaudeville, hardly existed in the tony resort towns.

Erik needed an insider for the spa bookings. He placed advertisements in the *Prager Tagblatt* for an experienced secretary and impresario. Among the dozens of applicants was Erich Juhn, the Secretary-General of the Jewish National Fund of Czechoslovakia.

Like Hanussen, Juhn was an unlikely *Luftmensch* who dabbled, more or less, in the same low professions as the clairvoyant: as a director and producer for a traveling children's theatre, a journalist, and film editor. Before the war, Juhn consorted with Rubini in Vienna. As a member of the Austrian Writers Union, he managed to spend his wartime service as a reporter for the *Bosnischen Post* and even wrote about Lance Corporal Steinschneider's wondrous dowsing experiments.

Juhn ran into Hanussen again during the Breitbart wars in Vienna and yet again in Prague when he engaged the Polish Samson for Zionist fundraising purposes. The peripatetic agent spoke six languages and had active links to most of the main galleries and lecture halls of Central Europe. He managed Theodor Lessing's extensive book tour and, for two years, supervised summer retreats in Karlsbad for Prague's Zionist leagues.

In the letter resumé Juhn included a photo, which he acknowledged was unattractive, and identified himself, in a comic postnote, as a Jew.

Erik enjoyed Juhn's vivacious cynicism and mocking self-image. This man was a youthful Peppi. Hanussen proposed a test: if Juhn could devise a stage venue in Karlsbad within one month, the temporary impresario would receive twenty percent of the profits from the ticket revenue and ten percent of the consultation session fees.

Juhn made the bookings in Karlsbad and arranged for other performances in Marienbad, Kometan and Teplitz-Schönau for July. Erik hired the clever Jew as his secretary, but neither of them luxuriated much over their contractual relationship. Hanussen's "parapsychological" lectures lacked originality or elite appeal. Interest in such presentations was noticeably ebbing. At the time, audiences responded better to opera tenors, and even preferred symphonic concerts over occult séances.

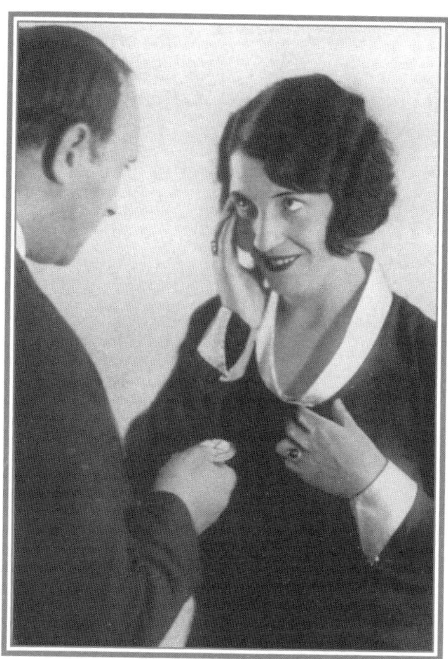

Leopold Thoma hypnotizes Frau Dagma

Frau Dagma, the Woman with One Thousand Eyes

Hanussen experienced an epiphany that completely redirected his career and world-view. At the Karlsbad Orpheum, Erik watched, with Juhn and 800 guests, a cheap variety act. "Frau Dagma," billed as an Indian seeress, performed a prophetic-clairvoyant number with her secretary, the "psychologist" Karl Kraus (born Karl Weber). A former protégé of Thoma in Vienna, Dagma (then known as Megalis II) began with the usual telepathic parlor tricks. The second part of the evening, however, contained a fascinating innovation: spectators were requested to write the dates and places of important personal events on plain paper sheets and hand them to the secretary during the intermission. Kraus then read the times and locales to Dagma, who seemed to intuit the nature of the secret incidents.

This clairvoyant stunt excited the audience in a way that Erik had not witnessed since the war. Dolled up in a white-silk sari with her eyes covered in black blindfold, Dagma paced the stage as Kraus mouthed the mysterious scribblings. Suddenly Dagma's arms groped through the air like a banshee possessed. The seeress twisted and convulsed as she delivered her prophetic visions from the unadorned dates and places on the slips: "a marriage," "I see a man . . . in bed," "there is a smell of death in these confines . . ."

The primitive enactment was revelatory and perversely explained to Hanussen his waning appeal. The average spectator had only one overriding concern: himself. People were engrossed with the occult for a reason; they wanted to know how they fit into the cosmic plan—not whether such a continuum was possible. Dagma and Kraus got the small-minded obsessions of an audience absolutely right: the metaphysical program must end on the prophetic and the personal. To talk about the reality of spiritual planes of existence or the scientific validation of ghosts was one thing, but to conduct a séance with every audience member as a potential "sitter" was something else entirely.

Juhn was no dummy. He understood, at least in theory, that Kraus and Dagma communicated through codewords and gestures to reveal the contents of the letters. Dagma, he surmised, could probably see through the fine black cloth. One question still remained: how did Kraus or Dagma ascertain the actual events from the spectators' mere indications of time and place? Not every envelope could be from abettors.

The Dane and his accomplice returned for a second night and later questioned Dagma's stage assistant. They learned about Kraus' codes and his detection of the dates and places. Kraus guessed the events, using Jenisch logic: most tragic accidents took place on factory floors and streets, marriages in halls or churches, births in hospitals, illness and deaths in bedrooms. Of course, the husband-wife duo made mistakes and followed blind alleys, yet Dagma's spectators wanted to believe in her clairvoyance, begged to be deceived. When the Indian mangled or faultily channeled a recollection, spectators quickly forgave her, and each psychic error could be seamlessly corrected with another grope, another whirl, a new declaration.

Hanussen Demonstrates the Gomboloy, 1928

An Inauspicious Premiere

Hanussen and Juhn decided to duplicate Princess Dagma's hokum displays of individual divination. Psychologically and materially, they needed a lift. Juhn rented the Karlsbad Stadt-Theater. During their first public presentation of clairvoyant prophecy, however, the novices stumbled disastrously.

Hanussen purchased a copper globe at a local glass and ceramic emporium and advertised himself as "The Copper-Ball Clairvoyant." He thought the mysterious object could substitute for the familiar crystal ball. After fumbling, he wound up using the black-and-red Gomboloy beads.

The Stadt-Theater production failed in every way imaginable. Juhn signaled Hanussen through a hastily designed, Labéro-like code. Still the Copper Clairvoyant could not remember the vocabulary or its combinations; he blindly conjured the audience's date-places and was wrong in ninety percent of his guesses. To make things worse—if statistically possible—two friends of Megalis II, the husband of the seer Madame Karolyi (Silverstein) and a Berlin stage magician, exposed Juhn's abetting plot and forced him to leave the hall.

Telepathic Post Act, 1928

Disgrace did not stop Erik's clairvoyant act. He rigorously memorized the codes. And he added his tried and true smirk to the act: humor, suspense, self-mocking irony, reckless improvisation, sham terror, scientific derision, and fakirism reshaped the evening.

Juhn also improved his part. During the breaks, he walked slowly and deliberately through the rows of spectators and gave them instructions on how to fill out sheets with dates and times. Juhn officially feigned disinterest in the nature of the events. On the contrary, he categorically refused to discuss the spectators' direct inquiries. For example, when someone asked, "How am I supposed to fill this out? It is about the suicide of my brother," the secretary answered, "Sir, it doesn't matter what kind of event it is, you simply write the exact date and the exact place of the event on the paper and hand it to me. I don't want to know any details!"

Juhn-Hanussen Stage Code (circa 1927)

AUDIO CODE

"Please" = a birth
"Please, silence!" = a murder
"Pst" = a fire
"Read" = burglary
"Silence" = death
"Thank you, please" = a wedding
"We require more silence!" = a major theft
"Will you read?" = a suicide.

VISUAL CODES

Holding letter in left hand = wedding
Holding letter in right hand = birth.
Crossing Arms and Legs = Doctor
Touch Head = Psychologist
Touch Ear = Ear Doctor
Hands in Pocket = Successful Merchant
Head turn = Lawyer
Lowering Arm = Merchant
Passing Hand over Hair = Poet
Putting Hands on Knees = Teacher
Straightening his tie = Judge
Yawn = Official.

Erich Juhn, **Leben und Taten des Hellsehers Henrik Magnus**
(Vienna: Saturn Verlag, 1930)

When Juhn could not discern a patron's story, he often returned the paper, admonishing the believer that only "significant events" were worthy of the Dane's expertise. At that point, the defensive audience member almost always imparted the essence of the hidden event—"But it concerns a fire and three deaths in my uncle's mill!" Sometimes, when Erik got details of past occurrences wrong, he challenged the veracity of the spectator's memory—"It happened on the third floor, not the second! Don't be stupid, Fräulein! Kindly, think!"—or he blamed the poor penmanship of the theatregoer. Amazingly, Hanussen's hectoring forced audience members to reinvent and correct their recollections or agree with him to prevent further embarrassment.

Week by week, Juhn and Hanussen polished and refined the occult production. Within just a few months, the show was vastly beyond the Dagma-Kraus original. It was practically flawless.

Fred Marion, 1932

Success in the Provinces

The tour and the consultation sessions brought in tens of thousands of kronen. Erik was lifted. The typical private reading cost around 100 kronen. A critic from Berlin's *Vossische Zeitung* saw one of the early productions in Karlsbad. She remembered Hanussen as "a common-faced man with a thick underlip, bushy brows and hands that always fidgeted. His main power was in his eyes—penetrating, mysterious—those of a hypnotist."

Juhn set up shop in Karlsbad's sister spa towns of Franzensbad and Marienbad and the lesser resort villages of Komotau and Teplitz-Schönau.

In Franzenbad, Erik befriended the Czech-Jewish mentalist and psychic detective Fred Marion (born in Prague as Josef Kraus). Marion had appropriated the term "television" and applied it to his telepathic ability to reveal the personal history of an object: where it was manufactured, how many owners it had, its influence on those who possessed it, and so forth. Marion's "television experiment" was basically the same induction technique of psychometry that Erik had achieved at Jacob Schlesinger's Night-Asylum. Hanussen added it to the clairvoyant program.

Erik brought Fritzi to the villa of Juhn's in-laws in Warnsdorf. As with his second wife, Hanussen wanted Fritzi to convert to Judaism before their marriage. His own wife a converted Jew, Juhn took care of Fritzi's religious instruction and the legal arrangements. (Hanussen and Friedl—which sounded more Jewish—formally wed on January 1, 1928 in a synagogue in the Bohemian village of Rumberg. Erich Juhn, of course, stood in as best man.)

As Erik's trusted confidant and private secretary, Juhn helped update their act, schooled the self-taught "professor" in foreign languages and phrases (Juhn would later work in the New York Berlitz School), corrected the Dane's sometimes less-than-genteel table manners, and acted as a shill for Hanussen's insatiable sexual appetite. (In every city, Erik granted one local beauty a free consultation in his hotel room with a voluntary or hypno-erotic finale.) Juhn organized Hanussen's notebooks and writings for a grandiose literary project, which the two writers had yet to decide to publish as an autobiography or a roman à clef.

Both maestro and secretary had contempt for their opponents and followers alike in the Bohemian countryside. Each group manifested the hypocritical qualities of the age: sanctimonious, miserly, ethnocentric, arrogant belief in science or superstition. Hanussen and Juhn fabricated a private language to describe this clientele. "Jaglers" (from "Ja") were potential Hanussen devotees. Autocratic professors, "free-thinkers," and narrow-minded inquisitors were called "Projas." Neurotic and insufferable believers in the paranormal were "Okkultjas." Doubters and other rigid sorts who formed the examining commissions were labeled "Prüfjas." Journalists were "Zeijas"; complainers who thought the entire Hanussen enterprise to be bogus "Querjas"; clients only interested in handwriting analysis, "Graphjas." And those

Image of Hanussen from 1928 Poster

who only demanded palmistry readings: "Chirjas." The "Helljas" were desperate patrons who wanted Erik to solve mysteries that the police had long given up on.

Juhn renegotiated his salary for twenty-five percent of the theatrical and consultation fees—a hefty 25,000 marks per month. He also persuaded his employer to hire a separate impresario, Adolf Walther Scimanczek, to rustle up information on village personalities and scandals from in-the-knows and police blotters the week before the production was to debut.

From October 1927 to February 1928, Hanussen performed in thirty towns in Bohemia and Moravia. Given a press reception in Prague, he told the left-wing journalist, Jan Susanka, that his political idol Josef Stalin would die an unnatural death on August 1, 1953, his prediction being a short five months off. Journalists and vice commissioners in Czechoslovakia were by and large antagonistic to the Dane and his séances, as Hanussen challenged all rules of traditional authority. His German-language presentations in the Sudetenland increased linguistic tensions in the Republic; his antinomian religious attitudes, always latent in spiritualism, managed to seep through. Pre-show advertisements—which included a large poster of Erik in full hypnotic grimace—revealed Hanussen's true menacing face, "a vampire of superstition."

Additionally. the financial drain on depressed small-town Bohemia, the unhealthy, anti-clerical, spiritualist excitements, that enveloped entire municipalites, not to mention an overall disregard for police methods and their infallibility could not have been welcome in the tenth anniversary of the Czech Republic. And unsubstantiated promises from Erik's consultation sessions, as well as accusations of hypnotic seduction from fathers, boyfriends, husbands, and hysterical young women followed Hanussen like a paper trail.

Psychic Detection Again

Marion reinvigorated Hanussen's interest in trance visualizations of kidnappings, burglaries, and homicides through telegraphy and psychometric induction. Psychic pronouncements worked well as sensational denouements in the shows and better still in the consultation sessions. Random crime and the search for missing persons had more than tripled in Central Europe since the Great War and reportage of them became a staple entertainment of the local and national tabloid press.

Hanussen's telepathic investigations into the savage crime wave was the one activity that the Bohemian police most objected to among his retinue of occult stunts—although it was also Erik's most socially useful undertaking. The Dane actually helped locate lost property and identify law-breakers and their accomplices in at least one dozen cases where the local police had mishandled or ignored significant evidence or minute clues. Even in incidents where Erik only alluded to architects of enigmatic crimes, he goaded the authorities to further their lackluster investigations.

Between October 1927 and February 1928, Hanussen was publicly credited with resolving at least five elusive murders and kidnappings. In Eger, Hungary, despite a legal prohibition, he correctly identified the killer of a teacher from Galtenstallung—a disgruntled student. Erik's uncanny hunch was later verified by Eger's police chief, a state lawyer, and the town's magistrate.

In Bratislava, a female corpse washed up on an embankment near the Danube. Police investigators had no signs to her identity or clues to the brutal circumstances of her death. A few weeks later, Hanussen referred to the mystery (already old news in the community). The murdered woman was from the Hungarian-speaking village of Tyrnau, he intoned in his altered hypnotic state. The innocent girl had come to visit her lover in the Czech Army. Then a fiend approached her in Bratislava and dragged her to the river, where he ravished and asphyxiated her. The rapist-murderer wore black boots and had two golden caps on his front teeth. The madman was still at large, he warned. News cameras and journalists captured the clairvoyant moment.

During a performance in Trautenau, a hesitant woman asked Josef Richter, a business agent, to deliver a note to Hanussen. The paper contained the time and address of an unsolved murder in Trautenau from some twenty years ago. Erik glanced at the note and then described the circumstances of the mysterious slaying in fantastic detail. He even related, with astonishing accuracy, the scene of the crime—a house that had since been demolished. Hanussen concluded with the pronouncement that the killer was still alive and residing nearby. An excited police inspector decided to reopen the criminal file. A few weeks later, the culprit was found and brought to trial.

Hanussen With Journalists, 1928

In Leipzig, a female student disappeared from the University, leaving a seven-year-old child behind at her boyfriend's fraternity house. Three days later, the woman's lover also vanished. A German author known as "Ch." contacted his old friend, a priest, and asked him to pursue the matter in Leitmeritz, where the boyfriend's family lived. The police clerk listened politely to the clergyman's tale but took no action. Where would he begin the search?

Hearing that Hanussen was adept at such matters, the priest incongruously showed up at one of Erik's consultation sessions. After receiving 150 Czech kronen, the clairvoyant declared that there was no kidnapping or coercion. He described the exact physical appearance of the lovers and their eight-room flat in Leipzig. (A few details were wrong here, yet most of the physical portrayals were strikingly consistent with Ch.'s story.) Hanussen believed the woman suffered a miscarriage and was on her way to Asia via Zurich and Rome. Before fleeing the University, she hid for three days in another apartment, he added.

Immediately following Hanussen's prophecy, the couple was arrested in Salzburg. The girl had miscarried and spent three days in hiding in Leipzig. The two were attempting to reach Switzerland with a final destination in the Orient. Only the prediction of a Rome stopover proved incorrect.

In February 1929, Hanussen performed in Aussig. A secretary of a mountain-climbing society handed Juhn the date and place of the knife murder of a close acquaintance. Erik described the crime precisely: the victim met a young man in a tavern one evening. Over drinks, the two decided to hike up an isolated mountain trail, and one climber was found dead the next morning. The killing received little publicity, but Erik was convinced that the prime motive involved revenge, not robbery, and the murderer had left the country. Hanussen's telepathic assessment was later corroborated by local authorities.

In Ostrau, Erik, speaking in trance-state, assured a high city official that his fifteen-year-old daughter, who had disappeared for two weeks, was in fact safe, and on the road between Ostrau and Troppau. Following the Dane's suggestion, police investigators retrieved the runaway teen. The father, Karl Burcik, maintained that Hanussen was a true clairvoyant and maybe something of a saint.

The most celebrated and profitable of Erik's psychic detections took place in Prague. Remembering Hanussen's investigative work for the Austro-Hungarian Bank in 1919, a claims agent for the insurance firm Riunione Adriatica di Sikurta contacted the miracle man in May 1928. Three years earlier, the Czech Kommerzialbank sent 10,000 American dollars in cash to the Banque du Credit Roumaine in Bucharest. The registered package arrived at the bank with its official seals intact but the currency had been replaced with clippings from a German electronics magazine.

Hanussen reasoned that the amateur thief worked inside a Romanian customs office in Satumare or Kaschau, was a radio and electrical hobbyist, and would have used the dollars to purchase a house in a German-speaking border village in Romania. He studied photographs from a lineup of postal inspectors in Kaschau.

Erik went into a trance and indicated the figure of one young manager, Ivan Lazar, as the likely culprit. The claims agent drove to Satumare and interviewed Lazar at home. His residence was indeed new and paid for in American dollars. After initial denials, Lazar broke and made a stunning confession, blaming the mail robbery on another mastermind in Kaschau. There, the claims agent spoke to Konstantin Bolea, a convicted felon and a former postal employee. Bolea admitted to nothing and a house-search by Romanian federal police uncovered little of value. But one room contained a number of electric apparatuses, all self-built—just as Hanussen predicted.

A few months later, the claims agent learned that Bolea was once employed by the municipal power station in Kaschau. Using Hanussen-like logic, the officer returned to the city and asked to see Bolea's old work desk. In the drawer were scraps of paper from the 1925 technical magazine that was substituted for the money. When presented with this new evidence, Bolea finally admitted his guilt. After four years, the Kommerzialbank case was closed, and Erik received a laudatory testimonial letter from the Riunione Adriatica and a reward of $1,100, eleven percent of the lost funds.

ERIK JAN HANUSSEN SÉANCE

A Typical Performance in a Czech Hall, circa 1928

1. INTRODUCTION

The crowd waits impatiently for the evening's marvels. On the stage stands a thick-set figure. He possesses a brutish face, a low forehead, a squat body, dark hair. Thick bushy brows fall over the eyes; a puffy lower lip adds to the vulgarity of the man's appearance.

For a moment he stands motionless on the stage. Then he begins to speak, in a pleasant, modulated, assured voice. His tone is quite ordinary, with a note of familiarity:

"I will not attempt to fool you. Nothing is further from my mind than to claim supernatural powers. I can't create miracles, I merely want to perform a few experiments—experiments which cannot be easily dismissed because science cannot explain them."

Hanussen explains that fifty years ago anyone who had dared prophesy the miracle of the radio would have been burned at the stake. Yet today we take this invention for granted. We know that a machine receives messages transmitted from distant points without any visible means of connection. Even if we don't quite understand it, we are no longer mystified by it. Why do people refuse to believe that the human brain, more delicate and complex than any mechanism, is not capable of doing the same? Because the learned professors wouldn't like it?

On this stage is one human brain, Hanussen's brain, which can do these things. How it works the master clairvoyant himself does not know. The fact remains that Hanussen is capable of receiving emanations from men and objects and events just as a radio set receives electrical impulses from a wireless transmitter.

Describing this as a mere trick is to be behind the times. It will not be long before we understand more about the strange phenomenon which today is lumped together under the heading of the occult.

Any spectator who can prove trickery on Hanussen's part during these experiments will receive a reward of one thousand marks.

Applause greets this speech. The man on the stage has won the sympathy of the public.

2. TELEPATHIC POST

The first half of Hanussen's program is methodical and lighthearted. He asks members of the audience to write on a slip of paper the name and seat-number of somebody present in the hall. The paper is then enclosed in a sealed envelope. Hanussen promises to forward the envelope by what he calls "Telepathic Post." Dignified matrons, bespectacled professional men, excited youths leave their seats to go up to the stage; Hanussen chooses a few who look as if they might be good subjects, and asks them to remain on stage.

He addresses one of them, "Please take my hand. I will cover my eyes and stuff my ears with cotton. I will only hold your hand. All you need do is to think of the place to where I am to go. Can you think hard? Of course, you can. We'll soon see. Concentrate on it, now. All you have to do is think: Turn to the right, Hanussen, stop for a moment, turn to the left, or whatever it may be. Concentrate on it with all your might."

Hanussen delivers all the telepathic envelopes to the proper parties. He never fails.

3. FINDING THE NEEDLE

Two committees are selected. The first panel accompanies Hanussen to a room outside the hall. The second committee (usually of women) hides the needle, say, in the mayor's cigarette case. The telepath returns to the podium and chooses a medium. He takes her hand, asks her to think of the placement of the needle, and guides her to it. This too is done with assurance and humor. The needle is always discovered.

4. PSYCHO-GRAPHOLOGICAL EXPERIMENT

"Psycho-Graphological Experiments" follow. A few distinguished citizens are asked to come on the stage and write their names on a blackboard. From that, the clairvoyant not only reads their character and reveals their profession and their hobbies, but also divines specific incidents from their lives, such as, for example, a quarrel between a professor and his dean.

INTERMISSION

The highlight of the séance is reserved for the second half of the evening. Before the intermission an announcement is made: Anybody who has knowledge of a particularly striking event, such as an accident or a crime, a birth or a wedding or a death, is asked to write the time and place of the occurrence with as much detail as possible on a slip of paper. During the intermission, Hanussen's secretary, Erich Juhn, takes the slips in the lobby.

By this time the tension among the spectators has reached a fever pitch. The Great Hanussen is about to pierce the veil of the past with his superhuman radio-brain, which can project itself into the distant past or future and which is able to absorb and interpret the mysterious waves emanating from events and objects long past or yet to come.

5. PLACES/DATES CLAIRVOYANCE

The bell rings. The audience rushes back into the auditorium. The curtain rises. Before the footlights stands Hanussen, but an entirely different Hanussen. Gone is his jovial demeanor. He is serious now, his face grave and tormented, one hand convulsively gripping a black blindfold and a string of beads. The stage is empty except for a single chair in the middle. Although the hall is absolutely quiet, Hanussen begs for silence. The most difficult part of his task has arrived. He is only human, he explains; he does not know whether he will succeed in his clairvoyant predictions. He must first fall into a deep trance. To achieve this state, he has brought his Gomboloy, a rosary-like strand used by Indian yogis.

While in trance, he will endeavor to call forth the events to which the slips refer. Once more he pleads for absolute silence. The experiment is fraught with danger to himself.

The audience is overcome with awe. Hanussen ties the blindfold over his eyes, sits down on the chair, and lets the Gomboloy slip erratically through his fingers. A low moan emanates from his mouth.

In the aisle below stands Juhn. A number of slips are held in his upraised hand. "What happened on January 27, 1897, at three o'clock in the morning at Charlottenburg, Kantstrasse 132, first floor?" he asks in a clear, penetrating voice.

Strained silence. Then Hanussen mumbles some unintelligible words. His voice suddenly fills the auditorium: "I see . . . I see a dark room. Nobody is there . . . no, someone is there . . . who is it? The man doesn't belong there! He is a burglar! Where are the people who live there? Something terrible is going to happen! The thief prowls through the house, goes into the rear room. For God's sake, the jewelry! Where are the police? . . . Police! . . . Too late. The thief has fled!"

A shudder runs through the hall. The secretary's voice asks, "Is that correct?"

"Yes," a shaken voice from the audience replies. 'Yes, that is correct," Juhn confirms.

Another slip is read. Again, the right answer. And so forth with the other slips. Rarely is the answer wrong.

Then the last slip is read. It refers to an incredibly complicated story of a mysterious crime and its solution, a story replete with so many minute particulars that the most obstinate skeptic yields, falls under the spell.

At the climax of his dramatic description Hanussen tears off his blindfold, as if he can no longer endure the vision he has evoked.

He jumps to his feet. He reels. His hand clutches at his chest.

Juhn rushes up to the stage, comes to his master's aid.

The spectators, carried away in a mass hysteria, give Hanussen an enthusiastic ovation, convinced beyond the slightest doubt that this man is a seer, that miracles do exist even if our vaunted science cannot explain them.

The curtain falls as the unsteady and spent soothsayer is directed into the wings.

Translated and compiled from Erich Juhn **Leben und Taten des Hellseher Henrik Magnus** (1930); Leopold Thoma, **Hanussen: Hinter den Kulissen eines mysteriösen Lebens** (1933); and Bruno Frei, **Hanussen: Ein Bericht** (1934)

Photograph and Cartoon of a Consultation Session

CHAPTER SEVEN

MIRACLE IN LEITMERITZ

1928-1930

Teplitz-Schönau

At the end of the Golden '20s, Teplitz-Schönau was considered the idyllic watering spot for families of Germany's nouveau riche and an agreeable playground for Balkan aristocrats on the move. The Sudeten resort town had more than its share of posh hotels, garden-restaurants, concert halls, body salons, rejuvenation clinics, and spas. The region's curative alkaline and saline springs, already celebrated when it was a garrison settlement before the Roman Empire's fall, were said to benefit sufferers of gout and rheumatism. The Dutch Queen Wilhemina kept a huge villa on the Teplitz mountainside and Russian noblemen frequented the city's gambling dens for much of the nineteenth century. Goethe and Beethoven once met on the town square.

In the post-World War One era, Teplitz was still hailed as the "Bohemian Paradise." Its picturesque sidestreets and forested hillsides had yet to be marred by factory chimneys or lumber mills. An outlet for local crafts and porcelain, free outdoor recitals—the city boasted a dozen choral and musical troupes—and the modern electric tramway to the Eichwald were widely advertised as the Teplitz' main attractions. Tourism was such an established feature of the place that few visitors balked at the city's peculiar entertainment tax that was levied at the railroad station.

The new ethnic fault lines and tensions that ran through Western Czechoslovakia, however, were visible here as well. It was not only the devout Czech peasants who despised the Jewish townspeople and traders, largely responsible for the petit bourgeois holiday trade; now the reigning *Ostmarkts* and Teplitz' Pan-German cultural societies incorporated the virulent anti-Semitic rhetoric that flowed from Munich and Vienna.

Even in liberal Prague, sixty miles to the south, the Lord Mayor Karel Baxa made his national political reputation as a race-baiting jurist. He was known as the only state lawyer in Austro-Hungary who in modern times prosecuted a case of Jewish ritual murder. An innocent Jewish cobbler from Eastern Bohemia was sentenced to life imprisonment but was later cleared of the preposterous, trumped-up charge.

The independent Czech Republic as a peaceable model of racial tolerance and harmony was mostly a League of Nations' fiction. Journalists and left-wing sycophants, desperate for good international news, intentionally conflated the personality of Czechoslovakia's humane and intellectual president, Tomas Masaryk, with its inhabitants, a majority of whom were lifted by Europe's wave of xenophobia and Jew-hatred.

A Portent of Doom

Hanussen performed several times at the cabaret in the Hotel Monopol in Teplitz-Schönau. His consultation clients, consisting mainly of Sudeten German landowners, including many war-widows, was a steady source of income.

After New Year's 1928, the Wizard of the Ages, newly content with his station, purchased another luxury sedan, an eight-cylinder LaSalle, and shelled out down payments for a modest house for Fritzi and apartments for Juhn and Scimanczek.

On February 9, however, Erik had a strange premonition. Disaster approached. Not just his livelihood but his very liberty was threatened. After the show in the Monopol greenroom, Hanussen told Juhn of his foreboding. He was ready to cancel the February 10 performance. His secretary counseled him out of it.

As predicted, the second evening unfolded in a strained atmosphere. Two Czech patrolmen appeared at the back of the cabaret and covertly scrutinized Juhn, who sensibly refrained from any obvious abetting. A visibly spent Hanussen answered four of the five date-place questions from the audience without assistance. One phony prophecy, however, was too good to pass up.

During the second intermission, a manufacturer in the audience, Franz Tomschik, wrote down the place and date of a burglary. The safe in his factory had been jimmied and broken into the night before. Sitting next to Tomschik was a plainclothes Czech prefect, Captain Hercik. The officer had been stalking Hanussen's performances in Warnsdorf and Eichwald. He noticed how Juhn and Scimanczek cajoled additional information from spectators and somehow communicated it to the master on stage.

Hercik told Tomschik of his suspicions and asked if he could tack some extraneous and fanciful details to his story. Tomschik agreed to the wicked artifice. It would be a true test of Hanussen's clairvoyance.

When Juhn strolled through the aisle searching for prospective cases, Tomschik waved his sheet in the secretary's direction. Studying the address and recent date, Juhn coolly objected that the mysterious incident would probably be too mundane or petty for the prophet. Tomschik pleaded that it involved a major theft from his plant and Captain Hercik began to pile on more and more invented particulars: Tomschik's night guard was shot and suffered bloody wounds. A dog was used to chase the robbers, and so forth.

By the time Juhn read Tomschik's time-and-place question to the Dane, Erik's prophesying was in high form. The place was a factory and the event dealt with an open safety box, he declared. Was that correct? Juhn barked to Tomschik. It was.

Then Hanussen described his vision. Last night, three culprits, one of whom worked for Tomschik, conspired to break open the industrialist's steel safe. Another of the crooks was a black man, a very dangerous figure. And around Tomschik's building, there was a protective fence, however, in a dilapidated condition.

Then Erik began to stroke the top of his head repeatedly and shouted, "I see the watchful eye of a brave and honest man ... Blood, blood ... The guard is dead!" Juhn asked Tomschik if that was correct. When Tomschik hesitated, Hanussen changed his prognosis. "He is not dead. Only injured!"

The session ended with the clairvoyant's prophecy that Tomschik would be robbed again in exactly four weeks. The Teplitz audience screamed its approval; they were exhilarated.

Hanussen staggered off as the curtain fell.

In the wings, Erik appeared to be in a physical state of panic. He rushed Juhn to the dining hall of the Hotel de Saxe, where they were staying. And during their late-night repast, Erik piled his bulky wallet, gold watch, diamond ring, and tie-clip on a cloth napkin and pushed the treasure trove to Professor Kameol, a local enthusiast of the occult. He implored the scholar to hand the valuables to Fritzi, who would pick them up in the morning.

Fifteen minutes later at midnight, doom, in the form of six armed gendarmes, materialized. Hanussen, Juhn, and Scimanczek were placed under arrest and roughly hauled off to Teplitz' precinct jail. Under the direction of Detective Ladislaus Havlicek, the three were placed in separate quarters that night and subjected to harsh questioning.

The charges against Hanussen and his gang were serious: fraud and larceny. Havlicek declared that clairvoyance did not exist, therefore all clairvoyants and their helpers were engaged in a conspiracy of racketeering and charlatanism. The complaint against the trio was initiated by Captain Hercik, based on Hanussen's description of the Tomschik date-place fabrication.

The three were incarcerated in Teplitz' tiny jail for nine days. Juhn and Scimanczek were freed on February 20 after giving separate testimonies. Both men proclaimed their innocence.

The Teplitz court could not rule out that Hanussen's private secretary and impresario might have been gulled—with the Bohemian audiences—into believing the swindler's mystic claims. Their dismissal was the first sign of the Czech authorities' judicial incompetence and illogic. How could Juhn, the clairvoyant's confederate and abettor, be ignorant of his master's wiles? Any qualified board of state attorneys would have demanded that Juhn be held behind bars until he agreed to testify for the prosecution or, at least, sign an incriminating deposition that could be used in further hearings.

Instead, Havlicek had Hanussen detained and isolated for another ten days and attempted to crack, over six punishing interrogations, the impostor's pretense to supernatural endowment. Erik did not break. He maintained his virtuous position, bided his time in the dank military prison cell, reading newspaper scraps (which Juhn secreted to him by passing the rolled pages from mouth to mouth) and mentally constructing his autobiography—a book that would gloriously conclude with his victory over his *Jenischmänner*-hating tormentors.

On March 2, the Dane was released from solitary confinement after posting a huge bail. For the next 864 days, Hanussen and his attorneys developed their ingenious defense for what would be known as the "last witch trial in Europe."

The judicial venue was changed to the Leitmeritz, a German-speaking village on the Elbe.

Gathering Evidence

Havlicek notified all the local precincts, requesting instances of complaints of fraud against the clairvoyant. Authorities in northwest Bohemia and Prague complied, but the paperwork took months. Indictments from eighteen cities and towns were finally assembled.

Hanussen's performance in Lobositz on January 28, 1928 was particularly infelicitous. The Dane chose twelve young women from the audience for his expert committee. During a fakir number, he punctured his cheek with a bicycle spoke, but he uncharacteristically bled from the wound. Members of the committee could not help but notice the stage mishap. To compensate for said accident and change the mood, Hanussen promised to make a donation to the local poorhouse and offered free consultations in his hotel suite for the female observers the following day.

One of the selected panelists, Marie Brunetzky, a pretty twenty-three-year-old German national, came to Hanussen's hotel room in the afternoon. After guessing her line of work from her polished nails, Erik stroked the manicurist's slim and elegant hands and read her palms. He offered the beauty a permanent job as his secretary for 1,500 kronen per month and began to kiss her fingertips. Marie panicked, believing that she was falling into a hypnotic trap and would soon be corralled as Erik's sex slave. The young woman bolted from the room and filed a charge against Hanussen for dishonest and immoral acts. Brunetzky's was the first of thirty-four names to be recorded as state witnesses against Erik Jan Hanussen-Steinschneider.

Havlicek and his legal team decided against prosecuting Hanussen on the stage deceptions. No money passed hands inside the theatre and all of Erik's proscenium tricks might be defended as standard music-hall fare. Besides, the detective was uncertain which stunts involved legitimate legerdemain.

Hanussen's chief attorney, Rudolf Wahle, maintained that his client possessed the gift of divine prophecy, like Therese Neumann. That and bogus fortune-telling, Czech police felt, could be disproved and litigated in a court of law. The most serious charges had to do with using religious tenets to shake down Czechoslovakia's naive believers in occult phenomena.

Bloodied but Standing

At first, Erik had only one fear: that Juhn would testify against him. When he discovered that his intrepid secretary refused to turn state's witness in February and was not even called to appear in Leitmeritz, Hanussen knew that he would win the game. (His seasoned attorneys were not so optimistic.) Fritzi, as foretold, took Erik's liquid assets, and fled to the Riviera; she returned to Warnsdorf after a few weeks. Scimanczek vanished completely, retreating to Vienna. Two years later, he reappeared in Leitmeritz.

After the February arrest, Hanussen was free, more or less, for the better part of 1928 and 1929. Havlicek managed to force a decree forbidding Erik's participation in public séances, consultations, or other occult affairs in Czechoslovakia. Juhn and the maestro, however, tactfully found ways around the injunction.

In May, they hired Diebel, the stigmatic miner. Hanussen appeared on stage in the role of a neutral and baffled conferencier. After stage problems with Diebel in Prague, Juhn engaged the services of another stage patsy, known as "Svengali." A hopeless alcoholic and hypnotist-cum-telepath, the Czech Svengali possessed all the correct permits to perform in the Republic's variety houses. Together, the notorious Dane and the third-tier spiritualist set up shop at the Hotel Ambassador in Prague.

Articles about the forthcoming court proceedings in Leitmeritz added spice to their productions. Max Brod and other members of the Prague intelligentsia found the Svengali-Hanussen act sufficiently outré and otherworldly. Both the Czech fantasy writer, Karl Capek, and the Austrian novelist, Ernst Lothar, penned ironic fictions about the haughty mystic and his down-at-the-law enterprises. Hanussen and his troubles made fascinating copy for authors of fiction and nonfiction alike.

During this period, Juhn's and Hanussen's association began to splinter. Erik treated all of his employees pretty much like parasitic servants or worse. Even his private secretary was the object of his verbal onslaughts. Juhn, however, refused to accept the maniacal insults, knowing that most of Erik's new prosperity and refinements came as a result of his labor and instruction.

After an unsuccessful show in Ober-Polaun in November 1927, a cranky and drunk Hanussen blamed Juhn for the fiasco that evening. The secretary uncovered no worthwhile gossip in the village and as a result the Dane's finale petered out dismally. During the limousine ride back to Gablonz, Hanussen asked the chauffeur to stop the sedan and discharge his confidant in the middle of the road. Juhn laughed. The limousine was just as much his as Erik's. Hanussen silently brooded through the remainder of the trip and fired Juhn the next day. The chauffeur removed Fritzi from Juhn's in-laws in Warnsdorf and Erik performed alone for a few days when he realized that the production required Juhn's magic. The two reconciled, but the emotional bond between the con-artists began to unravel.

The Preliminary Examination

The state prosecution attorneys in Leitmeritz were at a loss how to pursue the question of clairvoyance. The sensational core of their case depended upon their public entrapment of the Dane. They planned to pummel the arrogant mentalist with an endless parade of hostile witnesses. Then, before the Chief Justice, they would puncture Hanussen's alleged psychism, using reams of incontestable scientific evidence that refuted the possibility of divinely-inspired power. But the prosecuting lawyers could find no precedent in Czech jurisprudence. Only in Germany had such trials taken place and many of them were inconclusive. Havlicek appealed to Judge Robert Schalek, the presiding magistrate, for a solution.

Schalek did not know a single legal specialist in the fields of clairvoyance, telepathy, or graphology. At least, not in the Republic. The no-nonsense jurist was forced to assemble an ad hoc committee of experts from the universities in Bratislava and Prague. He selected Dr. Franz Seracky, a philosophy professor from the Psychotechnical Institute in the Masaryk-Academy of Labor, and Dr. V. Forster, the head of the Psychology Department of the National Defense Ministry. In turn, Seracky drafted two assistants from the Academy, Dr. E. Benda and B. Kosiner, a graduate student, to conduct the double-blind tests for extrasensory ability and telepathy.

Schalek cautioned his expert witnesses—as devoted academics in the recognized sciences, or Negativists in the occult debate—about their anti-supernatural bias. They were to accord Hanussen every courtesy and benefit during the court-ordered examination. Any prejudice on their part might sully and ultimately discredit the official proceedings.

At Seracky's request, Hanussen (with Juhn at his side) was interviewed and examined at a laboratory in the Marsaryk-Academy on December 19, 1928. The session was conducted in German. Seracky noted with some professional irritation that Erik appeared to be fluent in an array of exotic languages, like Arabic, Turkish, and Farsi, yet could hardly be understood in Czech, the first language of the scholars.

The Academy investigation began with a standard intelligence questionnaire. Hanussen scored highly. Although lacking a traditional middle European education, the self-taught clairvoyant deftly responded to the linguistic and mathematical puzzles. He knew history, music, literature, art, and could retain complex images and word sequences with remarkable ease. A list of 100 jumbled numbers were presented to Erik and, after studying them for a minute, he recited them back to the investigators. There were no mistakes.

The Leitmeritz Judiciary. Judge Robert Schalek (center)

Hanussen was then asked to exhibit his psychophysical prowess as described in old flyers from pre-Juhn days. The Ottakring fakir held his breath, went into deep trance, and demonstrated several Hatha yoga poses. This part of the examination was less successful. Erik's corporal skills had deteriorated considerably over the years. The carny's nocturnal habits had damaged his lungs and weakened his muscle tone. Try as he may, Hanussen failed as a variety-hall superman in Prague.

On December 27, Dr. Benda tested the accused's telepathic faculties. Hanussen held a Gomboloy as he was blindfolded. Juhn sat silently at the lab table and Kosiner read two place-dates. The first Erik guessed correctly. It was about a birth. The second involved a mock suicide attempt by a student in a kitchen apartment. The man pretended to cut his left forearm. Hanussen insisted that he saw several people in the domestic setting. One of them suffered from a severe ailment. Kosiner maintained that the incident was a solo activity and refused to accept the university observers in the kitchen doorway as participants. Inflicting a wound to one's self could not be designated as an "illness."

Juhn submitted signed testimony from police stations in Vienna (1920), Budapest (1923), Leipzig (1924 and 1927), Prague (1927), and Bremen (1928) that Erik helped to solve major crimes through psychic detection.

Despite the testimony and Hanussen's accurate assessment of the first date-place event—and near-clairvoyant description of the second—Seracky ruled in the negative. Erik Jan Hanussen-Steinschneider possessed no paranormal abilities. The controlled tests proved the accused was an impostor and a fake. The Academy's conclusions were consistent with the prosecution's charge. An official certificate from Seracky two weeks later was forwarded to Havlicek and the court in Leitmeritz.

In a pamphlet published by the League of Proletarian Free-Thinkers in 1931, Seracky wrote a detailed personal account of the Academy inquiry. He recapitulated Hanussen's second-sight experiments, but excised every single instance where the subject achieved a correct reading. Clairvoyance, in the Czech Free-Thinkers' philosophy, was anti-materialist and anti-Marxist, and was therefore not within the realm of human possibility.

The Accusation

On March 13th, 1929, one year and eleven days after Erik's arrest and arraignment, a formal indictment was issued, accusing Hermann Steinschneider (aka Erik Jan Hanussen) of duping "mentally impaired" citizens of the Republic through superstition and other deceptive means. Twenty-five "imbeciles" were bilked out of fees up to 200 kronen; nine lost between 200 and 2,000 kronen. Total loses were estimated in the thousands of kronen. Hanussen was in violation of Paragraph 201a of the Czech penal code. This statute protected the infirm and feeble-minded from material fraud resulting from confidence schemes and religious chicanery.

Hanussen was also charged with professional misrepresentation, a violation of Paragraph 320 of the penal code. In the registry of the Hotel de Saxe, he described his occupation as "private scholar," and advertising flyers promoted him as a "professor."

The state attorneys asked for another nine months to firm up their case. The prosecution had never dealt with parapsychological issues and needed extra time to assess the Academy experiments. These, Seracky assured them, would scientifically devastate the soothsayer's defense.

The trial in Leitmeritz was scheduled for December 13, 1929.

Solo

The Hanussen-Juhn quarrel continued unabated and took new forms. In Warnsdorf, Erik ranted against Juhn's adoring six-year-old nephew, Ernest. And during their Rhineland tour in the winter of 1929, which garnered substantial receipts, the Dane could not stop himself from humiliating his stalwart secretary. When his Bugatti needed water, he shrieked at Juhn and kicked him out of the car to find it, then drove off.

Juhn had enough. In June 1929, he toyed with the idea of absconding with the master's props or offering to assist Havlicek's inept prosecution team. Even then, the secretary also feared Erik's mercurial temperament and savage capacity for retribution. He drove instead to Wiesbaden, where he unloaded their properties. The partnership was formally dissolved a few days later. Juhn retired to their common villa in Warnsdorf.

Hanussen did not know it then, but it would be Juhn's vengeful disposition that should have concerned him. It would lead directly to his undoing as the Prophet of the Third Reich and contribute to his death in just three years.

The Leitmeritz Trial

Hanussen With His Supporters in Leitmeritz

For Leitmeritz' 15,000 inhabitants, the Hanussen trial was a Chamber of Commerce dream event. The inland city lived off an uncertain tourist trade and the trial engendered much favorable international attention. The hotels and beerhalls across from the courthouse were ideal forums for free-spending curiosity seekers and reporters at the watch for local color. Wahle provided the impatient stable of foreign journalists with tabloid tidbits of legal slapdashery and fascinating Hanussen ephemera. Newsreel directors from Berlin and Paris stationed their cameras in Leitmeritz' Hall of Justice. German radio stations attempted to broadcast the proceedings on a live feed. It was as if belief itself—and not just the occult—were on trial.

With Leitmeritz' citizenry, the prosecution of Hanussen took on other, noncommercial, meanings. The tightly-organized Jewish community formed a support movement for Herr Herschel Steinschneider, one of their own. Jewish innkeepers addressed the defendant solicitously as "Master" and provided Wahle's team with free dinners. At the town's trade school, a teacher polled his class over the issue of the clairvoyant's innocence or guilt. Eighteen students registered their support for Erik; only two—members of a nationalist Sudeten organization—rallied against the "Jew Hanussen."

The main trial opened on December 16, 1929, lasting only three days. Carloads of letters from Germany, Austria, and the Republic were delivered to Schalek's chambers. Hundreds offered to be witnesses for the prosecution or defense—400 letters alone were received by Hanussen's attorneys. The prosecution wanted to check virtually all of them.

Though four dozen witnesses were summoned to testify, the number changed by the day. Havlicek's original thirty-four was a fickle and unstable crew. Several came down with cold feet, others had changes of heart, and an ill-starred assortment began to embellish their stories so radically that they became liabilities to the prosecution. A few simply died. Wahle's list of defense witnesses varied, too. (In the end, seventy took the stand.)

A circus atmosphere reigned in the Leitmeritz courtroom even before the bailiff called for order. The state, the defense, the public, and the media, especially, all anticipated surprises.

After the gavel silenced the hall, Havlicek's indictment was finally read. He called the trial a simple case of fraud. Only the defense was unusual. Havlicek summarized fifteen of his thirty-four prosecution depositions to show that each "idiot" was swindled out of substantial funds through spiritual deceit and unethical dealings. Havlicek requested the maximum penalty of one to five years of imprisonment for the accused.

Wahle swiftly demanded a legal definition of "idiocy"—the word in Paragraph 201a that described the mental status of the plaintiffs. The criminal designation of an "idiot" was not the same as the medical term, the prosecution lawyers argued.

Havlicek's clients, sitting in the dock, were startled by the state's unkind portrayal of their intelligence.

Schalek set Wahle's argument aside as a subject best decided by experts at a later date. Wahle made a second appeal: all of the prosecution witnesses had to undergo court examinations for their alleged pathological condition as "idiots." Schalek promised to take the entreaty under consideration as well.

Several government officials and private clients were sworn in, and each described Hanussen's failures to uncover the sources of various crimes they had presented to him. Erik responded that psychics and detectives, no matter how gifted or experienced, could not be expected to have a 100% rate of success. The determining factor was in the percentages, which, he claimed, his documented record to be rather high. And in many of the cases cited, Erik maintained that he was not given a full opportunity to complete his telepathic mission. Plaintiffs balked when he pleaded for additional funds or time.

Hanussen appeared reasonable on the stand, but the first day ended in madness.

In the Air

The rhythm of a provincial Czech trial followed the back-and-forth pattern of prosecutory charges and rebuttals from the defense. At the end of Day One in Leitmeritz, however, something new instigated an alternating flow: the testimony of a "would-be Hanussen" and, in other sessions, "counter-Hanussens."

Franz Dietz, a merchant from Hennersdorf, took the oath as a prosecution witness. He claimed that during Hanussen's appearance in Franzensbad in July 1928, he too experienced mystic visions, as an amateur clairvoyant and spectator.

When Erik was given pieces of paper from the audience that he was supposed to interpret graphologically or identify the date-place event, Dietz whispered the answers to a friend before Hanussen could respond. In fact, Dietz swore that his pictorial apparitions were exactly the same as the seer's—only he saw them more quickly and was not in an altered state of mind.

A second witness from Franzensbad, Hans Lugert, a reputable businessman, substantiated Dietz' nutty assertion. Lugert, Dietz, and three of their friends came to see Hanussen at the Kursaal. At the conclusion of the psychometry part of the evening, an elderly woman in the audience handed Erik a sealed envelope with a faded letter inside. As the Dane clutched the envelope with trembling hands, Dietz turned to Lugert and told him of his divination: a twenty-one-year-old man had shot himself in the forest. Then Erik telepathically described the author of the letter. It was the lady's son and he was, sadly, deceased. Hanussen returned the letter to its owner and whispered a few more words to the woman, which caused her to tear up.

During the intermission, Lugert approached the bereaved mother outside the theatre and told her of Dietz' oracle, "Your son killed himself in a forest because of a love affair!" The shocked woman validated this revelation and hurried back into the hall.

In still another segment of the evening, the lady begged Juhn to take her son's letter back to Erik one more time. A sympathetic Hanussen described the house where her son worked, as well as his office and other personal details, including his self-inflicted death in a grove. The sobbing woman nodded an affirmation after each pause in the reading.

Lugert told the court that his group returned to witness a second Hanussen lecture. They brought a photograph of a group of soldiers on patrol. The picture was sent to Lugert by relatives who wanted Hanussen to tell them the fate of their missing son. Hanussen then described the appearance of the soldier, that he had a scar on his left shoulder, and that he died during an attack in northern Italy. (When questioned later, the family confirmed the scar.)

Lugert asked Erik about an old family tragedy involving arson and the death of his two siblings. Hanussen divined the nature of the incident and hazarded a guess what the burning building looked like. It was correct.

Schalek was intrigued by Lugert's story. Here was an intelligent man, the owner of a business, who believed in telepathy and extrasensory communication. The personal examples just cited were compelling instances of not only Erik's work but the undertaking of other clairvoyants.

Lugert defended his beliefs to the Justice by quoting Goethe and even explaining how Hanussen was hoodwinked by the Tomschik hoax. Clairvoyance, Lugert stated, was analogous "to looking into the soul." If fake details are added to a real event, naturally, the seer will conjure up a distorted picture. The same was true for a psychologist, physician, chemist, or a lawyer. Misleading elements had to result in an incorrect analysis; correspondingly, any other diagnosis would be truly fraudulent.

The simple rationality and guilelessness of Lugert's words broke the spell of Havlicek's prosecution strategy. To win, the state would have to do more than show that Erik's activities were merely cynical manipulations of prognostication, they would have to disprove magical thinking—or raw faith, the basis of religion.

Hanussen Reads His Testimony

When applause and jeers interrupted Lugert's bizarre testimony, Schalek silenced the courtroom repeatedly and warned that he would clear the benches of spectators if such occurrences continued. The Chief Justice admonished the Leitmeritz onlookers solemnly that they were not in a cabaret.

But he was wrong.

Day Two

The sworn affidavits presented on December 17 were valiant attempts to restore the dignity of the Czech state and court after Lugert psychologically derailed the proceedings. Prosecution witnesses faltered and seemed unsure if Hanussen had actually defrauded them after all. Judge Albert Hellwig, Germany's leading Negativist and noted expert on crime and telepathy, appeared shrill and exceedingly hostile to any paranormal beliefs, especially to Hanussen's claims.

Even the most assured witnesses from Havlicek's list of "imbeciles" stumbled.

A wealthy miller from Klein-Ezernosek, Emil Mader, recounted how he went to a Hanussen consultation session in a Leitmeritz hotel in December 1927. He asked the seer if it was an auspicious time to invest in grain. Erik requested 200 kronen for such information and, after an hour's delay, read Mader's palms. The miller was encouraged to take the risk and promptly bought two wagonloads of corn. The price of corn dropped precipitously, Mader claimed, and estimated his losses at 4,000 kronen. When his demand for a 4,200-kronen refund from Hanussen was ignored, he joined Havlicek's lawsuit.

Wahle called the head of the State Agricultural Agency in Leitmeritz to the stand. The government official totally contradicted Mader's testimony. The miller purchased the corn on September 12, 1925, not December 1927 as he testified in court. Another defense witness, Josef Stern, stated that Mader did in fact buy two wagons of corn from him around January 1928. The prices jumped overnight and the Klein-Ezernosek speculator made a nice profit of 2,000 per wagon. Only in the fall of 1928, after the statistics of the new harvest were announced, did grain prices tumble.

Schalek's assistant, Judge Lusk, questioned Hanussen how he could predict the rise and fall of commodities futures through chiromancy. Erik explained that lines in the hands reveal whether the client is about to lose or gain something. Yet how accurate could those readings be, Lusk wondered. Hanussen replied that in his experience, around seventy-five percent.

Havlicek protested that a seventy-five percent probability of success was a poor example of clairvoyance.

And so it went.

The Positivists

On Day Three, a young psychiatrist from Prague University, Dr. Artur Heller, was invited into the Leitmeritz courtroom. To counter Hellwig's anti-parapsychological testimony, Wahle wanted Schalek to hear from the Positivist wing of the scientific community. Heller had tested Hanussen at the Hotel Ambassador in May 1928. He prepared twenty notes, ten with places and dates and the other half with descriptions of the events. Heller tucked the papers in separate sealed envelopes and placed the stack on the Dane's table. In front of a second physician and two witnesses, Erik went into trance state. He guessed eight of the ten incidents correctly. One conjecture was absolutely wrong, and a tenth, which seemed false at the time, turned out to be prophetic: the subject afterward committed suicide as Erik foretold.

The normally skeptical psychiatrist characterized Erik Jan Hanussen as a demonstrable master of telepathy. Schalek inquired further. He wanted to know from Heller how established social scientists explained the phenomenon of telepathy. Heller confessed that he was uncertain of its physical or mental basis, although handwriting analysis, another one of his interests, was also discounted until recently as a sham Gypsy art. But graphology was slowly being accepted into the mainstream of Central European psychology as an important manifestation of expressive behavior and a key trait to personality.

Next, Wahle invited Dr. Walther Kröner, a homeopathic physician and the head of the Berlin Medical Society for Parapsychological Research, to testify. Kröner first met with Hanussen the previous day at the Red Crab Hotel. Present with the Positivist scientist and the telepath was Scimanczek. Erik studied Kröner's handwriting and began to tell him details about his childhood and adolescence. Kröner claimed the analysis was insightful and accurate. Next, Kröner displayed an unsigned letter from 1917. Hanussen at first thought it was written by a woman, then a feminine male. The author was Germany's Foreign Minister Walter Rathenau, a homosexual. Kröner affirmed Erik's attribution, and the telepath went on to describe a head wound—or a sudden death—that involved the writer. This was consistent with Rathenau's assassination in 1922. Finally, Kröner gave the dates and places of two war incidents. Hanussen surmised both correctly. According to the homeopath, the accused was right in four out of four controlled tests.

Kröner told the court that he had never observed such clairvoyant ability before. Hanussen belonged to a tiny circle of mediums who had been scrutinized and certified by recognized experts. The doctor concluded with a plea to Schalek. He prayed that the court would finally pass judgment on the existence of the paranormal and not punish those endowed with the gift of prophecy.

Havlicek practically leaped out of his chair. Kröner's evaluation could not be considered expert testimony. The man was a foreigner, a parapsychologist from Berlin, with a vested interest in the defense's position. Unlike Hellwig, Kröner was not brought to the House of Justice as an objective friend of the court. He was as phony as Steinschneider-Hanussen himself.

Judge Schalek called an end to the proceedings that afternoon and on the morning of December 19 announced an adjournment. There were too many new witnesses, some of whom had to be carefully screened by the court, and new legal aspects to the case. When Schalek asked for a rescheduling of the trial for February 1930, Hanussen stood up and vehemently objected. His work had been defamed and placed under suspicion for nearly two years. The seer demanded an immediate examination of his powers. The child-like desperation in his voice shocked everyone. Even Fritzi. Erik appeared close to a nervous collapse.

Schalek gathered his notes and exited. The House of Justice was cleared of all spectators, witnesses, lawyers, and the defendant. The second part of the trial was reconvened for May 22, 1930.

Interim

Leitmeritz' businesses were delighted by the trial's many delays. For twenty-seven months, the world would link one charming Bohemian spa-village with the relentless state pursuit of spirit communication and occultism. It meant more publicity, more small-town boosterism, and repeated rounds of tourism, all stimulated by a who-knows-what conclusion to the prosecution of the mysterious Hermann Steinschneider.

Erik quickly recovered from the immense psychological strain of the stop-start proceedings. Public tirades and traumas had no strategic value. He engaged Victor Frischauer as his newest impresario and decided to use the Leitmeritz interlude to shore up his reputation as a virtuoso mentalist. He wisely limited their travels to Germany, where the reception of his good works was buoyed by the extensive coverage from Leitmeritz.

On January 20, 1930, Hanussen assisted the Offenbach police in their hunt for the murderer of Ernst Henke, a merchant. Refusing to accept any fee, Erik divined the scene of the crime and the killer's M.O. A stenogram of Hanussen's trance-pronouncement was professionally made at the police station and Frischauer requested a letter, certifying the accuracy of Erik's visions.

At the sumptuous Krupp mansion outside Essen, Hanussen conducted a private séance. One of the iron magnate's friends wanted to know where he would be on his fiftieth birthday, on August 28, 1942. The blindfolded seer predicted that the aristocrat would be in Bombay, in exile with his Jewish spouse. The others, including the world-famous juggler Enrico Rastelli and his wife, the daughter of a Danish clown, also asked about their whereabouts on that day. Erik saw troops—British soldiers—on the march. There would be war in Europe and in the Pacific in the summer of 1942. Krupp's guests warmed to the Austrian soothsayer. They were greatly amused by his after-dinner prognosis of world conflict. And while they continued to pepper Hanussen with more questions about their personal destinies and the future of Europe, Frischauer dutifully recorded every word of the session.

In the winter and spring of 1930, much of Germany turned its attention to Düsseldorf, a city in the heartland of the Ruhr industrial belt. Seventy-nine women and children had been attacked by a hammer or knife-wielding maniac. Eleven had died and another dozen were horribly maimed. The assailant was no ordinary serial killer either; he mocked the police, leaving behind a mad trail of 2,000 clues and taunting riddles. The lust-murderer seemed to require blood from his prey in order to achieve sexual orgasm. Half of the corpses were discovered with puncture wounds on the neck, made by human teeth; their tiny torsos hacked and sexual organs eviscerated.

The terrified citizens and the sensation-mongering press labeled the serial killer the "Vampire of Düsseldorf" or the "Tiger of the Ruhr."

At first, the local police welcomed outside detectives, psychics, graphologists, and assorted crime-fighters. Two Berlin mediums were taken to a murder scene, but their conflicting descriptions of the fiend left the officers in a quandary. The clairvoyants were packed off to Berlin. A total of 300 amateur psychic sleuths, including Edgar Wallace, hoped to solve the crime and collect the 15,000-mark reward. None were successful.

By the time Hanussen attempted to identify Düsseldorf's Jack-the-Ripper, the Chief Crime Commissioner Momberg had utterly lost patience with telepathic detection. Sidestepping the pleas of the city fathers, Hanussen delivered a graphological analysis of the sadistic killer to the local papers on February 14, 1930. His reading uncovered twenty-six traits, among them: the criminal was homosexual, well-educated, severely nearsighted, blonde, a member of the railroad or postal union, overweight, a bicycle enthusiast and non-smoker.

On March 2, the Vampire wrote to the *Düsseldorf Freiheit*, confessing to two more brutal deaths and giving directions to their burial sites. The police reacted despairingly to the insolent challenge. Erik took the message, however, as a personal reply and responded with a series of dramatic letters to the demented criminal. In the *Dortmunder Generalanzeiger*, Hanussen begged the elusive demon to surrender to the authorities before contemplating his next attack or the seer would singlehandedly hunt him down. There was no escaping the psychic mind, Erik asserted; he already knew too much about the slasher's patterns and appearance.

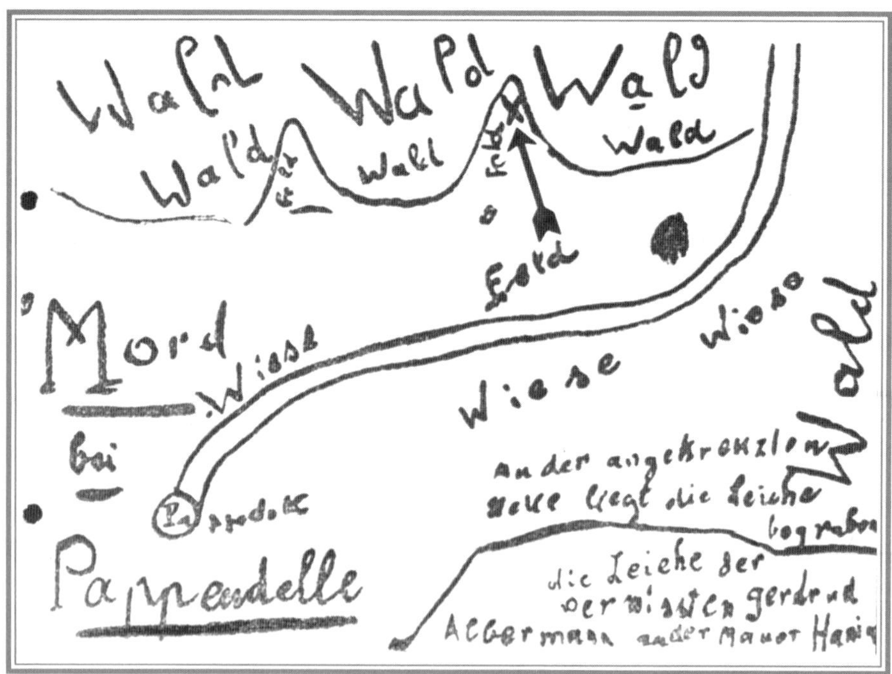

A Map From the "Düsseldorf Vampire," Which Indicated the Location of His Last Murdered Victim, 1930

The Prussian police and city's vice commission turned down the clairvoyant's offer to work with them. They would capture the ghoul through their tried and tested means only. Meanwhile, over three months, nine more young women and girls in Düsseldorf were savagely attacked.

A foolish misstep, not the city-wide dragnet, resulted in Peter Kürten's arrest, conviction, and beheading. On May 24, 1930, a twenty-year-old victim, after being fondled, persuaded the serial murderer that she had forgotten his address, where he dragged her. The next morning, she led the Düsseldorf police to Kürten's apartment. The case was finally closed.

Hellwig later claimed that none of Hanussen's published characterological descriptions corresponded to Kürten's physical profile or biography. Erik maintained the opposite. The truth, as always, was somewhere in between.

In March, April, and May, Hanussen performed twelve experimental evenings at variety halls in Göttingen, Potsdam, Berlin, Brunswick, and Dessau. The shows in Potsdam and Berlin were great successes, playing to audiences in the thousands; the ones in the smaller cities, less so. The "television," or psychometric part of the evenings yielded mixed results.

When a brooch was handed to Erik in Göttingen on April 28, for instance, he stated that it was purchased in 1864 and had been in the spectator's family for two generations. The owner denied its telepathic history. Hanussen pretended to repeat his statement, saying that the heirloom was purchased in 1864 and had been in another family's possession for one generation. The spectator protested this time that the seer had changed his story. Erik broke the contentious mood by complimenting the brooch owner, "You are an admirable adversary, sir!" Humor was part of the show too.

In Dessau, journalists estimated that fifty percent of Hanussen's readings and prophecies were verifiably false.

On the morning of May 16, Dr. Kröner telephoned Dr. Christoph Schröder, the head of Berlin's Institute for Metaphysical Research. Hanussen was in town briefly and Kröner hoped that Schröder could arrange a series of telepathic tests that evening. Schröder happily accepted—his journal, the *Zeitschrift für metapsychische Forschung*, had followed the Leitmeritz trial with keen interest. Unfortunately, the Institute's recording equipment was out of service. Hanussen agreed nonetheless.

Schröder invited four other scientists and asked them to bring envelopes with inscriptions of dates and places of significant personal events placed inside. The sealed envelopes were shuffled and arranged in a stack. When Frischauer and Hanussen arrived at 8:40 PM, a shorthand transcription of the examination began.

With a minimum of preparation, Erik matched the envelopes to the authors. He correctly foretold five of the eight date-place indications, guessed wrongly in two cases, and one envelope was discarded because of a procedural error. The last two envelopes belonged to Schröder.

Erik started with an inquiry. He asked a dozen questions about the metaphysician's note-card, which read "April 3rd, 1916. Eleven o'clock. Govem Street.

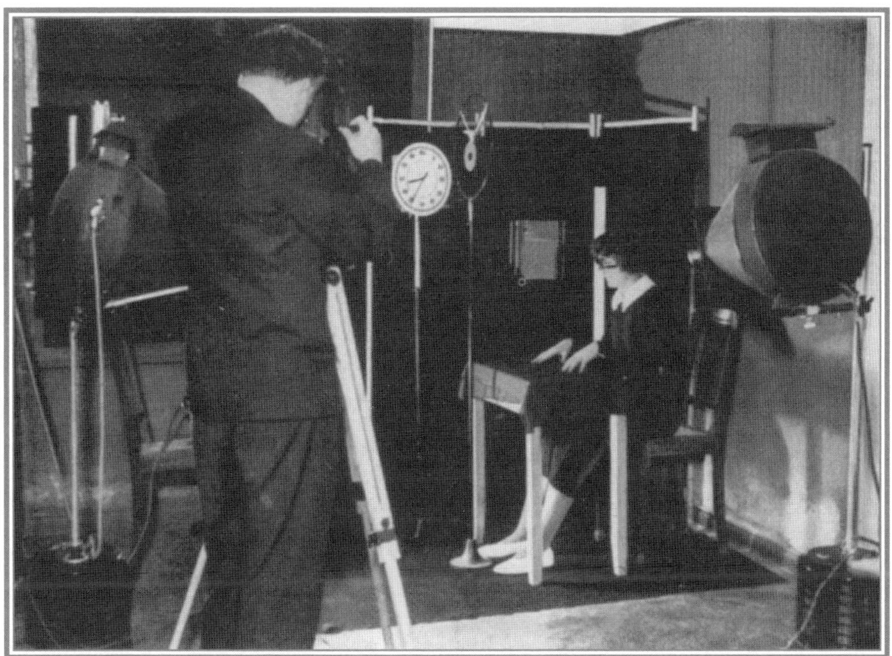

Dr. Christoph Schröder's Laboratory at the Institute for Metaphysical Research

Hanussen at the Institute for Metaphysical Research, May 16, 1930

Persia." The psychic saw a brawl and a fire. Schröder was on an expedition and had suddenly found himself in grave danger. He was injured. He sat on a horse or mule, attempting to escape. He wore a thick beard.

The aging parapsychologist was startled. The description fit perfectly with the time and place on the card. Schröder had been sent by the German government on a top-secret mission to Central Asia in 1916. The note referred to an attack on his mule-train by Persian bandits in Shiraz. Schröder never spoke about the wartime skirmish, not even to his closest associates, or wrote about it. Hanussen could have learned of the incident in only one way—through telepathic communication. The second note concerned an arduous safari to East Africa in 1912. Erik envisioned Schröder's deadly journey and descent down Kilimanjaro in fantastic detail. This too was magically correct and the information had been previously hidden from Schröder's acquaintances.

A few days later, after carefully reviewing the Institute's transcripts and pondering the controlled circumstances, Christoph Schröder, Germany's leading scholar of the paranormal, declared Erik Jan Hanussen a living medium. His psychic abilities were indeed genuine and beyond reproach.

Schröder had led hundreds of such investigations, traveled the world to observe shamans and gurus in their yurts and hovels, corresponded with the established metaphysical researchers in Europe and America, studied their experiments, but never experienced what he had that night. The beetle-browed Hanussen certainly looked like a fraud yet his skills were nothing less than authentic.

Round Two

The Leitmeritz trial reconvened on May 22, 1930 for six days. Judge Robert Schalek once again presided over the hearing and Professors V. Forster, Oskar Fischer, Franz Seracky, and Jan Simsa continued to act as judicial consultants. Fortunately for the defense, only Fischer was totally fluent in German, the language of the courtroom. The others followed the negotiations, though with considerable difficulty.

One of Schalek's magistrates, Judge Sulc, retired in December and was replaced by a Dr. Polak. Sulc's absence meant that all of the testimony from the first round had to be resubmitted and reconsidered by the court.

During the week, there were sixty-eight live witnesses and two sworn depositions. Among the returning prosecution witnesses were Marie Brunetzky (the finger-kissing episode); five plaintiffs who claimed Erik's palmistry sessions were fraudulent or misleading; five spectators who wanted refunds from the Bohemian performances; and eight disgruntled clients from the consultation sessions. The last group complained about Hanussen's incorrect diagnoses regarding missing children, errant husbands, failing businesses, suitable marriage partners, medical advice, location of lost watches, clandestine rivals, and murder suspects. In addition, Hellwig reappeared (but not as an expert witness) and three brainy townspeople explained how they fooled Hanussen by concocting invented places and dates or phony events.

Five of Havlicek's witnesses contradicted their earlier pre-trial testimonies. The wife of a railroad official, Luise Drbal, in fact did suffer from a nervous disorder, just as Erik foretold in a palm-reading. Anton Berger, a butcher's assistant, purchased a reading to find out about his future. Erik divined that he would have his own shop at age 25, meet a girl in 1928 and marry her, and live to be sixty. When confronted by Schalek about his earlier deposition, Berger became confused and admitted that some aspects of Hanussen's prediction had already come true. The engineer Max Rotter, who attempted to recover a suitcase lost in 1926, charged that Hanussen had swindled him out of 100 kronen. Under cross-examination, Rotter confessed that he forgot about Erik's promise to pay the cost of the valuables in the suitcase if he failed to restore them. A peasant, Adolf Modrey, inherited three keys from his deceased father and requested Hanussen's help in finding the matching safety deposit boxes. When the seer requested a ten percent reward for his efforts, Modrey balked. Under questioning, the peasant acknowledged that Hanussen had correctly determined the unusual construction and place of manufacture of the safes merely by fingering the keys.

Twenty-two witnesses testified for the defense. One woman convincingly claimed that Hanussen cured her son of stuttering after a one-hour hypnotic session. She had previously taken the boy to several Viennese specialists without success. And among the renowned physicians, only Erik Jan Hanussen refused payment. Six officials and laymen waxed eloquent about Hanussen's supernatural gift in uncovering murders, thefts, or kidnappings. A total of seven professors spoke of their positive experiences with Erik in the consultation room.

Dr. Max Ostermann, Franz Hlavinka, from the Austro-Hungarian Bank, and Dr. Abald Tartauga (aka Leopold Thoma) gave more prudent affirmations regarding Hanussen's escapades in Vienna. The trio accepted the possibility that the man possessed some superior, esoteric powers.

This time, Dr. Seracky questioned Kröner's credentials as a doctor and also insulted his parapsychological companion, Schröder, They were German and their publications on the occult more closely resembled fairy-tale primers than hard scientific analysis. Erik rose from the docket and shouted that Seracky was such a bumbling researcher himself that he was not even present during his own Leitmeritz experiments back in December 1929.

Judge Schalek silenced the room. However, the stodgy Berliners stormed out in huffy protest; they packed their bags and returned to Germany two days later. Schalek removed Seracky from the judicial panel.

Other witnesses—snooty academics, dignitaries from Hanussen's past, and maniacally incoherent clairvoyants—appeared before Schalek, but their testimonies and pleas neither helped the prosecution nor rallied the defense's position. They just increased the factors of weirdness. By mid-week, it was difficult for the hundreds of reporters to keep score.

The trial had stalemated.

The Miracle

On Day Five, Wahle made a request to call up twenty-two new witnesses for the defense. Clearly troubled, Schalek asked the lawyers to approach his bench. He was fearful that the trial was going nowhere. Kröner and Schröder had attempted to enter important, first-hand scientific materials in the proceedings. Now with their departure from Leitmeritz, the Berlin logs from the Institute of Metaphysical Research were no longer valid. The interrogation of more witnesses, pro or con, was unlikely to influence the judgment of the court at this late date.

Then, Hanussen, in an audacious "Believe-It-Or-Not" moment, volunteered to recreate his experiments in the House of Justice. It was the only way to break the judicial logjam. Wahle's eyes glazed over. (Erik remembered his lawyer's face breaking into tic-like spasms.) Schalek cautioned the accused about the pitfalls of such a demonstration. If Hanussen did not succeed in the paranormal tests, he would likely forfeit the entire case. Erik understood. Schalek's associates and prosecution team immediately agreed to the bizarre in-house examination.

Court was adjourned until early afternoon. High drama had come to Leitmeritz.

Fischer impaneled a board of expert witnesses. Hanussen's advocates and wife would be placed under tight supervision, so they could not signal the accused. And spectators would be readmitted into the courthouse by written invitation only. (In fact, so many tourists had an investment of time and money in the trial's verdict that the police decided to scratch the last restriction. The packed crowds had

Hanussen in the Courtroom

already overflowed the courthouse steps and foyer anyway. They were ready to push their way inside, no matter what was decreed.)

Eighteen police officers, armed with bayonets, surrounded the room.

Erik entered the hall, carrying a blindfold, cotton wadding for his ears, and a Gomboloy. Five exhibitions of clairvoyance were to be displayed: the Key Search, Graphology, Psychographology, the Date-Place Letters, and Psychometry.

A Czech Gymnasium professor, Dr. Klouek, and a local lawyer, Leo Töpfer, were instructed to hide a key somewhere outside the courtroom. The two went into a side chamber where Klouek placed a key in a flower-box outside the window sill. After they returned to the judge's bench, Hanussen touched Klouek's elbow and asked him to concentrate on the location of the secreted object. Hanussen thrust the man forward into the nearby room. Within five minutes, Hanussen returned victoriously holding the key.

The courtroom spectators applauded so loudly that Schalek made his old threat to clear the hall.

For the graphology test, Hanussen asked the judge to select three prominent individuals, including one of the prosecuting attorneys. They were to sign their names and scrawl two words of their choosing on a blackboard standing before the bar. Erik was taken out of the room while Schalek pointed to a local actor, a teacher, and Hans Bassler. Each got up and wrote on the blackboard. After a few minutes, Erik was returned to the court.

With striking detailed accuracy, Hanussen summarized the basic personality types and histories of the signatories. Although much of Hanussen's analysis veered toward the vague and commonplace, his characterization of Bassler was astounding.

Studying Bassler's script for several minutes, Hanussen announced that this man was a secret hedonist; he had suffered deeply from a tragic love-affair in his youth; his profession involved law in spite of an obsession with the outdoors; he was an avid collector of tiny objects; in 1917 and 1918 he underwent a severe crisis of faith; and finally, his affection for small animals was so great that he would endanger his own life rather than drive over one crossing the road.

Bassler reacted with giddy shock. Everything that Hanussen said was true except the part about animals. Bassler's father made him swear an oath never to keep pets and the adult Bassler abided by that childhood pledge.

Psychographology was next. Schalek handed Hanussen an envelope with a handwritten address. Erik said the few lines were not sufficient for an in-depth analysis. He requested to see the letter inside, which was passed to him. The seer labeled the author as a gentle soul. Schalek's assistant contradicted that assessment. The letter was written by a charlatan claiming to be an archbishop. Nonetheless, Erik maintained, the impostor was a likable person.

A second letter was selected as a substitute.

This psychographological reading went better. Hanussen identified the handwriting as belonging to a woman who was president of some company or organization. Schalek concurred. That was absolutely correct!

Both prosecution and defense teams were stunned. Schalek said nothing. He smiled majestically. Although smoking was forbidden in the Hall of Justice, Hanussen lit a cigarette for himself. He walked to the blackboard and drew the signatures of Richard Wagner, Beethoven, and the popular German cartoonist, Heinrich Zille. Professorially, Erik began to explain how the handwriting of these desperate individuals revealed their genius-like artistry.

Hanussen Leaving the Leitmeritz Courthouse

The courtroom spectators listened attentively. Hanussen now knew that he was on his way to winning the lawsuit in the most dramatic way imaginable.

Erik sat with his Gomboloy and slowly went into trance, as it was time for the telepathic events. A lawyer asked what happened on May 17, 1927 at four o'clock in the afternoon on Boreslauer Strasse. "A motorcycle accident," Hanussen intoned. Correct.

A second date and place from a physician. Hanussen

made some general statements, but he was unable to identity the event. The doctor was promoted by his university department on that day.

Finally, Bassler returned to the stand and gave a time and place. Hanussen described the birth of Bassler's son. The Prosecuting Attorney turned to the Chief Magistrate; Hanussen was right again.

Schalek canceled the Psychometric examination. He had heard enough. Havlicek and Wahle were instructed to prepare for closing arguments.

CLAIRVOYANT PROVES POWER IN CZECH COURT

Jan Hanussen, With Face Masked and Ears Stuffed, Demonstrates While Experts Wrangle.

Wireless to THE NEW YORK TIMES.

PRAGUE, May 28.—Jan Hanussen, one of th est-known clairvoyants in Middle Europe, was acquitted today of a charge of fraud at Leit-

On the following night at 11:45, Judge Robert Schalek read the Leitmeritz verdict. Erik Jan Hanussen-Steinschneider was absolved of all criminal charges.

The crowd waiting in the adjoining city auditorium went wild and accompanied Erik to his hotel suite for a spontaneous victory celebration. Throughout Leitmeritz, midnight champagne dinners were ordered in every restaurant.

The court's ruling on whether or not Hanussen truly possessed clairvoyant ability was unclear. That didn't prevent ecstatic journalists from making their own incredible conclusions.

Sensational front-page stories were phoned into Europe's largest newspapers: "MIRACLE IN LEITMERITZ! HANUSSEN ACQUITTED!"; "CLAIRVOYANCE EXISTS!"; "LEGALLY CONFIRMED: HANUSSEN CAN PEER INTO THE FUTURE!"; "COURT OF LAW: THIS MAN KNOWS ALL!"; "TRIUMPH FOR OCCULTISM!"

Hanussen later wrote that May 27, 1930 was the happiest day of his life.

On May 28, with Fritzi in tow, Hanussen boarded a first-class train to Berlin, the city that seemed to welcome him most. It was to be the clairvoyant's final engagement with history.

by Ernest Issberner-Haldane, Berlin

Women — Your Legs give you Away!

The Nine Types of Women's Legs:

1. The Normal (or Standard) Legs
2. Classy Legs
3. Ideal Legs
4. Variety (or Dancer's) Legs
5. Stick Legs
6. Champagne-Bottle Legs
7. Doll Legs
8. Elephant Legs
9. Fly Legs

Normal Legs exhibit total harmony and allow no space between the thighs. This leg shape characterizes a vital personality with a slight inclination toward comfort, motherliness, kindliness, and total devotion in love. This woman has a healthy amount of natural sensuality with strong erotic potential, has many friends, is temperate, and sensitive. She has an affinity for the finer senses; therefore, an interest in religion and the occult.

Classy Legs are the rarest form one can imagine. They obviously belong to a tall, slender body. The shape can be found in only one female in a million. Like everything that is wonderful and perfect, they are a sign of good racial hygiene. This form indicates a woman who is extremely attentive to detail, is intuitive and imaginative, has a fine sense of beauty and perfection, possesses a strong temperament and passion, and is artistically talented.

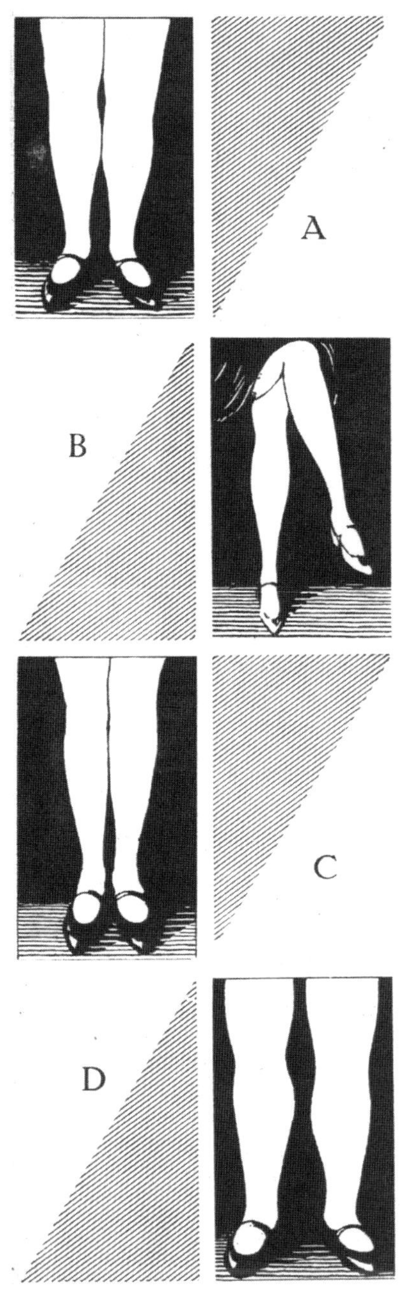

Her vitality, however, is not great but inwardly directed. She cannot be a common worker. Material endeavors do not interest her. She is better at giving advice and formulating plans.

Ideal Legs belong to slender and pleasant personalities. They are also very attractive and are probably the most common standard of beauty. Despite their beautiful formation, the thighs are imperfectly thin. They characterize motherliness, but without the power to conceive easily. The vitality of the female is not strong although she possesses much charm, tenderness, a preference for luxury and beauty, in addition to good taste. This woman has strong emotions and passion, a stable temperament and sense of devotion. She has a good heart, another product of racial hygiene. In general, she is artistic and has a high degree of self-awareness, decency, tact, and an independent life-style. She is the best type for intellectual companionship with men who are intellectual, professional, or spiritually advanced. Like the Classy-Legged woman, when she has marital problems, it is because the mate has not understood her disposition or desires.

Variety Legs are not necessity beautiful but display physical strength. The calves, instead of being soft, are sharply defined, muscular, and possibly hard. The ankles are strong and firm. One often sees such legs on the stage or circus arena. The woman can be characterized as flexible with a natural tendency for sports and the outdoors. She possesses a strong awareness of the physical world, is inclined toward malice, and, to a lesser extent, can be considered brainy. Being versatile and practical, she can overcome melancholic impulses but has an undeveloped imagination.

Stick Legs appear to run almost parallel from knee to foot. The calves are invisible. This woman is characterized by her excellent posture and mental faculties. She has a good sense of reality and the physical world, is a good hiker and loyal comrade. Her soul-vibrations (and soulful thoughts) are lacking. She may feign a beautiful pose but it will be superficial. Her basic temperament is rigid, stiff. She is a suitable companion, yet a poor lover. Even as a friend, she is good only for certain males. This leg-shape is common among hikers and college students.

Champagne-Bottle Legs are also referred to as "Ham Legs." The ankles are thin and the calves are excessively thick and heavy. The upper leg is also oversized. The knees are, for the most part, not angular but round like a ball. This female is motherly and affectionate, soft and sociable, devoted with a great deal of sensitivity and temperament. This woman has many friends, is home-loving, full of imagination and has a thoroughly positive view of life. Under some circumstances, she can be stubborn and energetic. She cannot be influenced or won over with flattery.

Doll Legs attract attention because of their delicate contours. The ankles are strong and smooth. The line of the ankle tapers imperceptibly to the calf and complements the knee. This woman is not usually interested in sports or intellectual, spiritual pursuits. She may possess a fiery temperament but it remains hidden and underdeveloped. Her legs stand firmly on earth although its owner lacks initiative and boldness, flexibility and cleverness. She is sociable, good-natured, and makes a loyal wife and cook. She is not mentally curious, wanting only a sense of domesticity and leisure. Rarely will she be a "battle ax."

Elephant Legs, which are also known as "Porterhouse Legs," have a noticeable form because of their stability and exceptional thickness. The ankles barely exist and the entire leg resembles a tree-trunk jetting

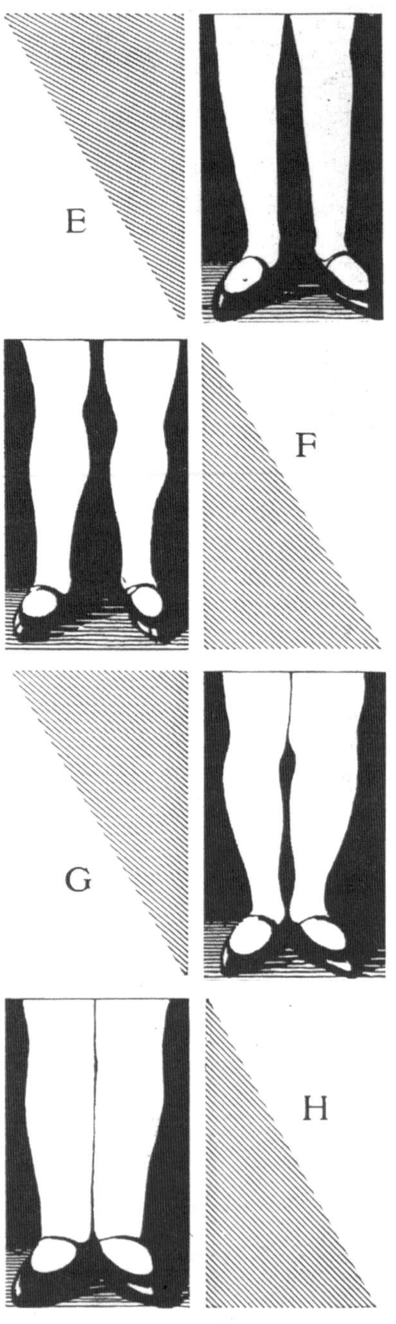

from the shoe. This female can be characterized by her good nature, devotion, sense of motherhood, and phlegmatic soul. For the most part, she is trustworthy, if often pedantic and close-minded (to the point of meanness and, frequently has tunnel-vision). She is suited for hard work. This female may attempt a vain interest in intellectual matters, including art and religion. But, let's face it squarely, the finer aspects of life are lost on her. She seeks peace and tranquility, loves a slow paced life without interruptions. She is superstitious and has no high racial background.

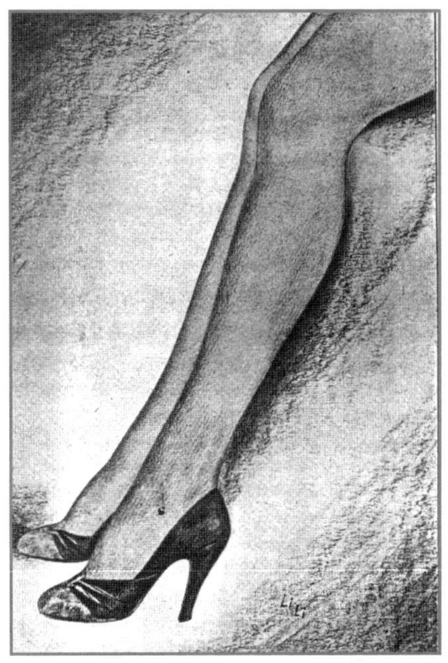

Fly Legs are immediately visible because of their abnormal appearance. There is only skin and bones. The calves are as skinny as the ankles. The upper legs always display a large space when the legs are crossed. (Usually a sign of rickets.) This woman is considered of be modern—that is "decadent"—because she has no calves or buttocks. This woman is characterized as sensible, but nervous. She is weak, yet highly intelligent. The lack of calf means that she is given over to perversity. Altogether, this woman is unfit for marriage or good breeding. Like a fly, she spreads contagion—the contagion of mental illness. Avoid her!

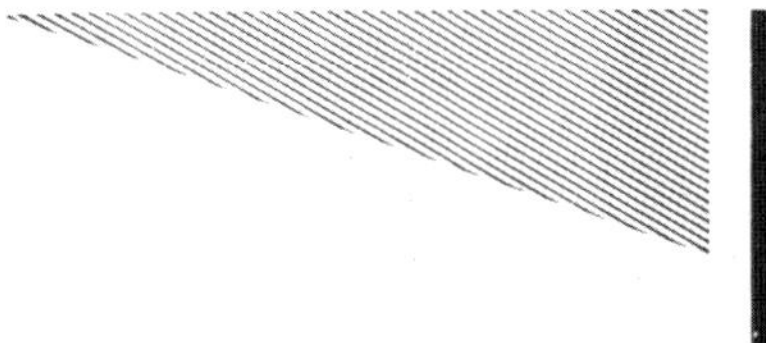

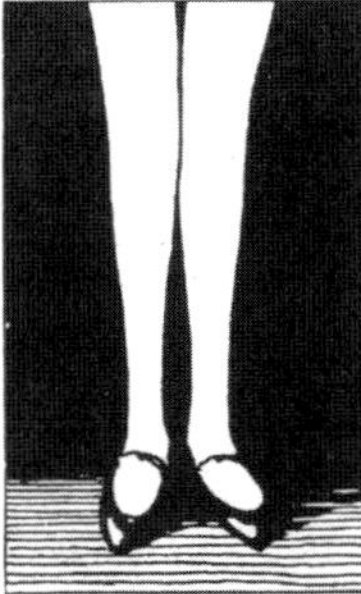

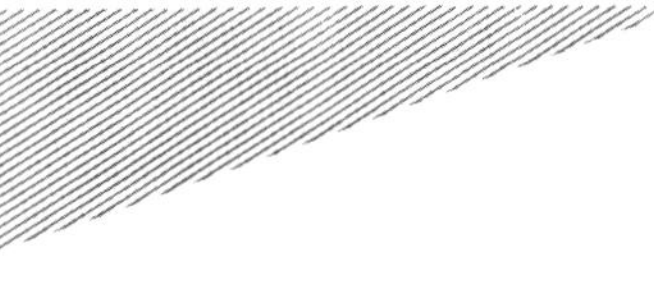

Cover of Max Moecke, **You Too Can Be Clairvoyant!** (1930)

CHAPTER EIGHT

CONQUERING BERLIN

1930-1932

Capital of the Occult

In 1930 Berlin was continental Europe's largest and most dynamic city. Its four million hard-driven inhabitants had long established an unique urban identity, defined by their solipsistic wit, nonstop cynical disposition, and an American-like spirit for innovation. In the years after the Great War, Berlin developed into an international center for finance, publishing, graphic design, fashion, modern architecture, avant-garde cinema and musical theatre. The metropolis also boasted a nightlife unlike any city before or since—with hundreds of restaurants, risqué dance emporiums, cabarets, and honky-tonks. Its erotic subculture included 120 registered gay and lesbian *Lokals* and dance halls; another seven catered solely to gender illusionists, shameless cross-dressers, and gawking tourists.

In 1930 German interest in the occult and supernatural had also reached new heights. Judging from the sales of books and journals specializing in spiritualism and other forms of esoterica—seven astrological weeklies alone competed for the serious horoscope crowd—the numbers of adherents and rabid believers in the mystic arts exceeded twelve million. Berlin alone was estimated to have over 20,000 fortune-tellers, astrologers, tarot-readers, hypnotists, crystal-ball gazers, fakirs, hollow-earth theorists, faith-healing quacks, stigmatics, yogic masters, trance-painters, chiromancers, and bizarrely costumed leaders of secret brotherhoods and doomsday religious cults.

Hanussen had much competition.

He quickly dismissed the storefront Gypsy types and all the lowbrow mesmerists and cranks, no matter how large a following they had assembled.

Josef Weissenberg Observing a "Healing Session," 1930

Josef Weissenberg was a case in point. At seventy, he had already created a vast occult empire, called the New Jerusalem sect, which included houses of prayer; healing clinics; various publications and newspapers, celebrating its man-god founder; a museum run by his daughter; and a getaway agrarian colony just outside Berlin. In addition, Weissenberg promoted his own holistic brand of foodstuffs, which his flock of 100,000 was required to purchase.

Weissenberg's homeopathic healers ("angel-sisters") prescribed Quark for all serious ailments. The yogurt-like cheese (cured in vats and exposed to airborne particles of horse manure) was life's elixir, the sectarians enthused. When a diabetic child died after the white cheese replaced insulin injections, Weissenberg maintained the New Jerusalem parents had simply not applied enough Quark to the boy's body. The walrus-mustached guru was a frequent defendant in the city's criminal courts and a Berlin original.

A New Adversary

More troubling to Hanussen and Frischauer were the activities of the parapsychologist Max Moecke. Billing himself "*The* Clairvoyant of Berlin," Moecke attained a devoted patronage within the city's fashionable clique and surprising credibility among Berlin's hard-nosed correspondents and magazine writers. The editors from the Ullstein and Scherl House publishing conglomerates doted on him.

Like Hanussen, Moecke had achieved a bit of global notoriety. In a piece circulated by the UPI, Moecke was credited with breaking the bank in grand fashion during an excursion to a Monte Carlo casino in 1929. His clairvoyant abilities were tested almost as many times as Hanussen, but Moecke possessed the dashing physicality of a movie star or celebrity boxer—with equally slippery charms.

Moecke conducted evening consultation sessions in a tony Berlin West apartment and was often surrounded by adoring young women and middle-range intellectuals. Adding to his status as a columnist in one of Germany's leading astrological monthlies, the metapsychic set up his own publishing arm in Stuttgart, where employees sold a series of mail-order promotional pamphlets and lessons in autoclairvoyance. And to secure an international standing, the Clairvoyant of Berlin had created an occult "World Federation for the Promotion of Culture" with offices in Newark and Vaduz (Liechtenstein).

Erik wanted to be Moecke or, at least, to overtake him. The unctuous Moecke struck first.

During a performance at the Berlin Beethovensaal on March 15, 1930, Moecke, unrecognized by the Danish seer, placed two photographs in a large envelope. Before it was sealed and delivered to the podium, the slick hometowner removed one of the pics. When Erik started to describe the missing photograph, Moecke challenged his vision. Hanussen stood on the stage in confusion for a few seconds, then quickly realized the con. He grasped the envelope tightly and asserted that it contained the headshot of the adversarial "Clairvoyant M." Erik's claque hissed at the crafty metaphysician and Hanussen requested Moecke's immediate departure. The Ottakring telepath was chastened, yet also relieved by the turn of events. The audience enjoyed the drama. Maddeningly though, it was not the last of Moecke.

In the spring of 1930, six of Berlin's daily newspapers published extremely unflattering reviews of Hanussen's "Experimental Evenings." Erik was denigrated in terms seldom applied to stage performers; he was labeled a low-life swindler, liar, and dangerous con-man. The normally staid *Berliner Volkszeitung* was disgusted with the Master's academic impudence; he treated the knowledgeable Berliners in his audience like "naughty children."

When Hanussen's lawyers demanded retractions and pursued the matter in civil court, Moecke appeared as an expert witness for the press. He testified that Erik was not a bona fide clairvoyant, like himself, merely a cagey provincial trickster. Arrivistes like Hanussen were besmirching the profession, the impervious clairvoyant stated.

Separate lawsuits and restraining orders were filed against Moecke by Erik's legal team in 1930 and 1931. They snared the World Federation clairvoyant in a libelous scheme to defame their client by reprinting a letter Moecke had forged on purloined stationery. They also publicized a nasty sexual harassment allegation made by Moecke's young secretary against her outwardly debonair employer. In the end, Moecke was prohibited from demeaning Hanussen's work. Erik, however, had more radical punishments in mind.

The Counter-Hanussen

As far back as 1924, small-town skeptics and teenage magicians tried their hand at imitating Erik or exposing his tricks. Starting with the Leitmeritz trial, their numbers increased. One amateur clairvoyant in the provinces promoted himself as "Eric van Janussen," another as "Hannussen" (with two "n"s). Their activities were quickly enjoined by Hanussen's busy staff of attorneys.

Wilhelm Gubisch proved more problematic. He was a "Counter-Hanussen." After Erik's arrest in Teplitz, Gubisch toured the variety houses and civic halls of Central Europe, riding high on the growing Hanussen bandwagon. During the first part of his program, called "Invisible Powers," the "spiritual enlightener" duplicated the Dane's routines: muscle reading, psychographology, palmistry-readings, and date-place clairvoyance, the whole production in miniature. Then, as the curtain fell for intermission, Gubisch announced over the audience applause, "Ladies and gentlemen, I have just deceived you!" In the second half of the show, Gubisch and his assistant revealed how each of the miraculous feats was achieved. The Counter-Hanussen evening concluded with a lugubrious warning about the nature of theatrical deception and religious belief.

Wilhelm Gubisch

Hanussen ignored the irritating showman-debunker for several years. Finally in the summer of 1931, he decided to do something about Gubisch. The "spiritual enlightener's" secretary communicated with his boss from the back of the hall through a hidden telephone connection. Gubisch heard the assistant's messages in a receiver that was concealed in his jacket sleeve. At Gubisch's performance in Liebnitz, Erik cut the telephone wire just before the grand finale to Part One. The Counter-Hanussen fumbled, his "psychic" line had gone dead. [See "'Clairvoyant' With a False Bottom," pp. 204.]

Still later, to blunt Gubisch's influence in Berlin, Erik published a pictorial exposé of the Counter-Hanussen's tricks. It may not have occurred to the Mental Wizard of the Ages at the time that doing so also revealed several of his own mentalist ruses.

The "Experimental" Evenings

Hanussen wasted no time establishing himself in Berlin, hiring Georg Lorant, the brother of one of Germany's most important publishers, as his publicist. Filled with fresh vitality, Hanussen was anxious to storm the capital on all fronts. His advisers urged a more cautious approach.

Hanussen performed six Experimental Evenings in Berlin during the first half of 1930. All of them played before enormous, sold-out audiences although they were essentially one-shot affairs in rented halls. Each show required a vast amount of backstage preparation and a constant flow of publicity and civic glad-handing.

The playbills usually listed nine experimental sections: "1) Telepathy, 2) Graphology, 3) The Gomboloy (round beads), 4) Facsimiles, 5) Graphology and

"Experimental Evening" at the Berlin Great Bachsaal, June 1930

Love, 6) Clairvoyance, 7) The Miracle of Konnersreuth, 8) Television, and 9) The Divining Rod." Yet none of the evenings contained all nine parts or followed the printed sequence. By varying and mixing the routines from show to show, impresario Frischauer hoped to attract many of the Hanussen faithful back to successive performances.

Dr. Kröner acted as the local emcee/wonder-struck scientist, welcoming the spectators to the special occasion. Kröner gushed over the phenomenon of Hanussen and outlined the status (or, after May 27, the results) of the Leitmeritz trial. Then with a cabaret flourish—"Ladies and gentlemen, be open and gentle with him!"—the Man Who Knows All was beckoned to the stage.

Erik delivered his standard and sober patter about the unknown powers of the human psyche. (This was sometimes interspersed with references to Therese Neumann.) After all the talk, a rapid-fire demonstration of the Telepathic Post or *The Spy* scenario jolted the evening forward.

Then Hanussen asked spectators to shout out names of famous historical or contemporary personages, known types like Goethe, Gandhi, Wilhelm II, or Mussolini. Erik repeated three or four of their responses and chalked, in various scripts, their names on a blackboard. (He claimed to have memorized five to six hundred signatures of the great and noteworthy.) Frequently, a spectator or two would loudly acknowledge the accuracy of the channeled handwriting. This was followed by a psychobiological dissection of the script and lettering.

Finding a Hidden Object on the Berlin Streets

Audience members were invited to have their penmanship analyzed as well. As many as sixty spectators (mostly young women) mounted the stage and Erik would choose a few susceptible types for his psychographological guesswork. (In the "Graphology and Love" number, which could substitute for the above, Hanussen inscribed the word "love" as a teacher, doctor, and merchant might, comically pointing out how each script displayed occupational differences.)

The high point of the production was invariably the Clairvoyance (or Psychometry) experiment. The Expressionist playwright Ernst Toller and the editor of *Die Weltkultur*, Carl Otto, both submitted personal articles to Hanussen. The histories of their objects were described in such wondrous detail that the writers themselves became part of the Hanussen debate. In Potsdam, a gimlet-eyed singer slipped a ring that she received from Max Reinhardt on one of Hanussen's fingers. Erik asserted that the ring did not actually belong to the singer but to another woman—an artist who suffered from depression and struggled with an addiction. The perky singer reacted with extreme shock: the former owner of the ring was in fact her friend Maria Orska, a stage starlet who had recently died from a cocaine overdose.

The Battle of the Books

Despite—or because of—their acrimonious squabbles and separation, Hanussen and Wahle had wooed Juhn all through Leitmeritz. The former secretary and confidant had been privy to all of Erik's tricks and back-handed schemes. Juhn also was in possession of documents that could land Hanussen in jailhouses in any one of five countries. Luckily, Juhn's fears of being slapped with a perjury suit (if he supported Hanussen) or facing the rancor from his former boss (if he didn't) were unfounded—as were Erik's pretrial anxieties. Havlicek never subpoenaed any of the Dane's associates.

Juhn and his family remained at Hanussen's villa in Warnsdorf. Coincidentally, Gubisch, also from Warnsdorf, began his Counter-Hanussen shows at that time. Although no one suspected it, Juhn was the clandestine source of Gubisch's showbiz exposés, the first act of Juhn's retributions.

The devious impresario brainstormed another venue and one that would exact a profit. Juhn would author a roman à clef that would reveal all the seamy sides of Hanussen's personality. He titled it *Leben und Taten des Hellsehers Henrik Magnus* ("The Life and Career of the Clairvoyant Henrik Magnus"). Juhn was proving to be a formidable enemy.

Henrik Magnus followed the bizarre chronicle of Hanussen's up-and-down existence as an entertainer and mystic. In part, it drew from Juhn's private notes and Erik's autobiographical project that the two had contemplated. Juhn even folded in some paragraphs from Hanussen's 1920 textbook *Gendankenlesen/Telepathie*. Naturally, most names of the real people were changed and other characters were formed from composites of lesser figures. Nonetheless, *Leben und Taten des Hellsehers Henrik Magnus* was unmistakably the life and career of Erik Jan Hanussen.

"The Clairvoyant's Séance" by Rumpelstilzchen (Adolf Stein)

I see Herr Erik Jan Hanussen only as a skillful artist, like all other so-called fakirs who have proven to be charlatans. But the city dweller, the less faith he has, the more he believes in telepaths, clairvoyants, chiromants and whatever they may call themselves. Even such a serious and capable businessman like the former bank director and Secretary of State Dernburg, who sits close to me, has wide-open unskeptic eyes. Or did he really only come because one has to join in the conversation when people talk about Hanussen?

The experimentator gives a long introductory presentation about "The Wonder of Konnersreuth," the stigmatic Therese Neumann, who—he makes me fall asleep—so he claims, puts the listeners in a condition of excitement, which apparently makes them believe in the supernatural.

Then the first experiment is on. Several ladies from the audience who possess "strong imagination" are asked onto the stage. Hanussen chooses four of them. Hmmm. They seat themselves facing us. It catches my attention that he passes behind them looking at their necks. Behind one of the four, he seemingly unintentionally lowers her cape a little bit, apparently to make sure about something.

"Please, ladies, close your eyes!"

Now he tells all of them, the first, the second, the third, and the fourth something which can be colorfully imagined. Number three seems to be "highly sensitive." A young movie actor in front of me, a skeptic, tells me that she has participated in other performances. Erik Jan Hanussen tells her in that she is in a hospital. While her eyes are closed, her body jerks. She convulses, she squirms, Is she in trance? Some of the audience believe it. They catch their breath.

And now the telepath orders all four ladies to imagine a man, a man who is dear to them. He tied to a lonely tree in an open meadow. and his back is bare. Next to him stands a sinister fellow swinging a whip who will crack it on the command of "One!" . . .

Brief silence.

"One!"

Like the crack of a whip, comes this word.

"I thank you, my ladies. Now open your eyes again! And please turn around!"

Look there, all four ladies have—a blood-red welt on their neck skin!

Trembling in the audience. Wild applause.

But I could only laugh, I spared myself from the rest of the experiments and left. The next is supposedly the following: Anyone from the audience can write on a piece of paper a precise date, a precise place, his full name and then Erik Jan Hanussen will tell him precisely what event took place, with all the details. But naturally, hundreds of papers can not be performed, that would take hours. Therefore Erik Jan Hanussen's assistant chooses a few. Enough, enough. Smugly, the "clairvoyant" tells that the Berlin Wintergarten, the great variety theater, offered him a salary of 60,000 Marks if he performed there for a month. Why not? He sure belongs to the variety theater! But no: he has no interests in making money, he says. Plain and noble.

Germania (April 24,1930)

In June 1930 the Viennese Saturn-Verlag, owned by Fritz Ungar, a childhood friend of Juhn, and employer of his writer brother Egon Juhn, announced the publication of Juhn's "novel." *Magnus* could not have been issued at a more commercially auspicious time. Its jacket displayed a Svengali-like Gubisch lurking over a helpless and hypnotized blonde maiden.

Hanussen's lawyers in Berlin took immediate action. They filed an injunction to ban the book as a libelous attack on their client. Magnus' clairvoyant acts were portrayed as contemptible stage deceptions and the main character was presented as a selfish monster, engaging in a host of reprehensible frauds and sexual improprieties. Moreover, the complaint charged that Juhn had plagiarized from Erik's published and unpublished writings, which he had stolen from Hanussen's villa in Warnsdorf.

The attorneys requested that all copies of *Magnus* be withdrawn from international distribution and destroyed. As for personal injury, they wanted Saturn-Verlag and Juhn to pay a fine of 10,000 marks and court costs.

The courtroom struggle started in October 1930 and ended three months later. Juhn received legal assistance from the Potsdam magistrate Albert Hellwig, Hanussen's most energetic nemesis, but to little avail. The Berlin judges found the accused in the wrong and awarded Hanussen's lawyers a complete victory. In April 1931, both Juhn and Ungar petitioned for bankruptcy protection and had themselves declared indigent.

While Juhn prepared for his defense in the summer of 1930, Erik pieced together his "unvarnished" autobiography, *Meine Lebenslinie*. He negotiated a substantial advance from Universitas-Verlag—15,000 marks, or "eggs" as native Berliners called them—and hired Leopold Thoma as his ghostwriter. The impressionistic memoir skirted Erik's complex relationship to his Jewish background, although it did nothing to deny it directly. (He certainly did not claim to be descended from Danish nobility.) The atmosphere and style of the book skipped from self-mocking humor to social invective to maudlin theatrical anecdotes to speculations on the paranormal. The narration, for the most part, seemed heartfelt and believable. Even Hanussen-doubters could have subconsciously found themselves supporting the indefatigible *Jenischmann*.

Among the most curious aspects of the *Bildungsroman* was its final chapter. A lonely author named Hermann Steinschneider visits a washed-out seer named Herr Hanussen in his ugly, cold hotel room. After paying for a consultation session, Steinschneider teases the weary clairvoyant. When asked who he is and what he wants to know, Steinschneider responds with the traditional rejoinder, "You tell me. I'm not the fortune-teller."

Then after answering his own inquiries, Hanussen waxes existential. Steinschneider may have thought that he came to find out about his financial destiny; yet the larger question concerns something utterly nonmaterial: his God-given gifts, his special place in history.

When Hermann returns to the benefits of money—it brings pleasures, friends, security in old age—the clairvoyant reminds him of the German fairy-tale about the Mountain-Spirit and the Magic Turnip Patch. With his supernatural wand, the desolate Mountain-Spirit can transform the lowly vegetables into loving friends and riches. But the metamorphosis is always temporary. In the end, all the people (really parasites and sycophants anyway), all the objects (cars, jewels, penthouses) revert to turnips, which shrivel back into the earth and turn to dust. In the end, death cannot be avoided.

The dispirited Steinschneider bids farewell to the busy, morose clairvoyant. As the man gets up to leave, Hanussen wishes Steinschneider much luck for his book's success.

Meine Lebenslinie hit the stores in Berlin at the end of November 1930, just before the Christmas rush. It sold surprisingly well.

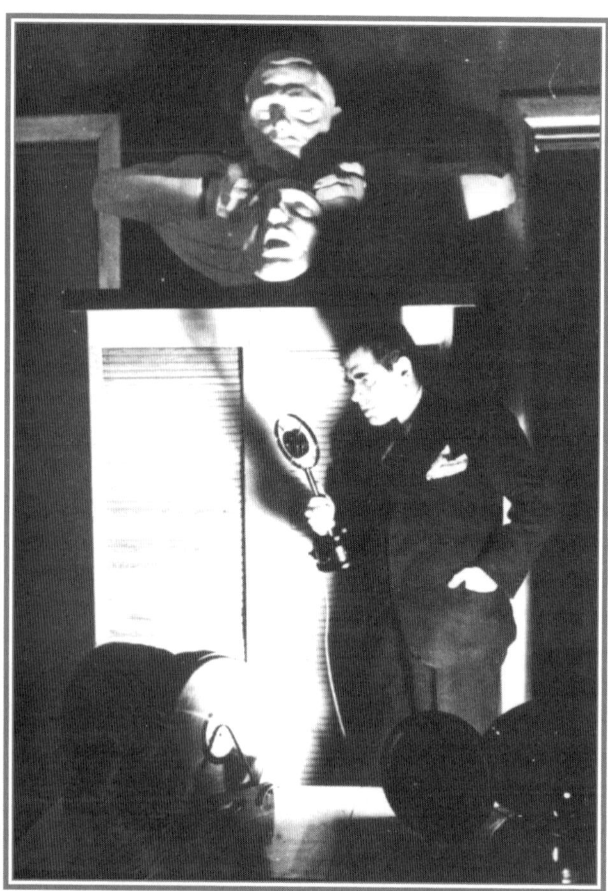

Hanussen Dictating His Autobiography, 1930

In Variety

In his first mystic foray after Leitmeritz, Hanussen had surpassed all expectations. Frischauer knew, however, that the Experimental Evenings in Berlin could not sustain the phenomenon. The steel-hearted metropolis had a notoriously scant attention span. Though ample, the indigenous occult audience was greatly specialized. Almost every daily newspaper had reported on the Danish seer in an article or two; what more was there to write about?

Frischauer wisely changed venues. He offered a twenty-minute version of Hanussen to the variety palaces. The venerable Scala took the first bite and heavily promoted the event. In the middle of September 1930, enigmatic posters were papered around Berlin's kiosks: "HANUSSEN COMES!" "SEVEN MORE DAYS!" "SIX MORE DAYS!"

The minor journalists who previously reported on the Hanussen evenings in the winter and spring had a personal stake in the subject. Most knew about Leitmeritz and the Moecke-Hellwig dispute. Writing about Hanussen gave them an opportunity to discuss other esoteric and spiritual issues. The 100 newspaper writers invited by Scala to the Hotel Eden on September 19, 1930, however, were basically entertainment critics and hotshot columnists. Berlin's finest—Egon Jacobsohn (from *Berliner Zeitung*), Hans Tasiemka (*Tempo*), Walther Kiaulehn (*Berliner Tageblatt*), Herbert Ihering (*Berliner Börsen-Courier*), Egon Lehrburger (*Süddeutsche Sonntagspost*)—had heard about the Dane but never attended any of his productions.

Erik made a sensational appearance at the Eden press conference. With appropriate ironic flourishes, he defined clairvoyance as an elevated point on Einstein's time-and-space continuum and demonstrated the use of the Gomboloy. During the Q-and-A session, Hanussen predicted good fortune for Germany's depressed industrial stocks and the nation itself. Huge radium deposits were about to be discovered in Bavaria, and the Polish Corridor would eventually be reincorporated into the Republic. Unemployment, in just a few months, would fall to insignificant levels. And a right-wing coalition, without the Nazis, would soon rule the country under a "democratic dictatorship."

Some reporters tossed off the entire Hanussen affair as yet another silly round of sideshow blarney; this occult thing was merely metaphysics for servant-girls. Others, like *12-Uhr Blatt's* PEM (Paul Markus), enjoyed the revelry. As a journalist, Markus confessed that he needed to facilitate such tabloid stimulations. A pretend prophet was hardly newsworthy; a true clairvoyant, on the other hand, was a bankable feature.

Hanussen headlined at the Scala during the week of September 20-26. Paul Tabori, a twenty-two-year-old Hungarian journalist with a family interest in psychic research, attended one of the evenings. (Between 1906 and 1944, Tabori's father studied parapsychology and unconventional religious occurrences throughout Central Europe. In the middle and late 1960s, when occult scholarship expanded overnight into a minor segment of America's fast-growing book market, Paul was considered among its most popular and prolific authors.)

The show made an indelible impression on Tabori. Erik chose three subjects from the audience. The first was Tabori's journalistic colleague, a reporter from the *Nachtexpress*. Hanussen announced that the writer had originally sought to be a lawyer but later failed in his exams; he played the horses, was two months overdrawn on his salary, and almost lost his position at the paper because of an indiscretion with his boss' fiancée. Tabori marveled at Hanussen's pronouncements. They were news to him and, as confirmed by his friend, true.

Next, Erik asked a rotund gentleman to the stage. His dinner jacket was the object of a psychometric analysis. According to the Dane, it lived through "sixteen weddings and twenty-one funerals." Hanussen comically revealed that the man was an undercover tax agent, who came to the revue in an official capacity. He was investigating the number of Scala tickets sold that night. Finally, the head of a private bank was called up to the podium. The clairvoyant switched moods, warning the man of an impending personal disaster. His establishment was about to go up in flames. There was still four minutes to save the place from incineration. Hanussen pushed the frightened banker toward a telephone in the wings. It was a good closer. [*Companions of the Occult*, (New York: University, 1965)]

Another performance was described by Hubert Bücken. Hanussen requested that the newspaper crowd in the front-row seats pick four candidates to be subjects for an experiment. Erik took one, an elder financier, and sat him on a chair. Standing behind the man, Hanussen rubbed his temples and whispered a hypnotic induction. The financier quickly slumped in his chair. "You are five years old," Erik announced. "It is Christmas and you have just received a ball as a gift. Play with the ball!" Like an agile, reckless child, the old financier skipped around the stage, chasing an imaginary ball. Over the waves of laughter emanating from the hall, Hanussen shouted, "Watch out! The Christmas tree!" The man-child tripped and started to cry; he reacted as if he had toppled the tree. Erik moved the story forward: "Now your father scolds you and locks you in a room there. You have to go to the toilet. Yet the door is locked! Do you see the vase on the table?" The financier nodded boyishly and lifted an imaginary vase. Before the man could unbutton his pants, Hanussen ended the scene and broke the spell. With a red face, the financier returned to his seat in the house. He did not understand why the spectators around him were shrieking and clapping.

Hanussen Reading Fan Mail

The next two men were hypnotized in believing that they were a feuding dog and cat. Again, Erik concluded with a haunting image. He placed an attractive young woman, the secretary for an editor of a large newspaper, into a trance. He pointed to a pillar near the cloakroom and informed her that it was her boyfriend, back from a journey. She ran to the column, embraced it, and began to kiss it all over. The voyeuristic audience watched transfixed as the poor girl opened her blouse and erotically rubbed against the post. After a few moments, Hanussen woke the secretary from the embarrassing suggestion. [*Meine Lebenslinie* (Berlin: Universitas, 1930).]

Ismet Dzino

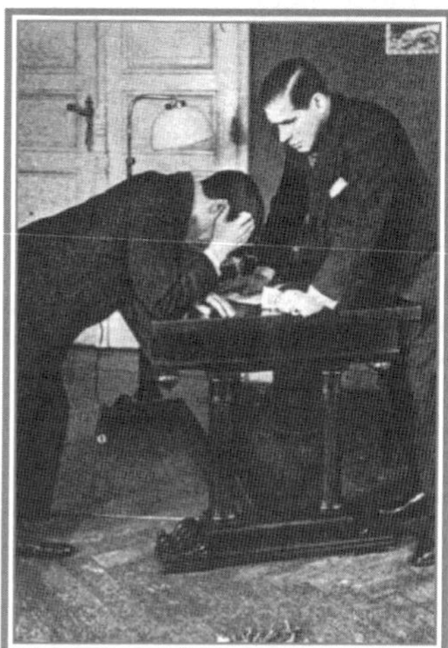

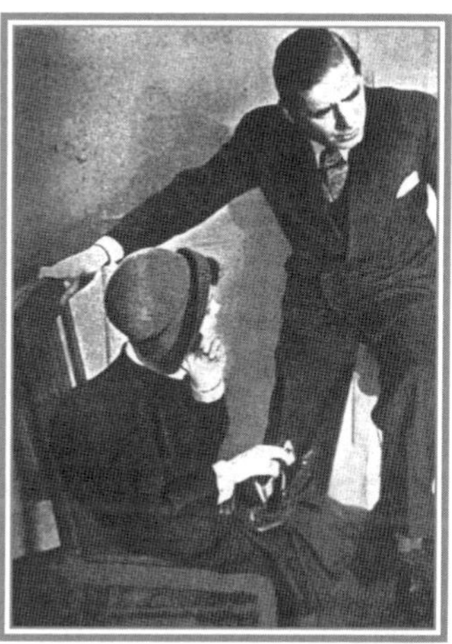

Three Consultation Sessions

Erik decided to replace Frischauer. He needed an *echte* Berliner for his consultation work. Frischauer had done well as an impresario and publicist. Still, Hanussen required more than a business associate; he yearned for a friend to accompany him on his nightly *Bummels* after the shows and sessions; a close-mouthed and resourceful lackey to open the office in the afternoons and conduct the indispensable back-alley researches; a trusted sidekick. In short, a Juhn without the ego.

At the bar in the Adlon Hotel, Erik found his man. Ismet Aga Dzino typified a whole class of male adventurers and knockabouts who subsisted on the edges of Berlin's seamy demimonde. Most had served in the Central Powers armies during the war and never fully adjusted to civilian life. Dzino's father was a famous oddity, the only Muslim commander in the Austro-Hungarian Army. Dzino himself fought in the Balkans and briefly worked as a detective. When Hanussen met the distinguished-looking "Turk," Dzino was heavily in debt and embroiled in an unpleasant love affair. The Bosnian jack-of-all-trades owed over 4,000 marks to casino managers, bookies, and other such Friedrichstadt "creditors."

Erik offered to cover all of Dzino's losses in exchange for his services as secretary and right-hand man. The bon vivant/gambler responded somewhat coldly and nonplused, which Hanussen took as a good sign. Dzino ultimately accepted the position. His involvement with the clairvoyant enterprise would later seal both Hanussen's fate and his own.

The Palais de Danse, a pleasure palace and dance hall on Behrenstrasse (formerly the Alkazar, formerly the Tempo! Tempo!), was one of Hanussen's favorite watering spots. Erik brought Dzino there one night and introduced him to Grace Cameron, an English-born beauty queen from Belgium. The gold-digging hostess had once spurned the Dane's attempts to seduce her. Hanussen reverted to clairvoyant mode and

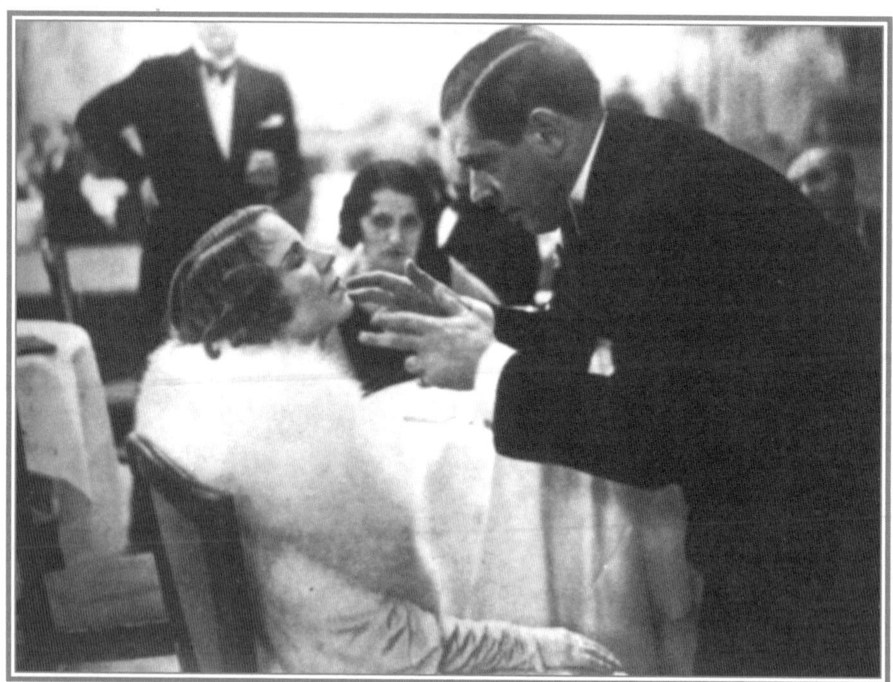

Hanussen Hypnotizing Grace Cameron

prophesied that Cameron would meet her future husband under a huge chandelier and, according to his reading of the stars, die under one.

That evening, the icy beauty queen came over to Erik's table and met Captain Dzino. The three laughed heartily as Hanussen ordered rounds of champagne; overhead stood a magnificent crystal chandelier.

Two weeks later, after a whirlwind courtship, two of Berlin's flotsam, the elegant Belgian and the elegant Turk, wed in Vienna.

Settling In

Prosperity altered Hanussen's lifestyle. He moved from the Eden Hotel, where he stayed with Fritzi since June, to an apartment on Westendalle. The couple quarreled openly over Erik's many affairs and ridiculous accusations that it was Fritzi who was cheating on him. They separated in the winter of 1930 and formally divorced in February 1932. Fritzi never responded to Hanussen's vicious detractors, who hoped that her inside knowledge of his duplicitous methods would help bring the Wizard down. In fact, Fritzi and Hanussen remained intimate friends. They still shared eight dogs.

On the stylish Kurfürstendamm avenue, Hanussen opened a private consultation parlor, where he dazzled, advised, cured, and befriended wealthy, eminent or spiritually inert Berliners. His fees, at 200 marks per session, were exorbitant by any standard, but the word on the street was good, very good. For legal protection, Hanussen's clients had to sign an agreement that acknowledged the clairvoyant's harmless advice as a private amusement. (The patrons had plenty of time to peruse the document's fine print. Dzino often kept them waiting in the Kudamm foyer for two or three hours.)

Hanussen soon counted among his inner circle the cultural elite of the city: singer and stage impresario Leo Slezak; the novelist Alfred Döblin, who had recently returned to his Hebraic roots; film starlet Lilian Harvey; the conferencier Paul Morgan; opera great Richard Tauber, whom Erik cured of his stage fright; Nobel Prize Laureate Thomas Mann; the fantasy writer Hanns Heinz Ewers; and the up-and-coming Jewish-Hungarian actor, Peter Lorre, who considered Hanussen a playful evening companion. In 1931, Georg Kaiser, another German Expressionist playwright, wrote a comedy about Erik, *The Clairvoyant.* The lead character was named "Sneederhan"—a scrambling of "Steinschneider" and "Hanussen"—and urged the Dane to play himself. Scheduling and legalities blocked the coup de théâtre.

Showcasing Berlin's greatest revue palaces, consulting for its richest and most illustrious citizens, emerging as the heady topic for all of its leading newspapers and pictorial weeklies, Hanussen was finally where he wanted to be: everywhere. He wrote an article on the Indian Mango Tree Wonder for the *Berliner Illustrirte Zeitung* (October 31, 1930) and explained how he unearthed the fakirs' trickery. At Berlin's Hoppegarten, the city's racetrack and haunting grounds for society ladies and their gigolo attendants, Erik handed out betting tips and gaming advice.

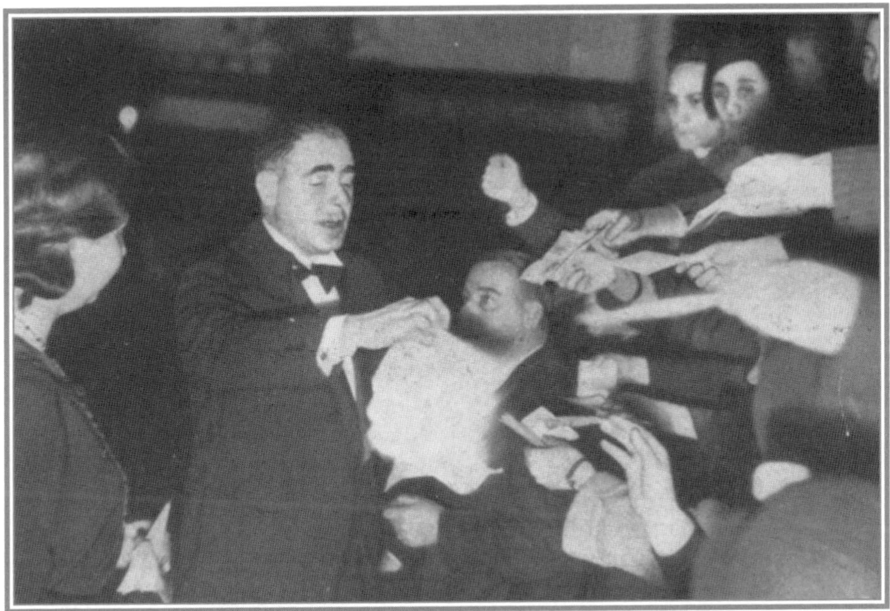

Hanussen Collecting Date-Place Notes. (Peter Lorre, Right of Hanussen)

His success wasn't enough. The man from the Ottakring required even more.

He procured a sanitarium where a panoply of occult cures was offered. He invented a hormonal cream to increase male virility and female desire. His new millions now secured him luxury cars, seven apartments, and a yacht (costing 30,000 marks) larger than any Rockefeller might ponder.

The Magister Ludi of Sex

In the celebrated nocturnal demiworld of Berlin of the early '30s, Hanussen was immediately recognizable by the bevy of stunning actresses at his side, each more beautiful than the next, each clustered in a net of jewels and attired in revealing dresses that the master himself had designed. A menacing retinue of six pistol-toting bodyguards in short brown overcoats hovered close by.

Women, who constituted the majority of Erik's patrons, regarded him as a mystic Don Juan and thrilled to be in his presence. Like the shopkeepers in Leitmeritz, they addressed him as "Master." It was a mutual admiration. Hanussen was slavishly dependent on their dizzying affections. He had the insatiable sexual appetite of a runaway teenager.

On his cabin cruiser the "Ursel IV" (nicknamed the "Yacht of the Seven Sins"), Hanussen paraded his new wealth excessively. Lavish feasts with drugs, like mescaline and peyote, that even sophisticated Berliners didn't know about, were the order of the day. Naked women and boys from every land mingled with Hanussen's selected coterie and later performed shocking revues when the Master himself was personally occupied. On the shore of Lake Scharmutzel, lucky neighbors observed the going-ons with binoculars.

Advertisement for Hanussen's Sex Creme, **Hanussen-Magazin** (January 1932)

After midnight, the cad-about-town demonstrated another private specialty: his ability to hypnotize women into sexual frenzy and then sustained orgasm. A German revue-dancer and film ingenue, Henriette Margarethe Hiebel, otherwise known on the nightclub circuit as La Jana,

The Ursel IV

often hosted the event and sometimes acted as a willing participant. Even for a Berlin accustomed to decadent displays, this was a bit much.

One "Seven Sins" affair became legendary. At a late-night party for film and theatre people, a wild young artist "Ruth" (probably the decadent painter Elfriede Lohse-Wächtler) begged Erik to hypnotize her to do something "unimaginable." Once Ruth was under his spell, Hanussen asked his august audience for suggestions. They agreed upon an American-style striptease, although none had actually

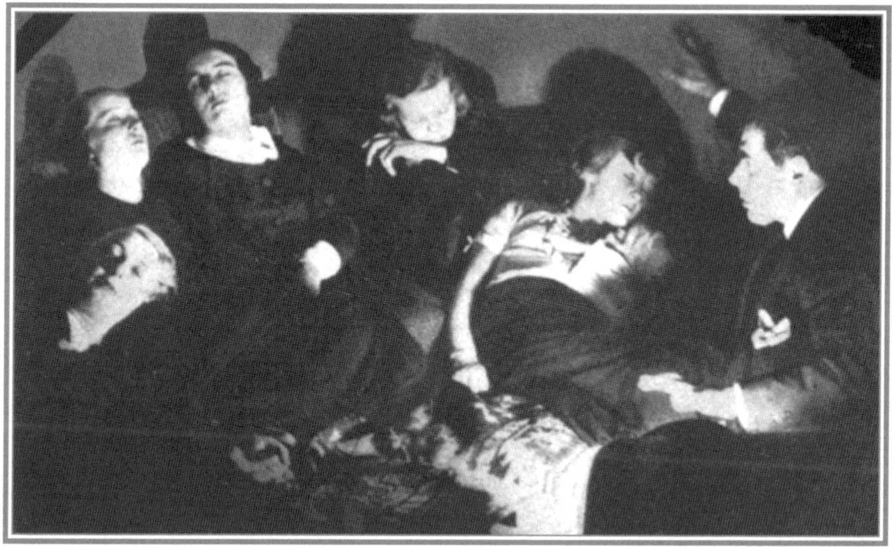

Hanussen Hypnotizing a Circle of Women

seen one before. Dzino put a record on the Victrola. Ruth shed her skimpy wares and pranced around the lower deck à la Isadora. After being awakened from her trance amusement, Ruth requested another hypnotic display with Max Reinhardt's in-house playwright, Ferdinand Bruckner, as Erik's next subject. The poet acquiesced unenthusiastically and was commanded by the hypnotiseur to sexually embrace Ruth. Like a horny automaton, Bruckner chased Ruth into a corner, kicked his pants off, and ravished her like a lusty stevedore in heat as their friends and colleagues roared.

Ruth proclaimed it was the best sexual experience of her life. Bruckner, however, recalled nothing about the episode. Among Berlin's literary set, the Ursel sex-game was rich café prattle for weeks.

And then there was the story of the beautiful Baroness. (Alternately identified as Verena Prawitz, Sybille Pongraz, or Barbara van Swieten, depending on the source, yet always described as twenty-seven years old in 1930.) She met Hanussen in 1927 and was informed at a private consultation that she would leave her loveless marriage to a baron in a few weeks and become Erik's paramour. Three years later, instead of the four weeks as foretold, she reappeared at Hanussen's office. The Baroness' disgust with the arrogant telepath had turned into an erotic obsession. Hanussen escorted her around town and introduced her to his party-mad friends on the Ursel. The Baroness stayed by Erik's side for slightly over one year. She was human proof of his Berlin success.

Opposition

A debate over the strength and veracity of Hanussen's omnipotent powers animated many brandy-and-cigar gatherings in Berlin's offices and boardrooms. But at the racetrack, in the stock exchange, and back in the variety hall and consultation room, the man had a Midas touch. Naturally with each bright-eyed convert, an equally passionate antagonist was born.

The newspapers were split on the question of Hanussen. Indirectly, it reflected their political agendas. The Socialist and Nationalist press went almost two to one against the outlandish occultist. Kurt Tucholsky, writing in *Die Weltbühne* (April 1930) under the pseudonym Ignaz Wrobel, had a grand time ridiculing "Der Hellseher." Hanussen was quoted as saying that the Weimar Republic, the German Communist Party, and the freedom of the press would all expire in two or three years. The middle-of-the-road publishing houses, if they weren't already supporting Moecke, endorsed the loony spectacle. The Nazis, however, had little time for such piddling stage chatter.

At first, the Communist dailies were quiet. Hanussen represented religion and magical thinking, and they opposed him. In November and December 1930, for instance, Hans Hein wrote a twenty-part series, "The Magicians from Berlin," for the left-wing *Welt am Abend*. Hanussen was Hein's first target and filled three and one-half segments. Erik's hocus-pocus fared no worse, in Hein's assessment, than

Weissenberg or Madame Sylvia's arcane machinations at their respective lairs.

Another Communist, Arthur Koestler, working as a science editor for the liberal Ullstein chain, decided to construct a different examination. He would test the gullible aptitude of the Hanussen patron, rather than the man himself. The twenty-six-year-old Hungarian wangled an invitation from Erik to meet with him at his private apartment at 17 Bendlerstrasse. (Koestler later described the refurbished 14-room suite as decked out tastelessly in lacquered "Neo-Gothic, Al Capone" fashion. Because he was there in the daytime, the journalist missed out on Hanussen's decorating trompe-l'oeil: a wall-sized pornographic mural that revealed itself only under incandescent illumination.)

With Koestler was the crusty head-porter from the Ullstein building and a female journalist. Erik wanted to loosen up the skeptics with a few drinks and demonstrate some preliminary telepathic tricks. Koestler sternly refused the friendly intro. The Puritanical scientist coveted only hard facts for his objective investigation into Psychometry and its adherents.

Hanussen briskly turned to the porter and demanded the set of keys from his left trouser-pocket. The man complied and Erik clutched the "contact-objects" with one hand and pressed his forehead with the other. In a trancelike voice, Erik told the story of the keys: there was a burglary, an act of violence, an inheritance by someone with a liver disease or chronic constipation, a healthy birth after personal anguish, a stupendous recovery from a lethal illness.

The porter shook his head. In the thirty years he possessed the keys, none of those incidents occurred. Koestler thought that he had his story. The other journalist was amazed, however. She maintained that every one of the mediumistic images the Dane just described took place in her apartment complex during the last twelve months. Maybe her proximity to the porter—she sat on his left side on the taxi ride to Hanussen's—had rubbed off on the keys. Koestler sighed. Mankind's thirst for miracles threatened corroborative laboratory evidence and his Scientific Socialism. [*Arrow in the Blue* (New York: 1952)]

Hanussen Parody: Man, "Why am I here? You're the Clairvoyant. You Tell Me!" **Der Querschnitt** (December 1932)

Empire of the Intellect

Hanussen wanted to be taken seriously. He begged to be known as something other than a celebrated clairvoyant. The Dane fancied himself as a true artist and social thinker. Like other overnight achievers without formal education, Erik longed for the respectability of the scholar and intellectual. He appeared with some frequency on German radio and allowed himself to be filmed and interviewed.

In March 1931, as a promotion for *Berliner Illustrierte Nachtausgabe*, Hanussen dictated an entire science fantasy novel about the destruction of New York City while in trance. Under Thoma's hypnotic control, Erik described a journey to the future, into the year 2320. Manhattan was about to be ravaged in a massive tidal wave caused by a government geological experiment gone awry. All that stood between the man-made deluge and the lives of millions was the mysterious character of Dr. Hermann Kennah. Known as the "doctor of death," Kennah, a German immigrant (and secret Jew), maniacally attempted to prevent the metropolis' doom with the application of his atomic ray apparatuses. In the end, he was unsuccessful. New York's skyline crumbled and its population was overcome in the watery devastation. The Hanussen-Thoma session, which received a goodly amount of reportage, was repeated over a seven-evening marathon. The results were recorded on 46 wax cylinders and preserved.

The unlikely intellectual continued to pontificate on the intricate finances of state planning and the likelihood of scientific breakthroughs, particularly in television photography and radioactive weaponry. Of course, there was a limit to newspaper and radio coverage of Erik's pronouncements. The man was an entertainer and a nutty one at that.

Publisher

Thoma Shows Hanussen the First Issue of **Die Andere Welt**, 1931

In the summer of 1931, after a tour of Danzig and the Netherlands interspersed with many difficulties and petty lawsuits, Hanussen purchased a Breslau printing firm. It was a first step, he hoped, in the creation of a self-promoting media empire. Erik hired a team of graphic artists, writers, and newspapermen. He gave the bimonthly journal the rather generic title of *Die Andere Welt* and later renamed it the *Hanussen-Magazin*.

The contradictions, anxieties, and murky tensions of Hanussen's world were apparent in its two issues. The magazines featured self-help and human interest stories framed in flashy tabloid styles with amusing graphics and carefully designed photomontage pictures.

Wonders for 50 Pfennig

Between the Zoo and the Kurfürstendamm

von Erik Jan Hanussen

Journalists are supposed to write about their fantastic adventures. Beside the reports they publish, writers also jot down their personal accounts how they got the story. These secondary descriptions—of surmounting enormous obstacles to obtain the necessary information—often provide the reader with lofty and instructive lessons.

My great mission was not merely to consult with the famous Seer Loni but to photograph him at work. This magician resides temporarily in a empty building on Joachimsthaler Strasse and makes his esoteric wisdom totally accessible to the broad populace for 50 pfennig. Other than Loni "the Soothsayer," one can discover in the huge room of the former restaurant a whole multitude of pleasures.

There is a roulette area for the common man. For a 20 pfennig wager, one can win 1.40 marks. One must be facile, however, to roll the little ball over the spinning roulette wheel at the precise moment. Only then will it fall in the proper slot. This, by the way, is no game of chance since, according to a posted sign, all games of chance are forbidden by law. Successfully tossing the ball into the right red or black slot is no more determined by chance than the mastery of medieval barbers curing the ill.

In another corner, there is a huge, electrical dial with numbers. Around the wheel is a menagerie of every kind of teddy bear. At that game, one can test his skill by guessing which number (of thirty-five) will stop dead at the top pointer. I do not know how many correct passes are required to win a halfway decent teddy bear. My understanding of this game remains somewhat limited.

On the other hand, I have rarely witnessed such an eloquent and hypnotic speaker as the man at the spinning wheel. He overwhelms one with his cascade of words, with his Mississippi-like outpouring of approbations. He can sucker anyone with his peerless descriptions of the one hundred teddy bears. All politicians should learn from this man. His "Bear-Spiel" has no match.

Next to the teddy bear table is a mystic pavilion, the entranceway to the tent of Loni the Soothsayer. This wigwam is decorated with a thousand emblems and images: the Zodiac signs of Cancer and Virgo, magic quadrants, and secret slogans like "Spitting is Officially Forbidden."

Loni wears a silver turban over his charmingly madeup face. His powdered cheeks have muttonchop sideburns penciled over them and his lips are painted deep red. I must say that Loni looked suspicious to me. Yet despite my first impression, he turned out to be a very good seer.

Standing outside the tent, Loni, the enigmatic midget, keeps a silent watch. Here my journalistic struggle began. Loni did not want his picture taken. I made him a tempting offer: in exchange for a few photos, I would give him a season pass to any of my consultation sessions, free and valid until Easter.

While Loni listened to my overture, the proprietor of the Joachimsthaler establishment suddenly appeared and asked me and my party to leave the premises immediately. Photographs are not allowed. We ignored his request and he called for a policeman.

Astonishingly, the hand of the law quickly materialized. The situation was about to become ugly. So I moved into the roulette area and sat down behind the croupier. He turned around and offered me a free round. By then I had won the sympathy of the gamblers around the table. They protested against the owner's hard-hearted treatment of me.

Afterwards I conversed with the teddy bear barker, who also supported me. He told the proprietor, "This man can photograph my booth as much as he wants. I have rented this space and he can photograph me if it pleases me." The owner examined my equipment and we ended our feud.

Now one naturally asks why did they try to stop us from taking pictures if the place is so harmless. They have their reasons. First, there are certainly many guests at the Zoppot am Zoo who do not want to have their presence advertised. Then there is the issue of gambling itself: games of chance are technically illegal, but tolerated in back-alley emporiums if discreetly run.

At the end of the evening, Loni read the cards of a woman he assumed was part of our crowd: "Fräulein, you paid me 50 pfennig from your purse and did not request your date to pay for it. In small things, a lady must always be generous. You don't allow others to care for you. When you go to the wash-room at a bar, I know, you do not even let your date hand you the required ten pfennig. From friends, one should always accept gifts of less than five marks." This Loni indeed possesses worldly wisdom.

As we were getting up to go, Loni said something that was very amusing. He probably recognized me at that point.

Because I arrogantly offered to tell Loni's fortune, he prophesied, I would be cast into Hell, my skull would tilt to one side and it would twirl around in a perpetual grin.

He concluded with this personal admonition to me, "Sir, one viper does not burrow itself into the eye of another viper."

More profound words I have never heard before or since.

Erik Jan Hanussen's **BW** (February 12, 1932)

Although its appeal was obviously directed at the devotees of the occult, Hanussen also aimed for a large, middle-class readership. Prominent writers and artists like Gerhart Hauptmann and Conrad Veidt furnished pieces on their experiences with the paranormal. Subscribers were encouraged to apply for memberships in the "Hanussen Society," where tickets to stage productions and items like the Gomboloy and a Hanussen 78 rpm disk were offered at a fifty percent discount. Clairvoyant workshops and discussion groups formed around the magazine.

In January 1932, Hanussen added to his publishing domain a new tabloid journal entitled *Berliner Woche*, the "Week in Berlin." Sounding nearly identical to an entrenched Berlin weekly, he was forced to rename it several times. Under any title, the venture was deemed a phenomenal success. In a mere nine months, circulation of the *Hanussen-Zeitung* skyrocketed to 38,000 copies then to 140,000 from an initial run of 8,000.

Erik's seamless mix of occult news, Berlin local color, entertainment listings, erotic graphics, and ironic treatment of the political scene attracted a wide readership. Hanussen frequently presented himself in the *BW* travelogues as both a bon vivant Everyman and a true Worker of Miracles.

On page 201 is a typical article. (Dzino, who accompanied the master on the comic excursion, is the mustached man, wearing the debonair hat.)

Although the *BW* established Hanussen as a man-about-town, his deep longing for social respectability remained unfulfilled. The Great One with an invented Danish pedigree, despite immense popularity and affluence, was still a mere showman—with a publishing outlet—to fashionable Berliners.

The smirking contempt that Erik often expressed directly to his adoring, downscale audiences was probably equally addressed to his private self.

But as Hanussen's fortunes rose, those of Germany fell.

The Crisis in Weimar

The economic downturn, which erupted in 1929, had not yet been contained. Long-established banks closed their doors permanently. Bankruptcies among the middle class and landowners soared. Shaken Ruhr industrialists slowed production. And, most threatening to the already weakened social fabric, unemployment rates tripled; eight million German workers were now without work or basic means of survival.

The political process had been stymied. At the national Reichstag and in the provincial assemblies, the traditional parties offered few lasting solutions. Their patrician bickering invariably canceled out whatever short-term bromides the resourceful bureaucrats could concoct. Absolutely no common ground was found as coalition-party cabinets shifted by the month and votes of no-confidence in the Reichstag became the seasonal resolution to the turmoil.

The German public responded to the deadlock in unique and sometimes unexpected ways. Big city thrillseekers intensified their pursuit of back-alley pleasures. Those ground down materially and spiritually by the endless civic chaos gravitated perilously into beckoning arms of religious fanatics and "kohlrabi" prophets like Weissenberg and his ilk.

Others, tens of millions, suddenly enlisted in or supported the extremist parties on the political fringe. More than three million militant workers swelled the ranks of the German Communist Party.

Adolf Hitler's National Socialists did even better, enlarging their 1930 Reichstag membership to 107. Previously only 12 Brown-Shirted representatives sat uneasily in that eminent body. In just two years, the radical Nazi movement had increased its electoral might by a factor of nine, or by seven and a half million new votes. The political pundits were stunned at these Reichstag tallies.

Sophisticated Berliners viewed Hitler as a hysteric *Auslander* and his Nazi zealots as little more than thuggish losers, hawking a senseless racist ideology, adorned with swastika-laced trinkets.

In 1932, however, heavily armed militias from rival Communist and Nazi factions roamed Germany's streets at will. Both thrived on agitation and public disruption. Riots and murderous violence followed them everywhere they appeared. Municipal police services, like the national politicians, seemed helpless against the sworn enemies of democratic rule. The Army continually threatened to reestablish order by the application of extraordinary measures.

Support for Nazi tactics fell. The electorate was having second thoughts about its campaign of nonstop terror and the Party coffers were effectively depleted by February 1932. Hitler's uncompromising stand to be appointed Chancellor, a virtual mathematical and political impossibility, was openly challenged by the Nazi movement's inner council. Talk of replacing Hitler as the Party's figurehead gained momentum. The future could not look worse for the long-suffering Führer.

Hanussen, like other Berliners of note, had more than a passing interest in the unstable political scene. He was frequently asked to comment on it, almost always giving upbeat predictions on the nation's glorious destiny. Yet he himself subscribed to no specific partisan stance.

The typical Hanussen's *BW* reader, he felt, had far more interest in learning the formulas for magnetic healing or how to achieve success and marital bliss through hypnotic suggestion. Hard news in his tabloid veered to exposés on the habits of ten-year-old prostitutes or mysterious facts about the kidnapping of Charles Lindbergh's infant son, or the astounding feats of Togo, the Telepathic Wonder Dog.

All of this changed on the morning of March 25, 1932, when Hanussen issued an electoral premonition.

"CLAIRVOYANCE" WITH A FALSE BOTTOM

by Erik Jan Hanussen

Where there is cheese, there are maggots. Where a courageous man goes his solitary way, the vultures circle: Erik Jan Hanussen takes aim at a certain Herr G and his personality as "the Enlightener." It would be superfluous to even speak of this man, unknown in distant circles, if the occasion weren't so convenient to debunk him and his kind once and for all. This occurs in the following letter, which Erik Jan Hanussen addressed to a journalist in the town where Herr G. had been drawing attention to himself.

—The editor.

Dear Sir:

It was most kind of you to send me your article on the Enlightener's séance, marked in red, which a certain Herr G. held in your town under the patronage of the People's Education Association.

With great pleasure did I read your three-column article with its bold heading, "Hanussen's Debunker." I could imagine the powerful impact this performance must have had on your town and its occult milieu. Since I have had the honor of speaking and experimenting at numerous occult lectures hosted by you, I feel obligated to reply to the otherwise uninteresting performance of the respective Herr Magician. All the more so, since you yourself once created extraordinary publicity for me during my tour of E. and printed the most flattering things about me. Therefore, I can understand the pang of guilt that you must feel when suddenly a man from Leipzig shows up in your town to disprove my clairvoyant experiments.

Let us first recapitulate what happened in your town: A short, corpulent man stepped forth as a clairvoyant. Apparently, he performed the most amazing occult experiments, recovered hidden objects, read thoughts from sealed letters—indeed, he even displayed the clairvoyant ability to predict the times and places of the events.

Everything was bewildering, since one observed here a first-class phenomenon, a man who demonstrated all the things that I myself, as a clairvoyant, once exhibited. The audience was enthused and responded with applause.

Then a horrible embarrassment was cast over the excited spectators when G. announced point-blank that he has fooled them—that everything he demonstrated was nothing less than a swindle and a fraud. I can imagine the shock that this exclamation must have triggered in the lawyers, doctors, teachers, engineers, and other intellectuals in the audience who never thought of themselves as born idiots. Certainly, it was not pleasant to be informed of this by some odd and utterly innocuous man.

Dear friend, your annoyance at your ignorance and alleged gullibility was so great that you attacked all occultism in your article.

But, sir, you are absolutely wrong. You were a victim to an artist who simply used your lack of expertise to feign cheap magic tricks, which can be had for pennies in any good magic store for occult phenomena. This utterly unskilled magician did not unmask clairvoyance, but rather demonstrated the purely undisputed possibility of feigning real phenomena by means of primitive tricks. In the company of professional magicians, G. most probably would be laughed off the stage.

I would naturally not consider it an art if I had three paid persons in the room who would respond "Yes" and "Amen" to everything in order to perform my amazing experiments. I would not consider it an art to read sealed letters if the contents of these were being transmitted to me over a microphone. It would be terribly easy for me and other clairvoyants to exchange slips of paper in a cupped hand.

Do you honestly believe, sir, that it would be possible for me to drag a microphone in my frock sleeve and under the table without being exposed? Do you believe that I use a hat with a false bottom when sharing the stage with Professor Dessoir or Ernst Toller? I am therefore giving you 15 minutes of instruction in "Clairvoyance with a False Bottom." Then, you will be able to hold enlightenment séances à la G. and hire yourself out to associations just like the "Enemy of Clairvoyants." Below, I will reveal the entire program of the so-called Enlightener:

1ST EXPERIMENT: THE MARKED ENVELOPES

G.'s "secretary" distributes a number of envelopes to the public and requests that questions of general nature be inserted in them. After a short while he collects them and then hands them to the "clairvoyant," who relates to the spectator details about their life that are often true.

EXPLANATION: The secretary takes envelopes from prominent people in the hall. In the case of a gentleman with a full beard, for example, he creases the left corner of the envelope; for a very corpulent lady, the middle. Once G. has collected the envelopes, he holds his forehead and begins: "This envelope is from a man with a very dignified appearance. Formerly he was smoothly shaven, now he wears a full beard. He appears to be a professor by occupation," etc. Or for a woman: "This envelope is from a woman whom I must warn of excessive use of obesity remedies." Most commonly, the "clairvoyant" describes two or three people whom he knows a lot about. This information is obtained earlier from his patrons, such as the chairman of the People's Education Association.

2ND EXPERIMENT: INTERPRETING DESTINIES

The "clairvoyant" selects a couple of elderly ladies, who appear to be extremely naive. Then he recites a few banal phrases: "You are good-natured and have experienced a lot. You have material worries." If a wedding ring is present, "Your husband is troubled at the present." With such county fair jokes I could naturally never survive one day. This patter suffices only for "People's Associations."

3RD EXPERIMENT: THE MOLE

In every presentation, the "clairvoyant" says to some man: "You have a mole on your left arm or on your leg." If it happens to be true—many people have moles—he is right. If not, he has simply erred.

4TH EXPERIMENT: NAME-GUESSING

The "clairvoyant" asks a lady to write her name on a slip of paper and then tightly clench the slip of paper in her hand. In order to demonstrate how to do the task, he, first, takes her slip in his hand and shows her how to hold it. Hidden in the hollow of his palm is another blank paper that has been folded identically like the original with her name.

EXPLANATION: When the woman clenches the slip of paper in her hand, he deposits with lightning swiftness the empty paper hidden in his palm into hers and takes the written slip, which he secretly reads—covered by the other papers—as he proceeds. (In the art of magic, this trick is called "Palmage.") To the astonishment of the spectators, he then guesses the name, hurries to the woman, takes the empty slip from her hand, acts as though he too wishes to check if it is true, and then lets the two slips disappear into his pocket.

Were someone to encourage the woman to open her cupped hand and expose the slip of paper, our "Clairvoyant" would be in a nasty situation, since the paper is blank.

5TH EXPERIMENT: THE MICROPHONE AND THE HAT WITH A FALSE BOTTOM

The Enlightener G. displayed the greatest audacity to conclude his evening with this cheap magic trick. If any real occultist dared deceive the spectators with a phony act of this sort, we would be sitting in a jail cell for some time. G. naturally has it easy. If he is caught, he can appeal, saying that he wanted to "expose" this deceitful practice.

He distributes five identical slips of paper to five spectators. On their paper, each writes a different question, which G. will answer in a clairvoyant state. When the notepapers have been filled out, G. collects them and takes a bowler hat from his secretary sitting in the front row or from another abettor and deposits the notepapers in the hat. Then G. takes the hat and starts to continue the experiment. Suddenly he grips his forehead as if scruples were forming in his mind, and exclaims, "Surely you are suspicious of this hat, ladies and gentlemen! Thus I shall take the notepapers out of the hat and pour them into an empty wine glass here, before your eyes."

He does so.

Yet G. carefully hands the hat to his secretary, who takes it and goes backstage or, as I myself once experienced in Leibnitz, walks right through the audience and carries it out of the room.

G. sits down at a table, props his head on one hand, and then removes the slips of paper one by one from the wine glass.

After short, seemingly strenuous contemplation, he begins to read aloud—as if telepathically—the contents of the unopened notepapers word for word, supplying each with some banal answer. The audience is enchanted.

Interestingly enough, G. never explains this trick; perhaps he is ashamed of branding people fools by means of such a hackneyed con. He leaves it up to the audience to rack their minds over it.

EXPLANATION: The hat in which G. collects the papers has a secret pocket which is not visible in the darkness. When G. tosses the spectators' question sheets into the hat, he skillfully pushes them through the secret compartment.

Also inside the hat are five blank slips of paper. When G. turns the hat over the wine-glass, the blank slips fall out. The secretary takes the bowler hat with the spectators' questions and disappears backstage. Behind the curtain is a microphone. It is wired to a small earphone that is hidden in the sleeve of the clairvoyant.

While Herr Enlightener supports his heavy head with his hand and strenuously contemplates the questions in the wine-glass, the secretary opens the slips of paper hidden in the secret compartment of the hat and broadcasts them to his master at the table on stage. Had you, dear writer, shouted "Stop!" when the assistant was leaving with the bowler hat, then you would have found the original questions in the secret compartment and blank papers in the wine glass. Try this next time G. gives a lecture.

In Leibnitz, where I enjoyed watching G.'s lecture, it did not work out so well. G. was forced to leave the stage without his famous finale. Today I can reveal why: I, maliciously and covertly, cut G.'s microphone wire.

Die Andere Welt #1 (October–November 1931)

CHAPTER NINE

THE MAN WHO IS NEVER WRONG

1932-1933

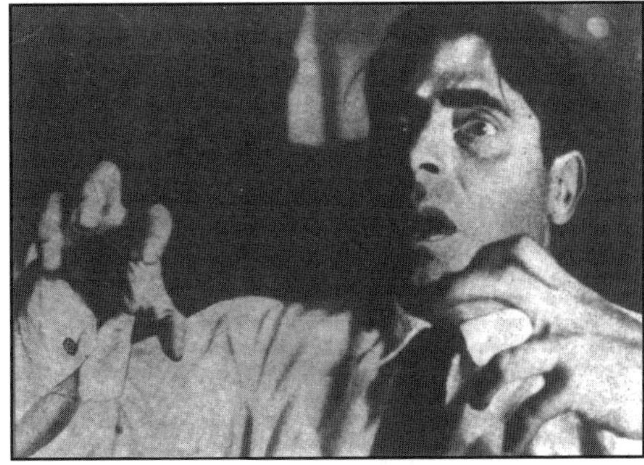

The Vision

In blazing, crimson typeface, *Erik Jan Hanussen's Berliner Wochenschau*, the weekly of esoteric knowledge, headlined on March 25, 1932 its newest sensational revelation: "HANUSSEN IN TRANCE PREDICTS HITLER'S FUTURE."

The cover story, in characteristic breathless prose, hinted that Adolf Hitler (still without German citizenship papers) would be appointed Reichschancellor in exactly one year's time. Furthermore, according to Hanussen's ecstatic vision, it would be Hitler's deadly foes, Fieldmarshal Paul von Hindenburg and his Nationalist allies, who would walk the Nazi Führer to General Bismark's exalted chair at the head of the Reichschancellery.

Hanussen's feature was a deranged and comical assault on conventional wisdom and common sense.

Undoubtedly, Berliners on their way to work that morning noticed the flaming red banner at their neighborhood kiosks and shook their heads sardonically. More than a few of them must have picked up a copy of the preposterous rag for the express amusement of their office mates. No one, it seemed, took Hanussen's latest portent seriously. No one, except the Führer himself, who was barricaded in the Hotel Kaiserhof with the last of his friends.

Hitler was known to be an extremely complicated and neurotic individual, even for the times. His firm belief in his historical mission and overall megalomania had much to do with the man's amazing seductive appeal. Hitler sustained his personal convictions, often against all objective reality, through a reliance on divine omens and banal Southern German folk superstitions.

From the misty portals of fate came Hanussen's timely vision.

The Führer made a note to contact the Danish clairvoyant and express his warm gratitude.

The *Berliner Wochenschau's* forecast of Hitler's future fell into two front and second-page parts: a summary of the editor's trance-vision and a horoscope by Maximilian Bauer. Hanussen emphasized that his weekly was non-sectarian and apolitical—two weeks earlier he published his predictions on Hindenburg's destiny; other editions would astrologically analyze Ernst Thälmann, the head of the German Communist Party, and his movement's future.

Since Leitmeritz, Hanussen had responded to a barrage of reporters' inquiries about Germany's political fate. In every interview, Erik predicted an extreme "jerk to the right" and the suborning of the Weimar constitution. By 1933, the Nationalist leaders would outlaw the Communist Party and rule by military decree. Delegates to the Reichstag would be replaced by a reactionary dictator and his confederates.

Hanussen rarely mentioned Hitler. In fact, his publications—like others in Berlin—pilloried the Austrian. In *Die Hanussen-Magazin* (January/February 1932), for instance, Hitler appeared as a Frankensteinish "Natural Wonder" merged with Heinrich Brüning, the persnickety head of the Catholic Zentrum Party, in a grotesque photomontage paste-up of the next cabinet. The second issue of the BW (January 22–29, 1932) featured a comic Man in the Street section, where famous people answered the searing question, "Can Polygamy Be Saved?" Hitler's invented reply had him foolishly addressing his many Nazi organizations and bureaus for racially sound advice and consent.

The thin-skinned Führer, if he knew about Hanussen's satires at all, could not have been pleased.

Erik Jan Hanussen's BW 20

Berliner Wochenschau

4. und 5. Lektion des Hanussen-Unterrichts:

Wie gefalle ich ihr? Wie gefalle ich ihm?

. 11 Redaktion: Berlin W 50 Kurfürstendamm 16 25.–31. März 1932 Fernsprecher: J 1 Bismarck 1635 Jahrgang 1932

E. J. Hanussen schildert im Trance

Hitlers Zukunft

Was wird aus Hitler?

Die Redaktion der „B. W." hat den ...essanten Versuch unternommen, mit ...Hellseher Erik Jan Ha...sen ein Experiment zu veranstalten, ...welchem ihm im Trancezustande die ...e nach der nächsten Zukunft des ...rers der NSDAP., Regierungsrat Adolf ... vorgelegt wurde. Es muß wohl

Juwelen in der U-Bahn

3000 Mark Belohnung

Börse:

Baisse-Stimmung

Die Börse wird die Tage vor Ostern sehr pessimistisch gestimmt sein. Die Kurse, die vorher etwas angezogen haben, werden sinken. Speziell in Farben gibt es Abschläge, auch in den Elektrizitätswerte-werten. Montan-Werte, die erst gestiegen

The March 25 article was quite different in tone. Although Hitler's political fortunes had taken a downward spiral, Erik implicitly understood the emotive staying power of the Nazi program. It was buttressed by its simplistic remedies and reliance on esoteric symbology and cult of personality.

Hanussen warned Hitler about his health and personal safety. An injury to his right hand might result in an infectious wound with long-term repercussions. Divisions within the Nazi camp, instigated by a close friend, would temporally endanger the cause. In the end, however, the Führer and his circle would emerge stronger and revitalized. Their Nationalist opposition would, over time, be blunted and defanged. Most importantly, Hitler should be aware that an assassination plot was about to be executed by a demented student.

If he could avoid these troubles, Adolf Hitler's star would certainly rise. Rise to the summit of his desires.

The Phenomenon of Our Time

Nothing materially followed from the *BW's* eccentric premonitions. On April 10, Hitler lost the Presidential runoff to Hindenburg by six million votes, although the ex-Kaiser's son, Crown Prince Auwi, in an SA Storm Trooper's uniform, campaigned furiously for the National Socialist cause. The Nazi paramilitary armies themselves were banned from German streets three days later by Brüning's new conservative government. Berlin's middle-of-the-road editors denounced their alarmist left-wing colleagues. The center had held.

Hanussen performed in Paris and toured western Germany for most of April. In Darmstadt on the 18th, he was the personal guest of Count Hermann Keyserling, the internationally acclaimed writer-philosopher.

Scherls Magazin, which fawned over the sophisticated Moecke since the late '20s, ran the ultimate humorous insult piece: "Be Your Own Hanussen!" in its April edition. (Erik's lawyers, of course, promptly sued for damages.) Ullstein's *Uhu* published a provocative photograph of Hanussen doing his magic on a mesmerized Grace Cameron.

Erik Jan Hanussen's Berliner Wochenschau continued to provide its hoi polloi readership with tabloid treats: the shady dealings of a Berlin bank owner, who was also a transvestite; "How To Attract Members of the Opposite Sex Through Hypnosis" (in three serialized parts); an ironic tour of the Hohenzoffern-Café, a local lesbian nightspot; occult cures for morphine addiction and smoking; profiles of Max Reinhardt and Gitta Alpar; Rumba lessons (with a diagrammed chart); more ad hominem attacks on Hellwig, Gubisch, Moecke and other "sexually

depraved" Berlin psychics; instructions on the use of the Gomboloy (chant "Ha-nu-ssen" as the circle of beads slips through the fingers; "Every ten minutes of Gomboloy equals three hours of restful sleep!"), and a fashion selection for stylish women based on their astrological birth-signs. There were also stock market tips, sports news, cabaret, variety, theatre and film reviews, and a backpage section for free graphological explication and clairvoyant advice for subscribers.

Photos of Session

At the end of April, Hanussen returned to performing at the prestigious Scala music hall. He received 550 marks for the engagement and an additional thirty percent for any daily box-office over 5,000 marks. The April revue included La Jana's Oriental ballet, comic acrobats, and a drama called "The Hand." Over the Scala's façade was a raised billboard of Erik's face. The marquee below read, "The Sensation of Berlin! The Most Famous Clairvoyant in the World: ERIK JAN HANUSSEN—THE PHENOMENON OF OUR TIME!!"

La Jana

The Hanussen act lasted an hour and was introduced by Thoma. Besides the normal telepathic stunts, Erik added "Fate-Balls," which were spheres tossed into the overflow hall. Whoever caught one could keep it, have it autographed, and receive confidential answers about their prospective destinies. In the playbill was an offering of 10,000 marks for anyone who could prove that the Dane used paid accomplices in the performance. Amateur detectives, of course, took the bait. No one claimed or received a reward.

"The Phenomenon of Our Time" broke Scala's records for attendance. The act was extended into May.

A Prophecy Fulfilled

After the May 15 Scala evening, Erik invited the Baroness to dinner. She declined, citing a previous engagement with Princess Lobkowicz, an old friend from Prague and the mother of the spirited young race-car driver Prince Leo Lobkowicz.

Invite them all, the ebullient Hanussen insisted. That would not be possible, the Baroness pleaded; the Prince was resting for the Avus Automobile Tournament. In addition, he was suffering from severe stomach cramps. Hanussen's wily mind spun. "How severe?" The Baroness reported that the Prince's condition was extreme and his predicament had to be hidden from public view.

Two days later, Hanussen called a press conference at the German Automobile Society, sponsors of the Avus event. Before the skeptical eyes of the Berlin newspaper corps, most of whom regarded Hanussen as a pressworthy joke, the seer made a shocking prognosis: not only would the Prince fail to place in the Avus, he would be involved in a fiery accident. Hanussen repeated his weird claim in his own paper that week.

On May 22, 1932, at the Avus Finals in Berlin, Prince Lobkowicz lost control of his Bugatti race-car after four minutes and smashed against a post, killing himself instantly.

The established newspapers went wild. Hanussen was no clown. In fact, maybe he had the power to actually see into the future. Journalists who previously parodied the clairvoyant suddenly sang his praises. For example, Fred Hildenbrandt, a reporter for the *Essener Wochenschau* and an old enemy of the Dane, utterly changed his tune. Overnight he wrote ecstatically about Hanussen and the Avus premonition.

Millions of rational-minded Germans followed the unfolding saga. Like the general press, the public scoffed at the Automobile Society's lame explanation: a small technical flaw caused the fatal wreck. Hanussen's prediction was made before two dozen neutral officials and reporters, his words were transcribed and published, the unlikely forecast came true. Berliners and other Germans were dumbfounded.

Prince Leo Lobkowicz

The Wreck of Lobkowicz' Bugatti

Support from the Right

The Communist press reported on the Lobkowicz racing death in a decidedly cynical tone. It was not a defective Bugatti or the stars that led to the mishap but Hanussen himself. The *Welt am Abend*, a Red Front daily, on May 28 blamed the Scala seer directly. His press conference prognostications merely grew into a dark "self-fulfilling prophecy." The Prince must have heard about the lethal warning and it adversely affected his Avus performance. The paper demanded a formal police investigation. The *Welt* even hinted that the Nazis were somehow behind the tragedy and Hanussen was the unanimous choice as "Reichs-Clairvoyant" of the clandestine Hitler government-in-waiting.

One day later, a National Socialist newspaper did pick up the sensational coincidence. The organ for Gregor Strasser's independent Nazi faction, *Die Schwartze Front*, ran the headline, "HANUSSEN, THE MAN WHO IS NEVER WRONG!" The editor-in-chief euphorically referred to Erik's March 25 vision and Bauer's horoscope of Hitler in the *BW*. The Danish soothsayer had proved his clairvoyant skills with Avus; now his predictions about Hitler's unstoppable rise and victory in January 1933 must be equally heeded.

The apolitical Erik Jan Hanussen had suddenly become a political commodity and pliant symbol for Germany's rapidly expanding extremist parties.

May 29, 1932 was a memorable day in German history for another reason. It marked the beginning of the Weimar Republic's dissolution. Hindenburg and General Kurt von Schleicher had secretly conspired to topple Brüning's center-right cabinet and tame the weakened, if implacable, Nazi menace by restoring freedom to its uniformed shock troops; Hitler had only to swear allegiance to the new right-wing government of Reichschancellor Franz von Papen. The Viennese-accented Führer and his Party faithful, in Schleicher's frivolous declaration, were merely "little children to lead by the hand." It was the first of many Nationalist blunders.

The SA and SS were back in the streets in June.

SA-Führer Helldorf

In general, Berlin was a poor source for Nazi fundraising and conscription. The unemployed and discontented youth of the metropolis (as well as its radical intelligentsia) veered strongly in their leanings toward the Communist Party and its colorful internationalist and pro-Soviet federations and associations. Most of Berlin's political reactionaries and monarchists supported the paramilitary Stahlhelm or the Black-White-Red coalition of right-wing Volks parties. In Germany's commercial and intellectual center, the Hitlerian movement, while a visible danger, seemed weak and disorganized. It boosted few indigenous leaders.

Count Wolf Heinrich von Helldorf was an exception. The black sheep of an aristocratic Prussian family, Helldorf was a Nazi insider and unrepentant libertine.

He was promoted to the rank of lieutenant in the war and joined the anti-Bolshevik Freicorp and later the Stahlhelm in the early '20s. In 1925, the politically savvy Junker changed his allegiance to the National Socialists.

As one of the highest-ranking SA leaders in Berlin, Helldorf established his notoriety for political mayhem by coordinating the first pogrom in the city's history in September 1931. On the evening of Rosh Hashanah, Helldorf's troops went on a rampage, smashing display windows of Jewish stores on the Kudamm and beating Semitic-looking passers-by who seemed dressed for the religious occasion. Embarrassingly, many of Helldorf's victims were Gentiles, including a contingent of "dark-skinned" diplomats from South America, innocuously taking in the big city's nighttime pleasures. Helldorf and his Nazi underlings were arrested and arraigned for Berlin's first major trial against National Socialist misbehavior—as a political institution—and collective violence. The Count was sentenced to six months jail time but was later acquitted on legal technicalities.

1940 Rendering of Hanussen and Helldorf

Helldorf also had a penchant for the black arts. He witnessed two of Hanussen's performances at the Scala in April and, like the majority of the two thousand spectators, left the variety house in open-mouthed amazement. Through a mutual friend—probably the Baroness or the actress Maria Paudler, both old girlfriends of Hermann Goering's wife, Emmy, from her salad days—he managed to secure an invitation to an Ursel soiree.

The depraved count must have liked what he saw. He palled around with Dzino and traded war stories and gambling strategies. He also observed the orgiastic proceedings. They did not disappoint. A few days later, Hanussen was Helldorf's guest at his villa on the Wannsee. The dissolute Junker confessed to the Dane how much he admired his lifestyle and asked him if he believed in the "Movement." Erik gave his typical, noncommittal reply: a true clairvoyant possesses no political beliefs, only the ability to read the stars and they were favorable to Helldorf and his associates.

Count Wolf von Helldorf

SA commander's second weekend foray on the Ursel created an unforgettable imprint on its participants and sparked a whole new round of smutty political gossip. Erik pulled out the stops. He called it "A Night in the Orient." The ritual-celebration centered around the Hindu love-goddess, Saraswati, the four-armed consort of Lord Brahma.

On the yacht's upper deck was an enormous phallic-shaped altar, the symbol of the Indian Lingam. The waiters were decked out in Persian garb as was a cobra snake-charmer. Ensuring that all were sufficiently provided with champagne and other intoxicants was Herr Maharaja Hanussen, attired in the turban and gown of a yogi master.

The blonde Baroness, after a hypnotic induction, embraced an imaginary love-partner and moaned convincingly on a white fur rug.

A smooth-skinned fourteen-year-old Indian boy, Kabir, was employed to assist Dzino with the phonographic entertainment and hand the naked bathers towels when they swam back to the boat. Erik yanked the boy from his station and had him dragged to the lower deck. He was accused of staring too closely at the ladies' exposed torsos. Kabir denied the charge.

Helldorf took over from there. He had the Indian servant stripped and tied to a tabletop. The Nazi Count commanded Dzino to assemble as many of the celebrants downstairs as possible. A skilled equestrian, Helldorf kept a handcrop concealed in his SA boots. For the edification of Hanussen's callous flock, the dashing aristocrat began to flagellate Kabir with a severe barrage of lashings. The beating was so strenuously administered that the helpless youngster passed out from pain.

Then, sensing that he may have transgressed even the Ursel's outer limit of sexual cruelty, Helldorf yelled, "All right, I'm a sadist! I admit it. We're all sadists! In the SA, my friends, one must learn to be desensitized to petty human compassion."

Erik escorted his raving champion of politico-erotic dominion to a private corner of the yacht. According to a curious society lady, who listened in on their agitated dialogue, they discussed for over an hour the theory of *Herrenmenschen*, the Nietzschean-Hitlerian notion of rule by superior men. Now it was Helldorf, not Hanussen, who was doing the seducing. (A fantastically detailed description of the night was first published in Bruno Frei's *Hanussen: Ein Bericht* (1934). It was unaccountably deleted from the journalist's supposedly unabridged 1980 reprint. Why the story was expunged is not clear; at least three other contemporaries reported on it.)

Into the National Socialist Orb

By the end of May 1932, nearly every order and branch of the National Socialist movement was facing a grim financial prospect. The vast amounts of money spent in March and April on organizing 120,000 rallies, producing propaganda pamphlets in the millions, electoral barnstorming (Hitler was the first German presidential candidate to travel by air), and salaries to support the private militias of the SA and SS had finally exacted its toll. The Nazis were more than a reactionary civic force. They were a revolution, a religion, with provincial headquarters, soup kitchens, meeting halls, barracks, storehouses, printing plants, and a fancy Brown House in Munich, where their Führer might find a respite from the perils of campaigning in a fickle constitutional republic.

When the bills from the April election came due, the Nazi financiers had no way to pay them. The 600,000-strong SA was hardest hit. Their wages had been slashed to Dickensian levels. The street thugs were impoverished, wretched, existing on less than three cents a day. Every week, Communist papers crowed that such-and-such a Storm Trooper in their city had come over to the proletarian side, where the ideology was humane and the potato soup thick and nutritious.

Hanussen in His Bugatti

Even the SA leadership could not cope. Helldorf had accrued 300,000 marks in gambling debts. Hanussen paid half of them off two days after the Night in the Orient and even lent the SA-Führer his Bugatti in order to settle his overdrafts at the Berlin banks in high style.

Other SA officers came begging at the Hanussen-Valhalla coffers. Wilhelm von Ohst, who embezzled 39,000 marks from the National Socialist lottery fund, borrowed just enough to stave off People's punishment. Karl Ernst, the one-time lover of Ernst Röhm and Helldorf rival, got funds and the use of Erik's LaSalle. Even the feared SA-Chieftain himself, Röhm, waited at Hanussen's private hairdresser each morning for his daily handout. For the Berlin-Brandenburg streetfighters themselves, Erik purchased a consignment of 400 military-style boots and donated free tickets to his performances.

Hermann Goering, according to postwar testimony, secured enormous sums from the multi-millionaire Dane. At a specially arranged séance, however, the old fighter pilot received bad news. Hanussen predicted great success for the Nazi Reich for several years, then its utter destruction. After that evening, Goering avoided all contact with Erik.

For Helldorf, Hanussen's largesse was a fantasy come true. He supplied the clairvoyant with twenty-five SA bodyguards and a trusted chauffeur. Only one thing confused the Count: why were there so many Jews around Erik? Except for Dzino, Thoma, and Bauer, the entire *BW* staff was Jewish, the Ursel guests and entertainers were largely Jewish, and Hanussen's closest friends appeared to be Jewish.

Erik brushed off the inquiry; the Jews were basically a good people, if sometimes a little deceptive. In fact, most Germans of the Mosaic faith were neither capitalists nor Communists, and some, like Helldorf and his comrades, were fun-loving, loyal citizens of the German Nation.

The answer did not sit well with the "Pogromist of the Kudamm." Wasn't the Danish seer aware of the Führer's rationale for Germany's defeat in the War? Didn't the Wizard follow Hitler's speeches in the National Socialist press?

Hanussen responded weakly; he would promise to do his best to disinvite known Jews and anti-fascists, like Richard Tauber and Paul Morgan. Yet some guests had disguised their origins so completely, it was impossible, even for a psychic detective, to uncover their blood heritage with certainty.

Count Helldorf accepted that response. It was one aristocrat speaking to another. Erik was naive in political matters and an honorable, if sometimes too good-hearted, gentleman.

In late June 1932, Helldorf offered to introduce Hanussen to the Führer himself. The two "miracle-men" would have to meet. Just as Hitler brought prophecy into politics, Hanussen blended politics with prophecy.

Hanussen agreed enthusiastically. Finally, his ideas were gaining the high recognition he so desperately sought.

Meeting the Führer

The exact day when Erik Jan Hanussen and Adolf Hitler initially met cannot be fixed precisely. All documents related to it were destroyed after 1933. The rendezvous unquestionably occurred in June or during the first week of July 1932. German historians agree, however, that the strange encounter physically took place at the Hotel Kaiserhof, Hitler's Berlin command post.

According to Fritzi's postwar statements, Hanussen telephoned her afterwards and excitedly referred to the Führer as "my pal Adolf." At the first meeting, Hanussen proposed the creation of a "University of the Occult" for the New Germany, and the fellow Austrian concurred that such as institution might be of great value in the *Führerstaat.*

In similar sworn testimony from the 1960s, Kurt Labatt, an old Café Louvre buddy visiting Berlin, recalled Hanussen speaking on the telephone with Hitler about the makeup of the *BW*'s latest headline. Erik claimed then that the Führer always consulted with him before any major electoral decision.

Otto Strasser, the brother of Gregor and ranking member of the Nazi Black Front, told Dr. Walter C. Langer, a psychoanalyst working for the Office of Strategic Services in 1942, that "Hitler took regular lessons in speaking and in mass psychology from a man named Hanussen, who was also a practicing astrologer and fortune-teller. He was an extremely clever individual who taught Hitler a great deal concerning the importance of staging meetings to obtain the greatest dramatic effect." (*The Mind of Adolf Hitler* [1972]). Although Langer confused the time frame—he reported that the conferences were held in the "1920s"—Strasser, who was certainly privy to all aspects of the Hitler-Hanussen connection, made it clear in earlier writings, in *Hitler and I* (1940) and in *True Detective Magazine*

Diktatoren und ihre Gegenspieler

Cromwell und Karl I. von England

Erik Jan Hanussen: Kreuz und quer durch die Welt

Hanussens BW Die Hellseher Zeitung

Bunte Wochenschau

20 Pf.

Nr. 30 8. September

ERSCHEINUNGSTAG: 8. UND 24. JEDES MONATS

Astrologischer Ratgeber

Deine günstigsten Tage im September

Mann meiner Träume — wo bist Du?

Die Sterne künden:

Hitlers größte Tage

Wie lange bleibt der Reichstag?

Hindenburgs unbegrenzte Macht

Vor großen Ereignissen — Entscheidung fällt im Herbst

Strasser — Göhring — Papen — Brüning. Was tut Schleicher?

(February–May 1942), that the intimate sessions actually took place intermittently during the summer months of 1932.

On July 8, the first photograph of Adolf Hitler appeared on *Hanussen's BW's* frontpage (no. 26). More strikingly, the newspaper's typeface was completely redesigned from the previous edition. All the words were now set in old-style Gothic lettering, Fraktur, the unwieldy, archaic national print favored by the Führer. The overall tone and makeup of the tabloid articles started to change as well: less entertainment news and Berlin profiles (too many Jews), more astrology and political analysis.

There were strings of horoscopic readings that parsed the fates of Hitler, Röhm, and Gregor Strasser; the fortunes of the German Olympic team in Los Angeles; the biweekly destiny of the struggling Nation; the movement of the constellations mapped against the signs of the swastika and Reichsmark; even the future of the Editor-Prophet himself. (Hanussen's stars, according to Bauer's July 24 chart, revealed that the seer still had to overcome an early mistake in life or humiliating stigma.)

Harry Price and Urta Bohn in Brocken

Goats into Men

1932 marked the centennial year of Goethe's death. It coincided with a burst of pre-Christian occult and black magic activities in the Weimar Republic. The Harz Mountain communities near Brocken, scene of the Walpurgis Night episode from *Faust*, in particular, were eager to host large-scale pagan fire-festivities and midnight processions. The heady brew of *Sturm-und-Drangism*, Aryan mystic services, peasant witchcraft, and Fasching parades was a transparent recipe for serious partying and a promise of high-voltage tourism.

In November 1931, the British "ghost-hunter" and psychical researcher, Harry Price, acquired (from a mysterious source) a hand-written, fifteenth-century German manuscript. It was known as the *Blocksberg Tryst*, the fabled ritual manual for "High German" necromancy. Price believed that the *Blocksberg Tryst* was Goethe's original source and inspiration for his poetic masterpiece.

The core of the *Blocksberg* manuscript involved the transformation of an unblemished white goat into a "youth of unsurpassed beauty." Besides an unguent made from bats' blood, soot, honey, and scrapings from a church bell, the rite required a full moon and the participation of a "virgin maid." It mandated a proper locale too, the "granite altar" on the highest peak in Central Germany.

When the Harz Goethe Centenary Committee heard of Price's discovery, they invited him to reproduce the black-magic séance outside Brocken (modern Blocksberg). The cautious professor and spiritualist was uncertain how to respond. After many postponements, he arrived in Brocken on June 17 with his friend, the philosopher C.E.M. Joad, and a randy assemblage of newsreel cameramen, paranormal scientists, and journalists. Urta Bohn, the gorgeous daughter of a Breslau psychologist and Scottish mother, enacted the part of the virgin. George Bernard Shaw wished them well.

The alchemical experiment in Brocken was a complete disaster. Price sounded hoarse when he read the Renaissance Latin incantations and visibly embarrassed when he invoked the sacred ancient formula; the moon never appeared from a bank of mist and clouds; the anointed kid-goat seemed distracted and repeatedly trailed away from the Magic Circle; and German reporters heavily doubted the purity of the comely Urta. No *Faust*-like metamorphosis occurred. Worse still for Dr. Price, the entire foolish affair was recorded on film for the delectation of British, French, German, and American audiences.

Hanussen, who had been tested by Price years back, urged the Britishers to come to Berlin, where he would try his hand at the Goethean ritual. And try it he did.

On midnight, June 21, at a chalked-off field in Tempelhof, in front of a Pathé sound camera crew and hundreds of Berlin merrymakers (including Valeska Gert and Leni Riefenstahl), Erik transformed the he-goat into a human. With the assistance of a "pure"

Hanussen Transforms a Goat at Tempelhof

Aryan maiden in a floor-length evening gown (possibly the Baroness), Hanussen covered the bashful animal with a white sheet and shouted, "Abracadabra." A flash of magnesium powder blinded the observers and out from under the sheet popped an exuberant midget, dressed in Bavarian peasant garb.

Price shook his head while the crowd shrieked. The cheery man in the lederhosen unmistakably symbolized one comic personage: the Nazi Führer, the elf-king of the Munich Brown House. Erik had changed Germany (the goat) into Hitler (the midget).

Judging from the reaction shots in the newsreel footage, the evening must have been great fun for its celebrants. The deeper meaning of the event, if any, however, probably varied from individual to individual.

The Communist Counter-Attack

Beginning in the late spring of 1932, the German Communist popular press obsessed over Hanussen. In an eight-month period, they printed over twenty-eight features on the notorious history of the alleged clairvoyant.

On May 25, Bruno Frei, the Viennese-born Jewish editor of the *Berlin am Morgen*, launched a vitriolic series entitled "A CHARLATAN CONQUERS BERLIN: WE EXPOSE THE SWINDLER-CLAIRVOYANT ERIK JAN HANUSSEN." In it, Hanussen was vilified as the "Prophet of the Third Reich" and "Hitler's Spiritual Father." Frei believed that Hanussen was Hitler's weakest link. A full-scale attack on Hanussen would unveil the irrationalism and occult basis of the Nazi ideology, further discrediting the fragmenting movement.

The opposite proved to be true. Contradictions in Hitler's theology, a mix of mysticism and advanced science, the pagan in the service of the corporate modern state, paralleled the longing of the German electorate for indigenous and radical solutions. Neither the left, center, right, nor the international press after them, clearly understood this.

Although the first of the *Berlin am Morgen* (*BaM*) attacks on Hanussen linked him with Hitler and the National Socialists, at that particular time in May, Frei had greatly stretched the truth. No personal connections were then known to exist. Yet, ideologically, the idea was tempting.

Frei told his staff that people who believed in Hanussen's clairvoyance were then, or would one day be, Hitler fanatics. Both German *Wundermänner* were disciples of Emile Coué, the nineteenth-century founder of modern hypnosis and miracle-healing. The smug heroes attained their glorious heights through audacious flattery, hocus-pocus, and psychological threats, through the subconscious power of suggestion. Marxist thought was built on rationality, prudent economical planning, mathematics, scientific methodology. The fascists could only appeal to voters through dark fantasy, guilt, astrology, hysteria.

In Frei's worldview, Hanussen was merely the entertaining counterpart of Hitler. The little Dane represented the soft underbelly of National Socialism.

The *BaM*, with its "paper sword," could derail the Nazi peril through the exposure and humiliation of the stage clairvoyant. Erik was an easier and more vulnerable target than the Austrian housepainter. As every good Leninist knew, evil must be eradicated at the very root, and the root of capitalism and its offspring, fascism, was religious belief.

The Communist strategy was indirect, skewed, and monstrously ineffective. Decades later, Frei came to regret the maneuver. Instead of hammering away at the Hitler clique squarely, his daily may have only pushed Hanussen, his three-million readership, and other occultist messianists into the Nazi camp. The twinning of the two "H's" may have been a disastrous "self-fulfilling prophecy," created by the Red Front press.

At first, Frei hoped the *BaM's* malicious tirades would force Erik into his normal course of action. That is, he would sue for libel. And, in court before the nation, the Communist attorneys would shred the seer, "the rest of the clairvoyant-filth," and their astropolitical reveries of fascist rule. Unfortunately for Frei, Hanussen ignored the attacks. He was busy performing in Amsterdam and the northern German provinces.

In Elderfeldt

The real Erik, unlike the evil mad genius of folklore, had some awareness of his predicament. In Elderfeldt, he crossed paths with an old companion, Frederick Marion. Both of their agents had simultaneously booked telepathic lecture-demonstration tours of Denmark the following season. The cheek-by-jowl competition was bad for business. The fellow mentalists needed to reset their calendar engagements to ensure full houses and vary their telepathic routines accordingly. As the lesser-known clairvoyant and also as a professional courtesy, Fred offered to withdraw. Erik's agent informed him later that Hanussen had already decided to void the profitable expedition.

Born Josef Kraus, Marion was a Jew from Austro-Hungary like Hanussen. Fred had stood up for the Dane in Leitmeritz and Erik returned the favor in his weekly by supporting Marion's legal defense in recent German lawsuits. In early August, when they spoke, the rumors about Hanussen and his service to Hitler were common knowledge. Marion was equally incredulous about Hanussen's Denmark cancellation and his feckless aid for the raving anti-Semite. The telepath from Prague assumed that there was an unwholesome link between the events.

Erik bared his soul to Marion. He was moody and nervous when talking about the Nazis. The Ottakring survivor was certain that Hitler would come to power in 1933. Marion recalled the following confession from Hanussen: "I've gone too far. I know that now. Nothing I can do will alter things. I've made plans to leave for America next year, but they'll never be realized. There's no way out for me." (*In My Mind's Eye* [1950]). The normally ebullient optimist sighed repeatedly and insinuated that his death had already been planned by political adversaries.

Meanwhile, Hitler's Party rebounded in the national summer elections. To paper over the Nazi-Nationalist differences, Papen had deposed the legitimately elected Socialist government in Prussia and prohibited the *Vorwärts*, the Social Democrats' main publishing arm. Papen's penchant for inane political mischief and conspiracies was already well established. In 1915, as a member of the German diplomatic staff in neutral Washington, D.C., he was expelled for concocting a cabal of schemes to blow up American cargo ships destined for Allied ports, poison the granaries that supplied the American Army Cavalry corps, and destroy the bridges and canals that linked Canada with New York State.

Reichschancellor Papen thought he could mollify the National Socialists with anti-Bolshevik decrees and kind words. Still the SA disturbances continued. Röhm's legions were gaining in their violent struggle with the Communist and Socialist paramilitary forces. In a single day, eighteen were killed and 200 wounded in the Red-Brown riots. Hindenburg's Nationalist coalition wondered openly if they could contain the unstable Bohemian Corporal with gentlemanly handshakes and pleas. The conservative center was obviously crumbling.

Herr Juhn Returns

Just when Frei had run short on anti-Hanussen rhetoric for his Red tabloid—Soviet-style atheist propaganda was declared illegal by Papen in July—a fellow *Auslander* came to the rescue. Juhn showed up at the *BaM* office with documents establishing Erik's Hebraic origins. This was the moment that Frei had waited for: Hitler, the defender of the German nation against the International Jewish Bankers, was himself under the spell of a duplicitous Jew. Berlin exposés did not get any more salacious.

And the materials had not gotten there too soon. Hanussen's bimonthly—now called *Hanussen's Bunte Wochenshau*—had been prescient in its short-term political prognostications. For instance, it correctly foretold a Nazi bloodbath in Hamburg days before the massacre erupted. And now the *BW* predicted the banning of the Communist Party, a Hitler victory in the Reichstag, and world catastrophe for the year 1940.

On August 13, one of Hanussen's part-time employees, Ernst Neumann, claimed in civil court that he was dismissed by Erik personally because of his religion, Judaism, and Neumann acknowledged that he was thoroughly disgusted with the veiled anti-Semitic tone of the "apolitical" occult paper.

The *BaM* embraced the tabloid irony the very next morning. Frei wrote that the Cagliostro of Weimar, the Mental Wizard of the Ages, the Führer's private Rasputin, himself was an abhorrent Israelite, born Hermann Steinschneider.

Neumann won the termination suit ten days later, receiving a five-month salary compensation, and Erik was forced to respond to *BaM's* Frei-Juhn revelation. The conjurer, this time, was trapped. He asked his lawyers to file an injunction and slander suit against the Communist paper. Depositions were to be submitted months later, on December 23, 1932, and criminal arraignments would follow.

Hanussen With the Police Commissioner of Copenhagen

In Foreign Lands

On August 30, Hanussen left Germany. The Ursel docked in Copenhagen. Danish tax authorities limited the soothsayer's activities to public gatherings and the municipal police hovered around him with a watchful eye; they were wary of anything German. Private consultation sessions were forbidden.

Erik performed four evenings at the Copenhagen Concert-Palace and was interviewed by a reporter from the leading Danish newspaper, *Politiken.* Hanussen bragged about his success in Leitmeritz, his biographical entry in the *Grosse Meyer* encyclopedia, and the "five million" members registered in the Hanussen Society.

The journalist reminded him that Hitler had over fourteen million admirers in Germany. Erik replied that the Führer's time had come; his ability to command such a disparate mass following was clear proof of his leadership potential. The clairvoyant repeated that he himself was not a National Socialist, only an anti-Communist patriot. The interview concluded on a humorous note: "Did the Hanussen Society have any particular greeting, like 'Heil Hanussen'?" "Not yet," the pseudo-Dane laughed.

Erik also wanted to take his traveling show to Oslo, but Norwegian authorities denied the Germans entry. Public exhibitions of hypnosis were considered detrimental to the upright citizens of the country and strictly prohibited.

On October 3, Hanussen appeared in Basel at the invitation of a Swiss psychiatric clinic. Géza von Cziffra, who was close to Erik at the time, believed the expedition to Basel was basically entrepreneurial. Hanussen was searching for a safe haven to deposit his millions in marks, kronen, guilders, and dollars. Cziffra also wrote that Erik became dangerously involved with another Dutch "Baroness" there and formed an uncomfortable *ménage à trois* with her lesbian companion. Neither the banking episode nor the love story can be substantiated.

At the end of October, Hanussen performed at the L'Empire Theatre in Paris. Although the fantasy writer Paul Heuzé introduced the evenings, the French audiences were not much taken with the Dane's telepathic act. They were fidgety and vocally critical. Erik later blamed the problem on language. His connection with the spectator, in order to achieve its deep parapsychological affect, had to be one-on-one; the soft-spoken French translator unintentionally broke the delicate esoteric bond.

Retracing His Path

Between the Swiss and French engagements in October, Hanussen visited Risa and their daughter Erika in Meran, Italy. He stayed for eight days at a hotel in the German-speaking community and spent much time with the twelve-year-old girl. For Erika, who still went by the surname Steinschneider, the week was magical, exhilarating. Erik bought her fancy dresses and a bicycle. He also told her that in the spring he would return to Meran and cart her off to Berlin, where they would sail together on his famous yacht. He would rechristen it the "Erika."

In a more serious mood, Hanussen implored the stately Risa to abandon her husband, Hans Fuchs, and flee with him and Erika to North America. Risa, of course, refused. She had enough of the Dane. His offer to convert to Catholicism seemed rushed and insincere. Hans was good to her and Erika, even if he was a known philanderer. Hanussen prophesied that the brewer-cum-industrialist would leave her in exactly two months for another, younger, actress.

Before Erik bade good-bye to his daughter, he gave Erika one of his photographs, signed it, and intimated that he had little time to live.

In December, Hans Fuchs took on a new paramour and formally separated from Risa. The former Viennese ingenue never wed again.

Black Magic for the Brown Shirts

Back in Berlin, Hanussen had to face the Jewish-Nazi dilemma. September 1932 had been the month for Hebraic outing. The dapper head of the fiercely Nationalist Stahlhelm and one-time Presidential candidate, Theodor Duesterberg, was attacked in Goering's newspaper, *Der Angriff*, as a hidden Jew. The aristocratic war hero claimed that he was shocked to learn that his father's mother was a full-blooded Israelite. Duesterberg acknowledged the genealogical blot and honorably resigned his post forthwith.

SA Man Reading **BW**

Trebitsch Lincoln—once an Anglican missionary in Montreal; a British MP for the Liberal Party; a Romanian oil magnate; a German double agent during the Great War; an informant for the anti-Bolshevik Freicorp; an early confidant of the National Socialists; a representative of various Chinese warlords in Europe; and an ordained Chinese Buddhist monk, seeking German souls and funding—was denounced in the Berlin press as a Hungarian Jew, an arch-rogue and international adventurer, born Ignacz Trebitsch.

Hanussen's BW defended Duesterberg and the colorful Hungarian Abbott "Chao Kung" as well as other recently designated "new Jews." Their ancestry and lineage was irrelevant to their character and national destinies. Nonetheless, it was tough sledding for the Dane.

The Communist monthly *Magazin für Alle* branded Erik's tabloid as the favored reading matter for Röhm's barbaric hordes. Conversely, three astrological newspapers with strong Nazi leanings, *Neues Deutschland*, *Die Neue Flagge*, and *Die Deutsche Astrologische Zeitung*, charged the *BW* with being insufficiently Aryan.

Rumors about Hanussen's genuine origins began to surface all through the fall of 1932. On September 3, another Jewish employee of the *BW* battered the clairvoyant/editor-in-chief, both physically in the newsroom with fisticuffs and legally in the courtroom with accusations of Jewish self-hatred. Even if "Hanussen-Steinschneider" were a Hebrew as claimed, the clairvoyant's lawyers argued, the newsweekly was merely reporting on the heavenly rotation of the stars and planets. Hanussen could not be held personally accountable if his mathematical ephemerides pointed to Nazi victories.

Later in the month, a Viennese chorus girl, Lizzie Bognar, chortled to everyone in her theatre crowd that the Aryan prophet had a circumcised penis. Dzino marched the nasty gossip to the Anhalter Bahnhof and shipped the chorine back to Austria on the first available train.

Erik soldiered on through September and October. The *BW* gave various hopeful forecasts for Germany's future: Hitler aligning with Hindenburg; the SA merging with the Reichswehr or the Stahlhelm; a fortuitous kabbalistic numerological analysis of Hitler's name (*Gematria*). There as also an ominous prediction. The September 24 issue of the *BW* (no. 31) featured a "Death-Horoscope" of the Reichstag. According to Dr. Wilhelm Baecker's chart, the unusual shifts of Uranus' orbit into the Twelfth House of the Sun was extremely inauspicious for the venerable institution. It portended "divine" destruction.

The Nazi press was far too busy with internal struggles between pro- and anti-Hitler factions to notice or respond to the Steinschneider-Hanussen revelations. The autumn months also saw the creation of a dubious marriage: Goering and the Communists. Both parties sensed the weakening of the right and center. They turned against Papen. SA rowdies started to harangue the Volks party rallies and, on November 2, they went so far to join hands with the Communist trade-unions to protect Berlin's transit-workers in the midst of a devastating wildcat strike.

Schleicher and "Old Man" Hindenburg were enraged. They wrote off Papen's regime as toothless saviors of the Republic and secretly began to woo Strasser and his Black Front away from the mad-dog elements of Nazidom. The Cathols and Sozis despaired; they suddenly realized that they had neither a voice inside the ineffectual cabinet nor one in the radical opposition. Leaders from the conservative splinter parties spoke gravely of uniting to overturn the Constitution and restore the Wilhelmian monarchy. Fearful of a bloody civil war and political anarchy, the Reichswehr moved troops to the outskirts of Berlin.

German democracy was given one last chance. National elections for the Reichstag were announced for November 6.

Despite a fourth spirited Nazi campaign in 1932, the electoral results startled Hitler, Goering, and Josef Goebbels, the Führer's propaganda chief. National Socialist support fell by a staggering two million votes and their war-chest emptied once again. The Communist Party surged regionally, picking up eleven parliamentary seats. And the ruling Nationalists increased their votes by one million.

The Red-Brown alliance in Berlin had confused the conservative-reactionary German electorate. One and one-half million citizens who voted for the Führer's party in July had stayed home. Ernst Röhm, the third force in the Nazi Movement, began, for the first time, to have doubts about Hitler's long-term strategy.

Erik spent the last two weeks of November in Hamburg, playing at the UFA-Palast. He soft-peddled his electoral divinations. The *BW*, expecting to replace Goebbel's *Der Angriff* as the preferred popular right-wing rag, moderated its tone. It ran features on color-healing and phrenology.

Schleicher had monumental problems forging a new majority in the Reichstag. He invited Hitler to be his Vice Chancellor. As always, the Führer refused any secondary position. He demanded the top post or nothing. Hindenburg made it clear that he would not even consider negotiating with the hysteric, Bohemian-born figurehead if Hitler insisted on carting the homosexual Röhm into his august chambers.

In early December, Schleicher hatched a scheme to unite the anti-Nazi Nationalists, the left-wing Catholic unions, the Socialist Democrats, and Strasser's Black Front into a "military-proletarian" coalition. Gregor Strasser agreed, breaking completely with the Hitler circle. Half of the National Socialist Reichstag deputies followed the sensible speaker's lead and discarded their swastika emblems.

Hitler was so confounded by the personal betrayal that, according to Goebbels, he "tore his hair" as he paced back and forth in his Kaiserhof suite. Things had never looked so bleak for the Movement. The Führer threatened suicide.

Exposed on the Left and Right

Frei's relentless assaults on Hanussen picked up steam in the last months of 1932. The Dane was described in the Communist tabloids as "Hitler's Jewish disciple," a "cultural disgrace," a "fraudulent adventurer," a "religious quack," "Adolf's *Kerl*," the "people's stupefier," and an "outrageous swindler."

On December 8, Erik's best and most trusted attorney, Dr. Alfons Sack, formerly filed an injunction against Kosmos-Verlag, the Red Front publishers of the *Berlin am Morgen*, and Alfred Hurtig, the editor of the *BaM's* sister newspaper, *Welt am Abend*.

To further imperil Hanussen's tottering reputation, Frei sent a personal letter to Goebbels, stating that Erik Jan Hanussen (aka Hermann Steinschneider) was not only a full-blooded Jew but the nephew of a rabbi from the Austrian ghetto of Pressburg. The incendiary allegation finally appeared in the December 12th issue of Goebbels' *Der Angriff*, where Hanussen was identified as a "Czech Jew."

Count Helldorf, now the titular head of Berlin's SA, was astonished to read the charge in his Party's main daily and felt personally threatened by the news. Could his leading benefactor and valued evening companion be an impostor named Steinschneider? Was it possible that the Führer's spiritual guide and stargazer, the man who bolstered the Party immeasurably in these last months of struggle, was an accursed Jew from Moravia? Helldorf lost no time finding out.

At Hanussen's private office on the Kudamm, the two met in the late morning. The customarily unflappable Nazi Count was officious, impersonal, and anxious in the extreme.

Erik, the old *Jenischmann*, smiled and fabricated yet another incredible genealogy for himself.

Yes, Frei's documents were authentic; however, the *Welt* and *BaM's* stories were not. Hanussen's parents were young Danish nobles, who died in a mountain-climbing accident in Moravia. Hanussen was adopted by a kindly Jewish couple in the nearby village of Prossnitz. That is why the master spoke a smattering of Yiddish and had a special affinity for Jewish artists and their friends.

When Hanussen produced phony adoption papers from a drawer, Helldorf sighed with relief. He telephoned the Führer and informed a disbelieving Goebbels of his discovery.

Der Angriff issued a short retraction on December 13. It reported curtly that according to "highly reliable sources," Hanussen was no Jew. It was his detractors, Frei and Juhn, who were engaged in typical Semitic chicanery. *Der Angriff's* court reporter was an inexperienced lad and had mistakenly copied the fake Communist charges into his notes.

The next-day correction in the evening *Der Angriff* already came too late for its provincial readers. SA troopers demonstrated against Erik's lecture in Breslau that evening. Hanussen returned to the safety of Helldorf's Berlin and remained there.

On December 21, Juhn submitted a notarized statement to Berlin's main municipal court. In the signed deposition, Juhn swore that, as Hanussen's impresario and secretary from June 1927 to July 1929, he was an active partner in Erik's sham clairvoyance productions. "Hermann Steinschneider" possessed no miraculous powers. Everything "magical" was accomplished through coded signals and stage tricks. Their variety routine was just a stencil of other occult rackets and counterfeit music-hall entertainments.

Two days later, the Kosmos-Hanussen libel hearings commenced. The Communist editor-in-chief Hurtig surprised everyone when he maintained that he was not responsible for the offending issues of *Welt am Abend*. It was a different *Welt* editor who approved the anti-Hanussen articles. The landcourt magistrate wanted to know why the defendant did not bring up this discrepancy earlier. Hurtig responded that this was his way of proving that Hanussen could not be a true clairvoyant.

At the beginning of the defamation trial, the Red Front attorneys forced Erik to enter his Czech passport into evidence. It read "Herschmann Steinschneider."

Naturally, Frei made political hay with the new court document. The *BaM's* holiday edition splashed "Herschmann Is His Name . . ." over its cover page. The Marxist cabaret troupe Die Wespen (in its final legal production) also satirized the Hebraic birth certificate of the defrocked Nordic prophet. ("Through the mighty Brown House, your astrological sign once ran. Today, however, the cosmos [Kosmos] informs us your name's not Erik Jan.") [Erich Weinert, *Das Zwischen Spiel* (Berlin: Verlag Volk und Welt, 1950)]

Against Sack's vehement professional objection, Hanussen settled the slander suite against the Kosmos-Verlag. The *BaM* was restrained from claiming that Hanussen-Steinschneider was a fraudulent clairvoyant or the nephew of Rabbi Daniel Prossnitz.

Encouraged by Frei, Juhn procured still more damaging items. He contacted Rabbi Fraenkel, the head of the Jewish Community Cultural Center in Rumburg. Dr. Fraenkel confirmed in a letter that Rabbi Ignaz Popper officiated in 1928 at Erik's marriage to Elfriede Charlotte Rühle in the Rumburg central synagogue. Hanussen's birth certificate, which Siegfried Steinschneider had deposited in Prossnitz, was located in the Jewish library there, and also a different version at the Jewish Document Bureau in Vienna. The two copies were forwarded to Berlin.

On January 13, 1933, Frei published a facsimile of the rabbinical letter to Juhn. It appeared in a front-page exposé in the *BaM*, under the heading "Hanussen with the Rabbi/Hanussen with Hitler." Frei also issued a booklet, co-authored with the Marxist writer Botho Laserstein, entitled *Wider den Hellseh-Schwindel! Der Fall des 'Hellsehers' Herschmann Steinschneider genannt Erik Jan Hanussen* (Berlin: Alfred Kiepser, 1933). It was a recapitulation of Juhn's research and the old *BaM* articles. Book publications were not subject to the newspaper injunctions.

January 1933 was turning into an ill-fated month for both the Führer and his Jewish astrologer.

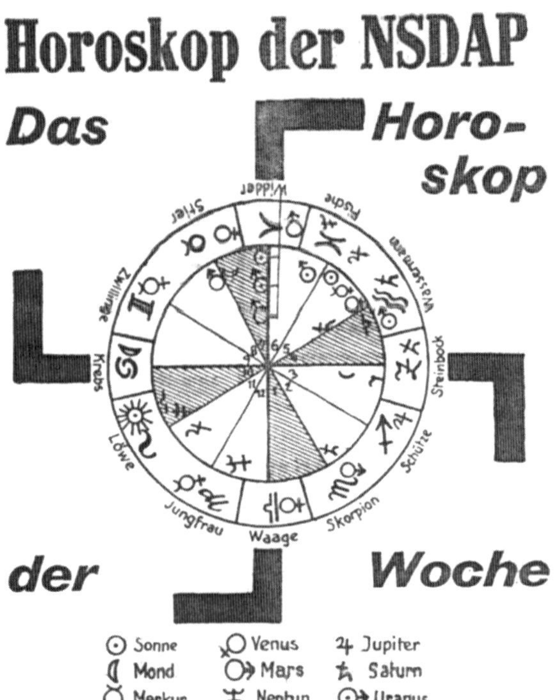

THE HOROSCOPE OF ADOLF HITLER

Cast by Maximilian Bauer.

Adolf Hitler's horoscope reveals he will receive a new burst of popularity from the "abyss." His Fiery Trigon has been rearranged with the movement of the Moon and Jupiter toward the Sun. The new pattern of the constellations in the Seventh through the Tenth Houses of his horoscope also shows that he will, over time, obtain a wide following and personal success, a new title and honors. These favorable signs began on February 15, 1932. But since the course of these changes are dominated by critical planet oppositions throughout March and April 1932, Hitler will neither achieve an electoral victory nor the Presidency.

Starting in March, ominous Saturn-Sun quadrates in the Fourth to the Seventh Houses are at work. Also, the Moon quadrate of Saturn moves into the Tenth (career) House on March 12. This greatly reduces his prospects for victory.

Furthermore, on April 4th (and especially around the 8th, 9th, and 10th and, to some extent, through April 20th), adversarial Uranus-Moon alignments in the First and Twelfth Houses will pass into his Sixth and Seventh Houses. This means that, until the planets right themselves in January 1933, Hitler will face extremely difficult times. During this period, the stars indicate that Hitler in particular as well as the entire National-Socialist Movement will encounter strong opposition. Hitler's struggle will not end without bloodshed. Also within his own Party, there will be rebellion and subterfuge against him and his leadership.

ADOLF HITLER

April 20th, 1889, 6.30 p.m., Braunau, Austria

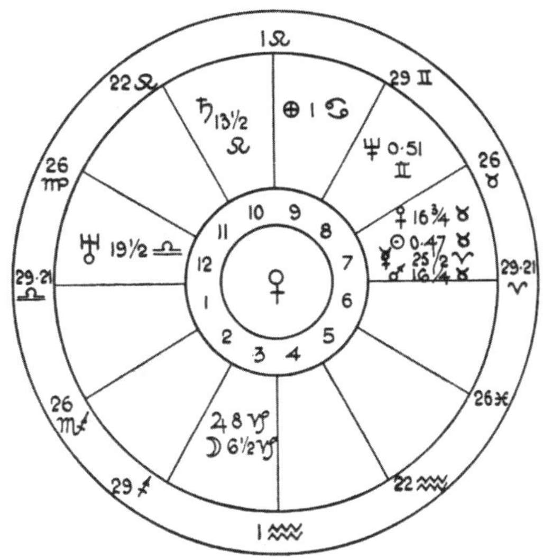

Main Aspects.

☉ □♄ △♃ ☌♂ ☌☿ △☽
☽ △☿ △♀ △☉ ☌♃ □♅
☿ ☍♅ △♃ ☌♂ ☌☉ △☽
♀ □♄ △♃ △☽
♂ △♃ □♄ ☌☉ △☽ ☌☿
♃ △♂ △☉ △♀ △☿ ☌☽
♄ ✱♅ □♂ □☉ □♀
♅ ✱♄ ☍☿ □☽
♆ –

Hanussen's Berliner Wochenschau #11 (March 25, 1932)

B. Molotow

der Vorsitzende der Volkskommissare der UdSSR., dessen Rede vor dem Zentralkomitee der Kommunistischen Partei der Sowjetunion wir heute veröffentlichen. (Seite 2.)

Berlin am Morgen

Einzelverkaufspreis in Groß-Berlin wochentags 10 Pf. Außerhalb 15 Pf.

5. Jhrg./Nr. 10 Berlin, Donnerstag, 12. Januar 1933

Redaktion, Verlag und Expedition: Berlin SW 68, Ritterstr. 75. Telefon: Dönhoff 7740 A 4 4971—73

Material für den heutigen Experimentalvortrag Hanussens im Bachsaal. Vielleicht kann der „Hellseher" auch dieses dunkle Problem aufklären:

Hanussen beim Rabbiner

Rabbinat und Matrikenführung der israelitischen Kultusgemeinde Rumburg

Z 27/32

Mit Bezug auf Ihr heutiges Schreiben wird Ihnen zur Kenntnis, dass die Eheschließung

Herrn Steinschneider-Hanussen mit Elfriede Charlotte Rühle am ersten Jänner 1928 im Tempel zu Rumburg in Gegenwart der Zeugen Erich Juhn, Schriftsteller in Warnsdorf, und Emil Förner, Verrich. Beamter in Rumburg, durch den derzeitigen Rabbiner Ignaz Popper stattfand.

Rumburg, 27. Dezember 1932.

(Stempel: Rabbinat u. Matrikenführung der isr. Cultusgemeinde Rumburg)

Der beeid. Matrikenführer: … Rabbiner.

Hanussen bei Hitler

Dämonen der Weltgeschichte

Kaiser Nero – Cesare Borgia

Astrolog. Ratgeber: Wer ist mein Typ

„Die Million im Regulus"

Nr. 10 8. Januar

Hitler vor der Offensive

Straßer bei Hindenburg

Verhandlung über Umbildung der Reichsregierung

Erst jetzt wird bekannt, daß Gregor Straßer am vergangenen Freitag, dem 6. Januar, eine Unterredung mit dem Reichspräsidenten von Hindenburg gehabt hat. Das Stattfinden dieser in der Reihe der politischen Unterhaltungen der letzten Tage nicht ganz unwichtigen Unterredung wurde bisher streng geheim gehalten, sie wurde in der Oeffentlichkeit erst bekannt durch eine an sehr versteckter Stelle erschienene Mitteilung in der Hugenberg-Presse von gestern abend. Zu der Unterredung selbst wird bemerkt, daß die „Behauptung, daß zwischen Hindenburg und Straßer bereits feste Vereinbarungen über eine Beteiligung Straßers an der Regierung getroffen seien", nicht den Tatsachen entspreche. Es habe sich „um eine erste Fühlungnahme gehandelt".

Die Mitteilungen des Hugenberg-Blattes sind in jeder Hinsicht aufschlußreich und bedeutungsvoll. Auch wenn noch keine „festen Vereinbarungen" über eine Beteiligung Straßers an der Reichsregierung zwischen Hindenburg und Straßer getroffen wurden, so beweist die Unterredung doch, daß Schleicher

den Plan einer Ergänzung der Reichsregierung durch Straßer nachdrücklichst weiter verfolgt.

Zudem hat die Unterredung genau zwei Tage nach dem Zusammentreffen von Papen und Hitler in Köln stattgefunden. Sie ist also auch als eine Demonstration an die Kreise aufzufassen, die sich bemüht haben, mit Hitler Sonderverhandlungen und Sondervereinbarungen über ihr Verhältnis zur Schleicher-Regierung zu führen. Es wird damit dokumentiert, daß Straßer nach wie vor der besondere Vertrauensmann Schleichers ist, und daß ohne Straßer eine Verständigung mit Hitler nicht in Frage kommt. Oder anders ausgedrückt: Hitler wird von Schleicher und Hindenburg nur dann in Gnaden aufgenommen, wenn er die Politik Straßers, nämlich die bedingungslose Unterstützung der Schleicher-Regierung, annimmt.

Hitler selbst ist bisher völlig ergebnislos nach Berlin gekommen. Die von ihm beabsichtigte Aussprache mit dem General Schleicher hat nicht stattgefunden. Wie wir erfahren, hat er sich zwar durch verschiedene Mittelsleute um ein Zusammentreffen mit Schleicher bemüht, dieser hat wohl zu verstehen gegeben, daß er zu einer Unterredung mit dem Nazi-Führer bereit ist, aber daß sie in diesem Augenblick nicht sehr erwünscht sei.

Der Canossagang zu Papen hat nichts genützt.

Schleichers Trumpf ist eben Straßer. Es steht fest, daß Gregor Straßer über einen festen Anhang von etwa 35 bis 40 nationalsozialistischen Reichstagsabgeordneten verfügt, die eine offene Frontstellung gegen Schleicher nicht mitmachen wollen. Unter dem Druck dieser drohenden Spaltung und der Reichstagsauflösung diktiert Schleicher dem Parteiführer Hitler seine Bedingungen. In der nächsten Woche wird Hitler seine Verhandlungsversuche wiederholen.

Bewährungsfrist für Schleicher

Unter diesem Druck Schleichers findet auch ein immer stärkeres Einschwenken der Nazis statt. So schreibt gestern der „Völkische Beobachter" in seiner Berliner Ausgabe:

The Rumberg Rabbi's Letter to Juhn **BaM** (January 12, 1933)

CHAPTER TEN
PROPHET OF THE THIRD REICH
1933

The Constitutional Crisis

Kurt von Schleicher, Hindenburg's designated Reichschancellor, had little luck assembling a working government in the winter of 1932–1933. The Social Democrats were divided about his unconventional overture for their participation in a left-right cabinet. After much debate, the Sozis pulled out of the negotiations. Germany no longer had a middle ground for stable rule. The next democratic administration had to be led by the first or second top-ranking party in the Reichstag; that is, either by the Socialists or the Nazis. Simple arithmetic demanded it. Short of a military coup or insurrection, there was only one political movement old Hindenburg could turn to now, the Sozi leadership believed: the anti-Bolshevik German party of humane Socialism.

Out of nowhere, the great schemer, Papen, still seething from his November humiliation, reentered the scene. He persuaded President Hindenburg that Hitler, reeling from the Reichstag defeat and the Strasser defection, could be induced to join the next government—as Reichschancellor. In their current enfeebled state, the Nazis could be yoked, civilized, and finally tamed.

The temperamental Führer, in a Nationalist-dominated cabinet, would have little real power or the ability to achieve his grandiose aims. Eventually, Hitler's diehard supporters would grow tired of his vacuous revolutionary promises and fade away. Or, there was the vain possibility that the National Socialists, once at the helm, would moderate their rabid programs and deal with Germany's hard realities, its failing economy, its Marxist rabble-rousers, its frustrated and wary Reichswehr.

The old man didn't know. No one knew. Everyone assumed that Adolf Hitler was finished as a viable factor in the German political arena.

The Final Hitler Sessions

How many times Hitler and Hanussen actually met in 1933—or in 1932—remains unknown. The Nazi erasure of the official records after June 1933 was so thorough that several German historians have speculated no rendezvous ever occurred. Publicly, they were seen together just once: when the Führer slightly nodded to the clairvoyant as he entered the Hotel Kaiserhof restaurant after New Year's 1933.

Bella Fromm, the widely respected political columnist from the *Vossische Zeitung* and one of the best sources for the behind-the-scenes diplomatic activity in Hitler's Berlin, reported on one of the Hitler-Hanussen encounters. The tryst took place at the Hotel Kaiserhof in the second week of January, shortly before the Weimar wheel of fortune was spun one more fateful time.

1940 Rendering of Hitler and Hanussen

Hitler, who had waited for the private session with great anticipation and dread, ordered Dzino to remain outside the suite. If Hanussen's prognosis was bad, the Führer hoped to conceal it from public knowledge. Erik began by dragging a chair to the center of the room and placing Hitler in it. The Dane studied the lance corporal's hands and felt the bumps on his scalp. He consulted some astrological keys.

The Nazi leader, according to Fromm, was frightened and awed by Hanussen's otherworldly demeanor. Erik's eyes suddenly glazed over, his body frozen in trance. After a long silence, as if spirit-guides were pointing to faint images of the future, the clairvoyant slowly articulated, "I see victory for you. . . . It cannot be stopped!"

"Hitler, completely taken in, started to tremble. He began to mutter something when Hanussen raised both his hands, apparently unaware that he was trying to speak. With due solemnity the fakir enunciated piecemeal, as though receiving the message in installments, that Hitler's destiny was in the stars, nothing could change it. He was fated to be supreme ruler of Greater Germany. At this Hitler, no longer able to contain himself, jumped to his feet and grasped Hanussen by the shoulders, which luckily woke him up so he could hear himself called 'P.G. Hanussen' (Party-Comrade Hanussen) and a man who was bound to succeed in life."

According to Dzino, who related the story to at least three associates, the Führer restated his summer promise to establish an Aryan "University of the Occult" with Erik as its dean and executive head. Goebbels, when he got word of the session, was outraged. In his *Angriff* office, he kept a thick and growing file on data relating to Hanussen's Jewish ancestry. ["I Spy on Nazi Plots," *True Detective* April 1942 and "Under the Nazi Terror," *True Detective* May 1942]

Reichschancellor Hitler

Papen pursued his wild, if ingenious, solution to the Weimar deadlock. In Cologne, before Hindenburg's son, Oskar, and Secretary of State Otto Meisner, Papen convinced the Führer to drop his extra-legal demands for National Socialist dominion. Hitler, now in high spirits, pledged to uphold the Weimar Constitution if the Old Man would approve his appointment to the Reichschancellory. The spinning political wheel stopped.

On the morning of January 30, Hindenburg handed the reins of power to Adolf Hitler. The Führer assumed the title of German Reichschancellor. For the SA and the common Nazi supporters, it was an absolute miracle. Although Papen limited the number of National Socialists in the eleven-member cabinet to two, Goering and Wilhelm Frick, Hitler appeared unconcerned about his restricted authority. ("The Chancellor in Handcuffs," one German diplomat quipped.) Hanussen's trance-prediction and Bauer's horoscope from March 1932 had come true.

Hundreds of SA, SS, and Stahlhelm battalions paraded through the streets of downtown Berlin that night. The Führer waved and heiled from his spotlighted

Hitler Waving to Supporters
From the Hotel Kaiserhof

balcony in the Hotel Kaiserhof to the endless paramilitary formations that chanted his name and returned his stiff-armed salute. The spectacular torch-light procession culminated in a midnight demonstration before the Brandenburg Gate.

To the international community, it looked like fascism had triumphed again. Another piece of the European landscape had opened its gates to totalitarian doctrine and the dictates of a race-spewing madman. Hindenburg, Papen, and their Nationalist partners begged to differ. It was they who outfoxed the volatile autocrat. In a few weeks or months, the destructive forces of both Communism and National Socialism would be blunted and checked.

For the Jews of Berlin, Hindenburg's tactical decision came as a profound shock. Nazi propaganda railed unceasingly against the perfidy of the Jewish people in Europe and their financial manipulations and cultural defilements. Even if Hitler's reign was short-lived, the political climate had turned disturbingly sour and physically menacing. Anti-Semitism provided the philosophical and emotional armature of the Führer's entire revolutionary cause.

It was time to make alternative plans.

Most of Hanussen's Jewish staff were doing just that. Like other probable targets of anti-Semitic Nazi terror, they mapped out extended winter vacations in Paris, Vienna, Prague, or Budapest. The cagiest among them transferred their German bank accounts to secure firms in Zurich and Geneva.

Hanussen, ignoring the advice of Dzino and his Jewish colleagues, chose an opposite course of action.

The Palace of the Occult

After New Year's 1933, Hanussen expanded his Berlin operations, acquiring a second magazine for political, aesthetic, and business analysis, *Die Kritik*, and leased a dilapidated mansion at 16 Lietzenburgstrasse for his long-awaited Palace of the Occult.

Tapping into his huge fortune and many artistic contacts, Erik directed the massive palatial reconstruction. And the results were impressive, magnificent, like a supernatural appendage to Versailles. Some journalists later compared to it an exquisite pagan temple, supplemented with the latest 1930s technology. The Victorian-style building was rewired for such innovations as indirect neon lighting and ubiquitous, miniature recording devices (concealed inside every column).

Inscribed on the Palace's Lietzenburgstrasse doors and in the passageways were mystic and astrological signs from the ancient Egyptian and Babylonian pantheon. Tiny wooden Indian prayer benches were set in the foyer. (This would be a resting-place for immobile, blue-eyed attendants in diaphanous garments of white and pale green.) Gold-leaf covered walls and circular rows of pure Carrara marble statues guided the visitor into a maze of dimly-lighted vestibules.

In the centermost chamber of the Palace, the Hall of Silence, a hydraulic lift was installed. This hidden contraption could hoist the master soothsayer fifteen feet in the air to the top of a massive domed ceiling. (All the better to consult with High Heaven about the profane affairs of his supplicants.) On the tiled floor, a colossal bronze sculpture of Hanussen, dressed in the toga of a Caesar, was erected. His elevated left arm was permanently cast into the Nazi gesture of victory. And by his side, two marble seeresses from classical mythology, the Oracle of Delphi and the Greek sorceress Sibyl, were tastefully positioned.

Hanussen designed an inner sanctum, the Room of Glass, for private readings. Surrounded by Buddhas and cages of deadly snakes and exotic reptiles, the invited guests were to sit at a circular table of glass and press their palms against its transparent face. Underneath the glass-top, a wheel encrypted with kabbalistic emblems, dates, algebraic symbols, and zodiac figures would revolve. When the dial came to a halt, Hanussen, on a swivel chair in the center, could then divine its occult meaning.

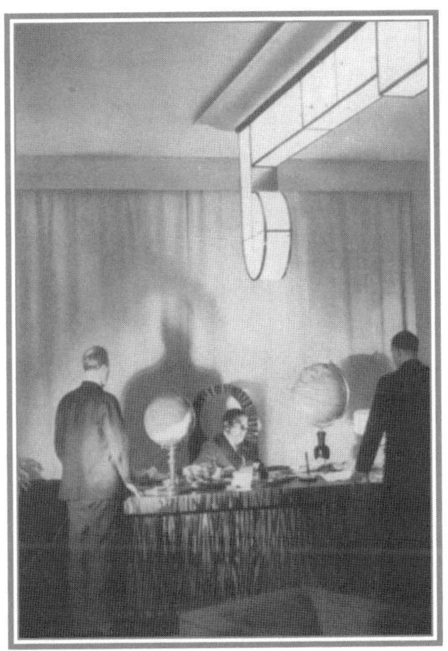

Hanussen in the Room of Glass

Hanussen at the Palace of the Occult, 1932

Hanussen and Iguana

The Palace took two months to build. Erik rushed the architects and craftsmen every week to complete the project in record time. The opening was announced for February 26, 1933.

The Tightening Noose

Six days before Hindenburg consented to the National Socialist-Nationalist union, Hanussen attempted to cover his political and racial tracks. In a full-page statement published in the January 24 edition of the *BW* (no. 39), Erik explained his personal backing for the Führer's party. It was entitled "In My Own Case!"

After disputing the long lists of Communist charges against him, Hanussen proclaimed to his readers that he was neither a Nazi nor a Communist, neither an anti-Semite nor a philo-Semite. "I respect every honest political tendency, ridicule no religion and no nation. I am equally indifferent to the Jews as they are to me."

Then his paean to National Socialism unfurled: "I have pledged to be first, with everything I own and am, to sacrifice at the altar of the German lands for Germany, if necessary and if the time comes. [. . .] I know that Adolf Hitler has already sacrificed everything for the National Ideal. I have seen SA-men in torn shoes and thin jackets, standing in the icy winds for hours in order to perform their duty; I have observed altruism, integrity, and true patriotism among the millions who stand behind Hitler and Hugenberg. Therefore, I have no choice but to show my respect and my gratitude, unhesitatingly—in spite of every obstacle—to serve the truth. It would not matter if I hailed from Honolulu or Krähwinkel, if my great-uncle was the Wonder-Rabbi Prossnitz or the Archbishop of Cologne."

The following issue of the *BW* (no. 40) on February 8 filled its cover page with a photograph of Hitler inside an astrological disk. The headline, underlined in red, shrieked, "Victory!" Beneath the Führer's head was an open letter from Erik Jan Hanussen. Again he announced that he was not a politician or ever wanted to be one. Still his prophecies had proved to be accurate. Except for his Marxist enemies, all of Germany was rejoicing in the miracle. Hanussen humbly concluded that his historical mission was at an end. The German nation was finally in the stewardship of able hands.

Erik spoke too soon. The "Prophet of the Third Reich" had not yet departed from the national stage. His adversaries on the left and right still had him in their sights.

For one, Frei did not leave Berlin. Through the Schleicher-Papen stalemate, through the Hitler nomination and Nazi revelry, and into the unsettled month of February, he remained at his office in the Kosmos-Verlag fortress. On the very day that the fortieth *BW* broadside hit the stands, the *BaM* countered with a reproduction of Hanussen's Viennese birth certificate. Frei wrote disingenuously that he was personally indifferent to Erik's Jewish pedigree. The editors of *Der Angriff* and the *Völkischer Beobachter*, however, were not. Hitler's spiritual adviser was a pureblood Hebrew.

One week later, Frei's *Berlin am Morgen* was banned from further publication. Juhn mailed a copy of Hanussen's Jewish marriage contract (a *Ketuba*) to the Führer's office in the Reichschancellery. Frei and Laserstein also petitioned the civic court for a counter-suit against Herschmann Steinschneider. The plaintiffs would determine, once and for all, that the so-called clairvoyant was both a fraud and the descendant of the *vunder-rebbe*. The court date was ordered for February 21. Sooner or later, the anti-Hanussen forces had to achieve their goal. The *Jenischmann* was too big a target.

When the attorneys for Hanussen and the *BaM* writers exchanged documents in court, however, there was utter confusion over Erik's birth name. The Prossnitz certificate read (in Yiddish) "Herschmann Steinschneider" and the Viennese paper had "Hermann Steinschneider" printed in German. Since Laserstein's lawyer had filed the Prossnitz version, the magistrate voided the suit/counter-suit cases and allowed for a four-week adjournment. The trial was to reconvene on March 21. Punitive damages were set at 30,000 marks.

Erik's attorney had bought some breathing room for his client but not much. Besides the Kosmos journalists, others were waiting for Hanussen's day in court with great anticipation.

A Warning

Some time in February, Erik was formally baptized as a Catholic and inducted into the SA. He was given an SA uniform, and a Nazi pendant was ceremonially affixed to the front of his Cadillac. Hanussen later received a card, certifying his official membership in the National Socialist Workers Party.

In doing so, Hanussen was following the lead of tens of thousands ambitious and enterprising Germans. (Few of them, one would suppose, had full Jewish lineage.) The numbers of newly-minted Hitlerites applying for Nazi membership across the nation had increased so precipitously that the Führer himself stopped the operation. The Johnny-come-lately stampede was not fair to the pre-January 30 faithful.

Hanussen spent the greater part of February out of public sight. Presumably he was at the Palace of the Occult, scrutinizing and overseeing last-minute details.

On Friday, February 24, a "Special Ballot and Struggle Number" of *Die Hanussen-Zeitung* (no. 42) appeared as an astrological guide for the Reichstag election to be held on March 5. This election was seen as a national plebiscite on Hindenburg's controversial resolution to make Hitler his co-partner. The most unusual political aspect of the issue was a feature called the "Death-Horoscope of the New Reichstag." Hanussen and Baecker each wrote about the pernicious movement of the planets over the next four days. Jupiter, Mercury, Uranus, and particularly Mars were about to invade alien Houses. It meant strong indications of Communist subterfuge and, in their appraisal, appropriate Nazi retaliation. No matter what internecine warfare transpired, each author claimed that the stars pointed inalterably to the "death" of the German Reichstag.

The Last Séance

The opening of Hanussen's Palace of the Occult on Sunday, February 26, was the prime social event of the topsy-turvy season. Besides the heads of Berlin's newspaper trusts, celebrities and politicians of every stripe begged to be placed on the VIP roster.

Erik's old fans, like the writer Curt Riess; Jules Marx, the artistic director of the Scala; Eduard Duisberg, his assistant; Fritz Jacobson, the variety publicist; Ewers; Prof. Rudolf Grossmann, the sketch artist and journalist; film star Siegfried Arno; Count Helldorf (in uniform); and his SA friends, including Ohst, made their appearance. There was also a retinue of aristocrats: Louis Ferdinand, the Prince of Prussia; Count Fassbänder with his wife; Prince von Reuss; and a White Russian gentlelady who asserted that she was the Russian Princess Anastasia Romanoff. (The Dane promised to authenticate her bloodline.)

Shortly before the evening began, Erik telephoned Hans Kahan, one of the *BW's* chief writers. He implored the Jewish journalist to attend the reception. Kahan had already prepared his emigration papers. Yet Hanussen needed him once again. The Prophet wanted to show Helldorf that he knew no difference between Mosaic-Germans and Aryan militants. Besides, Marx, Jacobson, and a dozen other Jews promised to come. Reluctantly, Kahan agreed to make a showing (and assist in the secret recordings of guests).

Upon their entrance to the Palace, Hanussen's male guests were given white rubber slippers to place over their shoes and the temple-priestesses enjoined them to absolute silence.

In the foyer and Hall of Silence, red candles flickered. An organist played Mendelssohn, switched over to Bach chorales, and—as Nazi-like searchlights flooded the room—the Funeral March from Beethoven's "Eroica" dramatically resounded. Servants entered with trays of fine champagne. Hidden wall-lights illuminated the place in darkened tones of grayish-purple.

Then, exactly at ten o'clock, clouds of greenish fog from an arched passageway swirled into the main hall.

Erik's sometime nemesis and newfound comrade, Joe Labéro, recalled the Maestro's extraordinary entry:

"Hanussen was not in sight. Then, concealed somewhere in the room, an organ began playing the thunderous music of Wagner. The lights dimmed and went out, leaving only a brilliant spotlight slashing down on the center of the floor. Slowly, the floor moved, a chasm appearing in it. Two panels moved back and a throne rose majestically to tower fifteen feet in the air. On an ebony-black throne was Hanussen, clothed in a scarlet robe. He was holding a large crystal, with colored lights flickering through it, and there was a half-dazed expression on his face. [. . .] Hanussen began to speak, his rich voice seeming to come from the walls. For the first thirty minutes he devoted himself to general predictions. I wasn't too interested and didn't follow him too closely, but a majority of the things I remember came true. He predicted the blood purge that was to come later and the war with England, Russia, and America." ["I Robbed Hitler", *Keyhole Detective Cases* #1 (March 1942)]

As he rested on the heavenly divan and stared at the crystal ball, Erik called out the names of individual guests and delivered otherworldly warnings and practical suggestions, which might permit them to sidestep fate's clutches.

The downbeat auguries certainly dampened the vivacious atmosphere. Hanussen's well-bred partygoers, however, were not about to offend their generous host. As soon as the lift descended, they applauded heartily and returned to their devilish repartee. Drinking, eating, general merrymaking, and guided tours of the temple's many architectural delights followed.

Hermann Hacker, the reporter for the *12-Uhr Blatt*, compared the opening-night extravaganza to an UFA science-fantasy film scene come alive.

Séance on the Night of February 26, 1933

Maria Paudler

At midnight, Dzino gathered about twenty guests and herded them into the Room of Glass. The Dane wanted to hold a private séance. Twelve of the elect took seats at the astrological table, the others hunkered down on stools around the room.

In one corner sat Maria Paudler, the blonde Czechoslovakian actress. She was apparently quite inebriated. Erik chose her to be his medium. Not wanting to disappoint the politically prominent gentlemen or high-society guests, Maria consented and Hanussen led her to an elevated platform.

First the "sitters" were asked to write down questions and place them in sealed envelopes. Erik took an envelope from an old noblewoman. He felt the contact-object and replied. Her letter concerned the health of a relative residing far away. She gasped. That was correct. The telepath assured her that the person in question would recover fully. Except for Helldorf, none of the sitters or the guests outside the circle had ever witnessed Hanussen at work. They were flabbergasted.

Then the Nazi Count handed Erik his sealed envelope. The clairvoyant shut his eyes and seemed to fall into a deep trance. He divined Helldorf's question: "Will our great plan to consolidate power succeed?" The Count's eyes widened. Hanussen responded affirmatively. It would.

On the tiny stage, Maria crouched in her chair and sipped champagne, which Dzino poured into her glass flute. She was enjoying the spooky parlor-game. Erik walked over to her and stared directly into her eyes. The drunken Maria giggled. Hanussen began to massage her temples and she became frightened and repelled by his touch. The actress thought that she might pass out from the wine and weird shadows that intermittently flashed from the rotating glass table.

Hanussen asked her what she saw. Maria closed her eyes. She saw red. The master clairvoyant wanted to know more. Could the red be flames? Maria straightened up. Yes, the red shapes could be flames. Flames from a great house. The blonde actress then fainted.

The Dane filled in the girl's prophetic image. "There are fires. I see a Great House is being consumed by flames."

The clairvoyant paused and stood frozen for a haunting moment. Dzino declared the séance over. As the sitters got up to leave, the secretary requested the journalists in the room not to report anything related to the Glass Room séance.

Exactly twenty hours later, the Reichstag erupted in flames. It signaled the first event that would lead to the Second World War.

"The Reichstag Is Burning!"

Just before ten o'clock in the evening of February 27, 1933, Helmut Heisig, the Detective-Inspector of the Berlin Police Department, Division IA, received an emergency telephone call. An agitated officer informed him that the Reichstag building was on fire. Thick clouds of smoke were seen billowing from its windows since 9:15 and now the main cupola itself was crumbling in flames. Luckily, Prussian police had already captured the culprit. He was a Dutch Communist.

The caller also told Heisig that fire brigades from the Linienstrasse Fire House were in action. Firefighters were, in that moment, attempting to contain what appeared to be very considerable damage to the nineteenth-century structure.

Hitler and Goering rushed to the crime scene in separate vehicles. The Führer appeared to be genuinely surprised and elated when he viewed the smoldering chambers. He hailed the arson as a "sign from heaven."

Hitler tramped up an unscathed stairwell to gain a better vista of the raging inferno. With him were Goering, Frick, Prince August Wilhelm, the Mayor of Berlin, the Chief of Police, the British Ambassador, and the London *Daily Express* journalist Sefton Delmer. Goering vouched that the outrage was the work of the Communists and his Prussian police were "ready for anything." The Führer reacted with insane anger. His face turned scarlet and he screamed over the sirens. "We will show them! [. . .] The German people have been soft too long. Every Communist official must be shot. All Communist deputies must be hanged this very night. All friends of the Communists must be locked up." [*The Reichstag Fire: Legend and Truth*, 1962]

Meanwhile at the police station, Heisig interrogated the bare-chested suspect. (His shirt was supposedly used to spread the conflagration.) The Dutch suspect spoke German fluently and confessed that he was the lone lawbreaker. The fire was intended to galvanize Germany's dormant working classes and spark their complacent leaders into an anti-fascist, Marxist revolt. The crazed man gave his name as Marinus van der Lubbe.

Van der Lubbe's confession presented the "handcuffed" Reichschancellor with something that he had ardently sought since 1923: a justification for absolute power.

On March 23, Hindenburg and the dithering Nationalists granted the Führer an extra-constitutional authority, the "Enabling Act." This allowed Goering's police force to arrest Communist Party members and other opponents of the newly-emboldened Nazi regime, suspend press freedoms, confiscate private property, and abolish all personal civil liberties. The war against the Jews was finally legalized.

The Reichstag in Flames

Adolf Hitler's dreaded Third Reich had come into being on that day.

Papen's Nationalists had only one firm judicial entreaty: an objective German tribunal had to determine incontrovertibly that van der Lubbe and his Bolshevik accomplices, in fact, had torched the Reichstag and conspired to foment a Communist revolution in Germany. Four others were indicted with the Dutchman and charged with high treason: Ernst Torgler, the speaker for the Communist Party in the Reichstag; Georgi Dimitroff, the Bulgarian Comintern apparatchik; and two lesser Bulgarian Communists.

The "Reichstag Fire Trial" promised to be one of the most significant public proceedings in modern German history. Testimony was to be held at the Supreme Court in Leipzig on September 21, 1933.

Questions Without Answers

One fact was incontestable. Van der Lubbe confessed to the criminal deed in the Berlin Police Station and never wavered from his story. The "antisocial vagrant" told Heisig that two days earlier he tried to ignite a welfare office in Berlin East, the downtown City Hall, and the old Imperial Palace. None of his attempts succeeded. The disabled—and probably mentally impaired—van der Lubbe could not be considered an accomplished arsonist.

Basic forensic questions arose: how could a foreigner break into the darkened Reichstag building undetected and, in a two-minute span, set some two dozen fires? The parliament assembly hall and its adjoining chambers were mammoth, oversized. Each combustible target had to be carefully selected and the fires artfully executed. The Dutchman's arsenal of tools consisted of cigar-store matches and a petrol can. Van der Lubbe's spellbound, lethargic, mumbling, empty-headed—almost robotic—behavior did not correspond to the vital enterprise.

There were other puzzles. What secret relationship did van der Lubbe have with the German Communist Party? (He was once a card-carrying member although he resigned in the late '20s. The political drifter was also an activist in other Marxist associations and briefly worked in the Weissenberg cult.) Who paid for the unemployed twenty-four-year-old's extensive European travels? And most enigmatic was motive. Only Hitler, among Germany's feuding national leaders, could benefit from the Reichstag's destruction. Torgler and his party comrades seemed totally unprepared for the revolutionary clarion call.

The German and international press smelled a rat. Still no plausible evidence pointed directly to the Führer or Goering.

And then there was the question of Erik Jan Hanussen.

The Great Plan

Three days before the Monday disaster, *Die Hanussen-Zeitung* heralded the Reichstag's "death." The Communists, under Mars' baneful influence, were planning lethal harm to the institution. The newspaper horoscope said the provocation would occur soon, certainly within days.

And at the Monday morning séance, the medium-hypnotist team of Paudler-Hanussen had specifically warned of a "Great Building" going up in flames. Over a half-dozen reliable people witnessed the event.

Dr. Franz Höllering, the editor-in-chief of the *12-Uhr Blatt* and the *Montag Morgen*, later wrote, in sworn testimony to the World Committee for the Victims of German Fascism, that he spoke with Hanussen on the telephone between 9:30 and 9:45 during the night of the Reichstag Fire. According to Höllering, Erik acted giddy and knowledgeable about the unfolding calamity. The editor told Hanussen that police had just informed his reporters that they had seized a Communist suspect. Höllering, like most of Berlin's newsmen, was skeptical about the claim. In the current climate, any left-wing threat was suicidal. Hanussen assured Höllering that the arson was definitely planned by the Communists and Germany would soon see a government counter-response. [Lord Marey, *Braunbuch über Reichstagsbrand und Hitler-Terror* (Basel: Universum, 1933)]

The prescient article, the spiritual vision, and the telephone conversation, taken together, can only be explained in a couple of ways. Hanussen's jeremiad was coincidental or the product of a veritably clairvoyant mind. Second possibility: Erik was apprised by Helldorf—or another Nazi agent—of the insidious undercover action and maniacally used it to promote his reputation and tabloid.

A third supposition is the most remarkable and, at first, strains historical credibility: Hanussen, without Nazi or Communist knowledge, instigated the Reichstag blaze himself, which nullified the Weimar Constitution and endowed Adolf Hitler with the unchecked hegemony of a German Caesar or a Napoleon Bonaparte.

Wilfred Kugel, in his *Hanussen: Die Wahre Geschichte des Hermann Steinschneider* (Dusseldorf: Grupello, 1998), the best source of documented Hanussenia, has brilliantly laid out the third rationale for Erik's timely predictions and Reichstag Fire conundrum.

The Dane hypnotized van der Lubbe, a homeless patsy Dzino discovered in a proletarian *Lokal*, and taught him the professional ins and outs of breaking and entering and advanced pyrotechnic feats—both Hanussen specialties. After a series of auspicious demonstrations, van der Lubbe was judged to be an able subject for the scheme. The willing Dutchman was shown blueprints of the Reichstag—the statehouse was one block from Erik's apartment—and taught how to use specially designed incendiary devices.

Which Nazis were privy to Hanussen's brazen plot at this point is still open to question. It is more than probable that Count Helldorf and a few of his aides participated in its history-shattering execution. Later events strongly suggest it.

The fantastic conspiracy has been advanced in print by ten authors, several of whom had intimate connections with Hanussen or Helldorf in the last two weeks of February 1933. First, Walter Korodi, a renegade SS officer, wrote about the Hanussen-Reichstag link after he escaped to Switzerland in 1934. Korodi maintained that it was Helldorf who brought van der Lubbe to the Dane for the hypnotic inductions. [*Ich kann nicht schweigen* (Zurich: Europa Verlag, 1936)] His revelation was independently confirmed by Dr. Gerda Walther, a noted parapsychologist who worked as a dowser in a top-secret project for German Naval Intelligence during World War Two. [*Tomorrow* (Winter 1956)]

The German novelists, Lion Feuchtwanger and Will Berthold, relying on personal accounts, made the van der Lubbe subplot the core of their romans à clef on Hanussen's Nazi machinations. [*Double, Double, Toil and Trouble* (New York: Viking Press, 1943) and *Hanussen* (Munich: Bastei-Lübbe, 1987)] Harry Schulze-Wilde and Cziffra both claimed to have witnessed the Dzino-van der Lubbe relationship firsthand or consorted with people who did.

Circumstantial evidence bears out Kugel and his forebears' narratives. The widow of the Reichstag Judge Wilhelm Bünger in 1966 recalled that Hanussen's name came up repeatedly in pretrial statements as an obvious influence on the van der Lubbe operation, but Nazi legal scholars exhorted the magistrate to excise any references to the Jewish clairvoyant. Van der Lubbe's own brother did not recognize Marinus during the trial. He appeared to be subhuman, physically unable to defend or explain his actions, in a post-hypnotic state. Court-appointed psychologists concurred with that assessment.

One bizarre aspect of the Reichstag Trial amazed everyone—and was captured on newsreel footage. Van der Lubbe, whose head remained stuck to his chest and whose voice was virtually inaudible, stood erect only once—when Count Helldorf,

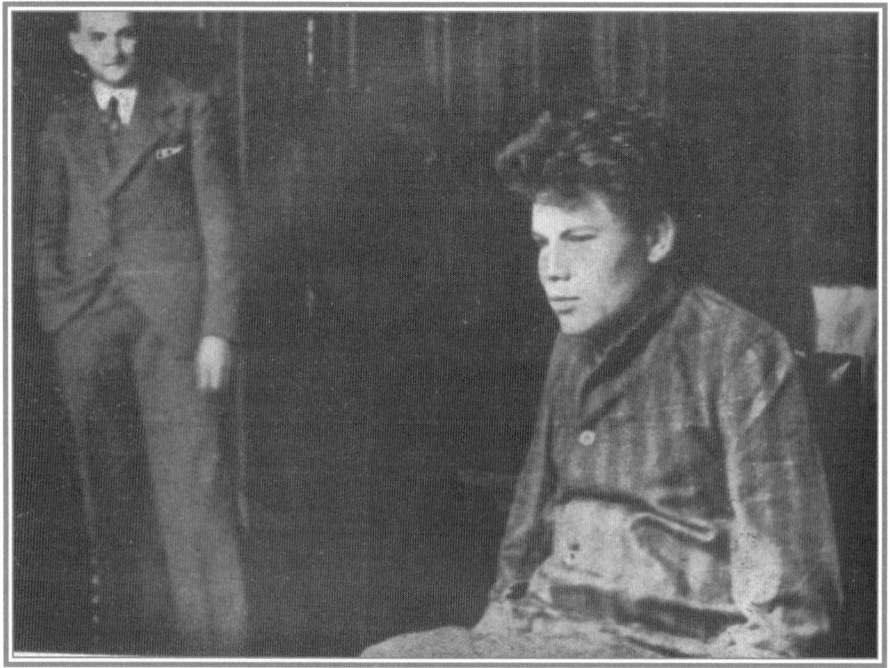

Marinus van der Lubbe in the Courtroom

Kreuz und quer durch die Welt:

Erlebnisse mit
Adolf Hitler im Felde

Die Hanussen-Zeitung
20 Pf.

No. 43

8. März

Nach dem Triumph
Hitlers nächste Mission

Was geschieht in den nächsten 14 Tagen:

Als Deutschlands Dornenweg begann
Horoskope der Urheber des Versailler Diktates:
Wilson, Poincaré, Clemenceau, Lloyd George

Erik Jan Hanussen: Die Unterschrift als Spiegel des Berufes

Kurfürst August der Starke und die Frauen

Bolschewismus ohne Maske: Horoskop der Rätediktatur in Bayern
Kurt Eisner — Toller — Eglhofer

testifying during cross-examination, commanded the condemned man to stand straight. Van der Lubbe, for the first time, changed his deportment. The Dutchman jerked upward like a puppet. No one knew what that meant.

In his characteristic broken-syllable monotone, van der Lubbe stated that he had never seen Helldorf outside the Leipzig courtroom. The lone beacon of revolution again muttered verbatim the Marxist banalities that Heisig and his lieutenants had first heard on the night of the arson. Equally puzzling, van der Lubbe could not corroborate his daily whereabouts after he reached Berlin on February 19, 1933.

Walther, an old hand at hypnosis, believed that Helldorf's voice returned van der Lubbe to his post-suggestive condition. This is consistent with Hanussen's description of the seemingly normal behavior of a Hypnotic Medium in "Are You a Medium or Hypnotist?" (pp. 18.)

Probable Motives

Erik Jan Hanussen's direct role with the Reichstag Fire and the installation of the Hitler dictatorship is still conspiratorial guesswork. The personal motives, however, for such an involvement are more clear.

Even after the Führer assumed the position of Reichschancellor, the clairvoyant had to contend with deadly enemies on the left and right. Frei, Laserstein, and Juhn had documentary proof of Erik's Jewish lineage and occult shams. Their day in court, March 21, was fast approaching. Goebbels and Goering were annoyed with the loose-talking pseudo-Dane and likely jealous of his proximity to their superstitious leader. Goebbels' dossier on the "Jew Hanussen" had expanded since Christmas, thanks to Juhn's contributions.

Short of abandoning his Palace, publications, and exalted status as "the Third Reich's Prophet," Erik could only go on the offensive. Bequeathing Hitler unmitigated power to rule Germany, he correctly inferred, would quickly result in the outlawing of the Communist Party. (It happened on February 28.) His *BaM* plaintiffs would be forced to flee the country before the March court proceedings. (They did.) The trio crossed the border to Czechoslovakia in March.

And since the Reichstag imbroglio was accomplished by him personally, through surreptitious means, Goebbels and company would be forever at Erik's beck and call.

Hanussen, the ultimate soothsayer, had failed to understand that his complicity in the Reichstag plot (or predictions of it), the huge amounts of money owed to him by Helldorf and his SA underlings, as well as films of Nazi orgies secretly recorded on the Ursel IV were all capital liabilities. Blackmail, the *Jenischmann* conveniently forgot, was very poor protection against murderous criminals.

The Dane's Communist antagonists were dispatched and scattered. His Nazi opponents, on the other hand, were more resolute to rid the world of this Jewish pest.

March 1933

The Scala booked Hanussen again for the entire month of March. He shared the stage with an acrobatic team, Large-Morgner; Grübers' Oddities; Patsy Marr, a dancer who performed upside down; the family comic act of the Four Rickys; an Arab high-jumper Omar; and the usual dazzling variety numbers. Erik received an honorarium of 850 marks for his twice-daily performance.

In a curious racial misstep, *Die Hanussen-Zeitung* continued to promote Kabbala as a divining source for the clairvoyant's fans. This was particularly unfortuitous since his newspaper, according to Egon Erwin Kisch, was only one of two issued to prisoners in the newly created concentration camp at Dachau. The other was the official National Socialist illustrated daily, the *Völkischer Beobachter*.

Count Helldorf and Nazi bigwigs continued to frequent the Palace of the Occult.

Although many of Hanussen's occult competitors were now on the run, Max Moecke, trading on his unblemished Aryan bloodline, attempted a comeback. He publicly mocked Hanussen as a greasy Semite. In early March, an SA squad trapped and cornered Moecke at the Romanische Café and lashed him with a bullwhip. (Heinrich Mann, the author of *The Blue Angel* and brother of Thomas, dramatized the cruel spectacle in a sketch for his anti-fascist theatrical anthology, *Szenen aus dem Nazileben* [1933].)

The second part of March did not augur well for Erik or his friends.

On March 20, Count Helldorf, who had been appointed High Police Commissioner of Berlin in February, was summarily dismissed from his post. Nazi

Prisoners During a Reading Period in Concentration Camp at Dachau

Minister of the Interior Hermann Goering informed him by telephone that his new position was one of equal value: Chief Police Commissioner of Potsdam, where one of his prime functions would involve the breeding of horses. Other SA officers in Hanussen's circle were suddenly reassigned or demoted.

Two days later, an old Viennese acquaintance, Toni Otto, the owner of the Scala's corner restaurant, the Grüner Zweig, warned Erik that two mysterious men, possibly Gestapo agents, had questioned him about the Dane's daily routine at the variety house. [PEM, *Heimweh nach dem Kurfürstendamm* (Berlin: Lothar Blanvalet Verlag, 1952)]

Hanussen knew that he had been reckless of late. He bragged to Ohst about his sessions with the Führer. When asked by the SA-Man about his impressions of the god-man, Erik tossed off that "Adolf looks more like an unemployed hairdresser than a Caesar." Word got back to the diplomatic corps, who grew more and more fascinated by the "Court Astrologer." [Bella Fromm, *Blood and Banquets* (Garden City, New Jersey: Garden City Publishing, 1944)]

Hanussen made still another foolish effort to bolster his Berlin prospects. On March 23, he appeared at the *Berliner Tageblatt* office at the invitation of Karl Vetter, its current editor. The Mosse establishment, like other Jewish-owned concerns, was in the process of being "Aryanized." Erik offered to purchase the prestigious daily, maybe even the entire publishing conglomerate. One of the SA officers handling the transaction, Ohst, laughed in his face. [*Heimweh nach dem Kurfürstendamm*]

Hanussen no longer had Nazi protection.

End Game

On the evening of March 24, 1933, a squadron of SA-Men showed up at Hanussen's apartment. The Prophet was about to depart for his nine o'clock appearance at the Scala. Dzino greeted the officers at the door and led them in. When Hanussen was informed that he was under arrest, the clairvoyant tried to pass it off as a practical joke. The commanding officer demanded all of the loan receipts that Hanussen had collected from his SA debtors. Hanussen quickly complied.

While a search was conducted of his bedroom and private safe, the Baroness and Hanussen's secretary, Elisabeth Heine, were told that the entertainer was charged with working in league with the Communists. Dzino telephoned Marx to cancel the evening performance.

The Scala MC made this announcement onstage: "Herr Hanussen has suffered a sudden nervous breakdown and had to be rushed to a sanatorium. He will not perform tonight. Those desiring a refund can obtain one at the ticket office tonight." [*Hanussen: Ein Berich*]

Hanussen was driven to Gestapo headquarters on General-Pape Strasse in his own red Bugatti. At the recently established station house, Erik faced a new charge: submitting a phony Aryan certificate in order to gain admittance to the Nazi Party. The penalty for such a deception was unstated.

After two hours of intense interrogation, the "Jew Steinschneider" was released. He returned to his ransacked apartment on Bendlerstrasse around one o'clock. In a near hysteria, Hanussen telephoned his closest confederates. Exactly at the moment when he implored his wife, Fritzi, to contact a lawyer, the phone line went dead. [*Hanussen: Die Wahre Geschichte des Hermann Steinschneider*]

Using an invisible ink, Hanussen penned his last letter. It was written to Juhn, temporarily settled in a Czech village safely outside the Reich. It read: "I have no time for long explanations, Erich. Let's be friends again at the end. I wasn't as shrewd as I thought, nor as stupid as you believed. But stupid enough. Yesterday they beat me till I was half dead. But half isn't enough for them. I know that without going into trance. You don't believe in clairvoyance—but the great Jagler [code name for Hitler] does. I've fixed up some notes for him that'll make him dizzy. That Rumburg God spelled my finish. I always thought that business about the Jews was just an election trick of theirs. It wasn't. Read carefully what my colleague Daniel has to say on the subject, in Chapters 11 and 12. Count the days, but only after they have destroyed a hundred temples in a single day—that's the time to start counting. The first date you get will mark the fall of the man who wants to become the ruler of the world by brute force. And the second date will mark the day on which will occur the triumphal entry of the victors. This is my farewell to you." [*Redbook Magazine* (May 1942), and *Something to Hope For* (New York: The Book of Gold, 1942)]

Hanussen left the seemingly blank note for the Baroness. He gave her instructions to hand-deliver it to Juhn. The former secretary, in turn, carried it with him to Vienna, the South of France, and eventually to New York in 1938. Pierre van

1940 Rendering of Hanussen's Arrest

Paassen published the missive in his follow-up article on the Jewish clairvoyant in *Redbook*. (Ernest Juhn, the nephew of Erich and a Hanussen insider, later authenticated the final communiqué.)

In the early morning on March 25, three SA-men broke into Erik's apartment and dragged him back to the Gestapo barracks. Waiting there were Rudolf Steinle, Kurt Egger, and SA-Führer Ohst. Each held a pistol. Hanussen was executed with three shots. Two struck him in the head. His lifeless body was robbed of everything except for thirty marks in bills and the corpse was dumped in a field north of Berlin. Ohst notified his superior Group-Führer Karl Ernst that the action had been successful.

On April 7, a farmer, Mathias Hummel, discovered the disfigured remains of Erik Jan Hanussen near the Staakower woods. (The face had already been ravaged by vermin and was nearly unrecognizable. Maggots swarmed over the wounds.)

Heine, Erik's chauffeur, and two friends were driven to the local morgue in Zossen and asked to identify the stylishly-dressed cadaver. It was Hanussen, to be sure. Despite the considerable injuries and swelling of the body, Heine recognized the face of her employer. Its rigid expression projected an expression of absolute horror.

During the ten days the Dane was declared missing, the Palace of the Occult (Room of Glass and all) and several of Hanussen's apartments were thoroughly looted.

The Berlin edition of the *Völkischer Beobachter* (No. 98) printed the following notice on April 8: "Dead body found under mysterious circumstances. The unidentified dead body of a man was discovered by workmen in a forest plantation between Neuhof and Baruth. The corpse, savagely mauled by game, thus unidentifiable, appears to have lain there for days and no personal papers were found on the man. The Berlin police crime squad assigned a commission to investigate the discovery. An unconfirmed rumor claims the dead body is that of clairvoyant Hanussen."

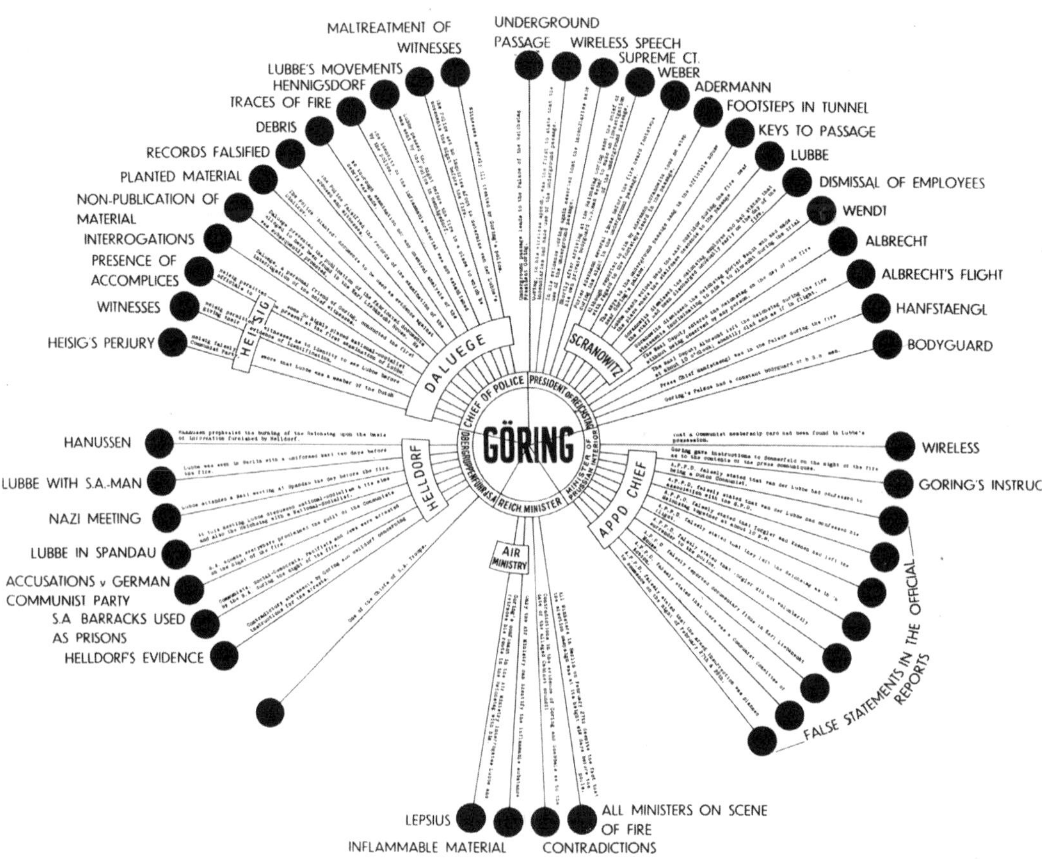

THE THREADS LEAD TO GÖRING

World Committee Chart Diagramming Inconstancies of the Nazi Charges Against Communist Leaders and Arson Links to Hermann Goering, **The Reichstag Fire Trial** (1934)

CHAPTER ELEVEN

AFTERMATH

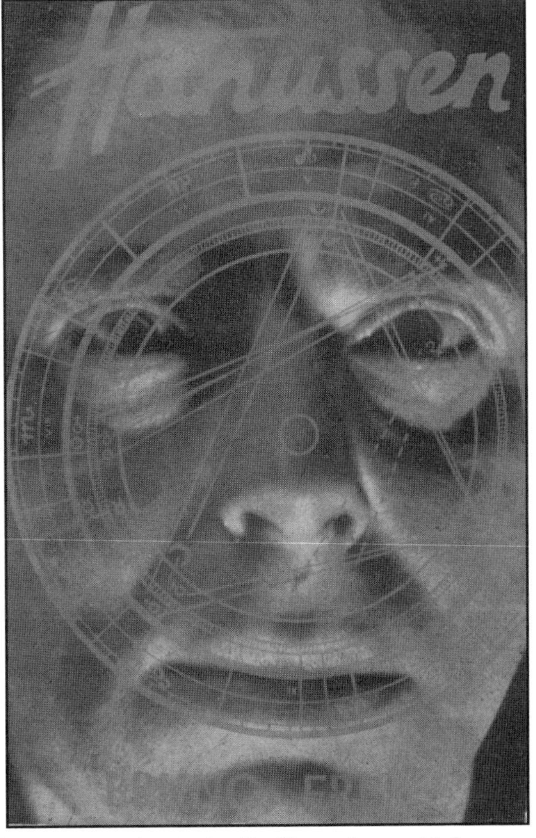

Last Rites

Announcements of Hanussen's murder by unknown hands appeared in all of the Berlin daily papers over the April 8–9 weekend. They were curt, unemotional, and, more or less, parroted the *Völkischer Beobachter* piece or the official police report approved by Criminal Commissar Hermann Albrecht.

A few suggestive details were added during the following week: the clairvoyant had many enemies in the Berlin underworld; he was challenged twenty-three times in court, he had countless lovers, some of whom were married. Hundreds of Berliners, from all walks of life, had cause to see the Dane dead. The style of execution, the placement of his body under a fir-tree, and the absence of forensic clues, however, pointed to a professional job. The Hanussen-Steinschneider case was consigned to the unsolved murder section of Albrecht's Police Headquarters. It would be one of thousands of unsolved murders over the next two years.

No mention of the SA, the Gestapo, or Goering's State Police was cited.

On April 11, 1933, Erik Jan Hanussen was buried in a Catholic cemetery in Stahnsdorf. At first, the SA wanted a private funeral in Zossen but Heine intervened. The priest who baptized the Dane conducted the service. It was a quiet, sad ceremony. Only six others attended. Among the mourners were Fritzi and Heine. The inscription on the tombstone read just "Erik Jan Hanussen." (The gravesite stands today untouched by vandals or wartime assault.)

Into the Whirlwind

Everyone associated with Hanussen was alarmed by the swift turn of events. The Group-Führer of the Berlin East Nazi unit, who was given the use of Hanussen's silver-green Cadillac, left the car in front of the Bendlerstrasse apartment. Inside were the keys and registration papers.

SA-Führer Karl Ernst also returned Erik's La Salle sedan. He professed that he could not accept any gift from a "known Jew." Hanussen's editor, Bauer, and the astrologer Baecker changed the name of *Die Hanussen-Zeitung* to the *Astro-Politische Rundshau.* The tainted and transparently pro-Hitler bimonthly lasted only a few issues.

Erik's surviving ex-wives and Jewish relatives attempted to claim portions of Hanussen extensive properties and bank accounts. The Nazi-dominated courts were unsympathetic.

The ubiquitous Baroness filled eight suitcases with Hanussen's valuables—mostly diamonds and jewelry—that she salvaged from his safes and hiding places and escaped to the Netherlands. One report had her living in New York City, where she owned and managed a ritzy French restaurant across from the Brooklyn courthouse. [*Hanussen. Hellseher des Teufels*]

Leopold Thoma published a series of articles on Hanussen's life and tricks, which he edited into a pulp-like booklet. It was published in the summer of 1933 but craftily diminished Thoma's professional and personal entanglements with the murdered clairvoyant. At the invitation of Alexander Cannon, a well-known British researcher on hypnotic induction and friend of Aleister Crowley, Thoma relocated to London. Where or how he spent his remaining years is unknown.

Joe Labéro also traded on his relationship with the Jewish trickster and revealed the origins of his magical stunts in a pamphlet published in 1933. SA officers viciously questioned Labéro and Freda, his half-Jewish wife, about their ties to Freda's brother, a leader in Munich's Communist underground. After a second unsuccessful interrogation, Freda was dispatched by Gestapo agents to a concentration camp, where she died of pneumonia. Labéro managed to smuggle his substantial wealth to a sympathetic bank in Amsterdam and eventually made his way to New York. He was one of the many Hanussen associates who wrote about the clairvoyant's friendship with the Führer.

"The Baroness"

Among Hanussen's cadre of associates, Dzino was the most vulnerable to Nazi persecution. Ernst wanted him out of the country pronto. The SA-Führer gave him the choice of one of Hanussen's luxury cars. Dzino took the Cadillac and fled with his wife to Vienna, where he began a new career as a croupier.

Max Moecke plotted to take control of Hanussen's inactive operations and ultimately be appointed Nazi Minister of the Occult. In the summer of 1933, Moecke created his own newspaper, *Die Moecke-Zeitung*, and occult union, the "New Spiritual League for Young Germany." He was arrested for embezzlement and briefly incarcerated. When a German law banning "witchcraft" was decreed in 1934, Moecke was immediately deported to Switzerland. He made his way across the Czech border, and back to Germany in 1937.

Max Moecke

From exile in Prague, Paris, and Mexico City, Frei continued his journalistic crusade against Hanussen and Nazism long after the seer's demise and after the many materials linking Herschmann Steinschneider to the Führer were thought to have been destroyed. The left-wing writer returned to Vienna after the war and continued to champion the Soviet cause. During the 1967 Six Day War, he had a change of heart. Rabid Russian invective against Israel and unwavering military support for the Arab cause pushed the Jewish journalist finally into the Zionist camp. Correspondingly, Frei began to reevaluate his 1932 attacks on the Jewish clairvoyant. For the first time, he wondered publicly if his strategy to humiliate Hitler through his association with an Ostjude had not actually hastened the Nazis' murderous anti-Semitic policies.

From Vienna, Juhn emigrated to America after fleeing the Anschluss, and became an instructor at the Berlitz Language Institute in New York City. With him, he carried Hanussen's secret diaries and other key documents. These revealed the enigmatic events that led to the Nazi takeover and last known source of Hitler's occult beliefs. Juhn died in 1973.

Van der Lubbe Confronting a Witness

Van der Lubbe was found guilty of the Reichstag arson after two trials in Leipzig and Berlin. Each trial was closely followed by the international press. The Dutch revolutionary was beheaded on January 10, 1934, three days before his twenty-fifth birthday. All of his Communist co-defendants were acquitted and allowed to leave the Reich.

Both the Nazis accusers and the World Committee for the Victims of German Fascism, a Communist front organized to defend Torgler and the Bulgarians, wanted to avoid or downgrade the subject of Hanussen's prophecies. Each side needed to blame the other directly for the Reichstag Fire and its results. If Hanussen bore any responsibility for the arson, the national show trial would undoubtedly lose its civic and emotional impact. Only National Socialism or International Communism could be the one champion of truth and the sole political victor.

Röhm, Ernst, most of the SA leadership that had befriended Hanussen, Georg Strasser, Schleicher, and two of Papen's closest aides were killed by orders from the Führer on June 30, 1934. The savage bloodletting was known as the "Night of the Long Knives."

Count Helldorf managed to avoid the massacre that morning. More than a decade later, on July 21, 1944, he assisted in a Wehrmacht conspiracy to assassinate Hitler at his Wolfsschanze retreat. The one serious and high-level attempt to eliminate the Führer failed. After a 16-day investigation, Helldorf and seven other staff officers were found guilty of state treason. They were hung from meat hooks and left to die in slow asphyxiation.

Hanussen's daughter, Erika, married an Italian aristocrat on August 18, 1943. Her senior by 22 years, Baron Jack Winspeare brought the young actress to Rome and managed to receive Papal protection for his ethnically Jewish wife. After the war, Erika performed on the Italian stage and early television. She played opposite Gina Lollobrigida and John Wayne in a string of Italian and international films.

Grace Cameron, Dzino, and their young son, Ismet Rudi, did not fare so well in Vienna. On September 22, 1937, under a chandelier—as Hanussen foretold seven years earlier—the three died from gunshot wounds. The Viennese and London tabloids played up the story as a double murder-suicide, with the edgy trappings of an occult curse. Depressed about his dire financial straits, Ismet shot his wife and child and then turned the pistol on himself.

Erika Steinschneider-Fuch, 1999

Cziffra had a different take on the mysterious tragedy. There was no hex pushing Dzino into dementia or suicide. The croupier and his family had been murdered by Nazi agents. Dzino, according to Cziffra who saw him twice in Vienna, had written a book-length manuscript that detailed Hanussen's role in the Reichstag affair. German-language publishing houses in Austria and Switzerland either doubted the veracity of Dzino's account or were scared of economic or physical repercussions from Hitler's Reich. They rejected the book. Word of Dzino's missive, naturally, got out.

The German Foreign Service, knowing the Palais de Danse legend still had currency among journalists, arranged the triple slaying to correspond to Erik's 1930 pronouncement. Cziffra also believed that all but one of Dzino's manuscripts were systematically destroyed by German operatives. [*Hanussen. Hellseher des Teufels*]

Why was Hanussen Killed?

The Nazi motive for Hanussen's murder, at first, seems obvious. The SA officers who ordered his execution owed him enormous sums of money. The Prophet of the Third Reich had incriminating materials on their after-hours pursuits and sexual predilections. Erik was a Jew who ingratiated himself with Hitler and Röhm. The loose-cannon entertainer somehow knew about the Reichstag incident. Probably he was a party to it and had to be removed before the Reichstag tribunal.

All or any of these reasons was cause enough to be liquidated in the early days of the Hitler regime.

There was even another worrisome aspect concerning Hanussen. He published a horoscope of Hitler on July 24, 1932 in *Erik Jan Hanussen's Bunte Wochenschau.*

The Man Who is Never Wrong predicted a violent end for his Austrian patron. According to Hitler's astrological chart, his Tenth House portended disaster. Jupiter was in extreme

Illustrierte Kronen-Zeitung. — Donnerstag, 23. September 1937.

Drei Todesopfer einer Familientragödie auf der Wieden.

Vor dem neugebauten Haus Mühlgasse Nr. 10 hält ein schwarzes Auto, ein Totenwagen. Zwei Sanitätsgehilfen kommen aus dem Haustor, sie tragen eine schwere Last, ein schwarze Truhe, die den Leichnam eines Selbstmörders birgt.

Es ist 4 Uhr nachmittags. Eineinhalb Stunden vorher, um halb 3 Uhr, war der Mann noch am Leben. Es lag in seiner Hand, sich selbst, seine schöne junge Frau und sein Kind vor einem fürchterlichen Ende zu bewahren. Aber der Unglückliche

Margret Grace-Dzino.

maßte sich an, über Tod und Leben der Seinen entscheiden zu dürfen.

Er hatte vor dem Selbstmord seine Gattin und seinen kleinen Jungen durch Schüsse aus einer Armeepistole lebensgefährlich verletzt.

Gräßliche Wunden entstellten das zarte, reizvolle Antlitz des armen Kindes. Als die Tragödie entdeckt wurde und als die Rettungsgesellschaft kam, den Opfern des Dramas beizustehen, da sah man, daß es für den Urheber der gräßlichen Ereignisse keine Hilfe mehr gab. Seine Gattin wies eine Einschußöffnung an der rechten Kopfseite und einen Durchschuß des rechten Unterarmes auf. Das vierjährige Söhnchen des Ehepaares war von einer Kugel getroffen worden, die von der Schläfe aus den Kopf durchquert hatte und eine gräßliche Ausschußwunde hinterließ.

Wenige Stunden nach der Tragödie hatten Mutter und Kind ausgelitten.

Man hatte in der Nachbarschaft die Schüsse fallen gehört, man sah, wie die Hausgehilfin mit dem Ruf

„Hilfe! Hilfe! Mord! Mord!"

die Treppe hinuntereilte, um Hilfe zu holen. Von allen Seiten strömten die Neugierigen zusammen, in dem sonst so stillen Gäßchen bildeten sich Ansammlungen von Menschen, die in Worten der Teilnahme und des Mitleids von der Tragödie sprachen. Kaum jemand wußte Näheres über die Familie, die nun ein so tragisches Schicksal erlitten hat, aber jeder sprach von der vornehmen, eleganten Erscheinung des Mannes, von der Schönheit der jungen Frau und von dem Liebreiz des vierjährigen Kindes. Manche, die näher in die Verhältnisse der Familie eingeweiht waren, fanden freilich Worte der Empörung über die unselige Tat des Familienvaters.

Er hatte seine Frau gequält, mit seiner Eifersucht verfolgt und dann, als sie dies nicht länger mitmachen wollte und ihn verließ, alles aufgeboten, um sie zur Umkehr zu bewegen. Sie kam zurück, ohne zu ahnen, daß sie damit ihr Leben verwirkt hatte. Ihr Leben und das ihres Kindes.

Der Mann, den seine maßlose Eifersucht dazu trieb, Frau und Kind zu töten und dann Selbstmord zu verüben, hatte in der Zeit, in der ihn seine Frau verlassen hatte, eine andere in der Wohnung aufgenommen. Und dennoch glaubte er sich berechtigt, zur Waffe zu greifen und drei Menschenleben zu vernichten.

Der Sekretär Erik Jan Hanussens.

Ismet Aga Dzino — dies der Name de Unglücklichen, der so Furchtbares verschuldete – ist der Sohn eines türkischen Obersten. Das Hau in dem er eine elegante Zweizimmerwohnung ge mietet hatte, steht auf den Freihaus gründen, es ist erst im Oktober des Vorjahr fertiggestellt worden. Die Familie Dzino war i Februar d. J. eingezogen. Da die Eheleute m den Nachbarn kaum je in Berührung kame wußte man in der Umgebung nichts Nähere über den Beruf des Mannes und über se früheres Leben.

Erst gestern erfuhren die Hausparteien, da Dzino bis zum Tod des Telepathen Eri Jan Hanussen dessen Sekretär wa

Ismet Rudi Dzino.

Illustrierte Kronen-Zeitung (September 23, 1937)

oppositional alignment to Saturn. So upsetting was this prediction that astrologers in the Third Reich, of whom there were many, found themselves expressly forbidden to repeat the 1932 claim. Most contradicted Hanussen's interpretation by altering the time of the Führer's birth by two hours.

The Clairvoyant Record

All of this leads to a final and, for scholars of the paranormal, grave question: WAS ERIK JAN HANUSSEN, IN ANY WAY, DEMONSTRABLY CLAIRVOYANT?

He failed to anticipate his own fate and was shown to use underhanded methods of divination throughout his career. Yet on hundreds of occasions, Hanussen correctly told the past activities and foresaw the futures of complete strangers.

In a two-part obituary published in the *Zeitschrift für metapsychische Forschung* (December 21, 1933 and January 24, 1934), Dr. Christoph Schröder provided one of the most intriguing assessments of Erik Jan Hanussen. After many professional and personal contacts, some of which Schröder found unpleasant or insulting, the parapsychological scientist began to make sense of Erik's telepathic abilities. They were verifiable. The man who utilized them, however, always appeared clownish, untrustworthy, a vain schemer.

According to Schröder, Hanussen thought that he was a fake, acted like a fake, yet was actually clairvoyant and possessed a Sixth Sense. The *Jenischmann* was so filled with self-loathing about his origins that he did not really comprehend his extrasensory gifts. Schröder had no other way of explaining Hanussen's work under strict laboratory conditions.

Hanussen, a true clairvoyant? One only has to look at the published accounts. In his "Astro-Political" columns printed in four major Berlin journals, Hanussen made the following prophecies in 1932 and 1933. (These were selected by van Paassen in 1942 for *Redbook Magazine*.)

- In the tenth year of his rule, Hitler will be betrayed by his most intimate co-workers. CORRECT.

- In August 1942, British troops will march through Denmark. NOT TRUE.

- Joseph Stalin will die an unnatural death on August, 1953. INCORRECT. (Stalin fell victim to a stroke on March 2, 1953.)

- Early in June 1942, the collapse of France as a great power will be complete. She will be stripped of all her colonial possessions and will be reduced to a status comparable to that of Austria after the Versailles Treaty.
  PARTLY CORRECT. (France surrendered to Germany in June 1940.)

- In 2000, paper money will be replaced with electric accounting. PARTLY CORRECT.

- The Japanese Army will burn Manila in 1942. CONFIRMED.

- In the final Reichstag elections the anti-Communist bloc will receive a 52% plurality. CONFIRMED. (The total percentage popular votes for the Nazis and Nationalist parties in the March 5, 1933 election was 51.9%.)

- Wars in the year 2000 will be fought with television monitors, instead of artillery and airplanes. INCORRECT.

- Germany's neighbors in 1940 will be England and Russia. PARTLY CONFIRMED.

- The capital of the world in 2500 will be Prague or San Francisco. UNCONFIRMED.

- Sometime in 1942, the Eiffel Tower will be carted away for scrap iron. INCORRECT.

- Invalids in the future will be killed by state agencies. CONFIRMED. (In the late '30s, the Third Reich established a policy of euthanasia for the physically defective.)

- Josef Goebbels will die in 1943. INCORRECT.

- Poland will be occupied and divided in 1939. CONFIRMED

- Radioactive weapons will determine the outcome of the next war. PARTLY CONFIRMED.

- In 2200, New York City will be destroyed in a massive tidal wave caused by a secret geological experiment gone awry. UNCONFIRMED.

CHAPTER TWELVE

Hanussen II

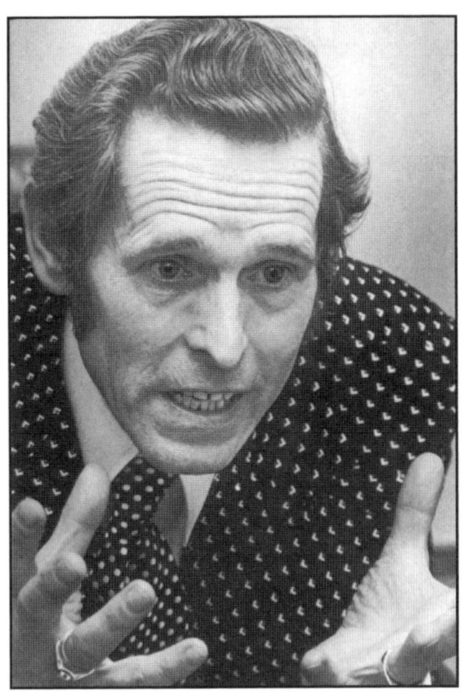

Willy Gerstel, who claims he is Erik Jan Hanussen's illegitimate son

Hanussen's name appears repeatedly on the Internet, and "Hanussen" ephemera can be found in places like eBay. Sometimes they are linked to German teleplays or feature films based on the clairvoyant's life, like the East German *Der Teufelskreis* (1955), O. W. Fischer's *Hanunssen* (1955), Istvan Szabo's *Hanussen* (1988), or, more recently, to Werner Herzog's *Invincible* (2001), the retelling of the Breitbart saga.

Two contemporary German entertainers, Gerhard Belgardt and Willy Gerstel, bill themselves as Hanussen—"Hanussen secundus" and "Hanussen II"—and have an interesting relationship to the original personality. For instance, Gerstel claims to be Erik's illegitimate son. Raised in a German orphanage in the '30s, Gerstel maintains that when he volunteered for the Wehrmacht at the end of the war, his mother and a priest finally revealed to him his true paternity; his father was none other than the Jewish magician Erik Jan Hanussen. After surrendering to American forces in northern Italy in 1944, Gerstel began to read fortunes as a pastime in a POW camp and discovered his predestined calling, that of a clairvoyant and prophet.

Today, Gerstel (as "Hanussen" or "Hanussen II") is the leader of an international spiritualist organization and the author of eight books on astrology. His headquarters is located in Las Vegas.

ENDNOTES

GENERAL SOURCES

Die Andere Welt (Breslau) (October–November 1931) [Edited by Erik Jan Hanussen].

Anonymous [Egon Erwin Kisch], "Nazidom's Rasputin," *True Mystic Science* #1 (November 1938).

Anonymous, "The Strange Destiny of Hitler's Pal," *Smash Detective* (August 1939).

Berliner Woche #1–4 (January 15–February 5, 1932) [Edited by Erik Jan Hanussen].

Géza von Cziffra, *Hanussen. Hellseher des Teufels* (Munich/Berlin: Herbig, 1978).

Erik Jan Hanussens Berliner Wochenshau #5–27 (February 5–August 7, 1932)

Bruno Frei, *Hanussen: Ein Bericht* (Strasbourg: Sebastian Brant, 1934).

Bella Fromm, "Under the Nazi Terror," *True Detective Magazine*, Nine-Part Series (December 1941–August 1942).

Erik Jan Hanussen, *Meine Lebenslinie* (Berlin: Universitas, 1930).

——— "Kreuz und quer durch die Welt," *Berliner Woche*, Five-Part Series (September–November 1932).

Hanussen-Magazin (Breslau) (January–February 1932).

Die Hanussen Zeitung #41–44 (February 16–March 24, 1933).

Hanussens Bunte Wochenshau #28–40 (August 8, 1932–February 8, 1933).

Erich Juhn, *Leben und Taten des Hellsehers Henrik Magnus* (Vienna: Saturn-Verlag, 1930).

Fred Karsten [Karl Pelz], *Vampyre des Aberglaubens* (Berlin: Verlag Deutsche Kultur Wacht, 1935).

——— *Hellseher-Medien-Gespenster* (Munich: Verlag Hohe Warte, 1952).

Wilfried Kugel, *Hanussen: Die Wahre Geschichte des Hermann Steinschneider* (Dusseldorf: Grupello, 1998).

Joe Labéro, *Wundermänner, Ich Enthülle Eure Geheimnisse!* (Leipzig: Verlag Wahrheit Ferdinand Spohr, 1933).

Christoph Schröder, "Erik Jan Hanussen," *Zeitschrift für metapsychische Forschung* (Part One-December 21, 1933; Part Two-January 24, 1934).

Leopold Thoma, *Hanussen: Hinter den Kulissen eines mysteriösen Lebens* (Berlin: Aufbau-Verlag, 1933).

Stuart Towne, "The Man With the Radio Mind," *True Crime* (August 1942).

Pierre van Paassen, "Prelude to a Tyrant," *Redbook Magazine*, Five-Part Series (April–August 1940).

——— "The Date of Hitler's Fall: the Prophecies of the Favorite Soothsayer of the Nazis," *Redbook Magazine* (May 1942).

Heinrich Wissiak, *Der Leitmeritzer Hellseher=Prozess Hanussen* (Teplitz-Schönau: Self-Published, 1931).

Author interviews and correspondence with Martin Ebon, Ernest Juhn, Henry Marx, Erika Steinschneider, and Phil Steinschneider.

INTRODUCTION

Heinrich Huter, "Hitlers Schicksalsstern!" *Neues Deutschland* (Dresden) (December 1, 1932).

Fritz Tobias, *Der Reichstagsbrand: Legende und Wirklichkeit* (Rastatt/Baden: Grote, 1962).

——— *The Reichstag Fire: Legend and Truth* (London: Secker & Warburg, 1963). Translated Arnold J. Pomerans.

Gerda Walther, "Hitler's Black Magicians," *Tomorrow* (Winter 1956).

CHAPTER ONE

Erik Jan Hanussen's 1930 autobiography, *Meine Lebenslinie*—most likely transcribed and partially ghostwritten by Leopold Thoma—is the best source of factual material on Hanussen's early years. Although Hanussen's adversaries and future biographers have ridiculed the popular book as a picturesque chronicle of unsubstantiated anecdotes and half-truths, nearly every hard reference to a time, place, and personal associates checks out today. Some aspects of Hanussen's life are conveniently ignored—like his Jewish ancestry and the existence of a first wife—and other events are jumbled in sequence. But, all in all, it appears to be an accurate, if untidy and occasionally self-serving, portrait of the man.

Phil Steinschneider, the grandnephew of Hanussen, has charted the only accurate genealogy of the Steinschneider family tree. With the assistance of other relatives in Europe and Erika Steinschneider-Fuchs, Hanussen's daughter, he has unearthed early documents, which he has generously forwarded to the author.

F. W. Conradi, *Magische Blätter und Blüten* (Berlin: Horster'scher Verlag, 1923).

Ludwig Hirschfeld, *Was Nicht im Baedeker Steht: Wien* (Munich: R. Piper & Co., 1927).

Wilma Abeles Iggers (ed), *Jews of Bohemia and Moravia: A Historical Reader* [1986] (Detroit: Wayne State University Press, 1992). Translations by the author, Káca Poláčková-Henley, Katherine Talbot.

Michael John & Albert Lichtblau (ed), *Schmelztiegel Wien: Einst und Jetzt* (Vienna and Cologne: Böhla Verlag, 1990).

J. Alexander Mahan, *Vienna: Yesterday & Today* (Vienna: Halm and Goldmann, 1929).

George Viereck, *Confessions Of A Barbarian* (New York: Moffat, Yard and Company, 1910).

CHAPTER TWO

Vaclav Borovicka's *Vrazda jasnovidce Hanussena* (1968) is the only major non-German account of Hanussen. Written at the time of the Prague Spring, the pop history adds little to our knowledge of Hanussen—it is vehemently anti-German—except for a few fascinating details on his 1923 New York trip and subsequent return to independent Czechoslovakia.

Géza von Cziffra's *Hanussen. Hellseher des Teufels* (1978) is easily the most problematic and unreliable of the principal Hanussen sources. A Hungarian screenwriter living in Berlin in the 1930s, von Cziffra actually knew Hanussen and his circle but produced a cleverly melodramatic account that contains invented documents and lugubrious characters from Hanussen's pre-Leitmeritz career. Some details from Hanussen's middle Vienna period complement Erik's autobiography.

Vaclav Pavel Borovicka, *Vrazda jasnovidce Hanussena* (Prague: Svoboda, 1968).
Ottokar Fischer, *Illustrated Magic* [1929] (New York: Macmillian Company, 1931).
Flowers Kollektion (Berlin: Psychologischer Verlag, 1905) [Book One: Personal Magnetism; Book Two: Hypnotism; Book Three: Magnetic Healing; Book Four: Mind Power].
Hans-Theodor Sanders, *Hypnose und Suggestion* (Stuttgart: Kosmos, 1921).
La Vellma [David Lustig], *Vaudeville Mind Reading and Kindred Phenomena* (Somerville, Mass.: R.W. Dodge, 1920).

CHAPTER THREE

Leopold Thoma observed Hanussen's first performances in wartime Vienna and introduced him to the German public in 1930. A professional hypnotist, retired detective, playwright, and feature writer, Thoma worked for Hanussen as an editor for his *Berliner Woche* in 1932. Immediately after Hanussen's death, Thoma published a series of articles about his personal relationship with the man in the *12-Uhr Blatt*. Reprinted as a sensationalist pamphlet, Thoma's biography was entitled *Hanussen: Hinter den Kulissen eines mysteriösen Lebens* (1933). A few sightings of Hanussen are incorrect: Thoma claimed to have witnessed Hanussen's first performance in the Viennese Konzert-Saal in 1917. It took place in April 1918. Also, Thoma concealed his lengthy employment with Hanussen.

Erik Jan Hanussen, "Die Wünschelrute," *Berliner Woche* #23 (June 17–23, 1932).
Hary Steinschneider, *Worauf beruht das—?! Telepathie, ihre Erklärung und Ausübung* (Cracow: Self-Published, 1917).
Hermann Steinschneider, *Was so über's Brettl ging . . .* (Olmütz: Josef Groák, 1915).
Dr. W. vom Bühl (ed.), *"Würu": Die Wünschelrute und der Findersinn* (Pfullingen in Württemberg: Prana-Verlag, 1928).

CHAPTER FOUR

Joe Labéro's *Wundermänner, Ich Enthülle Eure Geheimnisse!* (1933) was written in the last months of Hanussen's life but published shortly after his death. Labéro met Steinschneider in Vienna in February 1914 and instructed him in the secrets of muscle-reading, translated in this book. A few of his sightings of Hanussen—such as seeing him at the Circus Busch (Vienna) in December 1915—are incorrect. Harry did not perform there until September 1920 and was at the Eastern Front in 1915. Ten years later, writing under the pseudonym Hans Bleicher for the inaugural issue of the American monthly *Keyhole Detective Cases*, Labéro supplied another fascinating description of the Palace of the Occult's opening and more information regarding Erik's personal relationship to Adolf Hitler.

Hubert Bücken, "Die Jahre bis zum Ende," in Erik Jan Hanussen *Meine Lebenslinie* [Second Edition] (Berlin: Verlag Ullstein, 1991).
Erik Jan Hanussen, "Wie ich arbeite," *Neues Wiener Journal* (February 22, 1919).
——— *Schliessen Sie die Augen!* (Vienna: Nestroy-Verlag, 1920).
——— *Das Gedankenlesen/Telepathie* (Vienna: Waldheim-Eberle A.G., 1920).
Theresia Luksch, "Unpublished Diaries," (1919–1924).
Friedrich Mellinger, *Zeichen und Wunder* (Berlin: Neufeld & Henius Verlag, 1933).
Paola Giovetti, "Vorwort," in Erik Jan Hanussen *Meine Lebenslinie* [Second Edition] (Berlin: Verlag Ullstein, 1991).
Alexander Pilcz, *Über Hypnotismus, okkulte Phüanomene, Traumleben* (Leipzig and Vienna: Franz Deuticke, 1926).
Paul Schilder, "Psychopathology of Everyday Telepathic Phenomena," [1934] in George Devereux (ed), *Psychoanalysis and the Occult* (New York: International Universities Press, 1953).
Dr. Werner-Hagen, *Gedanken=Lesen und Hellsehen* (Pfullingen in Württemberg: Prana-Verlag, 1928).

CHAPTER FIVE

Marta Fara's syndicated series on her life with Hanussen appeared in three parts in the American tabloid *Saturday Graphic* in 1924. It is one of the first inside (and totally negative) exposés about Hanussen as a fraudulent showman and sadistic love partner.

Gary Bart, the grandnephew of Breitbart, and Dr. Sharon Gillerman have provided me with substantial materials regarding the Hanussen-Breitbart feud in 1923 and later writings on and by Hanussen.

Breitbart's Physical Culture Course (New York: Self-Published, 1926).
Siegmund Breitbart, *Muscular Power* (New York: Self-Published, 1924).
——— *Zishe Breitbart: Der Moderner Shimson Hagibor* (New York: Ferlag Hagvira, 1925). [Private translation from the Yiddish by Joseph A. Gordon]
Marta Fara, "My Life as Marta Fara, the 'Strong Woman,' Was Fake and Torture," *New York Saturday Graphic* Three-Part Series (September–October 1924).
Martha Farra, "Achtung," *Programm* (October 7, 1923).
Erik Jan Hanussen, "Can You Break Chains?" *Uhu* (January 1926). [From Gary Bart Collection]
——— "Mangobaumwunder," *Berliner Illustrietre Zeitung* (October 31, 1930).
"When Jan Hanussen Last Graced Vienna With His Presence," *Neues Wiener Journal* (June 1, 1930). [From the Gary Bart Collection]

Sharon Gillerman Collection. [Viennese newspapers from the January–March 1923 editions of *Arbeiter Zeitung, Der Abend, Illustrierte Kronen-Zeitung, Illustiertes Wiener Extrablatt, Kleine Volks-Zeitung, Krikerikl, Der Montag, Die Neue Presse, Neue Zeitung, Neues Wiener Journal, Neuigkeits Welt-Blatt, Reichspost, Der Tag, Wiener Morgenzeitung*, and *Wiener Sonn-und Montagzeitung*.]

CHAPTER SIX

Erich Juhn's 1930 *Leben und Taten des Hellsehers Henrik Magnus* was the first book-length account of Hanussen's pre-Berlin career. A roman à clef, it blended fictitious stories with actual source materials from Hermann Steinschneider's life. Juhn personally assisted Hanussen for two years in 1927–1929 as his secretary and used the clairvoyant's manuscript notes to construct his novel. Hanussen sued Juhn for plagiarism and libel. (Part of Hanussen's victorious legal settlement in 1930 and 1931 was the banning of the book and the pulping of the remaining copies.) Many of the factual descriptions of Henrik Magnus' adolescence were pure literary inventions by Juhn or simple inversions and had nothing to do the real history of Hanussen. Overall, Juhn's chronology was similar to *Meine Lebenslinie* and Magnus' general emotional and psychological development rings true to the life of the actual clairvoyant.

Ernest Juhn, the nephew of Erich, knew both Diebel and Hanussen from his childhood in Czechoslovakia and was exceptionally close to his uncle in the 1950s. The subject of Hanussen was a common theme at family meetings in New York.

Charles Fort, *Wild Talents* (New York: Claude H. Kendall, 1932).

Erik Jan Hanussen, *Das Gomboloy* (Gablonz: Self-Published, 1927).

——— "Fakir Zauber/Fauler Zauber," *Hanussen-Magazin* #2 (January–February 1932).

Bernhardt J. Hurwood, Strange Talents (New York: Ace Stra Book, 1967).

Christine Losso, *Über den Schatten Springen* (Bozen, Italy: Verlag Neue Südtiroler Tagezeitung, 2001).

Frederick Marion, *In My Mind's Eye* (New York: E.P. Dutton & Co., 1950).

Franz J. Polgar (with Kurt Singer), *Story of a Hypnotist* (New York: Hermitage House, 1951).

Rumpelstilzchen [Adolf Stein], *"Mecker' nich!"* (Berlin: Brunnen, 1926).

Johannes Steiner, *Theresa Neumann: A Portrait Based on Authentic Accounts, Journals and Documents* (Staten Island, New York: Alba House, 1967).

Josef Teodorowicz, *Mystical Phenomena in the Life of Therese Neumann* (London: B. Herder Book Co., 1940). Translated by Rev. Rudolf Kraus.

CHAPTER SEVEN

Heinrich Wissiak's *Der Leitmeritzer Hellseher=Prozess Hanussen* (1931) was a contemporary documentary account of the two-year-long court battle that contains additional details about Hanussen's youth and his itinerant apprenticeship. Befitting a court transcription, the descriptions of Hanussen's activities center around accusations of fraud from the beginnings of his career in Austro-Hungary to the time of the trial in Czechoslovakia. There are also positive biographical accounts from Hanussen, his attorneys, and expert witnesses working for the defense.

Karl Capek, "The Clairvoyant" [1929] in *Toward the Radical Center* (New York: Catbird Press, 1990). Translated by Peter Kussi.
"Clairvoyant Proves Power in Czech Court," *The New York Times* (May 29, 1930).
Ernst Lothar, *The Clairvoyant* [1929] (New York: Book League of America, 1932). Translated by Beatrice Ryan.
Franz Seracky, "Der Fall Hanussen und die wissenschaftliche Psychologie," in *Wissenschaft und Okkultismus* (Prague: League of Proletarian Free-Thinkers, 1931).
Christoph Schröder, "Erik Jan Hanussen," *Zeitschrift für metapsychische* Forschung (Part One-September 15, 1930; Part Two-October 12, 1930).

CHAPTER EIGHT

Wilfred Kugel's *Hanussen: Die Wahre Geschichte des Hermann Steinschneider* (1998) is the first objective investigation of Hanussen's life and a great scholastic undertaking. Trained as a physicist at Freiburg University, Kugel spent ten years locating Hanussen documents and articles, including correspondence and notes from Albert Hellwig's private archive. Kugel's understandable skepticism over Hanussen's autobiographical writings and reliance on the veracity of Juhn's banned novel and letters to Hellwig, however, have produced a number of mistakes in assessing Hanussen's career and place on the world stage. (Like other biographers before him, Kugel connects Hanussen's association with the Nazis months and years before such a tie was possible or made any political sense for either party.) His paper chase of Hanussen's reported activities after 1925 and archival Berlin research is, nonetheless, remarkable.

Martin Ebon, *Prophecy in Our Time* (New York: New American Library, 1968).
Essad-Bey, "Gespräch mit Erik Hanussen," *Der Literarische Welt* (August 7, 1931).
Wilhelm Gubisch, *Hellseher, Scharlatane, Demagogen* (Munich and Basel: Ernst Reinhardt Verlag, 1961).
Erik Jan Hanussen, "Sind Sie Medium oder Hypnotiseur?" *Der Andere Welt* (October–November 1931).
——— "Blick in das Jahr 1932," *Der Querschnitt* (December 1931).
——— "Sie können Handlesen!" *Hanussen-Magazin* #2 (January–February 1932).
——— *Der Untergang von New York* (Cologne: Smaragd Verlag, 1990).
Ernst Issberner-Haldane, "Frauen Eure Beine Verraten Euch!" *Hanussen-Magazin* #2 (January–February 1932).
Arthur Koestler, *Arrow in the Blue* (New York: Macmillian Company, 1952).
Siegfried Kracaucer, "Der Hellseher im Varieté," *Abendblatt* (May 28, 1932).

Fanny Moser, *Okkultismus: Täuschungen und Tatsachen* 2 vols (Munich: Ernst Reinhardt, 1935).
Carl Otto, "Einer der 'psychometrischen' Versuchstreffer vom-Hanussen-Abend im grossen Bachsaal, Lützowstrasse, 17. 6. 30," *Zeitschrift für metapsychische Forschung* (July 24, 1930).
Rumpelstilzchen [Adolf Stein], *Piept Es?* (Berlin: Brunnen, 1930).
——— *Das Sowies!* (Berlin: Brunnen, 1931).
Der Querschnitt (December 1932) [Issue devoted to the Occult with many references to Hanussen].
Otto Seeling, "Erik Jan Hanussen," *Zeitschrift für Parapsychologie* (May 1930).
Paul Tabori, *Companions of the Unseen* (Hyde Park, New York: University Books, 1968).
Leopold Thoma, "Hanussen," *Wissen und Fortschritt* (October 1930).
Florizel von Reuter, "Zum Problem Hanussen," *Zeitschrift für Parapsychologie* (September 1930).
Ignaz Wrobel [Kurt Tucholsky], "Der Hellseher," *Die Weltbühne* (April 1, 1930).

CHAPTER NINE

Bruno Frei, the editor of the Berlin Communist tabloid, *Berlin am Morgen*, spent much time with Juhn in 1932, preparing the most devastating onslaughts against Hanussen, exposing him as a Jew and a charlatan. Frei believed the Nazis' weakest point was their mystic ideology and naive racism. *Hanussen: Ein Bericht* (1934) was an biographical expansion of his 1932 articles and published in exile. Most of the early material in his biography is an interpretive summary of *Meine Lebenslinie* (withdrawn by Hanussen before his death) and Juhn's attacks. Frei later acknowledged in the 1980 reprint of *Hanussen: Ein Bericht* his anti-fascist screed was a much-distorted account and left-wing simplication of Hanussen's life and practices.

Josef Goebbels, *The Goebbels Diaries* (Garden City, NJ: Doubleday, 1948). Edited by Louis P. Lochner.
Erik Jan Hanussen, "Wird Hitler Reichskanzler?" *Hanussens BW* (July 24, 1932).
Albert Hellwig, "Misfortune of the Clairvoyant," *Umschau* (December 3, 1932). [From the Gary Bart Collection.]
Walther Karsch, "Erik Jan Strasser," *Die Weltbühne* #24 (June 1932).
H. Lehnert, "Schwarze Kunst die braune Wissenschaft," *Magazin für Alle* (October 1932).
Harry Price, *Confessions of a Ghost Hunter* (London: Putnam, 1936).
Christoph Schröder, "Erik Jan Hanussen," *Zeitschrift für metapsychische Forschung* (July 18, 1932).
Paul Tabori, *Harry Price: The Biography of a Ghost-hunter* (London: Athenaeum Press, 1950).
Hans Thyriot, "Vision im Kapitol," *Velhagen & Klasings Monatshefte* (October 1932).

CHAPTER TEN

Pierre van Paassen's "Prelude to a Tyrant," was published in *Redbook Magazine* (1940) on the intimate relationship of Hanussen and Hitler. Its treatment of the historical context of pre-Nazi Germany is superb. His basic sources were *Meine Lebenslinie* and Frei's *Hanussen: Ein Bericht* but he also managed to interview a few exiled Jewish associates of Hanussen, who were living in New York in 1940. Two years later, van Paassen received and quoted from personal Hanussen materials that were smuggled to Erich Juhn in 1933 and brought to America.

Anonymous [Walter Korodi], *Ich kann nicht schweigen* (Zurich: Europa Verlag, 1936).
Frank Arnau, *Täten auf der Spur* (Berlin: Verlag Volk und Welt, 1974).
Hans Bleicher [Joe Labéro], "I Robbed Hitler, *Keyhole Detective Cases* #1 (March 1942).
Robert Gordon Collier, *Something to Hope For* (New York: The Book of Gold, 1942).
Sefton Delmer, *Trail Sinister* (London: Secker & Warburg: 1961).
Georgi Dimitrov (ed), *Reichstage Fire Trial* (London: Bodley Head, 1934).
Ismet Dzino, "Das Hitlerjahre 1933," *Die Hanussen-Zeitung* (no. 43) (March 8, 1933).
Bruno Frei, "Hanussen," *Der Gegen-Angriff* #1 (April 1933).
Willi Frischauer, *The Rise and Fall of Hermann Goering* (Boston: Houghton Mifflin Co, 1951).
Bella Fromm, *Blood and Banquets* (Garden City, New Jersey: Garden City Publishing, 1944).
Hermann Hacker, "Privatseance bei Hanussen," *12-Uhr Blatt* (February 27, 1933).
Erik Jan Hanussen, "E.J. Hanussen Schildert im Trance: Hitlers Zukunft," *Erik Jan Hanussens Berliner Wochenshau* (no. 11) (March 25, 1932).
——— "In Eigener Sache!" *Hanussens Bunte Wochenschau* (no. 39) (January 24, 1933).
E.J. Hanussen and W. Baecker, "Das Todeshoroskop des Neuen Reichstags," *Die Hanussen-Zeitung* (no. 42) (February 24, 1933).
Lord Marey [World Committee for the Victims of German Fascism], *Braunbuch über Reichstagsbrand und Hitler-Terror* (Basel: Universum, 1933).
PEM [Paul Markus], *Heimweh nach dem Kurfürstendamm* (Berlin: Lothar Blanvalet Verlag, 1952).
Douglas Reed, *The Burning of the Reichstag* (New York: Covici-Friede, 1934).
Otto Strasser, *Hitler and I* (Boston: Houghton Mifflin Co., 1940).
Translated by Gwenda David and Eric Mosbacher.
——— "I Meet Hitler," *True Detective* (January 1942).

CHAPTER ELEVEN

Will Berthold's Weimar noir *Hanussen* (1951) was yet another roman à clef on the clairvoyant's life. Berthold's graphic use of real names and real events, unfortunately, allowed it to make a confusing leap from fiction to biography in the public's imagination. It was the basis of the 1955 German film *Hanussen* and probably restarted the Hanussen legend in Central Europe. (Paul Tabori, the otherwise respected Hungarian-British scholar of the paranormal and outsider history, incorporated many of Berthold's fictitious mystical and nasty assertions in his chapter on Hanussen in his *Companions of the Occult* (1968).

Anonymous, "Why Roehm Was Murdered," *Great Detective Cases* (September 1934).
Astro-Politische Rundschau #46–47 (April 24–May 8, 1933).
Will Berthold, *Hanussen* [1951] (Munich: Bastei-Lübbe, 1987).
Bunte Wochenschau #45 (April 8, 1933).
"Drei Todesopfer einer Familientragödie auf der Wieden." *Illustrierte Kronen-Zeitung* (Vienna) (September 23, 1937).
Lion Feuchtwangler, *Double, Double, Toil and Trouble* (New York: Viking Press, 1943). Translated by Caroline Oram.
John Godwin, *This Baffling World* (New York: Hart Publishing, 1968).
W. Hampel, *Schwärmer, Schwindler, Scharlatane* (Berlin: Verlag Neues Leben, 1961).
Walter C. Langer, *The Mind of Adolf Hitler* [1943] (New York and London: Basic Books, Inc., 1972).
Dusty Sklar, *The Nazis and the Occult* (New York: Dorset Press, 1977).
Nigel Trask, "Voodoo Murder Curse: Vienna's Baffling Mystery," *Master Detective* (January 1938).
"Wife and Son Shot Dead, Murderer Turns Gun on Self," *Daily Express* (London) (September 23, 1937).
Louis de Wohl, *I Follow My Stars* (London: George G. Harrap & Co., 1937).

INDEX

also available from feral house

WWW.FERALHOUSE.COM

VOLUPTUOUS PANIC THE EROTIC WORLD OF WEIMAR BERLIN

Mel Gordon

THE PERVERSE SPECTACLE OF WEIMAR BERLIN PRIOR TO THE THIRD REICH. "**VOLUPTUOUS PANIC** IS A PHENOMENAL, GUILTILY ABSORBING AND BEAUTIFUL COFFEE-TABLE SIZED MASTERPIECE. A MUST FOR EVERY PERV WHO WISHES THEY WERE LIVING BACK IN THE GOOD OLD DAYS, WHEN SEX AND PORN STILL HAD THE GOOD TASTE TO BE AS ELEGANT AS THEY WERE NASTY."— JERRY STAHL, **SHOUT MAGAZINE**

"THE SEXIEST – AND STRANGEST – VOLUME OF THE SEASON."

—**TALK MAGAZINE**

8 x 11 • 267 PAGES • EXTRAVAGANTLY ILLUSTRATED
ISBN: 0-922915-58-X • $29.95
AGE STATEMENT REQUIRED

STRUWWELPETER FEARFUL STORIES & VILE PICTURES TO INSTRUCT GOOD LITTLE FOLKS

Heinrich Hoffmann, Illustrations By Sarita Vendetta, Introduction By Jack Zipes

"THESE ARE DARK, MORBID, GRUESOME TALES – SO OF COURSE THEIR APPEAL TODAY IS TO ADULTS WHO'LL SEE IT MORE AS BLACK HUMOR AND GRAND GUIGNOL THAN EDUCATIONAL MATERIAL. . . .
SARITA VENDETTA IS A PRECISE DRAUGHTSMAN OF REVOLTING IMAGES DISPLAYING AN UNHEALTHY FASCINATION WITH DEATH, MAYHEM AND DECAY."—JOHN STRAUSBAUGH, **NEW YORK PRESS**

THE FERAL HOUSE **STRUWWELPETER** ALSO INCLUDES AN INTRODUCTION BY JACK ZIPES, THE ENTIRE ILLUSTRATED ENGLISH TRANSLATION OF **STRUWWELPETER**, WORLD WAR II-ERA BRITISH PROPAGANDA, **STRUWWELHITLER**, AND DESIGN BY SEAN TEJARATCHI.

8 x 11 • 176 PAGES • SPECIAL COLOR EDITION
ISBN: 0-922915-52-0 • $24

STRANGE CREATIONS ABERRANT IDEAS OF HUMAN ORIGINS FROM ANCIENT ASTRONAUTS TO AQUATIC APES

Donna Kossy

THERE IS NOTHING SO ODD AND PERVERSE AS THE FOLKLORE OF HUMAN ORIGINS. **STRANGE CREATIONS** PRESENTS ABERRANT FANTASIES AND MYTHS CREATED BEFORE AND AFTER CHARLES DARWIN – THE IMAGINATIVE CREATIONS OF DREAMERS, CULT LEADERS, AMATEUR SCIENTISTS, RACISTS AND ROGUES.

"KOSSY'S WORK OFFERS A RARE CHANCE TO TUNNEL INTO THE MINDS OF SOME OF THE MOST ORIGINAL THINKERS AROUND."—**WIRED**

6 x 9 • 257 PAGES • ILLUSTRATED
ISBN: 0-922915-65-2 • $16.95

TO ORDER FROM FERAL HOUSE: DOMESTIC ORDERS ADD $4.50 SHIPPING FOR FIRST ITEM, $2.00 EACH ADDITIONAL ITEM. AMEX, MASTERCARD, VISA, CHECKS AND MONEY ORDERS ARE ACCEPTED. (CA STATE RESIDENTS ADD 8% TAX.) CANADIAN ORDERS ADD $9 SHIPPING FOR FIRST ITEM, $6 EACH ADDITIONAL ITEM. OTHER COUNTRIES ADD $11 SHIPPING FOR FIRST ITEM, $9 EACH ADDITIONAL ITEM. NON-U.S. ORIGINATED ORDERS MUST BE INTERNATIONAL MONEY ORDER OR CHECK DRAWN ON A U.S. BANK ONLY. SEND ORDERS TO: FERAL HOUSE, P.O. BOX 13067, LOS ANGELES, CA 90013